# The History of the Royal Marines:
# The Early Years 1664–1842
# Volume 1

# The History of the
# Royal Marines:
# The Early Years 1664-1842
# Volume 1

Paul Harris Nicolas

**LEONAUR**

*The History of the Royal Marines: The Early Years 1664-1842*
*Volume 1*
by Paul Harris Nicolas

FIRST EDITION

First published under the titles
*Historical Record of the Royal Marine Forces*

Leonaur is an imprint of Oakpast Ltd

Copyright in this form © 2014 Oakpast Ltd

ISBN: 978-1-78282-419-0 (hardcover)
ISBN: 978-1-78282-420-6 (softcover)

**http://www.leonaur.com**

Publisher's Notes

# Contents

To

THE BRITISH NATION,

THIS RECORD

OF

THE SERVICES OF

THE ROYAL MARINE FORCES

IS

MOST RESPECTFULLY INSCRIBED BY

THE AUTHOR.

*Nequid Falsi Dicere Audeat,*
*Nequid Veri Non Audeat.*
Cicero

## CHAPTER 1

# From the Earliest Period to 1755

The earliest period any reference can be found to an establishment of soldiers embarked on board the ships of the royal navy which can be traced in the records of the Admiralty, is the following Order in Council of His Majesty King Charles II., dated 26th October, 1644:—

> Upon report from the Lords Commissioners for the affayres of His Majestye's Navy Royall and Admiralty of this kingdom, this day read at the Board, His Majesty was pleased to order and direct (amongst other things) that twelve hundred land soldiers be forthwith raised, to be in readiness to be distributed into His Majestye's fleets, prepared for sea; which said twelve hundred men are to be put into one regiment, under one collonell, one lieutenant-collonell, and one sergeant-major, and to be divided into six companies,—each company to consist of two hundred souldiers, and to have one captaine, one lieutenant, one ensign, one drum, ffoure serjeants, and ffoure corporalls, and all the souldiers aforesaid to be armed with good firelocks; all which arms, drums, and colours are forthwith to be prepared and furnished out of His Majestye's stores: the care of all which is recommended to the Duke of Albemarle His Grace, Lord Generall of His Majestye's Forces.

An order in Council, dated Whitehall, 1st April, 1668, sets forth—

> It is this day ordered by His Majestye in Councill, that his Grace the Duke of Albemarle, Lord Generall of His Majestye's forces, bee, and he is hereby authorised and desired, to draw and furnish such numbers of souldiers out of His Majestye's

Foot Guards for His Majestye's service at sea this summer as His Royal Highnesse the Duke of York, Lord High Admirall of England, &c. shall from time to time desire; to be delivered at Tower Wharfe on board such vessells as His Royal Highnesse shall appoynt to receive them, and thereupon his Grace doo cause the said Guards to be recruited as there shall be occasion.

Detachments from other regiments were occasionally embarked; and we find, in 1672, a company of the "Holland regiment under Captain Sidney" directed to proceed on board such ships as the Duke of York shall appoint. But the first regiment especially raised for sea service, was that of the Lord High Admiral of England, His Royal Highness the Duke of York and Albany's Maritime Regiment of Foot, raised in 1664; and it is so described in the return of the general review on Putney Heath on the 1st of October, 1684, and was thus commissioned:

*Colonel.*—Sir Charles Littleton.
*Lieutenant-*Col.—Oliver Nicolas.
*Major.*—Richard Baggett.
*Captains.*—George Littleton, Sir Thomas Custer, Edward Nott, Francis Ezod, Edward Harris, Samuel Scuddamore, Chichester Wray, Charles Herbert, Edmund Plowden.
*Lieutenants.*—Robert Crawford, Edmund Yarborough, Thomas Blechenden, Edmund Wilson, Robert Lloyd, Francis Hoblen, Francis Butler, John Thorn, George Rooke, Henry Hewys, Thomas Whaley, William Oglethorpe.
*Ensigns.*—Philomel Powell, Arthur Townshend, William Pearson, James Man, John Hill, Alexander Ewin, Thomas Man, William Somers, George Littleton, Francis Ezod, Joseph Whaley.
*Staff-Officers.*—Richard Beauvoir, *adjutant*; Tobias Legross, *quartermaster*; Samuel Tathan, *chirurgeon*; John Tathan, *chirurgeon's mate.*

This regiment, which consisted of twelve companies, without grenadiers, had yellow coats lined with red; and their colours bore the Red Cross of St. George, with the rays of the sun issuing from each of its angles.

About this time, titles of distinction were given to several regiments: Dumbarton's (the 1st Foot) was styled the Royal Regiment; the 1st Tangier (now 2nd Foot) the Queen's Regiment; and the 2nd

Tangier (now 4th Foot) the Duchess of York's. The 3rd was the Admiral's, or Duke of York's Maritime Regiment, which was sent to Holland in 1689, and incorporated with the 2nd Foot Guards. The Holland regiment, then designated "the Prince George of Denmark's," and the 4th in the British line, gained a step by the reduction of the 3rd, or Maritime regiment; and in 1708, on the death of His Royal Highness Prince George of Denmark, it took the name of the 3rd, or "Old Buffs," whilst the 31st regiment, raised in 1702, clothed in scarlet, with buff waistcoats, breeches, and stockings, was styled the "Young Buffs;" but the latter title has been long since laid aside. There is an exclusive privilege conferred, on the "Old Buffs" by the city of London, which was acknowledged so recently as 1840, when the minister intimated his intention of passing troops through the, city, and which is still retained by its descendants the Royal Marines, and the 3rd regiment of Foot.

It would be difficult, if not impossible, to trace the origin of this honour, as most of the archives of the city were destroyed in the great fire in 1666; but it is very evident that the privilege was granted to the "Old Buffs," (who, we may presume, were so designated from their being clothed in yellow); and probably from their being raised from the train-bands of the city. Moreover, the 4th regiment is described as having *flesh*-colour facings in the army list of Nathan Brooks in 1684; and in the Antiquarian Repertory of 1686, "red, lined with *ash-colour.*" Now neither of these descriptions give the Holland, or 4th regiment, a claim to the appellation of "Buffs," nor do we find it so styled until 1708, when it assumed that distinction, and discontinued the title of "Prince of Denmark's." Another circumstance confirms the claim of the Royal Marines to the precedence of the present 3rd regiment in the British line, which is here transcribed from the military memoirs of Major Donkin, published 1777.

The 3rd regiment of Foot, raised in 1663, known by the ancient title of the 'Old Buffs', have the privilege of marching through London with drums beating, and colours flying, which the city disputes—not only with all other corps, but even with the King's Guards going on duty to the Tower. It happened in the year 1746, that a detachment of marines beating along Cheapside, one of the magistrates came up to the officer, requiring him to cease the drum, as no soldiers were allowed to interrupt the civil repose. The captain commanding, (an intimate friend of mine) immediately said, 'We are marines.' 'Oh, sir,' replied the alderman, 'I beg pardon; I did not know it. Pray continue your route as you please.'

Here it is clearly defined to be the 3rd regiment of Foot *raised in* 1665, and not the Holland regiment, which became its successor in 1689, and which did not assume the designation of "Old Buffs" until 1708; nevertheless, as the Holland regiment was also raised by the city of London, the present 3rd regiment claims a similar privilege. The system of having soldiers exclusively for sea service, does not appear to have prevailed until 1693, when a draft for raising two marine regiments was presented to King William III.: who, by his order in Council of 22nd February, 1694, authorised their formation, subject to the following regulations:—

The number of officers, as well as their pay and that of the men, (with some trifling exceptions,) to be the same as those for the land forces.

The two regiments to be under the direction of the Lord High Admiral, or the commissioners for executing that office. None of the officers to be sea commanders, except the two colonels. When serving afloat, to be wholly under the command of the naval officers of the ships. Their cost and maintenance, &c. to be borne on the ordinary estimates of the navy.

Both regiments not to be on shore together: the regiment on shore to be quartered at or in the neighbourhood of the naval yards, in the following proportions:—four companies at Portsmouth, one at Sheerness, five at Chatham, two at Woolwich, two at Deptford, and one at Plymouth.

The men to be employed at the call of the commissioners of Chatham, Portsmouth, and Plymouth, and at the desire of the master attendant, or master-shipwright of the other yards where no commissioner resides; in heaving in or out of ballast, manning the cranes, removing goods and stores, laying cables and various other dock-yard duties,: for which they were to receive sixpence a-day in addition to their pay. The captain of the ship in which they served was required to send yearly to the Admiralty a list of the "names of such soldiers as shall in any measure be made seamen, and how far each of them is qualified towards being an able seaman."

Whilst serving on board, the men were to be borne on the books in a distinct list, and to be paid, as likewise on shore, by the captains of their respective companies, who were to receive the pay from their colonels.

There were several maritime regiments embodied between the years 1687 and 1698 subject to these regulations, but they were disbanded during the currency of 1697 and 1698. The expenses incurred by the maintenance of the maritime troops were classed with the estimates of the navy, and money was issued, from time to time, by warrant from the Lord High Treasurer to the Treasurer of the Navy, who placed it in the hands of a person especially appointed to receive it.

On the 18th of January, 1697, an order in Council granted half-pay to the officers of marines; but it was not defined if intended as a retaining fee, or as a reward for past services, nor has it been clearly ascertained up to the present day.

On the 4th of May, 1702, war was proclaimed against France and Spain; and the French king having advanced his grandson the Duke of Anjou to the vacant Spanish monarchy, Queen Anne, who had ascended the British throne, espoused the claims of the Archduke of Austria upon the Spanish sovereignty, and resolved upon sending a powerful fleet into the Mediterranean.

One of the first acts of her reign was a revival of the corps of marines. Her Majesty's order for levying this body was issued on the 1st of June, 1702, and was to this effect:—

> Our pleasure is, that six regiments of marines, and six other regiments for *sea service*, do commence and take place from the respective times of raising. And our further pleasure is, that the order given by our dearest brother, the late king, deceased, and such orders as are or shall be given by us, touching the pay or entertainment of our said forces, or any of them, or any charges thereunto belonging, shall be duly complied with; and that no new charge be added to this establishment without being communicated to our High Treasurer, or Commissioners of our treasury for the time being.

In 1702, Her Majesty was pleased to establish six marine regiments; they were put upon a different footing from those which were thought necessary at the beginning, but discontinued before the close, of the last war; for as the soldiers were formerly discharged from the regiments and entered on the ships books as foremast men, when they had qualified themselves to serve as such, and money allowed to the officers to procure others in their room, so now, when any of the marine soldiers died, or were otherwise missing, the companies were only made full by levy-money to the officers, without any regard to their being a nursery for seamen, which was one of the principal motives for the first raising of such a body of men. The charge of these regiments was defrayed by the navy, (as being part of the men voted by Parliament for sea service,) and money was issued out from time to time by the treasurer, by warrants from the Lord High Treasurer, to a person particularly appointed to receive and pay the same. The following articles for the government and conduct of these regiments were framed and adopted by Her Majesty in Council on the 12th of July, 1702.

They were to be employed on board Her Majesty's ships as there should be occasion, and quartered at, or as near as might be, to the dockyards when on shore, to guard them from embezzlements, or any attempts of an enemy. In all matters relating to their subsistence and clearings, when on board and on shore, they were to be paid in like manner as the land forces, and the same deductions to be made from them for clothing, and one day's pay, once a-year, from each officer and soldier for the hospital. They were to be allowed an equal proportion of provisions with the seamen, without any deductions from their pay for the same; and to have the same allowance for short provisions as the seamen, to be paid to themselves or their assigns.

Such regiments, or parts of them, as should be on shore, were to be mustered by a commissary or commissaries in the same manner as the land forces; excepting in this case, that they the said commissaries were obliged to allow at each muster on his or their rolls all such officers and soldiers as should appear to him or them, by authentic vouchers or certificates, to be put on board any of Her Majesty's ships or vessels; and that such part of the aforesaid regiments as should be at sea, might be paid while they were so. It was directed, that the commanding marine officer with them should, every two months, return to the commissary-general of the musters a perfect list of all the officers and soldiers on board each ship, signed by himself, and all the marine officers, expressing the times of entry, death, and discharge of each man; that so the commissary might compare the said lists with the monthly books sent to the navy office, and allow such of the officers and soldiers as should appear to him fit to be so allowed.

To prevent confusion, not less than fifteen marine soldiers, and with them an officer, were to be put on board of a ship at any one time, unless in cases of necessity. A particular paymaster was appointed, with power to solicit the arrears of the regiments, and to receive all sums of money from the Treasurer of the Navy; and immediately upon the receipt thereof, to issue the same to the respective colonels or their agents. He was also required diligently and carefully to adjust all accounts relating to the regiments, according to such muster-rolls as should be delivered to him by the commissary or commissaries; and those muster-rolls were to be allowed of, as sufficient vouchers for the charges in the accounts, and for making out debentures and warrants.

To enable the aforesaid paymaster to keep an office, and to defray the charge thereof, and of clerks and other contingencies, he was allowed sixpence in the pound, pursuant to the subscription of the respective colonels, which he had power to deduct out of all moneys issued to him, in the same manner as the poundage was deducted from the land forces. For rendering such parts of the regiments as should be on shore the more useful, Her Majesty declared it should be left to herself, or the High Admiral, to dispose of them at such places nearest to the several dockyards as might be judged most convenient. And since there might be occasion for labourers to despatch necessary works, Her Majesty empowered her High Admiral, or the commissioners for executing the office, to cause to be employed in the aforesaid dockyards so many of the marine soldiers as might be judged fitting, and to make them such daily allowance for the same, besides their ordinary pay, as should seem reasonable.

Brigadier-General Seymour was appointed by the Lord High Admiral to superintend the establishment. His particular duties were, to observe that the men were comfortably quartered; that the officers were attentive in their respective departments; and that the marine soldiers, when embarked on board of ship, were supplied with proper sea-clothes, and other suitable necessaries. A number of independent companies of marines were also raised for the express purpose of defending our West India possessions; to which quarter they were sent, and embodied into three regiments,

Charles, Archduke of Austria, being declared king of Spain, and acknowledged as such by England and her allies, Sir George Rooke was sent with a strong squadron of English and Dutch men-of-war to convoy His Majesty to Portugal. On his arrival at Lisbon on the 25th of February, 1704, after two days spent in adjusting the ceremonial, His Catholic Majesty was conducted on shore by the King of Portugal, and most of the royal family.

In compliance with the entreaties of King Charles III., the squadron embarked a division of troops under the command of the Prince of Hesse d'Armstadt, and sailed with a fleet of transports, under convoy, for the reduction of Barcelona, where they arrived on the 18th of May; and on the day following twelve hundred marines, four hundred Dutch foot, a company of Catalans, and as many volunteers as made up a total force of two thousand men, were landed under the Prince of Hesse. After remaining on shore the whole night, during which the Dutch had bombarded the place with some effect, His Highness, under the apprehension of being attacked by a superior force, caused the force to be re-embarked.

On the 21st of May the fleet sailed; and having passed the Straits on the 14th of June, was joined by the squadron under Sir Cloudesley Shovel in Lagos Bay on the 16th, when a council of war assembled to consider what service should be proceeded on; nothing decisive, however, was arranged, and Sir George again sailed for the Mediterranean. On the 17th of July, when in the road of Tetuan, it was determined to make a sudden and resolute attempt upon Gibraltar.

On the 21st of July the fleet arrived in Gibraltar Bay, and the marines, English, and Dutch, to the number of eighteen hundred, were landed under the command of the Prince of Hesse on the isthmus, to cut off all communication between the garrison and the continent. His Highness having taken post there, summoned the governor; who replied that he would defend the place to the last extremity. On the 22nd the admiral, at break of day, commenced a vigorous attack, and cannonaded the town with so much spirit, that fifteen thousand shot were expended in the course of five hours. This produced a correspondent effect, and Sir George Rooke, perceiving that the enemy were driven from the works at the mole head, ordered Captain Whitaker to arm all the boats, and attempt to make himself master of the enemy's fortifications; justly concluding, that if these were once occupied, the town must immediately surrender.

This order was no sooner issued, than Captains Hicks and Jumper, who were nearest to the mole, pushed ashore with their pinnaces; and having scrambled up into the fortifications, were actually in possession of them before the rest of the attacking party could arrive. The Spaniards, finding the works untenable, sprang a mine, by which explosion two lieutenants and forty men were killed, and sixty wounded. Notwithstanding this misfortune, the two captains maintained possession of the great platform until they were sustained by Captain Whitaker and the seamen under his command, who soon made themselves masters of a redoubt between the mole and the town. On this, the admiral sent in a letter to the governor; and on the 24th of July, 1704, that officer having signed a capitulation, the Prince of Hesse with the marines immediately possessed themselves of this important fortress.

This attack having been made on a Sunday, almost all the women belonging to the garrison were performing their devotions in a chapel about four miles distant from the rock, so that the besieging forces were between them and their families; and this circumstance hastened the fall of the place, for the citizens within strongly urged the governor to capitulate. The garrison was composed of two skeleton regiments only, but the strength of the fortifications, (the number of cannon mounted being upwards of one hundred pieces towards the sea,) and the two narrow passes of approach from the land, would have rendered it formidable to a less enterprising enemy. Our total loss was 61 killed, and 206 wounded.

The King of Spain being conscious of the importance of Gibraltar, obtained the assistance of a French fleet under M. de Pointis, to assist the Spaniards in carrying on the siege. The Prince of Hesse sent early advice of this circumstance to Lisbon; and consequently Sir John Leake with his squadron immediately proceeded to the relief of the place, and landed several engineers and gunners, with a body of 400 Marines; but finding that the French were approaching with a superior force, the admiral considered it expedient to return to Lisbon. Having refitted his squadron, he arrived at Gibraltar on the 25th of October, at a very critical juncture; for on that very night the enemy intended to storm the town on all sides, and had procured 200 boats from Cadiz, in order to have landed 3000 men near the new mole.

The Prince of Hesse persevered in defending the place against the combined efforts of the French and Spanish forces, until the 9th of March, 1705, when Admiral Sir John Leake, with a body of troops on board his squadron from Lisbon, again entered the Straits. The arrival of this succour determined the Spaniards to raise the siege, during which they had thrown more than 8,000 bombs, and upwards of 70,000 cannon shot, though to very little purpose. In a curious work published in 1707, entitled *The Triumphs of Her Majesty's Arms*, particular mention is thus made of the gallantry of the marines in the defence of Gibraltar:

Encouraged by the example of the Prince of Hesse, the garrison did more than could humanly be expected, and the English marines gained an immortal glory.

Captain Fisher of that corps, with 17 men, attempted to check the advance of 500 grenadiers of the enemy, after the round tower had fallen into their hands. This gallant officer was taken prisoner, rescued, and again taken by the enemy, who, though ultimately repulsed, carried their prisoner into the Spanish lines.

Sir Cloudesley Shovel and the celebrated Earl of Peterborough, having formed a juncture with their respective fleets, which had embarked 5000 troops, proceeded from Lisbon on the 22nd of June for Altea Bay, where they took on board King Charles of Spain, who pressed the earl to make an attack on the city of Barcelona and the province of Catalonia. Touching at Gibraltar, the newly raised regiments were exchanged for the veteran troops and marines; and the fleet arrived off Barcelona on the 12th of August, when 2500 men, exclusive of the marines, were landed, and the siege was undertaken.

On the 3rd of September, the Prince of Hesse proposed an attack on Fort Monjouic, situate on a hill that commands the city: it was accordingly assaulted and taken, but with the loss of the gallant projector of the enterprise.

After this success, the siege was pushed with vigour; the trenches were opened on the 9th, and batteries raised for fifty guns and twenty mortars. The bomb-vessels and eight ships, under Sir Stafford Fairbone, cannonaded the town, while the batteries and forts continued their fire on shore. On the 28th the garrison capitulated; and the surrender of this city so strengthened King Charles's party, that the whole principality, Rosas only excepted, speedily submitted. King Charles remained shut up in Barcelona, which was invested by the army under Marshal Thessé, until the 6th of May, 1706, when Sir John Leake, who had been joined by the Earl of Peterborough from Tarragona, arrived before the harbour. The king had been closely pressed, and Fort Monjouic retaken by the enemy; but this timely relief changed the position of affairs, and the siege was raised two days after their arrival.

The next object of attack was Carthagena, which immediately submitted; and a garrison of marines, under Major Hedges, was established for its defence. An attempt upon Alicant was then resolved upon, and the marines ordered to be withdrawn from Carthagena. On the 21st of July, all the marines of the fleet, with eight hundred seamen, were landed, and the bombardment commenced on the evening of the 22nd.

A detachment of the seamen under Sir George Byng rendered very essential service, by destroying the enemy's batteries opposed to the sea, mounting 160 guns. On the 24th of July the marines arrived from Carthagena, and were immediately landed. The ships having made a practicable breach in the round tower, situated at the west end of the place, and another at the middle of the curtain, between the mole and the easternmost bastion, the troops advanced to the assault on the 29th, when an officer, with fifteen grenadiers, who had rashly pushed on against the breach in the town, were repulsed before they could be supported. Captain Evans of the *Royal Oak,* at the head of some boats crews, was the first to mount in the breach; and these gallant fellows were rapidly followed by the whole of the forces, who were soon in possession of every post of importance.

Notwithstanding the preparations made for resistance, and the sharp fire kept up by the Spaniards from the houses, which had been loop-holed for their defence, our loss was inconsiderable, having only thirty killed and eighty wounded. General Mahoni, who had retired into the citadel with a garrison composed chiefly of Neapolitans, refused to capitulate until his defences had suffered considerably from the British squadron and bomb-vessels; but having sustained a heavy loss, he surrendered on the 25th of August.

On the 6th of September, the fleet under Sir John Leake sailed from Altea Bay, and on the 9th anchored before Ivica, which immediately tendered its submission to King Charles III. The expedition then proceeded to Majorca; and after throwing a few shells into Palma, the inhabitants compelled the viceroy to surrender. A captain and a lieutenant, with 100 marines, were placed in the garrison of Porto-Pin.

On the 5th of June, 1707, Sir Cloudesley Shovel, having joined Sir George Byng, anchored on the 28th between Nice and Antibes, about a league from the Var, with a fleet of forty-three men-of-war and fifty-seven transports. On the 29th an attack was made on the enemy's army, then entrenched upon that river, by 600 seamen and marines, who drove them from their position so suddenly, that the enemy laid down their arms and fled with the utmost precipitation. The Duke of Savoy with the allied army, consisting of 35,000 men, proceeded to Toulon, while the fleet under Sir Cloudesley sailed for Hieres.

It was not until the 15th that siege was laid to Toulon, and 100 pieces of cannon landed from the fleet. On the 4th of August the enemy made a vigorous sally, driving all the confederate troops from their works. On the 6th, the siege was raised and the army withdrawn, having sustained a loss of upwards of 1000 men in killed and wounded.

Sardinia was attacked on the 12th of August, 1708, and having been bombarded during the night, 1800 men including the whole of the marines, under Major-General Wills, were landed to attack the city; but the Spanish governor rendered any further measures unnecessary, by coming to a speedy capitulation. The whole were re-embarked and proceeded to the attack of Mahon, where they arrived on the 25th of August.

At this period two of the marine regiments were drafted, and both officers and men incorporated with the other four, now engaged upon this service. All the marines capable of duty were discharged from the ships about to return home, and employed in the reduction of this island. Fort Fornelli, mounting twelve guns, surrendered after a few hours cannonade by two of our ships; and Ciudadello, the capital, submitted without resistance, The batteries were opened on the works defending the town of Port Mahon on the 17th of September, and a lodgement having been effected under the walls of Fort St. Philippe, the enemy capitulated on the following day.

Thus was this strong fortress and important island gained by a force not exceeding 2400 men; while the garrison consisted of more than 1000 soldiers, with upwards of 100 pieces of cannon mounted, and having every requisite for a long siege.

The city and castle of Alicant, which had been taken by the remarkable valour of British seamen and marines, was at this time besieged by an army of 12,000 men.

The city is commanded by a strong castle, standing on a rock at a small distance from the sea. It now contained a formidable garrison under the command of Major-General Richards, who, after contending against the powerful army opposed to it, retired into the castle, which had hitherto been deemed impregnable. They sank three cisterns in the solid rock, and then, with incredible labour, filled them with water. The troops forming the garrison, which consisted of Sir Charles Hotham's regiment, with that of Colonel Sibourg, composed principally of refugees, and according to Gillespie a great proportion of the force being marines, exhibited the most heroic perseverance in maintaining the place. The besiegers attempted to undermine the rock upon which the castle stood; but this did not shake their resolution.

A partial explosion, which destroyed about thirty persons, did not intimidate them, and they bravely continued to defend themselves until the arrival of the fleet under Sir George Byng on the 4th of April. General Stanhope with the troops on board then promptly attempted its relief; but a heavy gale coming on, and being unable to gain any intelligence as to the state of the garrison, the commander-in-chief by a flag of truce proposed terms of surrender, which being acceded to, the brave remnants were re-embarked on board the fleet, which proceeded to Mahon, and afterwards to Barcelona.

A small squadron under Captain Martin arrived before the harbour of Port Royal, Nova Scotia, on the 24th of September; and on the 25th, Colonel Nicholson with a force of 2000 men, including 400 marines, proceeded to the attack of the place, opposed by a heavy fire from the batteries. Colonel Vetch, with 500 men, so lined the shore on the north side, that he protected the landing of the cannon and ammunition. The bomb-vessel drifting up with the tide, rendered important service during the first two days, and was so spiritedly supported by the military exertions on shore, that the governor capitulated on the 1st of September, and a garrison of marines was left in possession of the place, which was now named Annapolis Royal, in honour of Her Majesty, under whose auspices it had been subdued.

On the 13th of March, 1710, Sir John Norris arrived at Port Mahon as commander-in-chief of the naval force; and after some arrangements for transporting troops to attack the enemy in various quarters, he reached Barcelona on the 18th of June. An expedition was then directed against Cette, in the province of Languedoc, where the troops and marines were landed on the 13th of July. After a feeble resistance the place, with a fort mounting eighteen pieces of cannon, surrendered on the same day. Major-General Seissau, with the regiment of Stanhope, advanced towards Adge, which town was delivered up without resistance. The island of Cette was shortly afterwards recovered by the French Army, but our troops had previously been withdrawn.

In the early part of this year, 1711, it was resolved to make an attempt on the town of Quebec, the French capital of Canada; for which service Sir Hovenden Walker and General Hill were appointed commanders-in-chief of their respective forces. The fleet reached Nantasket, near Boston, on the 24th of June; and having prepared the provincial corps, and withdrawn the marines who garrisoned Annapolis Royal since its surrender, they sailed for the object of their destination on the 30th of July, and reached the Bird Islands on the 14th of August. After many fruitless attempts to ascend the river, with the loss of eight transports, in which 900 seamen and soldiers perished, and the fleet having been in imminent danger, a council of war determined:

21

That by reason of the ignorance of the pilots, and also the uncertainty and rapidity of the currents, it was wholly impracticable to go up the River St. Lawrence with the men-of-war and transports as far as Quebec.

It was therefore determined to abandon all further proceedings, and after leaving the provincial auxiliaries on their own coast, the expedition returned to England on the 9th of October.

Sir John Jennings assumed the command of the British fleet at Barcelona on the 20th of March. About this period, Joseph, Emperor of Germany died, and Charles III. of Spain, on succeeding to the imperial dignity, embarked on board the British fleet, which forthwith proceeded to Italy.

Peace was restored by the treaty of Utrecht on the 31st of March, 1713, allowing England to retain possession of Gibraltar, Minorca, and Nova Scotia, which were the fruits of our conquests during the war; and in effecting which, the marine regiments established during the reign of Queen Anne essentially contributed.

A great reduction of the forces took place during 1714, and the half-pay list for that year exhibits upon it the following regiments of marines: Lieutenant-General Holl's, Major-General Wills's, Brigadier Barr's, and Lord Viscount Shannon's.

In the first year, 1715, of the government of George I., it was judged proper to grant a signal mark of royal favour, in consideration of the extensive and gallant services of the marine regiments. Accordingly, all the officers attached to the corps of Lieutenant-General Holl, Major-General Wills, and Brigadier Barr, were restored to their rank and full pay, and were generally incorporated with the different corps of the line. Four invalid companies were also granted; but these regiments were again reduced, and it was not until 1739, when war was declared with Spain, that an order in Council of 12th December directed the immediate levy of six marine regiments, and the following colonels appointed to command them:

1st. Edward Wolfe, Esq. from 3rd Foot Guards; 2nd. Wm. Robinson, Esq., Lieutenant-colonel from Handyside's regiment of Foot; 3rd. Anthony Lowther, Esq. from 2nd Foot Guards; 4th. John Wynyard, Esq. from Colonel Tyrrell's regiment of Foot; 5th. Charles Douglas, Esq. from Colonel Howard's regiment of Foot; 6th. Lewis Ducie Morton, Esq. from 3rd Foot Guards. To render them immediately effective, and with a view to their perfect discipline, five men from each company of the regiments of Foot Guards were appointed as sergeants and corporals; and to hasten their completion, a bounty of one pound ten shillings was tendered to the first 1800 men of our regular army who should volunteer for this service. Early in 1740 three additional regiments were raised in America, when the Royal Standard was displayed at New York, as the port to which every volunteer marine was to repair.

It was supposed that the natives of that continent were better calculated for the service in that climate than the Europeans, and they were clothed in a manner well adapted for their duties. The colonels, lieutenant-colonels, and other commissioned officers were appointed by the Crown, except the captains of companies, who were nominated by the American provinces. Their uniform was camlet coats, brown linen waistcoats, and canvas trowsers. Colonel Spotiswood of Virginia, was colonel-commandant of the whole.

In January 1740, the six marine regiments received an augmentation of 2040 men, with one lieutenant to each company; twenty men were also added to each of the four companies of invalids, and another allowed to the retired marine establishment.

When Admiral Vernon was about sailing for the West Indies, his honest zeal for the public service induced him to offer the following observations, in an address to the Duke of Newcastle, on the value of marine soldiers.

> I could wish, indeed, we had each of us a company of regular troops sent on board of us, which would have strengthened us in numbers, as well as had their expertness in handling their arms, to have incited our seamen to the imitation of them. If we should come to a general war with France as well as Spain, I believe Your Grace will have already perceived, from the difficulty of manning these ships as they are, the necessity there may be of converting most of our marching regiments into marines; and if, as they become seamen, they were admitted to be discharged as such, that would make a good nursery for breeding them at a time we might probably find such a necessity for them.

These ideas appear to have been drawn from the system which prevailed in the sea service, prior to the formation of marine regiments, in the reign of Queen Anne, when they were entirely devoted to naval purposes; and as each individual became qualified to act as a foremast man, which was universally encouraged, he was discharged from his regiment, and entered upon the books as a seaman. Even under the present regulation of the service, great advantages would result from an increase of marines to the complement of each ship, instead of what is termed "landsmen and waisters." In case of emergency, a strong reinforcement might be embarked; and by the immediate equipment of ships, a powerful squadron could be sent to sea in perfect readiness to meet the enemy, with the advantage of having battalions well trained for both naval and military warfare, and capable of making a serious impression wherever their services might be required.

Vice-Admiral Vernon, with a squadron of five ships of the line, and one of fifty guns, sailed from Portsmouth on the 20th of July, and arrived at Jamaica on the 23rd of October, 1793, the day on which war was proclaimed in England; and embarking two hundred soldiers to serve as marines, he proceeded to Porto Bello, which was the destined object of his attack.

At the entrance of the north side of the bay, close by a steep rock, was a strong fort called the Castillo de Ferro, mounting seventy-eight guns, with a battery beneath of twenty-two. On the opposite side of the bay, and about a mile further up, on an eminence, stood Gloria Castle, consisting of two regular bastions towards the sea, mounting ninety guns, with a curtain between of twenty-two more, besides eight guns pointing towards the harbour. A little above this castle, near the other end of the town, lay Fort St. Jeronimo, a strong quadrangular redoubt; under the guns of which, and of Gloria Castle, all the ships of the fleet rode at anchor; and at the bottom of the harbour stands the town of Porto Bello, situated on the north coast of the Isthmus of Darien. On the 20th of November the fleet arrived at the place of its destination. The *Hampton-Court* took up her position near Castillo de Ferro, and was soon followed by the *Norwich* and *Worcester*. After firing several broadsides, on perceiving that the Spaniards abandoned their guns, the signal was made for landing; and the seamen and marines on reaching the shore, successfully scaled the walls, and immediately placed the English colours on the lower battery.

This was no sooner perceived by the garrison in the upper fort, than they hoisted a white flag, and surrendered at discretion. The *Burford* was engaged with the Gloria Castle until night; and on the morning of the 22nd it capitulated, when the British troops took possession of that fortress, and of the fort of St. Jeronimo. After destroying the fortifications, the squadron sailed for Jamaica on the 13th of December. Soon after this, Admiral Vernon bombarded Carthagena; and having entered the River Chagre, reduced St. Lorenzo, after destroying the castle and custom-house. He then returned to Porto Bello, and thence back to Jamaica. The intelligence of these successes diffused joy throughout the kingdom; and the Commons, in 1740, cheerfully enabled His Majesty to equip a very powerful fleet for the ensuing naval campaign. A camp was ordered to be formed on Hounslow Heath; while another was marked out in the Isle of Wight for 6000 marines, destined to be employed in the West Indies. In 1741 the House of Commons voted 40,000 seamen for the service of the year, together with ten new regiments of marines.

The fleet, which had assembled at Spithead under Sir John Norris, consisting of twenty-one sail of the line, proceeded no further than Torbay, and then returned to its former anchorage. On receiving intelligence that the Ferrol squadron had gone to the West Indies, and that the Brest and Toulon fleets were at sea, Lord Cathcart embarked with a large body of troops; and this formidable armament, amounting to one hundred and seventy sail, under Sir Chaloner Ogle, proceeded to the West Indies on the 26th of October. It had scarcely cleared the Channel before it was scattered by a violent tempest; nevertheless, the admiral pursued his voyage, and reached Jamaica on the 9th of January, 1741, where he found Admiral Vernon, who now commanded a fleet of thirty ships of the line, with a considerable proportion of frigates, &c, having about 15,000 seamen, with 12,000 troops, including six regiments of English Marines, and four battalions raised in America.

Touching at Dominica, to take in wood and water, on their passage to Jamaica, the expedition sustained an irreparable loss in the death of Lord Cathcart, a talented and experienced officer, who died of dysentery. The command then devolved on Lieut.-General Wentworth, a man of very moderate abilities, and of no experience. The fleet, now numbering one hundred and twenty-four sail, quitted Irish Bay, in Hispaniola, on the 25th of February, and anchored in Plaza Granda, which is to windward of Carthagena, on the 4th of March; but the commanders of the respective forces, as if determined to give the enemy time to recover from their surprise, remained inactive in the bay until the 9th, when the first division of the fleet under Sir Chaloner Ogle, followed by Admiral Vernon with all the transports, moved forward towards the entrance of the harbour, called Boca Chica, which was defended by several formidable batteries; while the third division, under Commodore Lestock, remained at their anchorage.

The *Norfolk*, *Russell*, and *Shrewsbury*, anchored close to the forts of

St. Jago and St. Philip, which, being silenced in less than an hour, were taken possession of by a detachment of British grenadiers. On the 10th, the regiments of Harrison and Wentworth, with six regiments of Marines landed on the island of Tierra Bomba, and having pitched their tents, they commenced erecting a battery against the castle of Boca Chica; but they soon found themselves exposed to the fire of a fascine battery on the opposite side of the harbour, on the island of Varu. The admiral immediately directed Captain Boscawen, with a party of seamen, to land a mile to leeward of this battery, which mounted fifteen twenty-four pounders, and was situated under a raised battery of five guns. Those gallant fellows soon gained possession of both batteries, and having spiked the guns, returned to their ships.

On the 22nd, General Wentworth opened a battery of twenty-four pounders on the castle; and on the following day Commodore Lestock, with five ships, attacked it by sea; and the Spaniards having remounted the guns in the fascine battery, it was a second time destroyed by the seamen. A breach being practicable in the castle of Boca Chica, it was entered by a detachment of grenadiers, without opposition; and the garrison of Fort St. Joseph also capitulated. Emboldened by this success, and perceiving that the enemy were preparing to sink their ships, the British boarded the Spanish admiral's ship, the *Gallicia*, and having destroyed the boom and opened a free passage, the fleet entered the harbour without molestation: the fortress of Castillo Grande, mounting fifty-nine guns, which protected the entrance, was abandoned by the enemy as soon as the ships approached.

On the 5th of April the troops landed at La Quinta, and General Wentworth pushed forward through a narrow defile to an open ground about a mile from St. Lazar, which fort entirely commanded the town of Carthegena, and was strongly fortified and defended by a numerous garrison. After much altercation between the two commanders, it was determined to storm this important fortress; and on the 9th, Brigadier-General Guise, with five hundred grenadiers and a thousand marines, advanced against the enemy's lines in front of the fort, followed by a body of Americans, carrying woolpacks, scaling-ladders, and hand-grenades. The troops pushed forward to the attack with great gallantry, although exposed to a heavy and destructive flanking fire; and on reaching the enemy's line, they rushed into the entrenchments, driving the Spaniards into the fort, over the draw-bridge which communicated with the lines.

But few of the Americans came up with the materials for further operations; and after an abortive attempt to scale the walls of St. Lazar by a small detachment, who were all cut to pieces, a general confusion ensued, and the troops were compelled to retire, with the loss of six hundred men, killed and wounded. It was then decided, in a council of war, that a re-embarkation should take place; and after destroying Castillo Grande, Vice-Admiral Vernon returned to Port Royal in Jamaica, where he arrived on the 19th of May. The loss sustained arose more from the effects of the climate, than in action with the enemy. Twenty-eight officers were killed, and seventy-seven died from disease and fatigue. Colonel Douglas, of the marines, was among the slain; and Lieut.-Colonel Cochran was promoted to the vacancy.

After the arrival of the troops at Jamaica, the mortality continued very great among them. Many changes took place between the regiments of foot and the marines, and promotion was established by rotation in the whole line. Within a few weeks the corps, originally Douglas's, included amongst its casualties three colonels, two lieutenant-colonels, and two majors. The fleet, consisting of eight sail of the line and twelve frigates, with more than forty transports, having taken on board a newly raised corps of 1000 negroes, who with the troops amounted to 3400 land forces, sailed from Jamaica on the 1st of July, and on the 18th anchored in Walthenham Bay, in the island of Cuba, which was immediately named Cumberland, in honour of His Royal Highness the Duke.

It was determined to attack the city of St. Jago, and the troops were accordingly landed: meeting with no opposition, they marched some miles up the country, and encamped on the banks of a navigable river. In the mean time, Admiral Vernon despatched part of his ships to blockade the port of St. Jago, and to watch the motions of the Spanish admiral, who was lying with twelve ships of the line at Havanna, a populous city on the west side of the island. But on the 9th of October, General Wentworth expressed his doubts of being able to proceed with the army, or to subsist much longer in the part they occupied. A council of war, held on the 9th, determined that it was impossible to proceed further into the country; and on the 7th of November another council, consisting of the land officers only, resolved on embarking the troops with all expedition. They were accordingly put on board the transports on the 20th, without any molestation from the enemy.

Thus ended the conquest of Cuba, the inhabitants of which, from the incomprehensible conduct of the British troops, were almost persuaded that they landed without any hostile intentions; for St. Jago, which was no more than four days march from Cumberland harbour, was weak in its defences on the land side, and might, therefore, have been easily surprised; and as there was no army in the country to oppose an enemy, it is difficult to conceive why it was not immediately attempted. After remaining four months on the island, the number of the British force was so decreased by disease, that probably in another month there would scarcely have been any left to bring home an account of this disastrous expedition.

The total loss of officers, at the close of the year, amounted to one commander of the land forces, five colonels, ten lieutenant-colonels, seven majors, fifty-five captains, one hundred and sixteen subalterns, and fourteen staff officers. Each of the marine regiments, which on leaving Europe consisted of more than 1000 men, were now so reduced, that, including the four battalions of Gooch's Americans, only 251 sergeants, 244 corporals, 89 drummers, and 2073 privates, remained fit for duty.

During the year 1741, the number of marine regiments was increased to ten, and the regulations of this establishment were very similar in their principles to those framed for the line: they were clothed by their colonels, who had the privilege of nominating officers for commissions. The number of men embarked on board the largest ships did not exceed one hundred, under a captain and three subalterns; and the smallest not less than twenty under an officer. The field-officers never embarked, unless the whole battalion was destined for a particular service.

Officers commanding marine detachments were required to make effective returns of them every two months, attested by the captains and pursers of each ship, in order to assist the numbers of the regimental companies, and to guide the recruiting service. The same deductions were made from them as in the army for clothing and Chelsea Hospital, whether embarked or not.

When attached to any ship, they were entitled to the same indulgences as the seamen, receiving their provisions without any deductions from their pay on that account; and they had short-allowance money, and the benefit of naval hospitals. When sent thither, either sick or wounded, they were deemed effective on their musters on shore, if producing a certificate from the surgeon of the ship, and another from their commanding officer at headquarters.

The paymaster-general issued the pay to the colonels of regiments, or their agents, and the paymaster of each settled the accounts agreeably to the muster-rolls from the commissary general; which muster-rolls, and the colonel's receipts, were sufficient vouchers for passing the paymaster's accounts, &c.

When brigaded abroad, they were paid precisely in the same manner as the army; but the arrears of officers of marines were longer withheld, and the captains of companies were exposed to peculiar hardships, particularly abroad, when they were often obliged to assign that portion of their pay at an enormous discount, in order to answer their temporary exigencies.

On the 15th January, 1742, the expedition arrived at Jamaica from Hispaniola, where they received a reinforcement of 2000 marines from England. It was then determined to make another attack on Porto Bello, and if successful, to march across the Isthmus of Darien, and take the rich town of Panama. After a delay of two months the troops embarked, and the whole fleet anchored in the harbour of Porto Bello on the evening of 28th March; but to the surprise of the admiral, the land officers considered, that as the season was far advanced, their numbers diminished by sickness, and the separation of some of the transports, they deemed it impracticable to pursue further measures. As there remained more than 2000 effective men, an army more than sufficient to have secured the treasure of Panama, and as there was no force in the whole country capable of meeting them in the field, this contemptible timidity is unaccountable; for in case of repulse they might have returned, without the least apprehension of being harassed in their retreat. The whole fleet sailed from Porto Bello in the early part of April, and arrived at Jamaica on the 15th of May.

In September Admiral Vernon and General Wentworth were recalled; and thus terminated this vast enterprise against the Spanish settlements in South America, in which enormous sums were expended, and 10,000 lives sacrificed without the least benefit to the nation. To the indecision of General Wentworth's character, and deficiency of that intrepid alacrity which inspires confidence in the soldier, may be attributed the cause of this inglorious issue. The naval commander was desirous to make the attack, but his contempt for his associate destroyed that cordiality which is so essential in all operations, and it abated the vigour which ought to have been exercised.

Previous to the departure of Vice-Admiral Vernon from Jamaica, measures were taken to put that island in the best posture of defence, and for having the fleet efficiently supplied with marines which arrangement required nearly all that remained fit for duty; consequently, the force was so reduced, that Sir Chaloner Ogle could only adopt a system of self-defence, as the Spanish squadron in the Havanna was now superior to his own.

In 1743, it having been represented to Sir Chaloner Ogle that the Spanish settlements of La Guyra and Porto Cavallo, on the coast of the Caraccas, were in a defenceless condition, the rear-admiral detached Captain Knowles with a small squadron to Antigua, where he was reinforced by some other ships; and 400 men of Dalzell's regiment, with 600 marines, were embarked on board the squadron. So little caution had been used to conceal the destination of this armament, that the governor of the Caraccas had two months' notice of the intended expedition, and, consequently, the fortifications were strengthened with the utmost care.

The squadron arrived off La Guyra on the 18th February, and about noon the attack commenced. Before one o'clock p. m. the ships had all anchored, and were warmly engaged with the batteries, which kept up a well-directed fire, and created great annoyance by their red-hot shot. The British had great prospect of success until the leading ship, the *Burford*, had her cable cut; being much disabled in her mast and rigging, she fell out of the line, and drifting on board the *Norwich*, obliged her, and also the *Eltham*, to quit their position, and with the strength of the current the three ships drove a great way to leeward. This disaster gave the enemy fresh spirits, and the cannonade continued until a shell fell into their principal battery and exploded the magazine. Night coming on, the firing ceased, when the squadron, having suffered considerably, drew off, and on the following morning the commodore proceeded to Curaçoa to refit.

The service sustained a loss of one lieutenant and ninety-two men killed; Captain Lushington of the *Burford*, mortally, and 308 wounded. The town was almost reduced to ruins, their fortifications were greatly injured, and the Spaniards had 700 men killed and wounded.

The squadron being refitted, and having received a reinforcement of Dutch volunteers, sailed on 20th March from Curaçoa, to attack Porto Cavallo, and anchored under the Keys of Barbaret, on 15th April. The commodore perceiving that the enemy's batteries on Ponta Brava might be cannonaded with effect, directed the *Lively* and *Eltham* to anchor within pistol-shot; and before sunset these ships had effectually succeeded. The soldiers and marines, supported by 400 seamen, were then landed, and proceeded to gain possession of the batteries; but some confusion taking place, the troops hastily retired to the beach. The commodore having determined to attack the place with his whole force, the ships on the morning of the 24th took their positions as follows:—

*Assistance, Burford, Suffolk,* and *Norwich,* to batter the castle; and the *Scarborough, Lively,* and *Eltham* to cannonade the two fascine batteries. The firing continued until after dark, when the ships, being severely damaged, cut their cables and retired out of range of the enemy's guns. This fruitless attempt, with the loss of two hundred men in killed and wounded, led to a council of war on the 28th, when it was resolved to detach the ships belonging to the Leeward Island station, together with the detachment of Dalzell's regiment; and the rest of the squadron returned to Jamaica.

On the 3rd April, 1744, His Majesty published a declaration for the encouragement of the officers and crews of his ships of war, privateers, and letters of marque; by which the property of all prizes taken by ships of war was declared to belong solely to the captors, and the two last-mentioned were to be regulated by the agreements with their owners.

At this period, when the establishment of the marines was 11,556 men, an order was issued by the Secretary-at-War for the ten regiments to recruit with expedition; and to render them speedily effective, impressed men were allotted to each: and this expedient was also extended to many regiments of the line. In the bill for recruiting, a clause was inserted that every one who should voluntarily enlist in the land forces and marines, would be entitled to a bounty of £4, and might require his discharge from the service at the expiration of three years.

On the 8th of May, the *Northumberland* of 70 guns, Captain Watson, having chased from the fleet of Sir Charles Hardy, on the coast of Portugal, brought to action the *Mars* of 68, *Content* of 60, and *Venus* of 28 guns. After sustaining the fire of the *Mars,* Captain Watson bore down to the *Content,* then nearly a mile to leeward. This enabled the enemy to bring their whole force into action, as the *Mars* followed to support her consort. After a close engagement of upwards of three hours, the *Northumberland* being totally disabled and Captain Watson mortally wounded, the master struck the colours before either of the lieutenants could get on deck to assume the command. The enemy had 130 men killed and wounded. The *Northumberland* was carried into Brest, having sustained a loss of 18 killed, and 30 wounded.

On the 3rd of October the *Victory* of 110 guns, commanded by

Admiral Sir John Balchen, having separated in a heavy gale from the fleet cruising off Ushant, foundered on the Caskets, near Guernsey, and the admiral and all on board perished.

On the 9th July, the *Lion* of 50 guns, Captain Piercy Brett, cruising in the Bay of Biscay, sustained a very gallant action with the French 64-gun ship *Elizabeth*. After engaging from 5 a.m. until 10 a.m., the *Lion*, having her mizen-mast and most of her spars shot away, was totally incapable of making sail, and her opponent made off. The *Lion* had 55 men killed, and 107 wounded; among the latter, her captain, all the lieutenants, and the master. Of the enemy, the captain and 64 men were killed, and 140 wounded. Lieutenant Walter Graham of the marines behaved so conspicuously, that, by the recommendation of the First Lord of the Admiralty, he was promoted to a troop in the 4th regiment of Dragoons.

As soon as it was determined to make an attack on Louisbourg, Commodore Warren was directed to proceed to Canso from the Leeward Islands, to take command of the naval operations. On the 4th of April, 1746, the levies from New England were encamped on Canso Hill, to await the arrival of the rest of the troops; while some ships of war, with several large privateers, continued off the harbour of Louisbourg, in order to cut off all supplies. On the 23rd of April, Commodore Warren, with the *Superb* 60 guns, *Eltham* 40, *Launceston* 40, and *Mermaid* 40, arrived at Canso, and after conferring with General Pepperell, the squadron proceeded off Louisbourg; and on the 29th the troops, amounting to 4000 provincials, and 800 seamen and marines, were conveyed to Garbarus Bay, about four miles distant.

On the 30th, 2000 men landed, and beat back the enemy who had opposed their debarkation; and on the following day the commodore landed the remainder of the troops and the marines from the ships, and they were formed into two separate encampments; one on the south side of the harbour to attack the city, and that on the northern against the grand battery. During the night of the 1st of May our picquets set fire to some storehouses; and the French, conceiving that the whole British force was advancing, retreated precipitately into the city. The enemy's works were quickly occupied by the British, and continued to be held in defiance of all their efforts to regain them. The force on the north side of the harbour had pushed their advances to within two hundred yards of the city by the 12th of May, and the cannonade was spiritedly maintained from some heavy ordnance on an eminence called the Green Hill, and a fascine battery mounting twenty-eight

32

guns. The siege was carried on under great difficulties; but every thing was well conducted, and some important captures by the squadron of ships bringing supplies from France, accelerated the fall of the colony of Cape Breton.

A force of 200 marines and 300 Americans embarked in the boats to attack the island battery at midnight, on the 23rd of May; but owing to a dense fog, they failed in effecting a landing. On the 27th, another detachment, consisting of 150 marines and 200 provincials, proceeded on this enterprise; but the enemy were prepared for their approach, and opened a heavy and destructive fire on the boats: nevertheless, the troops pushed gallantly ashore, and persevered in their efforts to scale the walls until sunrise; by which time they were so reduced in number, as to be compelled to surrender themselves to the enemy.

On the 12th of June, by great exertion, some cannon were planted on a cliff which commanded the platform of the island battery; and after forty-nine days of unceasing exertion, Louisbourg capitulated, and with it the whole dependency of Cape Breton, which was accomplished with the loss of about 100 men, while that of the enemy exceeded 300. The reduction of this settlement was of great importance to Great Britain, as well as to our North American possessions: it freed the northern colonies from a powerful neighbour, overawed the Indians of that country, and secured the possession of the province of Nova Scotia. At the same time, it distressed the French in their fishing and navigation, and removed all apprehension of encroachment or rivalship with our establishments on the coast of Newfoundland.

Ever since the institution of the marine regiments in 1739, commissions were purchased and sold, although they always bore an inferior value to those of the army. In 1746 a perquisite arose to the colonels from the disposal of the appointments of second-lieutenants, when their recommendations were approved of by His Majesty; and such commissions usually produced to those officers from £250 to £280; while ensigncies in the line sometimes yielded as much as £400. The great expense which had accrued in the maintenance of the land forces and marines, led to the appointment of a committee of inquiry. In this investigation it appeared that the colonel of a marine regiment had a greater emolument than an officer commanding a regiment of the line, arising from the comparative superiority in their numbers, and the articles of clothing being of an inferior quality.

A squadron of six sail of the line, under Admiral Lestock, with a fleet of transports conveying a military force of 5000 men under

Lieutenant-General St. Clair, sailed from Plymouth on the 14th of September, 1746, destined to make an attack on the port of L'Orient. On the morning of the 20th, the troops landed in the bay of Quimperlay, about ten miles from Port Louis, without sustaining any loss. Early on the 21st the general began his march, leaving the corps of marines, under Colonel Holmes, to assist in landing the stores and artillery. The army was divided into two columns; the first arrived at the windmill near L'Orient early in the evening, and were shortly afterwards joined by the other division. Preparations were made for bombarding the town; and after a fruitless parley with a deputation from the inhabitants, who proposed terms for the surrender of the place, considerable damage was done by our artillery; but the enemy, taking advantage of the delay in our operations, assembled a formidable force, which induced the Lieutenant-general to withdraw his army, and the re-embarkation was effected, after sustaining a loss of 150 men killed and wounded.

On the 4th of October, the troops landed on the peninsula of Quiberon, and took possession of a fort mounting eighteen guns. After destroying all the forts and guns, as well as those on the islands of Houat and Hedic, the army re-embarked, and the expedition sailed for Ireland. In the gradual increase of the army during the present war, the marines became incorporated with the line, and the 44th regiment was styled the 1st Marines.

The following is a detail of the field-officers of each corps, all of which were quartered in the vicinity of the principal seaports of Great Britain:

| No. of Regiment. | | | Colonel. | Lieut.-colonel. | Major. |
|---|---|---|---|---|---|
| 44th or 1st Marines. | | | G. Churchill. | N. Mitchell. | J. M'Donald. |
| 45th | 2nd | " | Robt. Frazer. | J. Leighton. | T. Matthews. |
| 46th | 3rd | " | C. H. Holmes. | P. Damar. | W. Brown. |
| 47th | 4th | " | C. George. | P. Hutchinson. | J. Read. |
| 48th | 5th | " | C. J. Cochran. | C. Whiteford. | J. Stuart. |
| 49th | 6th | " | —— Laforey. | C. Gordon. | C. Leighton. |
| 50th | 7th | " | H. Cornwall. | J. Paterson. | R. Bendish. |
| 51st | 8th | " | J. Duncombe. | T. Cunningham. | J. Brewse. |
| 52nd | 9th | " | C. Powlett. | G. Walsh. | —— |
| 53rd | 10th | " | Sir A. Agnew. | C. Pawlett. | C. Durand. |

These regiments, when complete, were supposed to consist of

1000 rank and file, with ten companies in each battalion; and at this period, the whole of the forces upon the British military establishment amounted to 85,600 men.

The French, persisting in their plan of operations, resolved to make another attempt to recover Cape Breton; and a squadron was equipped for that service, consisting of one ship of 74, one of 66, three of 52 guns, and four frigates, under Commodore De la Jonquiere, with several transports, amounting altogether to thirty-eight sail. Admiral Anson, with eleven sail of the line and three ships of fifty guns, sailed from Plymouth on the 9th of April, 1747, and on the 3rd of May fell in with the fleet of M. De la Jonquiere, off Cape Finisterre. After a smart action with the advanced ships of the British fleet, in which the enemy lost 700 men killed and wounded, five ships of the line and nine of the convoy were captured. The British loss amounted to 520 in killed and wounded.

On the 6th of October, a French fleet of merchant-men under Commodore Letendeur sailed from the isle of Aix for the West Indies, under convoy of nine ships of the line and several frigates; and on the 14th, off Cape Finisterre, they fell in with a British squadron, commanded by Rear-Admiral Hawke, of thirteen ships of the line, including two of fifty guns. The commodore, finding it impossible to avoid an action, directed a sixty gun ship and the frigates to proceed with the convoy; and then formed his squadron in order of battle. The action commenced at noon, and was continued with great spirit until night; by which time six sail of the line had surrendered. The commodore, in the *Tonnant* of 80 guns, and the *Intrepid* of 74, made their escape. The British had 154 killed, and 558 wounded. The enemy's loss amounted to 800 in killed and wounded. The order of the Bath was conferred on Rear-Admiral Hawke, and the thanks of parliament voted to the officers, seamen, and marines of the squadron.

In the early part of this year, His Majesty directed that the several regiments of marines which were then existing, or might afterwards be raised, should for the future obey such orders as they, from time to time, might receive from the lords commissioners of the Admiralty. The present constitution of the corps may in some degree be dated from this period; but it was not until 1755, that the marines were embodied in companies, at the respective divisions, as will be presently shown.

The navy of Spain was now reduced to twenty-two ships of the line, and that of France to thirty-one; whilst the navy of Great Britain amounted to 126 sail of the line and 75 frigates. Admiral Boscawen, who had sailed from England the previous November with a squadron of four ships of the line and two fifties, left the Cape of Good Hope on the 18th of May, having been reinforced by 400 Dutch troops, and arrived at the island of Mauritius on the 23rd of June. Finding the enemy fully prepared at every point, and considering that the dangers of approaching the land would probably involve a great sacrifice of men, the admiral determined on proceeding to the coast of Coromandel, to undertake the siege of Pondicherry; and he arrived at Fort St. David's on the 29th of July, where he was joined by the squadron under Vice-Admiral Griffin. The united force amounted to six sail of the line and four ships of fifty guns, with several Company's ships well armed, exhibiting the greatest marine force that had ever been seen in India, with an army of 5220 men, of which 880 were marines belonging to the squadron.

The troops landed and were put in motion on the 8th of August, and on the 11th they met some opposition from an advanced corps of the enemy; but nothing of importance occurred, until it was deemed essential to carry the fort of Arian Coupan, which appeared a mere outwork, but was fatally found to be of considerable strength, being fortified with a cavalier at each of the angles, with a deep dry ditch full of pitfalls, and a covered way. The attack was made by 700 men, composed of the grenadiers and picquets of the army, who were met by such a heavy discharge of grape and musketry, and a galling fire from two batteries on the opposite side of the river, that they were compelled to retreat. By this time they had sustained a loss of 150 men, with many valuable officers. Major Goodere of the artillery, who commanded in this unfortunate attack, was mortally wounded, and his loss was severely felt, as he was the person on whom the admiral relied for conducting the operations against Pondicherry.

This repulse did not deter the British from making another attempt: 1100 sailors landed and brought up battering cannon, and on the 17th a battery of four guns opened on the fort; but the distance was too great, and whilst the British were occupied in constructing another battery, a desperate attack was made on their entrenchments. Although at first it was attended with some success, the French were eventually driven back, and their commanding officer taken prisoner. Regular approaches were carried on for some days, when an accident happened to the enemy on the 30th, by means of which, possession was gained of the place. A large quantity of powder having exploded, blew up the fort, and killed upwards of 100 men; and the enemy consequently destroyed the remainder of the fortifications, and retreated to Pondicherry.

The British troops were employed repairing the fortifications, and endeavouring to render the place tenable, until the 25th, when the army advanced, and encamped within two miles of Pondicherry. The operations were now carried on at the north-west side of the town, and communication being opened with the ships to the northward of it, everything requisite for maintaining the siege was landed. Early in the morning, the advanced guard of about 100 men, and consisting principally of marines, was attacked by very superior numbers, headed by their principal engineer, M. de Paradis, who was mortally wounded, and the enemy repulsed with the loss of 120 men.

It is related that a woman fought in the ranks as a marine, who was named Hannah Snell,[1] a native of Worcester. She enlisted at Portsmouth in Colonel Fraser's regiment, and embarked on board the *Swallow*, one of the squadron under Admiral Boscawen, when she behaved with distinguished courage, and received a ball in the groin, which she herself extracted two days afterwards. Eleven other wounds in both legs rendered her removal to the hospital at Cuddalore absolutely necessary, and having returned home in the *Eltham* frigate, her sex was not discovered until she obtained her discharge. She afterwards wore the marine dress, and having presented a petition to His Royal Highness the Duke of Cumberland, obtained a pension of thirty pounds a-year for life.

It was not until the 26th of September that the batteries were completed; but they were so inferior to those of the enemy, that two ships were warped nearer to the shore. The water being too shallow to admit of their producing much effect, they were withdrawn on the 28th, with the loss of Captain Adams, of the *Harwich*, and one seaman. The approaches had now reached within 800 yards of the covered way, but on account of an inundation, they could advance no further on that side. Some new batteries were erected by the British, whilst the army having greatly increased their fire, had dismounted nine pieces of cannon.

The admiral perceiving that little impression had been made on the defences of the place, and that the troops were becoming sickly, called a council of war on the 30th of September; which, taking into consideration that when the rains set in, the low country would be overflowed, and apprehensive of difficulty in removing the artillery and stores, combined with the danger likely to arise to the fleet if they

1. *The Female Soldier,* two accounts of women who served and fought as men, by Hannah Snell & Anonymous is also published by Leonaur.

remained on the coast, were of opinion that the siege ought to be immediately raised, especially as there were 700 men on the sick list.

Several days were occupied in destroying the batteries, embarking the cannon, and removing the sick and wounded to the hospital-ships. This being completed, the army began its retreat, which was much impeded by the rains that had already set in, and which it would have been almost impossible to accomplish had it been deferred two days longer. The loss sustained in this expedition amounted to 757 soldiers, 43 artillery men, and 265 sailors: in all, 1065 Europeans.

The garrison of Pondicherry consisted of 1800 Europeans, and 3000 *sepoys*; their total loss did not exceed 250 men. The failure was attributable to the delay in advancing on Pondicherry, and the ill-advised measures that were pursued. Had the attack been directed against the north side, they could have carried on their operations even to the foot of the glacis, there being no inundation to stop them; and the camp might have been placed at a due distance from the batteries, and so close to the shore, that the supplies from the fleet might have been landed under their protection. The miscarriage of the British before Pondicherry tended to lower the nation in the estimation of all the powers in Hindostan, and the French were in consequence considered of the highest military reputation.

On the West India station, Rear-Admiral Knowles embarked 240 men of Trelawney's regiment on board the squadron, with an intention of making an attack on St. Jago de Cuba, and sailed from Port Royal, in Jamaica, on 13th of February; but the northerly wind blowing unusually strong, the ships could not reach their destination. It was therefore determined to attempt the French settlement of Port Louis, on the south side of Hispaniola. The British squadron, consisting of seven sail of the line, and one of fifty guns, arrived off this place on the 8th of March, and immediately proceeded to cannonade the fort, mounting seventy-eight guns, with a garrison of 600 men. The ships moored in a close line ahead, within pistol-shot of the walls; and after an uninterrupted fire of three hours, the place surrendered, when Major Scott, with the troops and marines, landed and took possession. Our loss amounted to 70 men, killed and wounded; among the former were Captains Rentone and Cust of the navy. After destroying the fort, the whole force re-embarked.

On the 29th September, the same squadron, when near the Havanna, fell in with six Spanish ships of the line from Vera Cruz. After an engagement of several hours, in which the British had 59 men killed and 120 wounded, and the enemy 86 killed, and 197 wounded, the *Conquestadore* of 64 guns was captured, and the *Africa* 74 subsequently destroyed.

The navies of France and Spain were now so reduced as to be no longer formidable, and this may be truly said to have been the only advantage gained by the war; for by the treaty of peace, concluded in the present year at Aix-la-Chapelle, all the conquests made by Great Britain from France and Spain were to be restored. So that after a long and sanguinary contest of nearly ten years continuance, and increasing the national debt to eighty millions sterling, the condition of Great Britain was little better than when hostilities commenced; and that important matter which had been the occasion of this expensive war,—the right of British ships to navigate the American seas without being searched, was not even mentioned. Our claim to the province of Nova Scotia was to be left to the discussion of commissioners to be named for that purpose; and this last article, not being properly settled, was mainly the cause of another war.

A bill was introduced into Parliament by the minister, "For reducing into one act the laws relating to the navy;" by which the half-pay officers were to be rendered subject to martial law. The sea-officers presented a petition to the House of Commons, requesting to be heard by counsel; and although the minister mustered sufficient strength to reject the petition, he thought proper to relinquish this unconstitutional attempt.

Amongst the many reductions that took place during 1748, and the early part of the ensuing year, was the total extinction of the regiments of marines, the officers of which were placed on half-pay. At this time the comparative rank between the navy and army was established; and an order was issued for an exact conformity of dress throughout the naval service.

The Earl of Halifax, who presided at the Board of Trade, formed a design for establishing a colony in Nova Scotia, and grants of land in that province were offered to every rank in His Majesty's land and sea forces, with an extension of privilege and property to those taking their families with them. This project was so much approved of, that 4000 adventurers sailed from England under the protection of Colonel Cornwallis, who landed in the harbour of Chebuctou on the 21st of June, 1749, in the neighbourhood of which they built a town that was named Halifax, in commemoration of their liberal and humane patron.

The French were displeased with this assertion of our right; and by way of counterbalance, they attempted to form a settlement on the island of Tobago, in the West Indies. In consequence of a firm remonstrance to the court of Versailles, the measure was abandoned; yet they continued to assert their claim to St. Lucia, Tobago, and other neutral islands. In North America their encroachments were so offensive, that the British subjects bordering on the French settlements were loud in their complaints to the government. After repeated remonstrances by our ambassador at Paris, commissioners were appointed by each nation in 1750, to settle the limits of Acadia, or Nova Scotia. These functionaries met in Paris, and continued their conference until 1753, during which time the Indians bordering on the British dominions in North America, were instigated by the French to commit acts of violence on the inhabitants of our back settlements; and in 1752 the Spaniards resumed their practice of interrupting our navigation in the West Indies. In 1753 the French erected a chain of forts along the lakes of Erie and Ontario, so as to connect their settlements on the Mississippi with Canada; and at length, having crossed Lake Champlain, they built a fort at Crown Point, in the province of New York.

Notwithstanding these flagrant acts of hostility, the court of London continued to receive assurances of the friendly disposition of the French government; but early in 1755, the British ministry were undeceived in their reliance on those professions of good faith, by certain information that a considerable fleet was preparing to sail for America from the different ports of France, with a formidable number of troops on board. The British minister, roused at this information, ordered an immediate equipment of men-of-war; and in the latter part of April, Vice-Admiral Boscawen, with eleven ships of the line, sailed for America, and was shortly afterwards followed by Rear-Admiral Holburne, with six ships of the line and one frigate.

The government had received subsequent intelligence that the French armament consisted of twenty-five ships of the line, sixteen sail of which, with troops on board, under the command of M. Bois de la Mothe, who having detached four of the line and two frigates for Louisbourg, the remainder proceeded to Quebec, where they safely arrived, with the exception of the *Alcide* 64, and the *Lys* of 20 guns, which were captured on the 8th of June, after a gallant resistance, by the *Dunkirk* and *Defiance* of 60 guns.

This action may be considered the commencement of the war, for as soon as it was known in Europe, the French ambassador left London, and orders were issued by the British Government for making reprisals.

## CHAPTER 2

# From the Year 1755 to 1775

In the early part of 1755, a levy of fifty companies of marines was ordered; they were now for the first time formed into three divisions, stationed at Chatham, Portsmouth, and Plymouth, being under the immediate control of the Board of Admiralty, and an Act of Parliament was passed for their regulation while on shore.

From this period, the corps of marines has constituted a part of the military force on the peace establishment. The sale of commissions was abolished, yet the interchange of appointments in the army continued to take place; but this system was soon altered, and the promotion was confined to regular rotation, which regulation has been enforced ever since. Every appointment was notified from the Admiralty, and appeared in the *London Gazette*; but the practice of its being thus officially announced was discontinued, and it is only within a short period that the publication of the promotions in the marines has been resumed.

In the early part of 1756, the French collected a considerable force on the coast of the British Channel; and although these preparations excited great alarm in this country, they were made merely to divert our attention from the armaments in the Mediterranean: nevertheless, it was sufficient to cause so much excitement, that Hessian and Hanoverian troops were brought over to assist us. Amongst the additional reinforcements, 9138 marines were voted in Parliament; and in order to complete the establishment, thirty additional companies were ordered to be raised. The expedient of a land impress was resorted to, by passing an "Act for the more speedy and effectual recruiting His Majesty's land forces and marines." But it was suspended on the 13th of May by royal command.

As it now became apparent that the French, in preparing an armament at Toulon, meditated an attack upon Minorca, it was deemed expedient to reinforce our garrison on that island. Admiral Byng was ordered to proceed with ten ships of the line to the Mediterranean for that purpose; and the 7th regiment of Fusiliers being ordered to embark on board the squadron, the marines were sent on shore to make room for them. The expedition sailed from Spithead on the 6th of April, and arrived at Gibraltar on the 2nd of May, 1757, where it was joined by the squadron under Captain Edgecumbe, who after landing a captain, two subalterns, and 110 marines, with 150 sailors, to assist in the defence of Minorca, had been driven away by the appearance of a French fleet of twelve ships of the line, under Admiral De la Gallissionaire.

Admiral Byng having refitted his ships, and taking with him those under Captain Edgecumbe, quitted Gibraltar on the 8th of May, and arrived off Minorca on the 18th, with the intention of throwing succour into the castle of St. Philip; but learning that the enemy's fleet was not far off, he considered it prudent, from the circumstance of having no marines on board the squadron, and the ships being but badly manned, to retain the troops; consequently, the garrison was left to depend upon its own resources. The hostile squadron was shortly afterwards discovered by our look-out ships; but it was not until the 20th that both fleets formed their lines of battle, when the British bore down to the attack.

The action was vigorously maintained by the rear division under Rear-Admiral West, until the *Intrepid* had her fore topmast shot away; the wreck falling on the foresail, the ship became ungovernable, and rendered it necessary for those astern of her to heave all aback. This accident caused an opening between the van and rear divisions, which exposed the former to the enemy's fire. The ships ahead were now directed to support the rear of our fleet, when the enemy, taking advantage of the confusion that prevailed, kept edging away, and being better sailers than the British, they avoided a renewal of the engagement. The number of ships engaged was equal, but those of the enemy were generally of larger dimensions, carried more guns and more men. Our loss amounted to 43 killed, 168 wounded. The enemy had 38 killed, and 181 wounded. The *Defiance* bore the brunt of the action, having her captain and 13 killed, and 45 wounded. Our ships suffered so much in their masts and rigging, that the admiral, after collecting his crippled ships, found it expedient to call a council of war; and on that decision the squadron proceeded to Gibraltar, leaving the brave defenders of Fort St. Philip to their fate.

In the early part of May, the French fleet, of which we have just spoken, sailed from Toulon, and landed 15,000 troops on the island of Minorca. The siege of Fort St. Philip had lasted seventy days, during which the British endured excessive fatigue in defending such extensive fortifications with so inconsiderable a force. On the 25th the enemy stormed the works at several points, but with partial success; the firing continued from ten at night until four the next morning, when Marshal De Richelieu beat a parley, for leave to bury the dead and remove the wounded. A suspension of arms was agreed upon, but the enemy took this opportunity to strengthen the lodgements they had made, by throwing a number of men into them; whence they communicated by subterraneous passages with all the other outworks, and even with the body of the place itself. This dastardly act of treachery, so unworthy of the character of a military nation, led to the immediate capitulation of the garrison, the whole force of which amounted to no more than 2760 men, and their loss was 93 killed, and 340 wounded.

Admiral Byng was recalled, and tried for not doing his utmost to destroy the enemy; on which charge he was found guilty, and sentenced to be shot; but the court considered that his misconduct did not proceed from want of courage or disaffection, and they therefore most earnestly recommended him to His Majesty's clemency. Notwithstanding this humane consideration, the sentence was carried into execution at twelve o clock on the 14th of March, 1757, on board the *Monarque*, in Portsmouth harbour.

Twenty companies were added to the establishment of the marines, to complete the parliamentary vote of 11,419 men. On the 8th of September Admiral Hawke, with sixteen ships of the line, seven frigates, and fifty-five transports, conveying ten regiments of foot, two of marines, and a proportionate train of artillery, sailed from Portsmouth to make an attack on the port of Rochefort. Part of the fleet, which had been detached under Vice-Admiral Knowles, anchored in Basque Roads on the 23rd, and on the following morning this division, consisting of seven sail of the line, entered the roads of Aix. After an hour's cannonade the troops took possession of that island, which, though possessing fortifications planned by the celebrated Vauban, were so dilapidated as to be incapable of defence, and there were only six guns mounted in a battery, *en barbette*.

After several days, it was determined to make an effort to destroy the shipping and arsenal at Rochefort; but no sooner had the troops embarked in the boats to proceed on that service, than the attack was relinquished, and on the 29th the fleet returned to England.

A further augmentation this year of thirty companies, completed the establishment of marines to 14,845 men. On the 28th February, 1758, the *Monmouth* of 64 guns, Captain Gardiner, having chased from a squadron under Admiral Osborn when off Cape de Gat, brought to action the French 84-gun ship *Foudroyant*; and, notwithstanding the great disparity of force, maintained a gallant action, which lasted from nine in the morning until one in the afternoon, when this powerful ship, after receiving a broadside from the *Swiftsure*, struck her colours, having lost her main and mizen masts, with 100 men killed, and 90 wounded. The *Monmouth* lost her captain, and 27 killed, and 79 wounded. The *Foudroyant* mounted twenty-four and forty-two pounders, whilst the *Monmouth* had only twelves and twenty-fours. The marine officers of the *Monmouth* were captain James Austin, and Lieutenant George Preston.

In order to frustrate the intentions of the French government, in the equipment of armaments to relieve their American colonies, Admiral Hawke, with seven ships of the line, was despatched to Basque Roads, where he arrived on 3rd April, and anchored inside the isle of Aix. The enemy's squadron of five ships of the line cut their cables and ran ashore; but they were afterwards by great exertion dragged through the mud, and got into the *Charente*. On the 5th, the admiral sent 150 marines, under Captain Ewer, to demolish the new works which the enemy had erected on the isle of Aix; which service being effected, he re-embarked in perfect order.

On 9th March a small squadron under the command of Captain Marsh, which sailed from Plymouth, having on board 200 marines under Major Mason, and a detachment of artillery commanded by Captain Walker, arrived off the entrance of the Senegal River on 24th April. The governor of Fort Louis endeavoured to oppose their passing the bar; but the French were beaten back, and a landing of the troops speedily effected. Preparation was made for attacking the fort, which is situated on a small island about twelve miles up the river; but proposals were submitted by the governor to surrender the colony. On the 2nd May, Major Monson, with his marines, took possession of the fort, in which was a garrison of 240 soldiers, with 90 pieces of cannon. The squadron then proceeded to attack the island of Goree; but their force proving insufficient, the attempt miscarried.

Admiral Boscawen, with twenty-three ships of the line, several frigates, and a fleet of transports, conveying 12,000 troops under Major-General Amherst, sailed from Spithead on the 18th of February, and arrived at Halifax on the 9th of May, whence he sailed on the 28th; and this fleet, numbering together 157 sail, anchored on the 2nd of June in Gabareuse Bay, about two leagues westward of Louisbourg. Chevalier Drucour had taken every possible precaution to prevent a surprise, by throwing up entrenchments and having batteries along the coast. In the harbour were five ships of the line and five frigates, three of which were sunk at the entrance during the siege. The garrison consisted of 2500 troops, besides 600 armed inhabitants.

For several days the surf ran so high, as to render it impossible to land the troops; but on the 8th the weather became more moderate, and the soldiers were in the boats at break of day. Under cover of the fire from the frigates and smaller vessels, they moved towards the shore in three divisions. The enemy reserved their fire until the boats were close to the shore; but the calmness and intrepidity of the British overcame all obstacles, although the surf was so great that many of the boats were destroyed. Brigadier-General Wolfe jumped into the sea, and being followed by his whole division, who were instantly formed into line, they drove the enemy at the point of the bayonet. The other two divisions following their gallant example, the French fled in great confusion, leaving seventeen pieces of cannon and two mortars, with their ammunition, in the hands of the British; and before night the whole army, with its cannon and stores, were landed, and the town regularly invested. The governor destroyed his out-posts, with all the buildings within two miles of the ramparts, and prepared for a resolute defence.

On the 12th General Wolfe, with 1200 men, was ordered to march round to the north-east harbour, where he erected a powerful battery, which silenced the fire from the island. On the 25th the marines were landed, and being formed into a battalion, took post at Kennington Cove; and on the 30th they were successfully engaged with the enemy. On the 28th the French sank a ship of the line and three frigates at the mouth of the harbour, to prevent the entrance of our squadron. The army underwent great fatigue in carrying on the approaches, which were considerably advanced, when an accident afforded them an unlooked-for relief, and greatly distressed the enemy: on the 21st of July a shell from the lighthouse battery having set fire to the 74-gun ship *Entreprenant*, she immediately blew up, and the *Capricieux* and *Celèbre*

45

of 64 guns taking fire, they were also destroyed. In the night of the 25th of July 600 seamen, under Captains Laforey and Balfour, pulled into the harbour, and boarded the *Prudent* 74 and the *Bienfaisant* of 64 guns, and carried them, without much resistance: the former having taken the ground was destroyed, but the *Bienfaisant* was brought triumphantly away. On the 26th of July the garrison of Louisbourg capitulated, and the islands of St. John and Cape Breton were ceded to His Britannic Majesty.

A squadron of four ships of the line, two frigates, with 600 troops, sailed from Cork on the 9th of November, and anchored in the road of Goree on the 24th of December. On either side of the bay was a small fort, with several batteries extending along the shore, mounting in the whole 100 pieces of cannon; and the garrison consisted of 300 regulars, and about the same number of negro inhabitants. On the morning of the 28th, the troops were ordered into the boats, ready for landing; and the ships having taken their stations, opened a heavy fire, which was returned by the enemy with great spirit. After this cannonade had been maintained for several hours, the governor surrendered at discretion; upon which Keppel landed all the marines of the squadron, and took possession of the island.

In November, the *Buckingham* of 64 guns, Captain Tyrrel, accompanied by the *Weazle* sloop, being near Guadaloupe, discovered a fleet of nineteen sail, under convoy of the French 74-gun ship *Florissant* and two frigates. After a running fight, in which the *Buckingham* was annoyed by the frigates, Captain Tyrrel closed with the *Florissant*, and the action was maintained with great determination on both sides. Captain Tyrrel received a wound which compelled him to resign the command to Lieutenant Marshall, who fell gloriously, and the second-lieutenant continued the engagement until the French colours were hauled down.

The *Florissant* had 180 men killed, and 300 wounded; whilst the *Buckingham* had only 7 killed, and 17 dangerously wounded. The. British ship was so much disabled in her masts and rigging, that the *Florissant* escaped during the night. Captain Tyrrel thus speaks of the conduct of the marines:—

> Captain Troy, at the head of the marines, performed the service of a brave and gallant officer, cleared the poop and quarter-deck of the enemy, and drove her men like sheep down the main-deck.

An expedition under Commodore Moore, sailed from England in the latter part of 1758, consisting of nine ships of the line, a frigate, four bombs, with sixty transports containing six regiments of foot. 800 marines were embarked in the squadron, commanded by Brevet-Colonel Rycaut, of the Portsmouth division, and it was intended that they should have been formed into a battalion to co-operate with the land forces, but the commodore altered this arrangement, and landed the detachments as it became necessary; consequently, the services of Colonel Rycaut were dispensed with. Dr. Beatson remarks, that:

> Colonel Rycaut, of the marines, was deprived of all command, whereby that useful corps was never permitted to land and act with the land forces, which was a very great loss to the army.

They arrived at Barbadoes on the 3rd of January, 1759, whence they sailed on the 13th, and entered the bay of Fort Royal, Martinico, on the 15th. Early on the following morning, the Bristol and Ripon attacked a battery of seven guns on Negro Point, which they soon silenced, and the marines from both ships were landed; who, climbing up the rocks, entered the fort and hoisted the British colours. At four o clock, the signal being made for disembarking the troops, they were immediately conveyed to the shore, under cover of the fire from the ships, and landed without much opposition; but finding it impracticable to bring the cannon sufficiently near for attacking the town, the forces re-embarked, in order to proceed to St. Pierre. When they arrived before that place, new difficulties arose, which occasioned a council of war.

The commodore had no doubt of being able to reduce the town; but as the troops had suffered greatly by disease, and the probability of the ships being so disabled in the attack as to prevent them from availing themselves of their success to undertake further operations, he recommended that they should proceed against Guadaloupe. The fleet arrived on the 23rd of January before the town of Basseterre, the capital of the island, a place of considerable extent, defended by strong batteries towards the sea; and on an eminence to the southward of the town stands Fort Royal, mounting forty-seven pieces of cannon. The chief engineer was of opinion that this fortress, from its elevation, was impregnable to the squadron; yet a council of war determined on the attack, and the ships took up their positions at nine a. m. on the 23rd,— the *Lion* 74 abreast of a battery of nine guns; *St. George* 90, *Norfolk* 74, and *Cambridge* 80 opposite the citadel, and kept up an incessant cannonade until five p.m., when the fort ceased firing. At ten a.m., the *Panther* 50 brought up close to the royal battery in the town, of twelve guns, and continued engaging for several hours, unassisted by the *Burford* 70, who was to have supported her; but owing to some accident she did not reach her station, nor take any part in the action.

The *Rippon* 60 ran so close to the shore, that she grounded; and in consequence of the *Berwick* 64 relinquishing her station on the approach of some vessels on fire, she became exposed to the battery of St. Nicholas, of seven guns, as well as that of Morne Rouge, mounting six guns *en barbette.* The *Rippon* having suffered considerably from an explosion, which blew up the poop and set the ship on fire, made the signal for assistance: on which the *Bristol* 50 ran down, and took a position between her and the St. Nicholas battery; the marines at the same time taking the militia in the trenches in flank, soon dispersed them. In the evening the bomb-vessels threw shells into the town, which set it on fire, and the magazines blew up with a terrible explosion. The only officer killed was Lieutenant Roberts of the marines, on board the *Norfolk*; and among the wounded, Captain Trelawney of the *Lion*, Lieutenant Curies of the marines of the same ship, and Lieutenant Chandy of the marines of the *Rippon*; with a total of 30 killed, and 60 wounded.

On the 24th the troops landed without opposition, took possession of the heights, and, the 61st regiment having marched into the citadel, hoisted the British colours. The country was far from being reduced to submission; it abounded in mountains and defiles, and the inhabitants were determined to defend their possessions to the last extremity. The French commandant, M. Nadau d Etreuil, posted himself in a deep cleft in the mountains, which entirely commanded the passage into the Capesterres, the richest and best cultivated part of the island, which was very difficult of access, the whole environs being intersected by deep ravines. On the 26th a summons was sent by the British, which the commandant rejected with firmness. Some skirmishes took place, in which the 61st regiment had an opportunity of distinguishing itself, in attacking the enemy's entrenchments.

It being resolved to reduce Fort Louis on the Grand-terre side of the island, the squadron, under Captain Harman of the *Berwick*, moved on to the attack on the 13th February. The cannonade lasted five hours, during which every house was burnt, a breach made in the walls, and the batteries silenced along the shore. The troops then got into the boats, and Major Campbell with his marines, and some companies of the Royal Highland regiment, with great difficulty landed. Finding that their ammunition was mostly destroyed, they drove the enemy at the point of the bayonet, and after a severe struggle carried the fort, with all the batteries.

The death of General Hopson changed the plan of operations; for his successor, Major-General Barrington, re-embarked the troops, after leaving a garrison in Fort Royal and blowing up the other works. On the 7th of March the fleet sailed for Fort Louis, on the Grand-terre side of the island, where the whole had arrived by the 20th. The commodore receiving information of the arrival of a French squadron of eight ships of the line, under M. de Bompart, the army was left to its own energies, and the marines returned to their respective ships. As their numbers were much reduced, a detachment of troops was added to their strength, and on the 13th of April the squadron sailed for Prince Rupert's Bay. On the 1st of May Guadaloupe capitulated, and the example was followed by Desirade, Saintes, and Petite-terre; and on the 26th of May, Mariegalante likewise surrendered.

A fleet of twelve sail of the line, under M. de la Clue, sailed from Toulon in the early part of August, and five of these, with five frigates, soon afterwards separated. On the 18th, the squadron fell in with a British fleet of fourteen sail of the line, two of 50 guns, and several frigates, under Admiral Boscawen, who immediately made the signal to chase and engage in line of battle ahead.

The advanced ships commenced firing upon the enemy at 2h. 30m. p. m., and closing with the *Centaur* of 74 guns, compelled that ship to surrender, with the loss of 200 men killed and wounded. The pursuit continued during the night, under favour of which two of the enemy escaped, and at daylight only four were to be seen, about five leagues distant from Lagos Bay. The *Ocean* of 80 guns, and *Redoutable* 74, ran on the rocks, and were destroyed; but the *Téméraire* 74, and *Modeste* 64, were brought away. M. de la Clue died of his wounds, and was buried at Lagos. The British sustained a loss of 56 men killed, and 196 wounded.

The fleet under Sir Edward Hawke having taken refuge in Torbay during the heavy westerly gales, Admiral Conflans took the earliest opportunity to put to sea with the French fleet, from Brest. On the same day the British admiral sailed from Torbay, directing his course towards Quiberon, and on the 20th of November the enemy's fleet was discovered by our look-out ships. At this time it was blowing hard, with a heavy sea; and although the shoals and rocks on the coast were imperfectly known to the English pilots, Sir Edward Hawke zealously persevered in his endeavours to bring the enemy to action. The British fleet consisted of twenty-three ships of the line and ten frigates; that of the enemy, twenty-one of the line and five frigates. At 3 h. 30 m. p.m., the van of the British began engaging the enemy's rear, as their advanced ships led round the Cardinal rocks.

About 4 p. m., the *Formidable*, bearing the flag of Rear-Admiral Verger, after a gallant defence, struck her colours. The *Thesée* foundered in consequence of shipping a heavy sea in her lower deck, and the *Superbe* shared the same fate. The *Héros* surrendered and came to anchor, but it was blowing so hard that no boat could be sent to take possession. Darkness coming on, the enemy fled towards their own coast; seven of their line of battleships, after throwing their guns overboard, got into the River Vilaine, whilst the British anchored under the island of Dumet. When morning appeared, the ship of the French admiral was discovered to be on shore, and she was soon afterwards burnt by her own crew. The *Essex* and *Resolution* ran on the Four-reef and were wrecked, but most of their crew were saved. Our total loss in this memorable battle was no more than one lieutenant and 39 seamen and marines killed, and 222 wounded.

In the East Indies the British arms were equally triumphant. A French squadron of eleven ships of the line, under M. d'Aché, appearing on the Coromandel coast, Vice-Admiral Pocock, with seven of the line, immediately proceeded thither; and on the 2nd of September the French ships were discovered, but it was not until the 10th that they were brought to action. Although nothing decisive resulted from this contest, our loss amounted to no less than 118 killed,—66 mortally, 122 dangerously, and 263 slightly wounded. Among the killed was Captain C. Michie of the *Newcastle*, Captain Gore and Lieutenant Redshaw of the marines, and Lieutenant Elliott of the *Tyger*.

Extensive preparations were now making in all the French ports for the invasion of Great Britain, and several men-of-war, transports, and flat-bottomed boats were getting ready in all the ports. Havre-de-Grace, and the other harbours on the coast of Normandy, prepared for the expedition against England, whilst another division of the flotilla was to proceed from Dunkirk, and make an attempt on the coast of Scotland; and a third embarkation, destined for Ireland, was to be made at Vannes, in Brittany, The Duke D'Aiguillon had the command of the land forces, and a powerful squadron, under Admiral Conflans, was to secure their landing. To counteract these machinations, Admiral Hawke with a large fleet cruised before Brest, leaving a detached force to watch the bay of Audierne, and a squadron under commodore Boyce was stationed before Dunkirk. In the month of July, 1760, rear-admiral Rodney bombarded Havre with great success, setting fire to the town in several places, and he destroyed all their preparations for the invasion of England.

In this year, twenty-seven sail of the line and thirty-one frigates were captured from the French, and eight ships of the line and four frigates destroyed; whilst England, during the various operations, lost no more than seven ships of the line and five frigates. In addition to these reverses, the commerce of France was seriously reduced by the loss of Quebec and Guadaloupe.

In consideration of the signal services rendered by Admirals Boscawen and Sir Charles Saunders, His Majesty instituted a new establishment of marine officers, entitled "General and Lieutenant-General of Marines;" and shortly afterwards three post-captains in the navy were selected for the rank of colonel.

The following officers were the first who held those appointments:—

|  |  | £/Per Ann. |
|---|---|---|
| Admiral Boscawen | General of Marines | 2000 |
| Sir Chas. Saunders, K.B. | Lieut.-General | 1200 |
| Sir Piercy Brett, Bart. . | Col. of Portsmouth Div. | 800 |
| Hon. Augustus Keppel. | Col. of Plymouth Div. | 800 |
| Viscount Howe | Col. of Chatham Div. | 800 |

The appointment of a major-general was subsequently added to the establishment.

This arrangement, at once humiliating and disrespectful to a corps which had ever supported its military character with credit and honour, created universal dissatisfaction. It was a wound that rankled at the very heart of the service; and it continued to be so sensibly felt as a mark of reproach, that in 1777 the corps resolved to memorial the lords commissioners of the Admiralty, respecting the injustice of placing officers of the navy over them; and justly remarking upon the incompetency of naval officers to take command of troops in the field. This remonstrance was forwarded by Colonel Mackenzie, with a strong letter addressed to the Earl of Sandwich; but neither that application, nor the many subsequent expressions of discontent, could obtain redress. The emoluments of these appointments continued to be enjoyed by naval officers until the year 1833, when this degrading system of sinecures was abolished; but even then the entire advantage did not revert to the corps, and but an inadequate proportion of the amount fell to their lot in the distribution of the good-service pensions.

In this year the British navy amounted to one hundred and twenty ships of the line: seventeen of that number were in the East Indies, twenty for the protection of our West India islands, twelve in North America, ten in the Mediterranean, and sixty-one on the home station. The establishment of marines was increased to one hundred and thirty companies, amounting to 18,365 men.

The French squadron under Thurot, which had sailed from Dunkirk and taken refuge in the harbour of Gottenburg, in Sweden, and which originally consisted of five frigates, having on board 1200 soldiers, sailed from that port for Bergen; and on the 5th of December, having parted company with one of the squadron, they directed their course towards Ireland. It was not until the 21st of February that Thurot effected a landing at Carrickfergus with 600 men, and made the garrison under Colonel Jennings prisoners; but learning the defeat of the fleet of Conflans, and finding that a body of regular troops was approaching, they re-embarked and immediately sailed for France.

A few hours after quitting the British coast, three ships were seen bearing down upon them; which were the English frigates *Æolus* 36, Captain Elliott, with the *Pallas* and *Brilliant* of 32 guns, Captains Clement and Logie. An action was maintained with great spirit for an hour and a half, when the *Marechal de Belleisle*, of 44 guns, was boarded and captured by the *Æolus*, the gallant Thurot having fallen in the action. The other ships were also captured, and taken into the English ports. The British loss was only 5 killed, and 41 wounded; that of the enemy 300 killed and wounded.

Shortly after the victory gained by Colonel Coote over General Lally at Wandewash, a squadron of six ships of the line under Rear-Admiral Cornish, reached Madras; and as the French squadron under M. d'Aché had not appeared on the coast, the admiral was at liberty to assist in reducing the French settlements. Colonel Coote with the army marched to attack Waldour, and block up Pondicherry, whilst the squadron proceeded to form the siege of Carical, where it arrived on the 28th of March. At five in the morning Major Monson, with 300 marines and 50 pioneers, landed about four miles from the place, and marching directly up to it, took possession of the town early on the following day. Finding themselves annoyed by the redoubt of Fort Dauphin, some shells were thrown by the British, which induced the enemy immediately to abandon it, and retire to Fort Louis. Reinforcements from Trichinopoly having arrived, the place was invested on the 3rd, and the British erected several batteries.

On the 5th, Major Monson, learning that the garrison was likely to obtain relief from Chilanbrun, summoned the commandant to surrender: the proposition was acceded to, and the French troops surrendered as prisoners of war. The marines, after assisting at the reduction of two other posts, were re-embarked in the early part of May.

Rear-Admiral Stevens, having assumed the command of the fleet, landed the marines at Cuddalore on the 29th of August, and on the following day they joined the army. Colonel Coote was superseded in his command by the promotion of Major Monson; but the latter was so severely wounded, that Colonel Coote resumed his office, and continued to direct the operations against Pondicherry until its surrender on 16th January, 1761.

A very gallant action between the *Biddeford* and *Flamborough* of 20 guns, Captains Skinner and Kennedy, and the French frigates *Malicieuse* of 36, and *Opale* of 32 guns, was fought on the 4th of April near Oporto. The enemy, perceiving the inferiority of the British ships, bore down upon them at about seven in the evening, and a close action continued until nine o'clock, when the enemy shot ahead. The firing was renewed as soon as the ships had repaired their rigging, and it was maintained until eleven; when the French frigates made sail and escaped, leaving the British ships so much disabled as to be incapable of pursuit. The *Biddeford* had her captain and 8 men killed, her lieutenant and 25 wounded. After the death of Captain Skinner, Lieutenant Knollis fought the ship until he was mortally wounded, and the master gallantly continued the action until the enemy made off. On board the *Flamborough* Lieutenant Price of the marines and 5 men were killed, and 10 wounded.

Rear-Admiral Rodney continued very actively employed on his station off Havre-de-Grace, keeping the enemy's coast in a constant state of alarm, and attacking their convoys whenever they dared to venture out of their ports.

Admiral Boscawen was stationed with a strong squadron in the Bay of Biscay, and so effectually blockaded the harbours of Brest and Rochefort, that the French were unable to reinforce their possessions in North America. Sir Edward Hawke, who relieved Admiral Boscawen in September, pursued the same plan of operations, and maintained the proud pre-eminence of our naval power.

A secret expedition, commanded by Major-General Hodgson and Commodore Keppel, consisting of twelve battalions of infantry, two battalions of marines, and a train of artillery, amounting to nearly 10,000 men, sailed from St. Helen's on the 29th of March, 1761, escorted by ten ships of the line, eight frigates, three bombs, and two fire-ships; and this fleet arrived in sight of Belleisle on the 6th of April. The island had been put into the best state of defence, batteries were erected at every position that afforded a practicable place for landing, and a strong garrison occupied the citadel, under the command of the chevalier De St. Croix.

Early in the morning of the 7th, the fleet passed the south end of the island so near the shore, as to afford an opportunity of reconnoitring the coast and fix on a proper quarter for landing. The ships anchored at noon in the roads of Palais, and the principal officers of both services proceeded to the northward, to make further observations; but they found the enemy so extremely on the alert and well prepared at every point, that it was difficult to decide where a landing could be effected without great risk and sacrifice of lives. Early in the morning of the 8th, dispositions were made for debarking the troops; and the *Dragon* and *Achilles*, with two bombs, sailed round to the bay of Port Andeo at the southeast end of the island, followed by the commodore in the *Prince of Orange*, with the troops in the flat-bottomed boats.

A battery, which opened upon them from the point at the entrance, was soon silenced, and the boats pulled towards the shore in three divisions, conducted by Captain Barton of the navy. The enemy was posted on the sides of a steep hill, the base of which was cut away to prevent the possibility of attempting the works without scaling-ladders. The troops made good their landing; but all their efforts to ascend the hill proving unavailing, a retreat was the only alternative.

On this occasion Generals Crawford and Carleton were conspicuous for the gallantry they displayed in leading their divisions to the attack, and the latter was wounded in the thigh. One of the boats landed at some distance from the rest, with a company of grenadiers under Captain Erskine; who, from not being supported, was driven back with great loss, after a determined resistance, in which their gallant leader lost his life. The fire from the ships effectually covered the retreat of the troops; but the weather became so tempestuous, that the transports got foul of each other, and many boats were destroyed.

54

The loss sustained in this attack amounted to nearly 500 in killed, wounded, and prisoners.

During these operations, a diversion was made by Sir Thomas Stanhope at Sauçon, in order to draw the enemy's attention from the main attack. This detachment consisted of the 96th and 97th regiments, and the battalions of marines. As soon as the weather became moderated, the utmost diligence was used to repair the damages the fleet had sustained; and a reinforcement having arrived, it was determined to make another descent at Fort d'Arsic, under the direction of Major-General Crawford. In order to second these operations, two separate attacks were to be made; the first by Brigadier-General Lambert, near St. Foy, and the other at Sauçon by the force which had recently arrived. Early on the morning of the 22nd, the ships of the line took their stations to cover the landing; and having silenced the batteries, the boats with the troops advanced in two divisions, in close order, until abreast of their respective points of attack. The enemy, supposing that Fort d'Arsic would be first attempted, did not adopt measures for the defence of the stupendous rocks, which offered such natural obstacles to the invaders.

Brigadier Lambert's division, to which the battalions of marines under Colonel Mackenzie were attached, advanced under this high coast; and Captain Patterson at the head of the grenadiers of the 19th regiment, immediately supported by Captain Murray with a company of marines, climbed these rocks unperceived by the enemy. Other troops soon followed their intrepid example; and reaching the summit, they formed upon it, and were soon attacked by a regiment of infantry. Contiguous to the ground occupied by our men, there was a wall that offered an eligible post of defence; whence the small force of the British, by keeping up a steady fire, checked the enemy, until they were reinforced by Brigadier Lambert at the head of the grenadiers of the 30th regiment, and the remainder of the marines under Colonel Mackenzie, who immediately attacked the enemy, and drove them back to the top of the hill, where they had some field-pieces.

Captain Sir Thomas Stanhope, perceiving the successful efforts of this detachment, instantly supported them with all the armed boats of his squadron: at the same time the division of troops designed to attack Fort d'Arsic, pushed on to unite with those under Brigadier Lambert; who finding himself thus reinforced, moved up the hill, drove the enemy back upon their main body, and captured three field-pieces, with some prisoners.

Our loss did not exceed thirty men: Captain Patteson of Beauclerc's regiment, Colonel Mackenzie and Captain Murray of the marines, were wounded. By five in the evening the troops were all on shore; and the army, after advancing three miles into the country, took post on an eminence during the night. In order to retard the march of the troops, the enemy broke up the roads, destroyed the bridges, and after withdrawing from the batteries along the coast, blew up their magazine.

Early on the 23rd, General Hodgson moved the army towards the town and citadel of Palais; and although the French had evinced an intention to dispute our progress, they fell back without further resistance, and shut themselves up in the redoubts and citadel. The weather being very unfavourable for landing the cannon, and the stores essential for the attack of the place, General St. Croix availed himself of the delay by constructing six redoubts, which it would be necessary to possess before the approaches could be carried on against the fortress. On the 2nd of May our batteries opened, and their effect was soon apparent. During the following night the enemy made a sortie with 400 men, carried one of our advanced works, and made General Crawford with his two *aides-de-camp* prisoners. Following up their success, they advanced against the trenches, which they attacked with much vigour; and the contest remained doubtful until the arrival of a party of marines under Captain David Hepburn, who drove them with the bayonet, and forced them to retire with considerable loss.

As it was found necessary to carry one of the enemy's redoubts which impeded the approaches, a heavy fire of shot and shells was kept up during the night; and on the morning of the 13th a detachment of 200 men, composed of Loudon's regiment and marines under Captain Carruthers, advanced upon the enemy, and after a sharp contest again drove them with the bayonet. Observing the panic which ensued, Captain Carruthers pushed forward and took possession of two other redoubts, which the French abandoned, and fled into the citadel. Major Nesbitt of the 69th regiment, having reinforced our detachment with 370 men, they were soon masters of the whole of the redoubts, the enemy abandoning them on the approach of our troops.

In this attack, Major Nesbitt and nine men were wounded, and four killed. The enemy suffered severely in killed and wounded, and 100 men were taken prisoners. Following up these successes, General Hodgson made a lodgement in the town, and compelled the enemy to withdraw into the citadel, from which all communication was cut off from the continent by the exertions of the squadron: the place was now so closely invested, that there was no longer a doubt of the surrender of the garrison. Nevertheless, M. de St. Croix resolved to defend the place until the last, and his conduct throughout, reflected the highest honour upon himself and the French arms.

By the 16th the batteries were completed, and the citadel played upon by the unremitting discharge of 40 mortars, 10 howitzers, 1 thirty-two-pounders, 20 twenty-four-pounders, and 10 twelve-pounders; besides field-pieces to clear the enemy's work by ricochet firing.

From this period until the 7th of June the approaches made rapid progress, and a breach having been reported practicable, preparations were making to storm, when M. de St. Croix proposed to capitulate. Terms were agreed upon, and on the 8th the citadel was taken possession of by the British troops: the garrison marched out with the honours of war, and were conveyed to the nearest port in France. When the place was first invested, their strength amounted to 2600 men, but it was now reduced to 1678; by which it appears their loss was 922 men. The British Army consisted of 13,000 men, and of that number 1000 were marines. The loss sustained, between the 22nd of April and the 7th of June, was 13 officers and 300 rank and file killed; 21 officers and 480 wounded: among the latter, brigadier-general Howe. During the siege there were many instances of intrepidity and courage deserving of notice:—

Captain Wright, having under him three companies of marines, held a post of great consequence, from which he received orders to retreat; but this gallant officer, knowing the importance of maintaining his position, took upon himself the responsibility of remaining, and by resolutely holding his ground he repulsed the enemy. Another instance of the kind is recited of Lieutenant Lachlan Cuthbert, of the army, who had charge of a battery, and though abandoned by his men, continued firing the guns until supported; and he then compelled the enemy to retire with considerable loss. The following orders were issued sometime after the surrender of the island:

General Hodgson has the greatest pleasure to acquaint the officers and soldiers under his command with His Majesty's satisfaction in the spirit, patience, and cheerfulness with which they have sustained the fatigues of this siege.

Commodore Keppel, in his public letter to the right-honourable Mr. Pitt, says:

Major-General Hodgson, by his constant approbation of the battalion of marines landed from the ships and put under his command, gives me the pleasing satisfaction of acquainting you of it, that His Majesty may be informed of the goodness and spirited behaviour of that corps.

At this period the marines wore caps similar to those of the fusilier regiments; and from that circumstance the French, in describing the troops whose valour had been most conspicuous, designated the battalions of marines "*les petits grenadiers.*" Their gallant conduct elicited the most flattering encomiums from both commanders-in-chief; and the British Government, to commemorate their distinguished services during these operations, authorised the corps to adopt the proud emblem which now encircles the globe emblazoned on the colours of the royal marines.

A squadron of four ships of the line, under the command of Commodore Sir James Douglas, sailed from Basseterre, Guadaloupe, on the 4th of June, having a division of troops on board, commanded by Lord Rollo. They arrived at Roseau, the capital of Dominica, on the 6th, and finding the inhabitants opposed to their landing, the ships anchored and silenced the batteries. The troops then landed under cover of the fire of the squadron, and formed in excellent order on the beach, while a detachment moved forward and took possession of the town. Lieutenant-Colonel Melvill, at the head of the grenadiers, seized a flanking battery, which the enemy abandoned on his approach; and following up his success, that gallant officer led the troops in driving the enemy from all their positions. The governor, M. Longprie, with the second in command, were made prisoners, and the island submitted on the following day.

On the 8th of January, the *Unicorn* of 32 guns, Captain Hunt, when cruising off the Penmanks, captured the *Vestale* of 32 guns, after an action of two hours, in which she had 5 killed and 10 wounded; among the latter, Captain Hunt, mortally. Captain Bois Bertelot, of the *Vestale*, was also mortally wounded. First-Lieutenant Charles Shearer, and Second-Lieutenant Thomas Phillips, were on board the *Unicorn*.

The *Seahorse* of 20 guns, Captain James Smith, when off the Start, sustained a very spirited action on the 10th of January with the French frigate *Aigrette* of 34 guns, which lasted an hour and a half within pistol-shot. The *Seahorse* had 11 killed, and 38 wounded. On the *Unicorn* making her appearance, the French ship made sail and escaped. Lieutenant of marines, Evan Cameron, was on board the *Seahorse*.

On the 30th of January the *Venus* 36 guns, Captain Harrison, and *Juno* 32, Captain Philips, captured the French frigate *Brune*, of 36 guns. The *Venus* was engaged with the enemy's ship upwards of two hours, and had 4 men killed, and 18 wounded. On the *Juno* coming up and firing a few guns, the *Brune* struck her colours; having 19 killed, and 39 wounded. Lieutenant John Evins of the marines, was serving on board the *Venus*.

On the 24th January the Richmond 32 guns, Captain Elphinstone fell in with the French frigate *Felicité* of 32 guns, Captain Donnel, off the Hague, and brought her to action. Both ships took the ground, and continued to engage until the enemy fled from their quarters, and escaped to the shore. The *Felicité* had nearly 100 in killed and wounded; among the former, her captain. The *Richmond*, 3 killed, 13 wounded. The *Felicité* was destroyed on the following day. The officers of marines were First-Lieutenant William Spann, and Second-Lieutenant John McCulloch.

On the 23rd of January, the *Minerva* of 32 guns, Captain Alexander Hood, when off Cape Penas, captured the French sixty-gun ship *Warwick*, (having only 34 mounted,) Captain Le Verger de Belais, after a gallant action of four hours. The *Minerva* lost her foremast and bowsprit, and her loss amounted to 14 men killed, and 34 wounded. The enemy had her fore and main-top masts shot away, and lost 14 men killed, and 32 wounded. Shortly after the action, the other masts of the *Minerva* went by the board.

On the 13th of March, the *Vengeance* of 26 guns, (nine and four-pounders,) Captain Nightingale, after an action of five hours, captured the French 40-gun frigate *Entreprenant*, mounting 26 guns, (twelve and nine-pounders,) with a loss of 5 killed and 24 wounded. Second-Lieutenant David Coutts was serving on board the *Vengeance*.

On the 13th of August, the *Bellona* 74 guns, Captain Robert Faulknor, and the *Brilliant* 36 guns, Captain Loggie, off Vigo, sustained an action with the French ships *Courageux* of 74 guns, Captain D. Lambert, and the *Malicieuse* and *Hermione* of 32 guns. After a contest, which lasted from twenty-five minutes past six until seven in the morning, the *Courageux* surrendered, with the loss of 200 killed, her captain mortally, and 110 wounded. The frigates made their escape as soon as they saw the fate of their commodore; but they had both been sharply engaged with the *Brilliant*, which ship had 5 men killed, and 16 wounded. Captain James Sabine, and First-Lieutenant Nathaniel

English, were serving on board the *Bellona,* whose loss amounted to no more than 6 men killed, and 25 wounded.

The prospect of a war with Spain roused the British nation to make vigorous preparations; and the Parliament in November 1761, voted for the following year 70,000 seamen, including 19,061 marines, comprised in 135 companies.

The failure of the expedition against Martinique in 1759, did not discourage the minister from making a further attempt for the reduction of that colony, which still furnished a considerable resource to the declining commerce of France. The plan for prosecuting this important conquest had been laid down by Mr. Pitt, and the succeeding administration maintained the same project. Eleven battalions having been ordered from New York, they sailed for Barbadoes the end of October 1761, under convoy of a squadron commanded by captain Darby, of the *Devonshire*; and in December, Rear-Admiral Rodney, with several ships, united with this force. On the 14th four battalions arrived from Belleisle under Brigadier Rufane, and on the 24th the troops, commanded by General Monckton and Lord Rollo, arrived in Carlisle bay. The armament now consisted of 14,000 land forces and a fleet of 16 ships of the line, with several frigates and 4 bombs.

On the 8th of January a division of the fleet silenced the batteries in St. Anne's bay, and part of the army landed; but finding it impossible to reach Fort Royal from this spot, it was determined to remove the ships with the army to St. Lucie, on the opposite side of the island, thence march across the isthmus to Gross Point, so as to be able to reach Pigeon Island, and thus enable the ships to anchor on the east side of Fort Royal, and assail the citadel; but from the difficulty that presented itself in transporting cannon and stores, the plan was relinquished.

It was, however, determined to attempt the reduction of Pigeon Island from the east side; and the squadron having silenced the batteries, two brigades of foot under Generals Haviland and Grant, and a corps of light infantry commanded by Lieutenant-Colonel Scott, landed at Ance d'Arlet, and marched to the heights opposite Pigeon Island. On the 10th, Captain Harvey in the *Dragon* proceeded against Grand Ance, and having silenced the battery, landed a few seamen with all his marines, who carried the fort, and held it until relieved by a battalion under Lieutenant-Colonel Melville. After destroying the works in St. Anne's bay, the commanders of the expedition, finding it difficult to extend the operations in that quarter, proceeded to Ance d'Arlet, and, uniting with Brigadier-General Haviland, they directed their course to the bay of Fort Royal, where the fleet came to an anchor.

Early in the morning of the 16th, the ships moved to their respective stations, and having silenced the batteries, the troops pushed for the shore, and made good their landing in Cas de Navières Bay. Early on the 17th, the remainder of the army disembarked, together with the marines, who were formed into two battalions of 450 men each, and attached to the brigade of General Rufane. The army encamped upon the heights above Le Cas des Navières, and detachments were employed in throwing up works for protecting the passage of the troops through the intervening ravines, in their advance upon the entrenchments at Morne Tortenson.

On the 24th, at daybreak, the troops moved forward under cover of the batteries, the grenadiers under Brigadier-General Grant taking the lead; whilst Brigadier Rufane on the right, with his brigade and the marines, were ordered to attack the redoubts along the seacoast, supported by 1000 seamen in flat-bottomed boats. Lord Rollo's brigade supported the grenadiers, and General Walsh, with his force, assisted the movements of Lieutenant-Colonel Scott with the light infantry in his endeavour to get round the flank of the enemy, which he effected, whilst the grenadiers drove them from post to post until they arrived upon their left flank, and the enemy was finally driven from their position. By nine o'clock our troops were in possession of the several redoubts on Morne Tortenson, the enemy retiring in great confusion to Morne Garnier, a still higher hill, and separated from Morne Tortenson by a deep ravine, which post was strongly fortified, and considered to be of great importance.

General Haviland, with his brigade and two battalions of Highlanders, with some light infantry under Major Leland, were directed to make a passage through the ravine, and cut off a detached corps of the French. They soon drove the enemy, and the light infantry possessed themselves of a post opposite to Morne Garnier; while the division of grenadiers and Walsh's brigade kept possession of an upper plantation, and the marines, which General Monckton had taken from Brigadier Rufane, were posted to cover the road between the two plantations,

On the 25th, the batteries on Morne Tortenson opened against the citadel of Fort Royal; and the fire from Morne Garnier was so annoying, that it became expedient to attack this post. On the 27th the enemy, in force, moved out under cover of their batteries, and attacked the two corps of light infantry and Haviland's brigade; but they were received with firmness, and repulsed. The ardour of the British troops led them to pursue the enemy across the ravine, and seize their batteries, where they took post, and were presently reinforced by the brigade of General Walsh and the division of grenadiers under Brigadier Grant. Before nine that night, the light infantry under Major Leland were in possession of Morne Garnier, which completely commanded the citadel.

On the 30th of January, the batteries on Morne Tortenson were opened upon the citadel; but finding that the distance was too great, it became necessary to possess Morne Capuchin, which was within four hundred yards of the place. Whilst preparations were making to carry this into effect, the French garrison proposed to capitulate, and terms having been agreed upon for the conveyance of the troops to France, the garrison, consisting of 800 men, marched out with the honours of war on the morning of the 5th of February. The governor-general, M. de la Touche, had fallen back upon St. Pierre, with an intention of holding out, but he soon surrendered; and Captain Harvey having landed the marines from the squadron, with 500 seamen, in the harbour of Trinité, the whole island submitted to the British Crown.

This conquest, which added so much lustre to our arms, was obtained at the expense of 7 officers, 3 sergeants, and 86 rank and file killed; and 32 officers, 20 sergeants, and 337 rank and file wounded; while the loss of the enemy exceeded 1000 men. The islands of St. Lucia, St. Vincent, and Grenada, fell soon after the surrender of Martinique, and by these acquisitions the colonies of Antigua, St. Christopher's, and Nevis were secured from any hostile intention of the enemy. Great Britain thus became quietly possessed of that chain of islands, extending from the eastern point of Hispaniola, almost to the continent of South America.

An expedition, consisting of five ships of the line and fifty transports, under Admiral Pocock, for the reduction of the island of Cuba, sailed from Spithead on the 5th of March, and arrived at Barbadoes on the 20th of April, whence it proceeded to Martinique, and on the 26th anchored in the bay of Cas de Navières. The army, after receiving reinforcements, was divided into five brigades, and the necessary arrangements being completed, the expedition took its departure on the 6th of May. Between that period and the 23rd, it was joined by the squadrons of Captains Harvey and Sir James Douglas; and on the 27th the fleet, now amounting to 200 sail, bore away for the old straits of Bahama, and arrived off the Havanna on the 6th of June. At this time the garrison of the Havanna consisted of 4610 regular troops, 9000 sailors and marines of the twelve ships of the line in the harbour, with 14,000 militia and people of colour, forming a total of 20,610 men.

The army having effected a landing about six miles to the eastward of the Moro without opposition, moved towards the Havanna; but a considerable force showing a disposition to dispute the passage of the Coximar River, the fort was silenced by the fire of the *Dragon*, and the troops passed unmolested. During this time Sir George Pocock made a feint with the marines on the Havanna side, in order to divert the enemy's attention. On the 10th the *Belleisle*, Captain Knight, was ordered against the Chorera Castle; and on the following day Colonel Carleton carried the redoubt which defended the Cavannos. On the 13th, Colonel Home, with 300 light infantry, and two battalions of marines under Majors Campbell and Collins, landed at the Chorera, to secure a footing and engage the enemy's attention on that side.

Owing to the thinness of the soil upon the Cavannos, the approaches against the Moro went on so slowly, that it was not until the 29th that our batteries could open upon the Moro and the shipping. In order to lessen the fire on the land side, the admiral ordered Captain Harvey, with the *Dragon*, *Cambridge*, and *Marlborough*, to attack the Moro castle. On the 13th of July they took their stations, and the cannonade was kept up without intermission from eight in the morning until two in the afternoon. The *Cambridge* was so much cut up, that it became necessary to order her to withdraw: her captain, William Goostrey, and 23 men were killed, and 95 wounded.

The *Dragon* was soon rendered incapable of keeping her station: her loss amounted to 16 killed, and 37 wounded; and the *Marlborough* had 2 killed, and 8 wounded. The Moro, from its elevated situation on a steep rock, had great advantage over the ships, and they also suffered from the galling fire of the Punta, as well as the other batteries. Although this bold attempt had little effect on the fortifications, it nevertheless diverted the enemy's attention from our operations on the land side; but as soon as the cannonade ceased on board the ships, the enemy returned our fire with increased vigour.

On the 2nd of July our batteries renewed the attack with great success, but they were somewhat impeded by a fire breaking out, occasioned by the dryness of the fascines; nevertheless, before the evening the enemy's batteries had suffered so considerably, as to be only capable of making a return from two guns. On the 3rd the fire broke out afresh, and continued until the 5th, destroying in a few hours what the labours of five or six hundred men had produced during seventeen days. This misfortune was severely felt, for the hardships of the siege were grown almost insupportable: sickness and fatigue had reduced the army to half its original number; and no less than 5000 soldiers and 3000 seamen were incapable of duty. The scarcity of provisions and water aggravated all their other sufferings, but the timely arrival of Sir James Douglas on the 12th, with reinforcements from Jamaica, and Brigadier-General Burton on the 28th, with the first division of troops from North America, re-animated the gallant fellows who had endured so much privation and fatigue.

On the 30th of July, about two o clock in the afternoon, two mines were sprung, and a breach made in the bastion, which being deemed practicable, the troops, led by Lieutenant Charles Forbes of the Royals, ascended to the assault with the greatest resolution, and soon drove the enemy from every part of the ramparts. The Spanish governor, Don Louis de Velasco, exerted himself to the last in defending the fortress, and in his endeavours to rally his men he was mortally wounded. The loss of the enemy amounted to 130 killed; 400 threw down their arms, and were made prisoners. The Marquis Gonzales, second in command in the Moro, was killed in his gallant though ineffectual efforts to defend his post.

The possession of this fort, after a hard struggle of forty-four days, gave great satisfaction to the troops, who had so cheerfully borne the fatigues of this protracted siege, and whose labours did not relax until the capitulation of the enemy on the 12th. The fortifications were mounted with 250 iron, and 104 brass ordnance, besides 12 mortars. Exclusive of the three ships of the line sunk at the entrance of the harbour, there were nine in an effective state, and two on the stocks.

In the distribution of prize-money for the capture of the Havanna, the commander-in-chief received £122,697. 10s. 6d.; next in command, £24,539. 10s. 1d.; major-gen., £6816. 10s. 6d.; field-officer, £564. 14s. 6d; captain, £184. 4s. 7d.; subaltern, £116. 3s.; whilst the private soldier had only £4. 1s. 8d. Total amount, £368,092. 11s. 6d.

A squadron, under M. de Ternay, of two ships of the line and two frigates conveying 1500 infantry, which sailed from Brest in the month of April to make an attempt on our settlement at Newfoundland, reached their destination on the 24th of June. The troops were landed in the bay of Bulls, and having summoned the officer commanding Fort William, the chief defence of St. John's, its feeble garrison surrendered. A detachment was sent to take possession of Trinity and the island of Carbonera, but their conquest extended no further; for captain Graves, who was then at Placentia, in the *Antelope*, immediately landed his marines, at the same time apprising the commanders at New York and Halifax of his situation, and requesting their support.

Lord Colville soon arrived with some ships from Halifax, and after disembarking his marines, as a further reinforcement, he sailed in search of M. de Ternay; but previously sent an officer and thirty marines from the *Syren*, to the island of Boys, which prevented it from falling into the enemy's hands. During this period, the works of St. John's had been much strengthened by the exertions of the French garrison, who took the precaution of laying a boom across the entrance of the harbour, to prevent any ship of force entering it. As soon as the intelligence of the French being in possession of St. John's reached America, General Amherst detached a force, which arrived on the coast of Newfoundland on the 11th of September, and landed in two battalions, under the direction of Lieutenant-Colonel Amherst, who, after several days skirmishing with the outposts of the enemy, invested St. John's on the 16th; on which day the dense fog that prevailed enabled M. de Ternay, with his squadron, to steal out of the harbour unobserved. On the 17th, Colonel Amherst opened a mortar battery against the fort, and on the 18th the garrison of St. John's capitulated.

The expedition against the Philippine Islands, suggested by Colonel William Draper, was one of the boldest and most important of our successes during the war. The Spaniards in this colony, confiding in their remote distance from Europe, persuaded themselves that no attack would ever be deemed practicable; and lulled by this security, they entirely neglected keeping up a regular military force for their own protection.

The Philippines, or Manillas, form a principal division of that immense Indian archipelago, which consists of above twelve hundred islands, extending from the nineteenth degree of north latitude, to the shores of New Guinea and the great southern continent. The Philippines, which form the northern-most cluster of these islands, are some of the largest and richest in the world, and were most happily situated for commercial intercourse with Asia and America; receiving European goods by the way of the Cape of Good Hope, and connecting the traffic of China, Japan, and the Spice Islands with that of Europe and America. The principal island is Manilla, or Luconia, which is three hundred miles in length, and ninety in breadth. The capital is Manilla, having a spacious harbour on the south-east of the island, where the galleons used to arrive annually, and sail for Acapulco in America, with treasure and valuable merchandise. On the declaration of the war with Spain, Colonel Draper was despatched to India in the *Argo* frigate, with instructions to take command of the land forces to be employed against Manilla, having rank of brigadier-general, and he arrived at Madras in the latter part of June.

The troops consisted of the 79th regiment, a company of artillery, 600 *sepoys*, and about 300 other native troops; to which were added 700 seamen, with 19 officers and 319 rank and file of marines, forming a total of 2330 men. The squadron under Vice-Admiral Cornish, consisting of eight ships of the line and three frigates, with two large transports conveying this force, sailed on the 12th of August, arrived at Malacca on the 19th, quitted that place on the 27th, and arrived at Manilla harbour on the 23rd of September. After an ineffectual summons, preparations were made for the debarkation of the troops; and about six in the evening of the 24th the boats, in three divisions under the direction of Captains Parker, Kempenfelt, and Brereton, pulled for the shore, covered by the fire of the frigates, which dispersed the enemy that had assembled on the beach. The violence of the surf destroyed many of the boats, and damaged the ammunition, but no lives were lost; and the troops, having formed upon the beach, moved forward and took possession of the village of Malata, distant about a mile from the enemy's works.

On the 25th a detachment occupied the fort of Pulverista, which the Spaniards had abandoned; whilst Colonel Monson pushed forward with 200 men, and possessed himself of the church of Hermita, situated near the city. This post was of much consequence, both from its strength and the shelter it afforded from the heavy rains that had already set in, and the 79th regiment, under Major Moore, was therefore ordered to reinforce it. The seamen were indefatigable in their exertions in landing the stores and artillery through the dangerous surf, in which Lieutenant Hardwick was unfortunately drowned.

The marines were left at the Malata, in the neighbourhood of the Pulverista, preserving a communication with the advanced forces; at the same time, whilst securing a retreat, they protected the stores and artillery, and, to use the words of Colonel Draper:

> The men, from the good conduct and example of their officers, behaved very well, and were of great use upon all occasions.

The battalion of seamen was stationed between the 79th regiment and the marines; a detachment advancing within three hundred yards of the town, who maintained themselves in the church of St. Jago. On the 26th of September the Spaniards made a sally from the garrison; and 400 men under Chevalier de la Fayette, having with them two field-pieces, with which they occupied a church on the right of the British, then commenced a cannonade upon their flank; but Colonel Monson with the picquets, reinforced by a small party of seamen, attacked them so sharply that they were driven back into the town, and their retreat was so precipitate that they left one of their guns on the glacis. A summons was sent to the governor; but he returned a spirited answer, expressive of his determination to defend his trust as became him.

Had the valour of the garrison corresponded with the declaration of their leader, the town would have had nothing to apprehend from an enemy, whose operations, from their inferiority of numbers, were confined to one corner of the place, leaving two-thirds of it open to all manner of supplies. The front attacked was defended by the bastions of St. Diego and St. Andrew, with a ravelin which covered the royal gate; and there was a wet ditch, covered way, and glacis. These bastions were in good order, mounting a great number of brass cannon; but the ravelin was not armed, and the covered way out of repair; the ditch did not extend round the bastion of St. Diego, and the glacis was much too low.

By great exertions three batteries were raised, which opened on the town with some effect; and on the 29th the *Elizabeth* and *Falmouth* took positions as near as the depth of water would permit, to second the operations of the army by enfilading the enemy's front.

On the 1st of October the weather grew so tempestuous, that the whole squadron was in great danger, and all communication was cut off with the army; but notwithstanding the heavy rains, the troops and seamen continued their exertions so effectually in completing the battery for the twenty-four pounders and a mortar, that all the guns were mounted by the 2nd. On the 3rd a fire was opened upon the left face of St. Diego's bastion with such effect, that in a few hours the twelve pieces of cannon on it were silenced, and the enemy compelled to retire. The Spaniards, finding that their fortifications were no longer tenable, projected a sortie, and before daylight on the 4th a 1000 Indians, armed with bows and arrows, and lances, attacked the cantonment of the seamen with great fury; but they were met with such determined firmness, that on the arrival of a reinforcement of the 79th regiment, the enemy was driven back with the loss of 300 men.

A second attack was made by another body of Indians, supported by a strong detachment of the Spanish garrison, who attacked the church of St. Jago and drove the *sepoys*; but the European troops maintained their post with great firmness, and at length defeated the assailants. This was the enemy's last effort: only 1800 of the Indians continued their assistance to the besieged, the remainder returning to their homes. Our batteries kept up their fire with renewed spirit, which was but weakly retained from three or four embrasures in the curtain, and before night these defences were in ruins.

A little after daybreak on the 6th, the different corps had taken their stations for storming the place, and under cover of our artillery they rushed on to the assault. Lieutenant Russell of the 79th, with 60 volunteers, led the way, supported by the grenadiers of that regiment. Next to the pioneers came the battalion of seamen, sustained by two grand divisions of the 79th regiment, and the troops of the East India Company formed the rear. Thus disposed, the assailants, to the number of 2000 men, mounted the breach with great rapidity; the enemy giving way, and offering no opposition until they arrived at the gate of the town, where a resistance was made by 100 men, who were all put to the sword. The governor, with his officers, retired to the citadel, but were glad to surrender at discretion, as that place was incapable of defence. The port of Cavite, and the other dependencies of Manilla, were surrendered to the British, and Captain Champion, with 100 marines and as many *sepoys*, was ordered to take possession of the citadel.

Throughout the whole of these operations the greatest cordiality prevailed between the two services, and no conjunct expedition was ever conducted with more resolution and professional skill, than the conquest of the Philippine islands. The loss sustained during the siege was less than could have been expected from the nature of the service. It amounted to one naval officer, and three of the army killed; one company's officer drowned; 13 seamen and marines, 75 soldiers killed, and 6 wounded; 1 officer of the navy, 3 officers of the troops, 20 sailors or marines, and 87 soldiers wounded: lieutenant Spearing of the marines among the latter. Commodore Siddeman, in attempting to enter the river in his barge on the morning after the capitulation of Manilla, was unfortunately drowned, with five of his people.

Brigadier-General Draper was made a knight of the Bath, Admiral Cornish created a baronet of Great Britain, and the thanks of Parliament were voted to those officers and their subordinates who were concerned in the conquest of Manilla.

On the 21st of May, the *Active* and *Favourite* sloops, cruising off Cadiz, captured the Spanish treasure-ship *Hermione*, from Lima, with a cargo which, with the value of the ship, amounted to £544,648. 1s. 6d.; the share of the treasure gave the captains each £65,053. 13s. 9d; lieutenants, £39,014. 2s. 3d.; and a private marine, £484. 2s. 5d.

On the 29th of August, the *Æolus* of 32 guns, Captain Hotham, chased two ships into Aviles bay, near Cape Penas, and on the 2nd of September stood in to attack them. On rounding the point, the largest ship, mounting 32 guns, opened her fire, supported by a battery of three guns, situated on an eminence within the point. At 3 p.m., the *Æolus* anchored with a spring on her cable, and directing her fire both on the ship and battery, soon drove them from their guns: the crew, taking to their boats, abandoned the ship, which having ran aground, was destroyed. The battery continuing to annoy the frigate, Lieutenant Campbell with his party of marines landed, drove out the enemy and spiked the guns. The other ship having removed higher up the bay in shoal water, Captain Hotham stood out from the anchorage without sustaining any loss.

We have not space to relate the various naval exploits of 1762, in the course of which year the British captured upwards of one hundred and twenty considerable prizes, and this success gave frequent occasions for the display of our professional superiority. Since Spain had undertaken this fatal war, she had lost twelve ships of the line, besides frigates. Eighteen of the line and thirty-six frigates were captured from the French, and fourteen ships of the line and thirteen frigates destroyed. On the other hand, two British frigates were captured by the French, and three destroyed by the enemy; whilst thirteen sail of the line, with fourteen frigates, were accidentally lost; but no English ship of the line fell into the enemy's hands.

During this memorable war, the marines took part in every exploit of honour and danger, and they served in every naval action, except the drawn Battle of Minorca. On all occasions their discipline and firmness was a subject of the highest commendation, and they never failed to maintain a subordination worthy of imitation.

The preliminaries of peace, which were signed on the 3rd of November, and ratified in February of the following year, closed the services of the marines for a long period; and a very considerable reduction took place, for in 1763 only 16,000 men were voted for the sea service, including 4287 marines. This circumscribed establishment produced so much discontent in the corps, that it gave rise to numerous memorials to the Board of Admiralty; but those remonstrances met with so little success, that many officers were induced to quit the service and enter the army, where some obtained the highest rank.

In 1770 affairs of a very serious aspect called the attention of the British Government to the disturbed state of her American colonies, in consequence of a real or pretended right on the part of Great Britain to impose internal taxes. The stamp-act was so exceedingly unpopular, that its repeal was absolutely necessary to appease the people; and the tax on tea imported into America was so obnoxious, that every means of opposition to the measure was resorted to.

In October, ships laden with tea having arrived at Boston, New York, Philadelphia, Charlestown, and Rhode Island, conveying altogether 2200 chests, the people assembled at different places to concert measures that would prevent the importation, and to compel the consignees, at the risk of their lives and property, to relinquish their employments. In these assemblies, resolutions were passed derogatory to the legislative power of Great Britain; and on the 18th of December a number of armed men, under the disguise of Mohawk Indians, boarded the ships, and threw their valuable cargoes into the sea; but at New York the tea was landed under the protection of the men-of-war.

On the 7th of March, 1774, His Majesty sent a message to Parliament, requiring immediate measures for securing the execution of the laws, and just dependence of the colonies upon the crown of Great Britain. The minister at the same time introduced a hill to take away from Boston the privilege of a port, as a punishment for their refractory conduct: reinforcements were sent thither, and General Gage was appointed governor of the colony. This restriction on of the inhabitants of Boston raised a spirit of rebellion throughout the continent of America; all were agreed in resisting the collection of any internal tax not imposed by their own assemblies, and to suspend all commercial intercourse with the mother-country until their grievances were fully redressed. Deputies were soon afterwards appointed from each province to attend a general congress at Philadelphia, which assembled on the 5th of September, 1774. Among their first resolutions they acknowledged their dependence, but insisted on their privileges; consenting to those acts of the British legislature which regulated their external commerce, yet insisting, that according to the English constitution, the people had a right to participate in their legislative council; and as the

70

colonies, from various causes, could not be represented in the British Parliament, they were entitled to a free and exclusive legislation in their respective provincial assemblies, in all cases of taxation and internal policy. They recommended to the several provinces the establishment of a national militia, and to raise money for paying those who should bravely hazard their lives in defence of the privileges of America.

In the latter part of 1774 the Americans were making great preparations for resistance; and they scrupled not to declare their intention of attacking Boston when the ice became strong enough to bear them; but as it did not freeze sufficiently hard during the winter, the disaffected postponed their plans until the spring of 1775.

To prevent being taken by surprise, the neck of land which leads into Boston from Roxbury, was carefully fortified by the British and Admiral Graves, by placing the *Somerset* in the ferry-way between the two towns, overawed the inhabitants of Charlestown, and prevented any attack from that side. The fleet under Vice-Admiral Graves, consisting of four sail of the line and a great many smaller vessels, was greatly dispersed, but so disposed as to afford all the protection possible to His Majesty's loyal subjects in the colonies.

General Gage, on receiving intelligence that a quantity of military stores had been collected at Concord for supplying the rebel troops, ordered a detachment, consisting of the grenadiers and light infantry of the army, under Lieutenant-Colonel Smith of the 10th regiment, and Major Pitcairne of the marines, to be embarked in the boats of the squadron; and on the evening of the 18th of April, they were conveyed up Charles River, and landed at Phipp's Farm, whence they advanced with rapidity towards Concord; but the country had been apprised of their intention, and before the break of day the inhabitants were assembled in arms.

Lieutenant-Colonel Smith detached Major Pitcairne, with six companies of light infantry, to secure two bridges on different roads beyond Concord. On their arrival within two miles of Lexington at four o clock in the morning of the 19th, the major received intelligence that a body of 500 armed men were assembled, and determined to oppose the king's troops; but when they came within a short distance of the Americans, the latter filed off towards some stone walls on the right. Major Pitcairne then called to them to disperse, and on attempting to surround and disarm them, they fired upon our troops; upon which the light infantry, without being ordered, fired and killed several of the country people. Shortly after this occurrence, Lieuten-

71

ant-Colonel Smith, with the troops under his command, joined Major Pitcairne, and the whole force reached Concord at nine in the evening. Captain Parsons was detached with six companies of light infantry to secure a bridge at some distance from this place, which was guarded by three of these companies, whilst the remainder destroyed all the military stores in the neighbourhood.

The alarm had now extended, and General Gage, learning how the troops had been opposed, sent a reinforcement of eight companies of the 4th, and the same number of the 23rd and 49th regiments, with some marines and two field-pieces, under the command of the Earl of Percy. This was a fortunate circumstance, for no sooner had the detachment under Lieutenant-Colonel Smith begun their march from Concord to Lexington, than they were assailed by a heavy fire from all sides, which continued without intermission until they met the detachment of the Earl of Percy. The fire from the fieldpieces at first checked the Americans, but their increasing numbers hung upon the rear of the English force until they reached Charlestown. On this occasion 1 lieutenant and 64 rank and file were killed; 2 lieutenant-colonels, 2 captains, 9 lieutenants, and 165 wounded; and a lieutenant with 27 men missing.

The marines of the squadron under Lieutenant-Colonel Johnstone were landed, to assist and cover the retreat of the detachment, who under protection of this assistance, and the commanding station of the *Somerset*, passed over to Boston without further molestation. Exaggerated accounts of the affair at Lexington were eagerly carried to every province, which so encouraged the spirit of resistance to His Majesty's authority, that it produced a determination not to supply the ships and troops with stores or provisions. All communication by land being stopped by the rebels, two vessels were employed to convey despatches to New York and Halifax. The Americans continuing to increase in numbers, they attacked Noddle's Island, and drove off the cattle, after destroying the buildings of every description.

The congress having resolved to form an army of 30,000 men, issued regulations for raising and maintaining this force. On the 24th of May a reinforcement arrived at Boston from Ireland; and on the 26th, Major-Generals Howe, Clinton, and Burgoyne in the Cerberus from England.

The following is an extract from the marine-battalion orders of the 20th of May, 1775:—

The Right-Honourable the Lords Commissioners of the Admiralty, having directed a reinforcement of marines to serve under Major Pitcairne in General Gage's army, consisting of 2 majors, 10 captains, 27 subalterns, 2 adjutants, 1 surgeon, 2 assistant-surgeons, 28 sergeants, 25 corporals, 20 drummers, 600 privates, the commanding officer deems it necessary, for the good of the service, to form the whole under his command into two battalions:—

| Officers in 1st battalion. | Officers in 2nd battalion. |
| --- | --- |
| **GRENADIERS.** | |
| Thomas Avarne, capt. | George Logan. |
| William Finney, 1st lieut. | Alexander Brisbane. |
| George Vevers, 1st lieut. | Francis Gardner. |
| **FIRST COMPANY.** | |
| Stawel Chudleigh, capt., | Hon. John Maitland, capt. |
| Richard Shea, 1st lieut. | Jesse Adair, 1st lieut. |
| Hewes, 1st lieut. | Roland Carter, 1st lieut. |
| **SECOND COMPANY.** | |
| Stephen Ellis, capt. | Charles Chandless, capt. |
| James Robertson, 1st lieut. | Fenton Griffiths, 1st lieut. |
| P. D. Robertson, 2nd lieut. | Henry D Oyley, 2nd lieut. |
| **THIRD COMPANY.** | |
| Thomas Lindsay, capt. | Thomas Groves, capt. |
| William Lycett, 1st lieut. | John Hadden, 1st lieut. |
| David Collins, 2nd lieut. | Titus Conyers, 1st lieut. |
| **FOURTH COMPANY.** | |
| William Forster, capt. | Samuel Davys, capt. |
| William Graham, 1st lieut. | Walter Nugent, 1st lieut. |
| Isaac Potter, 2nd lieut. | Robert Carey, 2nd lieut. |
| **FIFTH COMPANY.** | |
| Robert Ross, capt. | Edward Henvill, capt. |
| Charles Steward, 1st lieut. | Thomas Biggs, 1st lieut. |
| Jonas Mathews, 1st lieut. | James Lewis, 2nd lieut. |
| **SIXTH COMPANY.** | |
| William Sabine, capt. | George Elliott, capt. |
| B. M Donald, 2nd lieut. | Alex. M Donald, 1st lieut. |
| Henry Tantum, 2nd lieut. | John France, 1st lieut. |
| **SEVENTH COMPANY.** | |
| J. H. Branson, capt. | Archer Walker, capt. |
| William Creswell, 1st lieut. | James Anderson, 1st lieut. |

Thomas Trollope, 2nd lieut.    Robert Moore, 2nd lieut.

## EIGHTH COMPANY.

John Perceval, capt.              John M Fie, capt.

Aaron Eustace, 1st lieut.         Sir J.Dalston,bart.,lstlieut.

Thos. Woodcock, 2nd lieut.    Francis Dogherty, 1st lieut.

## LIGHT INFANTRY.

W. Souter, capt.                  Archibald Campbell, capt.

William Pitcairne, 1st lieut.    John Dyer, 2nd lieut.

Philip Howe, 2nd lieut.          N. H. Nicholas, 2nd lieut.

## ADJUTANT.

John Waller, 1st lieut.           John Fielding, 1st. lieut.

## QUARTERMASTER.

J. Pitcairne, 1st lieut.           Thomas Smith, 1st lieut.

Captain David Johnston, superintendent, adjutant, and deputy-paymaster to the 2nd battalion.

—— Hill, surgeon to the 2nd battalion; William Tervant and —— Silven, surgeon's mates.

The following regulations for the payment of companies were notified in the battalion orders of the 3rd of June:

> The right-honourable the lords commissioners of the Admiralty having directed, by their letter to Major Pitcairne of the 2nd of March last, that the captain of marines commanding companies on shore at Boston should pay their companies in the same manner as practised by the land forces, the captains or commanding officers of companies will receive from Captain Johnstone, deputy-paymaster, one month's subsistence for the non-commissioned officers and private men of their respective companies, deducting 1s. 5½d. per week each for provisions and the usual stoppages, as directed by the Admiralty, viz:—

|                                   | s. | d.  |
| --------------------------------- | -- | --- |
| For one sergeant, per week        | 0  | 2   |
| For one corporal or drummer       | 0  | 1½  |
| For one private man               | 0  | 1   |
| Dollars to be taken at            | 4  | 8   |

> Captains are to give the deputy-paymaster complete monthly pay-rolls, accounting for the subsistence distributed to their companies, and specifying every particular casualty that has happened in each company during the preceding month, and to commence this day.

## CHAPTER 3

# From the Year 1775 to 1783

On the 8th of June, 1775, the American congress resolved:

The compact between the crown and the people of Massachu-setts bay is dissolved.

A proclamation was issued by General Gage establishing martial law, and offering pardon to all who should return to their allegiance excepting Samuel Adams and John Handcock. Matters were thus fast approaching to a crisis, and both parties prepared in right earnest for the struggle.

At this moment, the town of Charlestown was not occupied by either party; and the rebels, anticipating the movement of the king's troops, sent a large body of men on the 16th of June to erect works upon Bunker's-hill, and during the night they raised entrenchments, and constructed a formidable redoubt. On the 17th at daybreak the garrison of Boston was alarmed by a heavy cannonade from His Majesty's ship *Lively*, directed against the working-party on the hill; but as the Americans persevered in their labours with great firmness, General Gage considered it highly necessary to dislodge them from so important a position, and therefore resolved on an immediate attack.

The *Lively*, *Falcon*, and *Spitfire*, having anchored abreast of and below Charlestown for covering the landing of the troops, at nine in the morning the *Glasgow*, lying off Newpoint, and a battery of six guns and some howitzers, opened upon the rebels; but they perseveringly continued their work, nothing daunted by the heavy fire which was poured upon them. The Americans on the heights were in great force, and strongly posted in a redoubt, besides other works, on which they had mounted cannon. In the houses of Charlestown, which covered their right flank, they had also posted a large body of troops, while their centre and left flank were protected by a breastwork partly cannon proof; and these works reached from the left of the redoubt to the Mystic, or Medford, River. Ten companies of grenadiers and ten of light infantry, with the 5th, 38th, 43rd, and 52nd regiments under Major-General Howe and Brigadier-General Pigot, were embarked with great expedition, and landed about noon on Charlestown Point, under the protection of the ships of war, whose well-directed fire kept the insurgents within their works. The troops formed in perfect order, the light infantry under Brigadier Pigot posted on the right, and the grenadiers on the left; in rear of these the 5th and 38th regiments, and the 43rd and 52nd in a third line.

Major-General Howe, on examining the state of the enemy's defences, and observing fresh columns pouring in to their assistance, solicited a reinforcement, which soon joined him, consisting of some companies of grenadiers and light infantry, the 47th regiment, and the battalions of marines, who were led by Majors Pitcairne, Tupper, and Short. The major-general then formed the corps under his command into two lines, and immediately advanced towards the enemy's works. About half-past three o'clock a smart fire was opened from the field-pieces and howitzers of the British as the troops slowly advanced, and occasionally halting to allow the artillery to fire with greater effect. The light infantry was directed to force the left point of the breastwork, and take the enemy in flank; whilst the grenadiers were to attack in front, supported by the 5th and 52nd regiments.

Not a shot was returned by the enemy until our troops were close upon them, when they opened a destructive fire, which was so well maintained, that it somewhat staggered the assailants. For some time the British withstood this opposition, but their loss of officers and men was so great, that they recoiled a little and fell into disorder, until the animating presence of general Howe restored confidence, when the soldiers rallied, and again advanced upon the enemy.

At this time the left wing, from being much exposed to the enemy's fire from the houses of Charlestown, sustained considerable loss; orders were therefore sent to destroy the place, which was speedily effected by red-hot shot from the ships, and by Cape's-Hill battery throwing carcasses. General Howe now renewed his attack, and overcoming the various impediments thrown in their way, the British soldiers rushed into the entrenchments with the bayonet, and drove the gallant enemy from every part of the works across the peninsula, leaving five pieces of cannon in our possession. At the commencement of the action the rebels had above 5000 men, and their loss must have been considerable; but only 30 of the killed remained in the redoubt. In this hardly-earned victory, the loss on the part of the British amounted to 1 lieutenant-colonel, 2 majors, 7 captains, 9 lieutenants, 15 sergeants, one drummer, and 191 rank and file killed; 3 majors, 27 captains, 32 lieutenants, 8 ensigns, and 758 privates wounded,—making a total of 1054 in killed and wounded.

The marine battalions sustained more than its proportionate share of casualties:—

First battalion; Major Short, Captain Stephen Ellis, Lieutenants Richard Shea and William Finnie, and 17 men killed; Major Pitcairne, mortally, Captains Thomas Avarne, Stawel Chudleigh, and David Johnstone, Lieutenant Ragg, and 57 men wounded.

Second battalion; Captain Archibald Campbell, Lieutenant Francis Gardiner, and 5 men killed; Captain George Logan, Lieutenants John Dyer, Alexander Brisbane, and 30 men wounded.

The reputation of the marines was never more nobly sustained than in this sanguinary contest. Their unshaken firmness was conspicuous, and the valour they displayed in closing with the enemy when some part of the attacking column wavered, gained them, not only the admiration of their comrades, but the commendation of their distinguished chief.

General Orders, 19th June, 1775.

The commander-in-chief returns his most grateful thanks to Major-General Howe for the extraordinary exertion of his military abilities on the 17th instant. He returns his thanks also to Major-General Clinton, and Brigadier Pigot, for the share they took in the success of the day, as well as to Lieutenant-Colonels Nesbitt, Abercromby, Gunning, and Clarke; Majors Butler, Williams, Bruce, Tupper, Spenlove, Small, and Mitchel, and the rest of the officers and soldiers; who by remarkable efforts of courage and gallantry overcame every disadvantage, and drove the rebels from the redoubt and strong-holds on the heights of Charlestown, and gained a complete victory.

The following interesting letter is from lieutenant J . Waller, adjutant of the first marine battalion, dated, Camp of Charlestown Heights, 22nd of June, 1775:—

My dear Brother,

Amidst the hurry and confusion of a camp hastily pitched in

the field of battle, I am sat down to tell you I have escaped unhurt, where many, very many, have fallen. The public papers will inform you of the situation of the ground and the redoubt that we attacked on the heights of Charlestown. I can only say that it was a most desperate and daring attempt, and it was performed with as much gallantry and spirit as was ever shown by any troops in any age.

Two companies of the first battalion of marines, and part of the 47th regiment, were the first that mounted the breastwork: and you will not be displeased when I tell you that I was with those two companies, who drove their bayonets into all that opposed them. Nothing could be more shocking than the carnage that followed the storming this work. We tumbled over the dead to get at the living, who were crowding out of the gorge of the redoubt, in order to form under the defences which they had prepared to cover their retreat. In these breastworks they had artillery, which did so much mischief; but these they were obliged to abandon, being followed closely by the light infantry, who suffered exceedingly in the pursuit.

The rebels had 5000 to 7000 men, covered by a redoubt, breastworks, walls, hedges, trees, and the like; and the number of the corps under General Howe, (who performed this gallant business,) did not amount to 1500. We gained a complete victory, and entrenched ourselves that night, where we lay under arms, in the front of the field of battle. We lay the next night on the ground, and the following day encamped. The officers have not their marquees, but are obliged to lie in soldiers tents, they being more portable in case of our advancing.

We had of our corps one major, 2 captains, and 3 lieutenants killed; 4 captains, and 3 lieutenants wounded: 2 sergeants, and 21 rank and file killed; and 3 sergeants and 79 privates wounded: and I suppose, upon the whole, we lost, killed and wounded, from 800 to 1000 men. We killed a number of the rebels, but the cover they fought under made their loss less considerable than it would otherwise have been. The army is in great spirits, and full of rage and ferocity at the rebellious rascals, who both poisoned and chewed the musket balls, in order to make them the more fatal. Many officers have died of their wounds, and others very ill: 'tis astonishing what a number of officers were hit on this occasion; but the officers were particularly aimed at.

I will just give you a short account of the part of the action where I was particularly concerned. We landed close under Charlestown, and formed with the 47th regiment close under the natural defences of the redoubt, which we drove the enemy from, climbing over rails and hedges. So we closed upon them; but when we came immediately under the work, we were checked by the severe fire of the enemy, but did not retreat an inch. We were now in confusion, after being broke several times in getting over the rails, &c. I did all I could to form the two companies on our right, which at last I effected, losing many of them while it was performing. Major Pitcairne was killed close by me, with a captain and a subaltern; also a sergeant, and many of the privates; and had we stopped there much longer, the enemy would have picked us all off. I saw this, and begged Colonel Nesbitt of the 47th to form on our left, in order that we might advance with our bayonets to the parapet.

I ran from right to left, and stopped our men from firing; while this was doing, and when we had got in tolerable order, we rushed on, leaped the ditch, and climbed the parapet, under a most sore and heavy fire. Colonel Nesbitt has spoken very favourably of my conduct, and both our majors have mentioned me to Lord Sandwich in consequence of it. One captain and one subaltern fell in getting up, and one captain and one subaltern was wounded of our corps: three captains of the 52nd were killed on the parapet, and others that I know nothing of. God bless you! I did not think, at one time, that I should ever have been able to write this, though in the heat of the action I thought nothing of the matter. *Adieu*, dear Jacob, yours,

J. Waller.

The provincials constructed works on an eminence on the continental side of the Charlestown-neck, directly opposite to the British troops on Bunker's-Hill, and by their frequent nightly incursions on the different islands, where the livestock for the British was kept, they added much to the distress of the army. In one of those daring enterprises they burnt the lighthouses at the entrance of Boston harbour; and when the principal one was under repair, protected by a detachment of marines, they surprised the party, and carried them all off to the continent.

In the orders of the 27th of September, the royal thanks were tendered to the forces in the following terms:

> The king has been pleased to order the commander-in-chief to express His Majesty's thanks, both to the officers and soldiers, for the resolution and gallantry with which they attacked and defeated the rebels on the 17th of June last, who had every advantage of numbers and situation; and more especially to express to Generals Howe and Clinton, and to Brigadier-General Pigot, the sense His Majesty entertains of the spirit, resolution, and conduct by which they distinguished themselves, to their honour, upon that day.

The battalion-orders of that day also contained a notification that, the king had been pleased to make the following promotions in his marine forces serving in North America:—

Captain W. Souter to be major, *vice* Short, killed in action.
Capt.-Lieut. Fras. Lindsay to be captain, *v.* Campbell, *ditto.*
    „    Robt. Ross to be captain, *v.* Ellis, *ditto.*
    „    David Johnstone to be capt., *v.* Souter, promoted.
First-Lieut. Jessie Adair to be capt.-lieut., *v.* Lindsay, *ditto.*
  „ Sir John Dalston to be capt.-lieut., *v.* Walker, returned home.
  „ Sir J. Hadden to be capt.-lieut., *v.* Ross, promoted.
  „ William Pitcairne to be capt.-lieut., *v.* Johnstone, promoted.
Second-Lieut. Jas Lewis to be first lieut., *v.* Shea, killed in action.

| | | | |
|---|---|---|---|
| „ | Robert Moore | *ditto* | „ Finnie |
| „ | Thos. Woodcock | *ditto* | „ Gardiner. |
| „ | Isaac Polden | *ditto* | „ Adair. |
| „ | Robert Carey | *ditto* | „ Dalston. |
| „ | Ronald McDonald | *ditto* | „ Hadden. |
| „ | Philip Howe | *ditto* | „ — |
| „ | Henry Tantum | *ditto* | „ Pitcairne. |
| „ | David Collins | *ditto* | „ Spencer. |

Voluntr. S. D. Bowman to be 2nd. lieut. „ Lewis.
It was further intimated:—

> That in consequence of the application of Major Pitcairne to have the same allowance for paying the companies of 1st and 2nd battalions of marines serving on shore in North America as the army, and that the captains should be answerable for the debts, &c,—the Lords Commissioners of the Admiralty are ready to give every reasonable mark of their indulgence, and are

pleased to consent that each captain commanding a company should be allowed after the rate of one shilling per day, being equal to the pay of two men per company, during their continuance on shore, as is practised in the army; and the deputy-paymaster is authorised to issue the same.

General Gage obtained His Majesty's permission to return to England, and on the 12th of October the command of the British land forces in America devolved on Major-General Howe.

The disaffected Americans, encouraged by their increasing strength, looked boldly forward to a successful struggle in establishing an independent government of their own; and animated by these hopes, they no longer confined their operations to defensive measures, but availed themselves of every opportunity of assailing their enemies. In this state of enduring firmness on the part of the Americans, the distressed army at Boston looked anxiously for reinforcements and supplies of provisions. On the 2nd of March, 1776, General Washington opened a battery at Phipps-Farm, and on the 5th some works were erected on Dorchester-Point, from which a fire was opened from a twenty-four pounder and a mortar with such effect, that the town was soon in a blaze. Finding it impracticable to dislodge the enemy from their new position, Major-General Howe was compelled to abandon the town, and the troops were consequently conveyed on board the ships.

The embarkation rather resembled the emigration of a nation than the breaking up of a camp: 1500 of the inhabitants, attached to the royal cause, encumbered the transports with their families, which, together with the scarcity of provisions, occasioned much discontent, and increased the jealous feeling that prevailed between the army and navy. As the British were unable to carry off their stores and heavy artillery, the cannon on Bunker's-Hill and Boston-Neck fell into the hands of the Americans, who reaped great advantage by our hasty departure. On the 17th of March, General Washington entered Boston in great triumph, and the British armament, amounting to 150 sail, proceeded to Halifax.

Amongst the augmentations to the British forces voted for the year 1776, 2378 men were added to the marines, making their total establishment 6665 men. The fleet, with the army from Boston, reached Halifax on the 4th of April, where they continued in expectation of succours from England until the 12th of June, and arrived at Sandy Hook on the 29th. On the 3rd of July, the grenadiers and light infantry were landed at Staten Island, without opposition, and the remainder of the army disembarked in the course of the day.

As the rebels were strongly posted, both on Long Island and at New York, having upwards of 100 cannon towards the entrance of the north river, the commander-in-chief resolved to remain in his present position, and not commence offensive operations until he should be joined by the force under Lord Clinton and the reinforcements from England. Lord Howe arrived at Staten Island on the 12th of July, and assumed the command of the fleet; and on the 14th, Commodore Parker, with the troops under General Clinton, arrived from the southward, which enabled General Howe to commence hostilities.

Preparations having been made for landing the troops in Gravesend bay, Long Island, the first division, amounting to 4000 men under Lieutenant-General Clinton, was conveyed to the shore on the morning of the 22nd of August; and the debarkation continued to be so well conducted, that before noon 15,000 men, with forty pieces of cannon, were disembarked.

After several encounters with the rebel force, the Americans were routed from the island on the 27th, with loss of five pieces of cannon, 2000 killed, wounded, or drowned, and 997 prisoners; whilst the loss of the British did not exceed 300 in killed and wounded. Captain Logan, 2nd battalion of marines, was killed; Lieutenant Nugent, 1st battalion, wounded; and Lieutenant Ragg, 2nd battalion, made prisoner.

In the month of July, 1777, General Howe passed over with the army to Staten Island, and preparations were made for an attack on Philadelphia. On the 23rd, the armament, consisting of thirty six battalions, and a powerful artillery, sailed from Sandy Hook, and on the 31st arrived off the entrance of the Delaware; but finding that the rebels obstructed the navigation of that river, the fleet proceeded up the Chesapeake on the 14th of August, and the troops were landed at Elk Ferry on the 25th. On the 3rd of September our troops began their march, whilst Washington, who had returned from the Jerseys to the defence of Philadelphia with 13,000 men, lost no opportunity of harassing them in their progress, without bringing on a general engagement; but several actions took place before our army entered Philadelphia, of which city they took possession on the 26th of September.

Lord Cornwallis immediately gave directions for the erection of three batteries for 6 twelve-pounders and 4 howitzers, to act upon the enemy's shipping that might approach the town; but before these batteries could be completed, two frigates, a number of galleys, gondolas, and other armed vessels, came up from Mud Island, and attacked the lower battery of two guns and two howitzers, the largest frigate, the *Delaware*, anchoring within 500 yards, and the other frigate somewhat more distant, whilst the other vessels took suitable stations. About ten in the morning they commenced a heavy cannonade, but the tide ebbing, the *Delaware* took the ground; upon which, the four battalion guns of the grenadiers did such execution, that in a short time she struck her colours, and was taken possession of by captain Thomas Avarne with his company of marines. The grenadiers of both marine battalions had been incorporated with those of the army previous to leaving Halifax, and formed part of the force which entered Philadelphia.

Lord Howe, on being apprised of the progress of the army, proceeded with the fleet to co-operate with the land forces, and anchored on the western or Pennsylvania shore. The passage to Philadelphia was however rendered still impracticable by the Americans, who had constructed numerous works to interrupt the navigation of the river. The principal of these were strong-batteries on a low and marshy island, at the junction of the Delaware and Schuylkill, and a considerable fort at Red Bank, on the opposite shore of New Jersey.

In the deepest part of the channel between these forts, they had sunk several ranges of frames, composed of transverse beams firmly united, and of great weight and strength. About three miles lower down the river were similar machines, commanded by guns on the Jersey shore, and both were supported by floating batteries, a number of armed vessels, and some fire-ships. At the suggestion of Captain Hammond of the *Roebuck*, two regiments were detached to dislodge the enemy from Billing's Point, the principal place of strength on the Jersey side. This service was effectually performed, whilst Captain Hammond, after a sharp contest with the enemy's marine force, removed the *chevaux de frise*, and opened a narrow passage through the lower barrier.

General Howe now ordered batteries to be thrown up on the Pennsylvania shore to assist in dislodging the rebels from Mud Island, and detached a strong body of Hessians to carry the redoubt at Red Bank; at the same time His Lordship moved the men-of-war near Mud Island, which was the main object of attack. Both these operations were unsuccessful: the Hessians were repulsed with great slaughter, and the ships, unable to produce any effect upon the island, were compelled to quit their position. The obstructions placed in the river by the Americans had so materially altered the channel, that the *Augusta* of 64-guns, and *Merlin* sloop, unfortunately grounded, and both were destroyed .

Those untoward events did not deter the British from making another attempt, and the Americans were equally persevering in strengthening their points of defence. The *Isis* and *Somerset* passed up the east channel, and attacked the enemy's works in front; whilst several frigates drew up against a newly erected fort near Manto Creek, and two vessels, mounting 20 four-pounders, having made their way through a narrow channel, enfiladed the principal works. The cannonade continued the whole of the 15th of November, but towards evening the fire from the fort began to slacken, and the enemy perceiving that measures were taking for assaulting their works, set fire to everything that could be destroyed, and escaped under favour of the night. The forts on the main land were also silenced, and their capture afforded a considerable quantity of artillery and military stores to the victors. The enemy's shipping retreated up the river, but on being closely pursued they were burnt by their crews. These successes enabled the squadron to forward the supplies required by the troops, and secured them good winter-quarters in Philadelphia.

On the 27th of June an action was fought off the banks of Newfoundland, between the American frigates *Handcock* and *Boston*, of 32-guns, and the British 32-gun frigate *Fox*, Captain Patrick Fotheringham. After engaging two hours, the *Fox* was so much disabled that she could no longer contend against such superior force; and having sustained a considerable loss, she struck her colours. Among the killed was the Honourable James John Napier, Lieutenant of Marines.

The province of Nova Scotia being threatened with an invasion from the eastern parts of New England, Sir George Collier, with the *Rainbow*, *Blonde*, and *Mermaid* frigates, and *Hope* sloop, sailed from Halifax, and arrived at Machias on the 13th of August. On the following morning, finding that the enemy had assembled in force on each side of the river, whence they kept up a galling fire of musquetry, and also from the fort, it was found desirable to land the marines, who, after some resistance, routed the enemy; and the port, together with some stores and several small vessels, were destroyed.

On the 4th of September, a very gallant defence was made by the *Druid* sloop, mounting 14-guns, against the American frigate *Raleigh*, of 32-guns, in which Captain Carteret of the *Druid* and 5 men were killed; Lieutenant James Nicolson of the marines and 20 men wounded. The *Druid* formed part of the escort of the West India convoy, under the *Camel* of 20 guns and *Weazel* of 16 guns; but being five miles astern, she sustained the action without any support from her consorts. The *Raleigh* withdrew from this unequal contest, after having suffered severely.

The news of the defeat of General Bourgoyne's army produced such a change in the conduct of the court of Versailles with regard to the Americans, that it determined on the 16th of December, 1777, to acknowledge the independence of the United States; and His Christian Majesty was resolved to support that policy, even at a risk of producing a war with England. On the 13th of March, 1778, the Marquis de Noailles, the French ambassador, delivered a message from his court, expressive of its determination to maintain their commercial relations with America, and that measures had been taken in concert with the United States to maintain the dignity of the French flag, and effectually to protect the lawful commerce of their subjects.

This declaration was immediately laid before the House of Lords, with a message from the king, setting forth the perfidy of France, and contrasting it with his own steady adherence to the faith of treaties. Both houses replied to the message in a high strain of indignation and resentment against the restless ambition of the French court. The British ambassador having been recalled from Paris, the Marquis of Noailles left London, and immediate measures were taken to prepare for hostilities, impress warrants issued, and the militia embodied to the number of 30,000 men.

While these preparations were going forward in Europe, nothing decisive occurred in America, and both armies continued in their winter-quarters. As the spring approached, General Howe sent detachments to open a communication by which provisions might be obtained for the army; and on the 7th of May, Major Maitland, with the 2nd battalion of light infantry, embarked in flat boats, protected by some armed vessels, to destroy the American ships lying in the river between Philadelphia and Trenton: two frigates and some smaller vessels were burnt, together with various magazines and storehouses.

Sir William Howe having obtained His Majesty's permission to return to England, Sir Henry Clinton arrived at Philadelphia on the 8th of May, and having assumed the command of the army, the first operation was to evacuate Philadelphia, pursuant to his instructions. This measure was deemed necessary, to enable the British forces to resist the united efforts of the Americans and their new and powerful allies. On the 18th the army proceeded to Gloucester Point, and having crossed the Delaware in safety, it continued its march to New York without interruption, until the 28th; but from that period the rebel force kept close to the royal troops, continually harassing their retreat. On the 5th of July the army crossed the Navisink, over a bridge of boats, to Sandy Hook, and then moved up to New York, while the fleet anchored at Staten Island.

The French admiral, D'Estaing, with twelve ships of the line, sailed from Toulon on the 13th of April, and pursuing their course to America, arrived on the coast of Virginia on the 5th of July. On the 11th, they appeared off the northern shore of New Jersey, and anchored off Shrewsbury-inlet on the following day. To oppose this formidable force, Lord Howe had only six sail of 64-gun ships, three of 50, and two of 44 guns; yet, notwithstanding this inferiority of strength, there was such an earnest desire to meet the enemy, that 1000 volunteers from the transports presented themselves to man the fleet, and the troops were equally zealous to embark as marines, where their services might be required.

Lord Howe made the necessary disposition of his fleet to resist any attack of the enemy, and on the 21st of July the movement of the French admiral seemed to indicate an immediate battle; when, to the astonishment of the British, M. d'Estaing bore away to the southward. On the 8th of August the French fleet anchored at Rhode Island, after cannonading the town and batteries as they passed, having reached Lord Howe of the enemy's position, he proceeded with a determination to save the garrison in Rhode Island, and on the 9th the British squadron made their appearance. On the morning of the 10th, the French fleet stood out to sea, followed by the English squadron; and after remaining two days in sight of each other without any opportunity of engaging, the fleets were dispersed by a violent gale of wind, in which several ships were dismasted.

The French fleet, after again appearing off Rhode Island, took refuge in Boston bay, where they were followed by Lord Howe; but as no attempt could be made upon the enemy in their then situation with a prospect of success, the British admiral returned to Sandy Hook.

Vice-Admiral Byron, with two of his crippled ships, which were the only ones of his scattered fleet of eleven sail of the line that reached their rendezvous in America, arrived at Sandy Hook from Halifax on the 26th of September; and after refitting his ships, that officer sailed for Boston on the 18th of October, in search of M. d'Estaing. A few days after he had put to sea, his squadron was greatly injured by a violent storm, when the *Somerset* was wrecked on Cape Cod, and the

*Culloden*, from being dismasted, was forced to bear away for England.

Commodore Hotham, who had been detached from Staten Island with a small squadron, conveying 5000 troops under Major-General Grant to afford reinforcements to our colonies, reached Barbadoes on the 10th of December, where he joined Rear-Admiral Barrington. It having been determined to make an immediate attack upon St. Lucia, the army landed without much opposition on the 12th and 13th, and on the 14th gained entire possession of the island. Just as this was accomplished, Admiral d'Estaing's fleet of twelve sail of the line, and several frigates, made their appearance, and found the British squadron placed in line across the entrance of the bay, protected by heavy batteries on either point of land at the entrance of the *cul-de-sac*, where they were twice attacked by the French squadron on the 15th; and on the following day the enemy disembarked about 8000 troops in Choc Bay, but were repulsed by Brigadier-General Medows, with the loss of 500 killed, and 1100 wounded. M. d'Estaing made no further attempts on the island, nor did he renew his attack on the British squadron; but on the 28th, having re-embarked his troops, the fleet returned to Martinique.

The arrival of Admiral Byron just after the repulse of M. d'Estaing, enabled the British fleet to assume a superiority over that of the enemy; and although means were adopted to draw them to an engagement, they remained in the security which the harbour of Port Royal afforded them.

The marines serving with the army at Halifax were formed into one battalion, by an Admiralty order dated January 1777, under Majors Souter and Maitland, with the under-mentioned officers:—

*Captains,*—Avarne, Elliott, McDonald, Pitcairne, D. Johnson, and Griffiths.

*Lieutenants,*—Ragg, Vevers, Stewart, Saul, Ewing, Moore, J. Lewis, Bowman, F. Lewis, Jacobs, Shea, Gilbert, Dyer, Short, Howe, Simins, Kempe, M Donald, Tantum, Trollope, Eustace, Carey, Meredith, and Creswell.

Dr. Boyles, *chaplain.* John Waller, *adjutant.*

Thomas Smith, *quartermaster.* Charles Hill, *surgeon*; James Silver, *surgeon's-mate.*

This battalion being ordered for embarkation on the 30th of August, Major-General Massey delivered in public orders of that date the following testimony of his approbation:—

The commander-in-chief cannot part with the marine corps without telling them he was pleased with their soldier-like appearance at the review of yesterday; and now has the pleasing satisfaction to say, that he has had the honour to command that corps for above two years without ever hearing of a court-martial in it, or ever rebuking an officer or soldier. He will therefore make such a report of that respectable body of men as they merit; and now wishes officers and soldiers plenty of prize-money, and makes not a doubt but they will always contribute to the glory of His Majesty King George's arms.

In consequence of a petition from the lieutenant-governor in council of the province of Nova Scotia, requesting that the battalion might be continued on shore, the commander-in-chief was pleased to intimate his compliance with their wishes in public orders of the 7th, when the thanks of the council were conveyed to Major Souter in the following letter:—

Halifax, 10th September, 1778.

Sir,

I have singular pleasure in obeying the request of the members of His Majesty's council, by conveying to you and the rest of the officers our acknowledgments and thanks for the good order and discipline observed by the battalion of marines under your command, during the whole time they have been on duty in this town. I have the honour to be, sir,

Your most obedient humble servant,

Richard Bulkeley.

Major Souter:

The battalion soon after sailed for England.

A very gallant action was fought on the 3rd of November, about sixty leagues E. S. E. of Cape Henry, between the *Maidstone*, Captain Gardner, mounting 28 nine-pounders, and the French 40-gun frigate *Lion*, Captain J. Michel. After engaging for more than an hour, the *Maidstone* had sustained so much damage in her sails and rigging that she brought to, to repair damages; but the action was renewed with such vigour from noon until 1 p.m., that the *Lion* struck her colours, with the loss of 8 killed, and 18 wounded. On board the *Maidstone* 4 men were killed, the captain and 9 men wounded. The officer of marines on board the *Middleton* was Second-Lieutenant Henry Bromley.

The celebrated song of a favourite vocalist, "the Saucy Arethusa," is familiar to our readers, but perhaps it is not generally known that the ballad originated in the following gallant encounter. The *Arethusa* of 32 guns, Captain Marshall, when cruising to the westward of the Lizard on the 17th of June, with the fleet under Admiral Keppel, was ordered in chase of a strange sail, which proved to be the French frigate *Belle Poule* of 36 suns. Hostilities not having been declared, the French captain was requested to accompany the British frigate to the admiral; but as he peremptorily refused to comply with this proposal, Captain Marshall fired a shot across the Frenchman's bows, which was instantly returned with a broadside, and a sharp action continued for two hours, when the *Arethusa* was so much disabled as to be incapable of following her opponent, who stood away to the French shore, having 48 killed and 50 wounded. The *Arethusa* had 8 killed and 36 wounded. First-Lieutenant Joseph Driffield was serving on board the *Arethusa*.

As soon as information reached Madras that hostilities had commenced against the French, the presidency caused preparations for an attack on Pondicherry. Major-General Munro had the direction of the force for that service, and on the 8th of August the troops under his orders encamped at Red Hill, about four miles from the place of attack, whilst Sir Edward Vernon, with one ship of 64 guns and three small frigates, blockaded the port. Shortly after his arrival the French squadron under Commodore Tronjolly, consisting of a ship of 64 guns and two large frigates, with two armed country ships, made its appearance. Chase was immediately given, and on the 10th the British bore down and brought them to action, which continued until the former were so much disabled in their masts and rigging, that the French squadron made sail on a wind, and escaped.

It having been determined to carry on two attacks against Pondicherry, the British broke ground on the 6th September, and on the 18th the batteries were opened, to which the enemy returned a very brisk fire. A gallery had been carried into the ditch from the southward, and a breach made in the bastion of l'Hopital, when it was resolved to pass the ditch by a bridge of boats, and to assault the place, whilst a simultaneous attack was to be made against the north side of the town. These arrangements having been determined upon, the marines and 200 seamen were landed from the squadron to assist in storming the place on the 16th of October; but M. Bellecombe, who had defended himself with great determination, proposed terms of capitulation.

A considerable augmentation in the marines now took place; the number voted by Parliament for the sea service was 70,000, of which 17,389 were marines,—being an increase of 5,500 men.

The *Apollo* frigate of 32 guns, Captain Pownall, being on a cruise on the coast of France on the 31st of January, 1779, at 1 p.m., when off St. Brieux, captured the French frigate *Oiseau* of 32 guns, but mounting only 26, after a gallant action of an hour and a half. The *Apollo* had 6 killed, her captain and 21 men wounded.

A secret engagement was entered into by Spain with France, as soon as the latter had concluded a treaty with our revolted colonies in America, and from that period preparations for war were making in all their ports; but it was not until the 18th of June that a proclamation was issued by the British Government, authorising the commencement of hostilities against Spain. On the 4th of June, a French fleet of twenty-eight sail of the line and several frigates, sailed from Brest: having formed a junction with the Spanish ships in Cadiz, the united force, amounting to sixty-six sail of the line, after cruising on the coast of Spain, entered the English Channel; and on the 16th of August this formidable armament paraded triumphantly for several days before Plymouth, while several of their frigates anchored in Cawsand Bay. The *Ardent* of 64 guns, Captain Boteler, standing down Channel, and mistaking the enemy for the British fleet, was captured in sight of Plymouth.

The combined fleet continued in the Channel until the 31st, when the wind, having veered to the westward, enabled Sir Charles Hardy, with thirty-seven sail of the line, to obtain a view of the enemy; but the weather becoming very hazy, the fleets lost sight of each other, and soon afterwards the combined armament took its departure.

Shortly after the surrender of Grenada, the French fleet under D'Estaing had been reinforced by a squadron from Europe, augmenting their force to twenty-six sail of the line. On the 6th of July Vice-Admiral Byron, being off Grenada with twenty-one ships of the line, gained sight of the enemy, and immediately made the signal to attack them. The superior sailing of the French ships enabled them to choose their distance, and by preserving their position, they prevented the British rear from getting into action. The firing commenced at seven in the morning, and continued till eleven; but it was renewed at half-past three, and lasted until sunset. The British had 183 killed, and 346 wounded, whilst the loss of the enemy amounted to 1200 killed, and 3500 wounded. First-Lieutenant of the Marines, Joseph Veale, was killed on board the *Sultan*.

On quitting the West Indies, Admiral d'Estaing, with a powerful fleet, proceeded to the coast of North America. His first object was to destroy the small force under General Prevost, and consequently to relieve the southern colonies from present danger and alarm; but the more important consideration was, a design to act in conjunction with General Washington in an attack upon the British force at New York. With this view the *Comte d'Estaing* anchored off the bar of Tybee, at the mouth of the River Savanna, on the 9th of September; and soon after his arrival the French troops formed a junction with the American forces from Charlestown under General Lincoln.

He then sent a haughty summons to the garrison at Savanna, demanding its immediate surrender; but General Prevost, having only a small part of his force with him, requested a short delay before he replied to the message. During this parley, a reinforcement of upwards of 1000 men, under Colonel Maitland, arrived from Beaufort; and on the 16th, after overcoming the greatest difficulties, this detachment joined the garrison at Savanna: their junction gave such encouragement to the besieged, that a message of defiance was sent to the *Comte d'Estaing*. On the 15th, the seamen having completed the landing of the cannon and stores, they were appointed to the different batteries under Captains Henry, Brown, and Fisher of the navy, whilst the marines were incorporated with the grenadiers of the 60th regiment.

When the town was first summoned, only ten guns were mounted; but by the great exertion of the troops, and the zealous assistance of the navy, nearly 90 pieces of cannon were now ready to oppose the enemy, and several vessels were sunk on the bar to prevent the approach of the enemy's ships. Whilst the French were preparing the batteries, their frigates advanced up the river to Mud-flat, and some ineffectual firing took place on the rear of the British lines. A sortie was made on the 24th, and again on the 27th; the first conducted by Major Graham of the 16th, and the other by Major Arthur of the 71st regiment, which did the enemy considerable mischief. On the 3rd of October the bombardment commenced from 9 mortars and 37 pieces of cannon on the land side, and 16 from their shipping, which continued several days with little effect. On the 9th, a little before daybreak, the enemy made a general assault upon the British lines. The attack was obstinately maintained, particularly at a redoubt on the Ebenezer road, when the greatest bravery was displayed on both sides: two stands of colours were actually planted, and several of the assailants killed on the parapet; but the enemy met with such determined resistance, that they could not force an entrance into the works.

At this critical moment, Major Glacier of the 60th, with the grenadiers of that regiment and the marines, advanced rapidly from the lines, attacked the enemy with the bayonet, and drove them from the ditches of the redoubt, as well as from a battery a little to the right of it: pursuing their success, they compelled the enemy to fly in great confusion over the abatis, and into the swamp. The advance of the British detachment was so rapid, that the three companies of the 71st regiment, posted at a short distance in order to sustain them, could not come in for a share in this brilliant affair. The French were repulsed on all sides, with the loss of above 1000 men in killed and wounded; including among the latter the *Comte d'Estaing*, and several officers of distinction. It was not until the 18th that the enemy had raised the siege; and as the fog cleared up in the morning, it was perceived that the French and Americans had abandoned their camps during the preceding night; and in their retreat they broke down all the bridges in their rear, to prevent pursuit.

The troops composing the garrison of Savanna acquired a brilliant reputation for the gallant defence of the place, and for the cheerful, yet determined spirit with which they set the enemy at defiance. On this occasion the greatest unanimity prevailed between the two services, and their heroic conduct gained them the approbation of their king, and country.

A squadron, consisting of the *Charon* of 44 guns, *Lowestoffe* 28, *Pomona* 28, *Porcupine* 16, and *Racehorse* 10, under Commodore Lutterell, proceeded to the attack of the fort and shipping at Omoa, on the Spanish main, and on the 10th of October they arrived in Cavallo bay. In the evening of the 16th, about 500 men, consisting of a small detachment of troops, with a party of seamen and the marines of the squadron, which were landed under the direction of Captain Pakenham of the *Porcupine*, immediately proceeded on their march to surprise and escalade the fort; but the roads were so bad, that the men were sometimes compelled to wade through the sea, in order to avoid the impenetrable thickets of mangroves. At other times they had to pass through lagoons and morasses, and narrow footpaths over the mountains, with precipices rendered dangerous by recent heavy rains.

Those difficulties so impeded their march, that at daybreak the troops were still two leagues from the fort. Captain Dalrymple ordered a halt for two hours, to refresh the men; and when the march was resumed, they were not only exposed to similar obstacles, but severely annoyed by the enemy's skirmishers: these were driven in, and in the evening Captain Dalrymple was enabled from the heights to ascertain that the fort was situated about half a mile from the town. On the 17th the squadron stood into the bay to attack the fort; but the wind falling, the ships became so disabled by the enemy's fire, that they withdrew without producing any result. On the 18th the guns were landed from the *Porcupine*, and placed on an eminence, from which they opened upon the forts; but so little effect was produced, that it was determined to storm the place. Accordingly, the *Pomona* was towed close in during the night of the 19th; and on the morning of the 20th, the other ships stood towards the shore, whilst the troops, in four columns, descended the hill, and at about four o clock they moved forward under fire of their own battery on the eminence. The troops advanced with trailed arms; and in order to animate them for the enterprise, the parole was "bayonet," and the countersign, "Britons, strike home."

The columns were at first staggered by the enemy's fire, but instantly recovering, they advanced to the foot of the wall, which was twenty-eight feet high, surmounted by a battery of five guns. The first ladder was broken by the flanking guns of another bastion, by which a midshipman was killed, and five men wounded. Two seamen were the first that ascended, and levelling their muskets at the Spaniards, produced such panic, that their comrades were enabled to follow them to the assault, before the enemy recovered their self-possession. These two gallant fellows were closely followed by the marines and seamen, who, with the "loyal Irish," leaped down the parapet, and drove the Spaniards into their casemates, whilst above 100 escaped over the walls, and out of the sally-port. The governor then came forward, and claiming protection for himself and officers, surrendered the garrison, as well as the register ships. The prisoners amounted to 355 rank and file, exclusive of the officers and inhabitants. Lieutenant Wightman of the marines was wounded on the evening of the 19th, when reconnoitring the fort.

On the 14th of September, the *Pearl* of 32 guns, Captain George Montague, cruising off the Azores, captured the Spanish frigate *Santa Monica* of 32 guns, after an action of two hours, with the loss of 8 killed, and 45 wounded. The *Pearl* had 12 killed; Lieutenant Fowke of the marines and 18 men wounded.

On the 25th of September, the *Serapis* of 44 guns, Captain Richard Pearson, in company with the *Countess of Scarborough* of 20 guns, sustained a very gallant action near Scarborough with the American frigates *Bon-Homme Richard* of 40 guns, *Alliance* 40 guns, *Pallas* 32 guns, and *Vengeance* of 12 guns, commanded by Paul Jones. Both the British ships were captured, after a gallant defence of two hours. The *Serapis* had 49 killed, 68 wounded; *Scarborough* 4 killed, 20 wounded. Lieutenant Samuel Wightman of the marines was among the wounded. The *Bon-Homme Richard* had 300 men killed and wounded, and she had suffered so severely, that she sunk the next morning.

On the 6th of October, the 32-gun frigate *Quebec*, Captain George Farmer, when cruising off Brest, brought to action the French 40-gun frigate *Surveillante*, mounting 28 twelve-pounders and 12 sixes. After a contest of three hours and a half, during which both ships were totally dismasted, the *Quebec* caught fire by the sails falling on the guns, and continued burning until six p.m. when she blew up, with her colours flying. Captain Farmer, who was wounded in the arm, with 150 men perished on this melancholy occasion. Lieutenant Roberts, with Lieutenant A.J. Field of the marines, the surgeon, 2 midshipmen, and 63 men were saved.

The commencement of this year presented very unfavourable prospects to Great Britain, and the war with her revolted colonies neither promised a speedy nor successful termination. The combined efforts of France and Spain, were eagerly employed in uniting their forces to support the resistance of America; and Holland, our ancient and natural ally, had with equal injustice lent her aid to the cause and interests of these powers. The two principal objects which engaged the attention of the ministry, were the relief of Gibraltar, and the protection of our colonies in the West Indies. Sir George Rodney was appointed to the command of a squadron about to proceed with the trade to the Leeward Islands, and on their way they were to succour the garrison of Gibraltar.

On the 27th of December, 1779, the admiral proceeded to sea with twenty sail of the line and nine frigates; and on the 7th of January, 1780, he detached the trade for the West Indies under convoy of the *Hector* of 74 guns, and two frigates. On the following day the British fleet captured a Spanish ship of 64 guns, with four frigates and fifteen sail of merchant-men, from St. Sebastian, bound to Cadiz: the latter being principally laden with flour and wheat, the admiral gladly conducted the prizes to Gibraltar. On the 16th of January, when off St. Vincent, a Spanish fleet was discovered, consisting of nine sail of the line, under Don Juan Langara: the signal was instantly made for a general chase, and for the ships to engage as they arrived up. About four o clock the *Defence, Bedford, Resolution,* and *Edgar,* commenced the action, but the enemy's ships were in such confusion, as to be unable to support each other; and about five p.m., just as the *Bienfaisant* was closing with an opponent, the Spanish ship blew up, and all on board perished. The pursuit continued through a dark and squally night, and at two a.m. on the 17th, all firing having ceased, the signal was made to bring to on the larboard tack; by which time six ships were captured, and the other two made their escape. The loss of the British amounted to 32 killed, and 102 wounded. Lieutenant Charles Henry Strachan, of the marines, was killed on board the *Edgar.*

On the 19th the fleet arrived at Gibraltar, and having landed the reinforcement and supplies for the garrison, the admiral sailed on the 14th of February for the West Indies with part of the fleet, and the remainder, under Rear-Admiral Digby, returned to England.

On the 27th of March, Admiral Rodney arrived at St. Lucia, and on the 2nd of April he proceeded to Martinique in quest of the *Comte de Guichen* with twenty-ships of the line; but finding all his endeavours to induce the enemy to come out and give him battle ineffectual, the British fleet repaired to Grosislet bay.

On the 15th of April, Admiral de Guichen, with twenty-three sail of the line, put to sea; and on the 16th they were pursued by the fleet under Sir George Rodney, who on the 17th brought them to action, notwithstanding all their efforts to avoid it. The engagement began about one o clock, and the firing continued until four in the afternoon. At the moment of running down to make the attack, the fleets were parallel to and nearly abreast of each other: the *Sandwich,* bearing the admiral's flag, with several of the centre division, stood for and engaged the ships opposed to them in the enemy's line, and Rear-Admiral Rowley, with the rear division, engaged the rear of the French fleet; but the van of the British, in its endeavour to reach the advanced ships of the enemy, had separated so much from the main body, that in order to collect the fleet, it became necessary to discontinue the action. The loss sustained by the British was 120 killed, 353 wounded; that of the French being nearly 1000 men, killed and wounded. Among the wounded were Captain Carey of the marines on board the *Montague,* and Lieutenant Heriot serving on board the *Elizabeth.* From the tenor of Admiral Rodney's letter, it is evident that he anticipated a more decisive result; and had he been properly supported, it is probable that he would have obtained better success.

95

After the repulse of *Comte d'Estaing*, in his attack on Savanna, Sir Henry Clinton was enabled to resume offensive operations; and an expedition, with a powerful armament, was resolved upon for the reduction of the province of South Carolina. Vice-Admiral Arbuthnot, with five ships of the line, two fifties, and several frigates, was to co-operate with his squadron; and accordingly, on the 26th of December, 1779, he sailed from Sandy Hook, accompanied by transports having the troops on board. The fleet, after receiving considerable damage in its voyage to the southward, did not get sight of the Carolina shore until the 1st of February, and then coasted along to Tybee, where it came to an anchor.

The American congress had conferred the command of their troops in the southern provinces on Major-General Lincoln, who took every possible measure to strengthen the defences of Charlestown against the threatened attack, by continuing the lines across Charlestown-neck, from Cooper to Ashley River. In front of these lines was a strong abatis and wet ditch, picqueted on the nearest side; and between the abatis and the lines, deep holes were dug at short distances from each other. Eighty pieces of cannon were mounted, and in the centre was a strong work, which might be considered the citadel. On the 9th of February the fleet sailed from Tybee, and arrived on the 11th at North Edisto. On the same day a division of the army landed in John's Island, and on the following morning the remainder disembarked.

On the 20th of March, the *Renown* 50, *Romulus* and *Roebuck* of 44 guns, being sufficiently lightened of stores and cannon to pass the Charlestown bar, anchored in Five-fathom Hole: at the same time the American commodore, Whipple, retired to Fort Moultrie, and soon afterwards caused the channel to be blocked by sinking six frigates and several merchant vessels, fitted with *chevaux de frise* on the decks. A boom, composed of cables and chains, was extended from the shore to the sunken vessels, defended by batteries mounting forty pieces of heavy cannon, and some ships of war were stationed inside the sunken ships ready to resist any attack; whilst the crews of the deserted vessels manned the guns, which had been landed and placed on the fortifications of Charlestown.

On the 29th of March, the army having landed on Charlestown-neck without opposition, moved forward on the following day, and on the 1st of April the British broke ground within eight hundred yards of the works of Charlestown. By the 9th of April, the batteries were ready to open their fire, and the admiral, having directed the squadron to weigh, entered the harbour in the following order; *Roebuck* 44, *Romulus* 44, *Richmond* 32, *Blonde* 32, *Virginia* 28, *Raleigh* 32; the *Sandwich* and *Renown*, 50, bringing up the rear. The ships maintained a well-directed fire upon Fort Moultrie, as well as on the batteries of Sulivan's Island, and in little more than two hours they anchored under James's Island: some spars were shot away, but the killed and wounded did not amount to more than 27. To prevent an approach to the Cooper River, the rebels sank eleven vessels in that channel, and placed the *Ranger* frigate with some galleys to defend the entrance. An ineffectual summons having been sent to General Lincoln on the 9th, the British batteries opened on the following morning, and they soon acquired a superiority over those of the enemy. Major Moncrieffe, the chief engineer, who had gained so much honour in the defence of Savanna, conducted the offensive operations against Charlestown with equal credit.

On the 18th, considerable reinforcements arrived from New York, which enabled Sir Henry Clinton to strengthen the corps beyond Cooper river, and Lieutenant-General Cornwallis was appointed to that command. On the 23rd, the second parallel was pushed to within 150 yards of the enemy's lines, and on the 24th a sally was made from the town; but the Americans were so effectually repulsed, that they never again quitted their works during the siege.

On the 29th of April, a brigade of 500 seamen and marines, under Captains Hudson, Orde, and Gambier, landed at daybreak at Mount Pleasant, and finding that the enemy abandoned the battery, they marched immediately towards Lampriere's Point; and on being re-lieved by the troops under Colonel Ferguson, they returned to Mount Pleasant.

It was now determined to make an attempt on Fort Moultrie; and on the night of the 4th of May, 200 seamen and marines having embarked in the boats of the squadron under Captains Hudson and Gambier, and passing the fort unobserved, landed before daylight. Immediate possession was taken of a redoubt on the east end of the island, whilst another division was ready to be transported thither from Mount Pleasant under Captain Orde; but the garrison surrendered on receiving a summons from Captain Hudson. On the 6th of May the third parallel was completed, close to the edge of the enemy's canal, and a sap was carried to the dam, by which means a great part of it was drained to the bottom.

Notwithstanding the fall of Fort Moultrie, and the possession of all the principal fords and ferries, the besieged continued to hold out with the same determination; and on the 8th they persisted in refusing the terms which were again proposed by the British commanders.

The batteries obtained such superiority over those of the garrison, that the besiegers, having gained the counterscarp of the part which flanked the canal, immediately passed it, and then began works extending towards the ditch of the place. The inhabitants now became so alarmed, that they induced General Lincoln to accept the terms proposed on the 8th, which stipulated that the rebel troops and sailors should remain prisoners of war until exchanged, and all the ships, stores, and guns to be immediately delivered up. On the 12th, Major-General Leslie took possession of Charlestown, and about 6000 men surrendered themselves prisoners. The total of the British troops employed under the Earl of Cornwallis before Charlestown amounted to 7550 men.

On the 15th of June the *Apollo* of 32 guns, Captain Pownall, being close in with Ostend, sustained a spirited action with the French privateer *Stanislaus*, of 26 guns, in which Captain Pownall and 5 men were killed, and 20 wounded. The beaten ship ran aground, and claimed the protection of neutrality. Lieutenant Edward Pellew, who succeeded to the command, thus expresses himself in his official letter:—

Lieutenant Mansfield, of the marines, was particularly active in assisting on the quarter-deck.

On the 10th of August the *Flora* of 36 guns, Captain W. P. Williams, off Ushant, captured the French 40-gun frigate *Nymphe*, mounting 32 guns. After engaging for upwards of an hour, the ships closed with each other, and the enemy attempted to board the *Flora*, but were repulsed by the British, who, rushing on the decks of their opponent, carried her after a short resistance. The *Nymphe* lost her captain and 62 killed, and 68 men wounded. The *Flora* had 9 men killed, and 18 wounded. Lieutenant Simon Busigny, who fell when in command of the marines on board the *Téméraire* in the Battle of Trafalgar, distinguished himself in boarding the *Nymphe*.

On the 4th of July the French frigate *Capricieuse*, mounting 32 guns, Captain Rensonne, was captured off Cape Ortegal by the British frigates *Prudente* of 36 guns, Captain the Honourable ——— Waldegrave, and *Licorne* 32, Captain the Honourable ——— Cadogan, after a gallant action of more than four hours, in which the French frigate sustained the loss of her captain, and 150 men killed and wounded;

but the gallantly defended ship was so shattered, that she was burnt by the captors. The *Prudente* lost 4 midshipmen and 13 men killed, and 31 wounded: the *Licorne*, 3 killed and 7 wounded. Captain Waldegrave thus reports the conduct of the marines:—

> In justice to Lieutenant Banks, of the marines, I must beg leave to observe to Their Lordships, that his party behaved with the utmost steadiness and bravery, keeping up a regular and constant fire from the beginning of the action, till necessity called them to the great guns, when they showed an equal share of spirit and good order.

On the 13th of August the *Bienfaisant* 64, Captain Macbride, with the *Charon* 44, captured the French private ship of war *Comte d'Artois*, mounting 64 guns, off the head of Kinsale, after a spirited defence of an hour and ten minutes, in which the enemy had 25 men killed, her captain and 35 men wounded. The *Bienfaisant* had 3 killed, and 22 wounded; and the *Charon*, 1 man wounded. The Officers of Marines were, Captain Benj. Adair, First-Lieutenant John Poulden, and Second-Lieutenant James Pool.

On the 7th of June, on the coast of America, the *Iris* 32 guns, Captain James Hawker, sustained a running fight with the French 36-gun frigate *Hermione*, in which the British ship sustained a loss of 7 killed; Lieutenant Bourne, of the marines, mortally, and 8 men severely wounded.

The *Pearl* 32 guns, Captain George Montagu, cruising off the Bermuda islands, on the 30th of September captured the French frigate *L'Esperance*, mounting 28 guns, after a running fight of two hours, with the loss of 20 men killed, and 24 wounded. On board the *Pearl*, Lieutenant Fowke of the marines and 5 men were killed, and 10 wounded.

Considerable augmentations were made in every branch of the military force, and the parliamentary vote for this year was for 90,000 seamen, including 20,000 marines.

The sufferings and privations of the inhabitants of Gibraltar deeply engaged the attention of the government, whilst it excited a lively sympathy throughout the British nation. The relief of the garrison was deemed indispensable; and on the 13th of March, 1781, a fleet of twenty-eight sail of the line sailed from St. Helen's having under its escort the convoys for America, and the East and West Indies, with ninety sail of transports bound to Gibraltar. The different convoys separated in their proper latitude, and Vice-Admiral Darby, with the fleet, arrived in Gibraltar bay on the 12th of April. The Spaniards continued the bombardment until the end of June from batteries mounting altogether 170 pieces of cannon; but notwithstanding their incessant cannonade, the British loss amounted to no more than 53 men killed, and 260 wounded.

On the arrival of admiral Sir George Rodney in the West Indies from New York, he received information of the commencement of hostilities against the Dutch, and therefore determined on attacking their West India possessions. On the 3rd of February the admiral, accompanied by a considerable military force under Major-General Vaughan, appeared before the island of St. Eustatius, and having summoned the governor, the colony surrendered, as did the small islands of St. Martin and Saba; but these possessions were soon recovered by a division of French troops from Martinique, when 68 pieces of cannon, and the garrison, composed of 670 men under Lieutenant-Colonel Cockburn, fell into the enemy's hands.

While Sir George Rodney was at St. Eustatius, he learned the approach of the fleet under the *comte*, De Grasse, and immediately despatched Sir Samuel Hood and Rear-Admiral Drake to windward with eighteen sail of the line, to intercept the enemy's fleet before they could form a junction with their squadron at Martinique. The British fleet proceeded off Fort Royal Bay, and continued to cruise there until the 28th, when the approach of the French was announced by the advanced ships.

A general chase was immediately ordered in line of battle ahead, and the pursuit continued during the night. On the following day the French squadron came out from Fort Royal bay, and formed a junction with Comte de Grasse, making their force twenty-four ships of the line, whilst our fleet was only eighteen; nevertheless, they avoided a close engagement. The van and some of the centre of the British were enabled to bring the enemy to action, but the attacking ships were exposed to very superior numbers of the enemy, and consequently sustained much damage. The *Russell* had suffered so severely, that she was obliged to bear away for St. Eustatius to refit; and the *Shrewsbury*, *Centaur*, *Torbay*, and *Intrepid*, were also much cut up.

The next day Sir Samuel Hood endeavoured again to bring the enemy to action, but the Comte de Grasse withdrew his ships, and returned to Martinique. In the month of May the French made an attempt to reduce the island of St. Lucia, a division of 2000 troops, under the Marquis de Bouillé, having effected a landing without opposition. On the following morning they attacked Pigeon Island, which was bravely defended by its little garrison, consisting of a company of the 87th regiment under Captain Campbell, and some seamen under Lieutenant Ralph Miller of the navy, who resisted the summons of the French general, and resolved to defend their post to the last extremity. The fortunate arrival of the *Thetis, Santa Monica, Sybille,* and *Scourge,* off the Carenage, contributed greatly to the preservation of the island, by landing the marines and a party of seamen, who were stationed in the batteries of the Vigie, whilst another detachment went to the assistance of the troops posted on Morne Fortunée.

On the 12th the Comte de Grasse anchored in Gros-islet bay with twenty-five sail of the line, and several frigates; but the fire from the batteries on Pigeon Island had so severely damaged seven of his line of battle ships, that the French fleet put to sea, and after anchoring in the bay of Trou Gascon, they re-embarked the troops, and returned to Fort Royal, Martinique.

On the 2nd of September Rear-Admiral Graves, with nineteen sail of the line, discovered the French fleet under Comte de Grasse lying anchored in Lynhaven Bay, in the Chesapeake, consisting of twenty-four ships of the line, which got under weigh on perceiving the British. As the fleets neared each other, the British wore round and brought themselves parallel with their opponents; and at 4 p. m. the firing commenced in the rear and centre, and continued until dark. The rear-admiral kept close to the enemy during the night, intending to renew the contest in the morning; but finding that several of his ships were much disabled, he was compelled to relinquish the idea. The fleets continued in sight of each other for the space of five days; but the French, who had the weather-gage, showed no disposition to close, and the British admiral, from the crippled state of his ships, had no opportunity to resume the offensive. On the 10th of the month the Comte de Grasse bore away for the Chesapeake, and on the following day anchored within the Capes.

The following is a statement of the killed and wounded, showing the officers of marines:—*Resolution,* 74 guns, 3 killed, 16 wounded. First-Lieutenant William Patten, Second-Lieutenant William Daws.

*Bedford,* 74 guns, 8 killed, 14 wounded. Captain David Cuming, First-Lieutenant George Vinter.

*London,* 98 guns, 4 killed, 18 wounded. Second-Lieutenant Ralph Clark, Second-Lieutenant Charles Reynolds.

*Royal Oak,* 74 guns, 4 killed, 5 wounded. Captain Wm. Bird, Lieutenant Thomas Thomas.

*Montagu,* 74 guns, 8 killed, 22 wounded. Second-Lieutenant William Buchan, Second-Lieutenant James Breedon.

*Europe,* 64 guns, 9 killed, 18 wounded. Captain Alexander Macdonald, First-Lieutenant Hugh Mitchell, Second-Lieutenant William Minto.

*Terrible,* 74 guns, 4 killed, 21 wounded. First-Lieutenant Carlton Atkinson, Second-Lieutenant Charles Hogan.

*Ajax,* 74 guns, 7 killed, 16 wounded. Captain Henry Tantum, First-Lieutenant Charles Green, Second-Lieutenant Richard J. Squire.

*Princessa,* 70 guns, 6 killed, 11 wounded. Captain William Foster, Second-Lieutenant Randal Myers, Second-Lieutenant Samuel Laban.

*Alcide,* 74 guns, 2 killed, 18 wounded. Captain Randal Macdonald, First-Lieutenant William Ramsay, Second-Lieutenant James Gower.

*Intrepid,* 64 guns, 11 killed, 35 wounded. Captain William Fleming, First-Lieutenant David Pryor, Second-Lieutenant William Home.

*Shrewsbury,* 74 guns, 14 killed, 52 wounded; Second-Lieutenant John Waters, Second-Lieutenant John King.

Total,—90 killed, and 246 wounded.

Shortly after the commencement of hostilities with Holland, the Dutch fitted out a squadron under Rear-Admiral Zoutman, consisting of one ship of 74 guns, one of 68, one of 64, two of 54, one of 50, one of 44, five of 36, one of 40, and two of 24 guns, for the protection of their trade in the Baltic. They were proceeding to the northward with a convoy under their protection, and when near the Dogger-bank, on the 5th of August, they fell in with the British squadron of seven ships of the line and six frigates, under Vice-Admiral Parker, who had likewise a large fleet of merchant vessels under convoy. The *Tamar* frigate was directed to proceed with the trade, and the British squadron made sail in chase of the enemy. Rear-Admiral Zoutman formed his ships in order of battle on the larboard tack, under easy sail, whilst the convoy lay a very little way to leeward; and the Dutch squadron thus resolutely awaited the attack, not firing a gun until their opponents were fairly alongside.

The morning was perfectly clear, with a slight breeze from the N.E., as the British bore down to the attack; and at about 8 a.m., when within pistol shot, hauled their wind together, and the action became general, After the battle had lasted three hours and forty minutes, the Dutch bore away to the southward, leaving their opponents in such a disabled condition as to be incapable of pursuit, with a loss of 104 men killed, and 339 wounded. From the best accounts that could be obtained, the Dutch had 142 men killed and 400 wounded. The *Hollandia*, of 68 guns, was so much shattered, that she sank on the same night.

British squadron on the 5th of September, 1781, showing the names of the officers of marines:—

*Fortitude*, 74 guns, Vice-Admiral H. Parker, Captain George Robertson, 20 killed, 67 wounded. Captain Francis Loighlin, Second-Lieutenants Charles B. Mosley, and William Thomas Chaters.

*Princess Amelia*, 80 guns, Captain J. Macartney, 19 killed, 56 wounded. Captain Alexander Malcolmbe, Lieutenant Thomas Thompson.

*Berwick*, 74 guns, Captain J. Ferguson, 18 killed, 58 wounded. Captain Duncan Campbell (wounded), Lieutenant Hugh Stuart (wounded), Second-Lieutenant Samuel Brown.

*Bienfaisant*, 64 guns, Captain H. Braithwaite, 6 killed, 21 wounded. Captain Josiah Ellicott, Second-Lieutenants James St. Clair, and George P. Ellicott.

*Buffalo*, 60 guns, Captain W. Truscott, 20 killed, 64 wounded. Captain George Ormsby, Second-Lieutenant P. Stapleton.

*Preston*, 50 guns, Captain A. Graeme, 10 killed, 40 wounded. Captain William Sharp, Lieutenant John Kennedy.

*Dolphin*, 44 guns, Captain W. Blair, 11 killed, 33 wounded. Lieutenant Cuthbert (wounded).

Total,—104 killed, and 339 wounded.

With six frigates and six smaller vessels, mounting altogether 716 guns; whilst the total of guns mounted on board the Dutch squadron amounted to 670.

An expedition against the Dutch possessions at the Cape of Good Hope, under the orders of Commodore Johnstone, consisting of two ships of the line, three of 50 guns, three frigates, and two sloops, with several Indiamen and transports conveying between 2000 and 3000 troops, sailed from St. Helen's on the 13th of March, and arrived in Port Praya Bay, St. Jago, on the 10th of April. Whilst lying there, in the security of a neutral port, they were attacked by a French squadron, under M. de Suffren, of five sail of the line, several frigates, with transports, having on board a number of troops and a formidable train of artillery. When this armament made its appearance, a considerable portion of the British crews were on shore, watering and embarking stock; but the commodore, on perceiving the designs of the enemy, called every body on board, and made the signal to unmoor and prepare for action. M. de Suffren, seeing the confused state of the British squadron, left his convoy in the offing, immediately entered the bay with his five ships of the line, and firing at the *Isis* as they passed her, three of the enemy brought up in favourable positions to engage the *Monmouth* and *Hero*; whilst the other two ships kept under weigh, firing at every ship as they passed. The action was maintained with so much spirit by the British, that they were soon enabled to make the enemy repent their treacherous attack, and to withdraw from the contest in a disabled state, pursued by the English squadron, whose total loss in this gallant defence was only 43 killed, and 130 wounded.

M. de Suffren proceeded on to the Cape, where he arrived on the 25th of June, and after landing 500 men to reinforce the garrison, bent his course for the East Indies. Commodore Johnstone, finding that an attempt on the Cape was rendered impracticable, conducted his fleet to Saldanha bay, where he captured four Dutch Indiamen; and having accompanied the vessels destined for the East Indies to a certain degree of longitude, General Meadows proceeded on to India with a proper escort, and the commodore returned to England.

In October an attack was made upon Negapatam by 3200 Company's troops, under the command of Major-General Sir Hector Munro, K.B., assisted by the squadron of five ships of the line under Vice-Admiral Sir Edward Hughes. On the 21st the marines disembarked from the ships, amounting to 443 men, officers included; and immediately joined the army at Nagore, on the sea coast. On the following day 800 seamen, under Captains Mackenzie, M'Coy, and H. Reynolds, were also put under the orders of Sir Hector Munro, and the artillery, with stores necessary for the siege, were with much difficulty landed through the surf.

The general, having invested the place in the best manner his scanty force would admit, determined on an assault; and on the 29th of October the strong lines which the enemy had thrown up were stormed, and carried by the steady and distinguished bravery of our troops. On the 3rd of November the approaches were commenced, and on the 7th a battery of 10 eighteen-pounders was ready to open. During the course of the siege the enemy made two desperate sallies with the greater part of the garrison, but they were beaten back with much loss. On the 10th the batteries opened with so much effect upon the bastion, in which a breach was to be made, that the enemy proposed to capitulate, and on the 11th of November both town and citadel were taken possession of by the British troops. The garrison consisted of 8000 men, but of these only 500 were Europeans; and about 2000 were the troops of Hyder Ali, who fled on the first charge made on the enemy's lines.

The loss sustained by the British during the siege of Negapatam was 28 killed, and about 100 wounded. The marines and seamen were re-embarked on the 24th, and on the 25th of October the squadron prepared for an attack of the Dutch settlement of Trincomalé, which however did not take place until the following year.

A severe action was fought by the *Nonsuch* of 64 guns, Captain Sir James Wallace, near the English Channel, on the 14th of May, with the French 74-gun ship *Actif*. The *Nonsuch* had chased from the squadron of Vice-Admiral Darby, and brought the enemy's ship to action at 10h. 30m. p.m., and after engaging an hour and a half close alongside, the enemy made off, pursued by her antagonist. At 5 a.m. on the 15th the *Nonsuch* renewed the action, which continued until the British ship was so much disabled, that the *Actif* made her escape. The *Nonsuch* had 26 men killed, and 64 wounded; and the French ship 15 killed, and 38 wounded.

On the 30th of May, at 5 a.m., the *Flora* of 36 guns, and *Crescent* of 28 guns, Captains W. P. Williams and the Hon. Thomas Pakenham, attacked two Dutch frigates near Ceuta, and after an action of two hours and a quarter, the opponent of the *Flora* struck her colours. She proved to be the *Castor* of 32 guns, having 22 men killed and 41 wounded. The *Flora* had 9 men killed, and 32 wounded. The *Crescent* engaged the other ship for more than two hours; but the enemy was so superior in force, that the British ship, after being greatly disabled, was compelled to surrender. The *Flora* came up in time to prevent the enemy from taking possession, and the latter, which was the *Brill* of 32 guns, then made off. The *Crescent* lost her mainmast, and sustained a loss of 12 killed, and 40 wounded. The frigates and their prize, after refitting at Cadiz, sailed for England, and on their passage both the *Crescent* and the *Castor* were captured by two French frigates.

Rear-Admiral Hood, suspecting that the Comte de Grasse would speedily return to the West Indies from the Chesapeake, left Sandy Hook on the 11th of November with seventeen sail of the line, and arrived at Barbadoes on the 5th of December, where he was joined by the *St. Alban's* of 64 guns. He again put to sea on the 14th with the whole fleet, and finding that the enemy were at St. Christopher s, he bent his way to Antigua, after being reinforced by the *Prudent* of 64, and *Russell* of 74 guns. The admiral then proceeded off Nevis, and on the 25th, at daybreak, the enemy's fleet was discovered to leeward on the larboard tack, standing to the southward in line of battle ahead, consisting of twenty-nine sail of the line, and two frigates. Rear-Admiral Hood, with his fleet of twenty-two of the line, manoeuvred as if intending an attack, by which means he drew the enemy further off shore; and when they were at some distance from Basseterre road, the British admiral made a push to occupy the anchoring ground the enemy had quitted, and having fortunately succeeded in this bold attempt, he saved the island from capture.

The Comte de Grasse, on perceiving his error, crowded after, and endeavoured to cut off the rear of the British squadron, which consisted of the *Russell, Resolution, Bedford, Canada, President,* and *Montagu,* and at about three o clock, he made a furious attack on those ships; but notwithstanding his vast superiority, after engaging for nearly three hours, he was compelled to draw off, and stand to the southward.

At daylight on the 26th, the French fleet were seen forming their line off Nevis Point, and at about 8 a. m. they stood towards the British squadron. At nine they began their attack on the van, and continued along the whole line, wearing round after they passed the sternmost ship, and then stood to the southward. At one p. m. the enemy tacked, and again standing towards the British, opened their fire upon the centre at 2 h. 50 m. p. m., and then proceeding on to the rear, they wore round as before. Neither of these attacks made much impression on our line, but the French suffered considerably. Captain Strickland, and Lieutenants Forster and Griffiths, of the marines, were wounded.

After the capture of Negapatam, the tempestuous state of the weather retarded the intended departure of the squadron of Sir Edward Hughes to attack the Dutch settlement of Trincomalé, in the island of Ceylon; but the squadron having embarked 30 artillery men, and 500 volunteer *sepoys,* put to sea on the 3rd of January, 1782, from the roads of Negapatam, and arrived in the bay of Trincomalé on the 4th. Early in the morning the marines, with 2 six-pounders, were landed, and soon afterwards 800 seamen were disembarked, followed by the *sepoys*; and before it became dark, the whole force pushed forward towards Trincomalé Fort. On the same night the grenadier company of the marines, led by Lieutenant Orr, made themselves masters of the fort, by forcing an entry through the gateway at the moment the governor was preparing terms of capitulation. The garrison consisted of only 3 officers and 40 men; but the possession of the fort was important to the future operations of the enterprise, as it commanded the only safe landing for stores and provisions from the ships.

On the 8th the seamen and marines carried a post situated on the top of a high hill commanding Fort Ostenburg, which fortress was also on the summit of a neighbouring eminence that commanded the harbour. Sir Edward Hughes, after sending a second summons to the governor without success, ordered the immediate preparation for an assault on the morning of the 11th. Accordingly the storming party, consisting of 450 seamen and marines, having on their flanks a party of pioneers, with 20 seamen carrying scaling-ladders, and a reserve of three companies of seamen and three of marines, supported by two field-pieces and the company's troops, advanced at daylight towards the fort. A sergeant's party of marines led the attack, and getting through the embrasures, the Dutch were soon driven from their works and the fort gained, with the loss on our part of Lieutenant George Long of the navy, and 20 sailors and marines killed; and Lieutenant Samuel Wolseley of the navy, Lieutenant Samuel Orr of the marines, officiating as brigade-major, and 40 men wounded.

The fort mounted above 50 guns, and contained a garrison of 400 men. In the harbour there were two valuable East-Indiamen, and 30 smaller vessels. Sir Edward Hughes, in his official report, thus expresses himself on the conduct of the marines:—

The whole of the officers who have been landed from the squadron for the attack of Negapatam and Trincomalé, have on all occasions manifested much honour, courage, and good conduct; and the private seamen and marines have acted with great steadiness and bravery.

Leaving a garrison in the fort of Ostenburg, the vice-admiral sailed for Madras, where he arrived on the 8th of February, and was informed of the arrival upon the coast of a French fleet, which made its appearance on the 15th, consisting of twelve ships of the line, six frigates, and eight large ships *en flute*; whilst the British were only eight of the line, and one of 50 guns, with one ship of 20 guns. Sir Edward immediately got under weigh in pursuit of the enemy, who separated on the 16th from their convoy, six of which were captured.

At 6 a.m. on the 17th, the French squadron under Commodore de Suffren were seen approaching under a crowd of sail; but the wind dying away, the action did not commence until 4 p.m., when they were engaged with the rear and centre of our squadron, but principally with the *Superb*, *Exeter*, and *Hero*. The engagement continued until dusk, when the enemy hauled their wind, and stood to the north-east. The *Superb* had 11 killed,—her captain, William Stevens, mortally, and 13 wounded. The *Exeter*, Captain H. Reynolds, 9 killed and 45 wounded: total 32 killed, 83 wounded.

The British squadron saw nothing of their opponents, and arrived at Madras on the 12th of March. After taking; on board supplies, they sailed for Trincomalé, and having been joined by the *Sultan* of 74 guns, and *Magnanime* of 64, from England, Sir Edward Hughes on the 30th kept his course, neither shunning nor seeking the enemy.

On the 18th of April, the French fleet was discovered to leeward in the north-east; but Sir Edward continued his course, whilst the enemy kept their relative position until the 11th, when the British, by bearing away for Trincomalé, allowed M. de Suffren to obtain the weather-gage, of which he profited; and on the 12th at daylight, the enemy were seen advancing under sail to the attack. After manoeuvring for some hours, they bore down in two divisions, five ships attacking the van, and the other seven, led by M. de Suffren against the centre of the British line, formed in order of battle on the starboard tack. The *Superb* was at first closely engaged by the French commodore and another ship of 74 guns, but they were so roughly handled that they stood on to attack the *Monmouth*; who, with her main and mizen-masts shot away, had suffered so severely that she fell out of the line to leeward, warmly engaged by her opponents, until the *Superb*, *Monarca*, and *Sultan* ran down, and covered the crippled ship from the destructive fire of the enemy. The cannonade continued until 6 p.m., when the French squadron drew off in disorder to the eastward; and the British ships shortly afterwards came to an anchor.

At daylight on the 12th, the French were perceived also at anchor about five miles distant; in which situation both squadrons remained several days repairing their damages, anxiously watching the motions of each other. On the morning of the 19th, the enemy got under sail and stood towards the British, but soon tacked, and making sail to the eastward, were out of sight by the evening.

The *Superb* and *Monmouth* suffered more than any other ships. The great loss of men of the latter is almost unequalled on board of a ship of her class; having 45 men killed, and 102 wounded. The *Superb* had two lieutenants, her master, with 56 men killed, and 96 wounded.

Lieutenants of Marines, Thomas Milrea of the *Monmouth*, and John Dixon of the *Burford*, were killed. The total loss in the British squadron on the 12th of April, was 137 men killed, and 430 wounded.

Although these actions were not decisively in favour of the British, yet they were of great importance in their consequences. Hyder Ali had relied on seeing our small squadron defeated by the powerful naval force opposed to it; but the result of these two contests, and the capture of the French convoy with the artillery and stores on board, deeply impressed the Indian princes with a conviction of the vast superiority of the British in all naval affairs, as well as of their invincible courage and fortitude: at the same time recalling to their recollection, the battles fought by the gallant Pocock against a superior force under Comte d'Aché, whom he compelled to quit the Indian seas.

M. de Suffren, having refitted his ships at Batacalo, returned to the coast of Coromandel in the early part of June; and having touched at the Danish settlement of Tranquebar, he proceeded to Cuddalore, which place had been strongly fortified by the French.

M. de Suffren, on learning that Sir Richard Bickerton was expected in the Indian seas from England with a reinforcement, resolved to make another attack on the force under Sir Edward Hughes, and in order to strengthen his crews, he received on board 400 French infantry, as many *sepoys*, and 300 artillery.

The British admiral sailed from the bay of Trincomalé on the 23rd of June, and anchored his squadron off Negapatam on the following day. On the 5th of July the French squadron made its appearance, on which the British put to sea and stood to the southward, in order to gain the wind of the enemy. On the 6th of July, at daylight, the French were discerned at anchor, distant about seven miles on the north-north-east, and the wind a light breeze from the south-west. At 6 a.m., the enemy having weighed and stood to the eastward, the vice-admiral was induced to form his squadron in line of battle ahead; and at seven a.m. the signal was made to bear up in line abreast, and for each ship to engage the one opposed to her in the enemy's line. At 10 h. 45 m. a.m. the enemy opened their fire, which was instantly returned by the British; and from 11 h. 10 m. to 35 minutes past noon, the engagement was general.

Shortly afterwards there appeared to be great confusion on board several of the French ships, and the *Brilliant*, the second ahead of M. de Suffren, had lost her main-mast. At this crisis, when fortune seemed to have decided the contest in favour of the English, the sea breeze sat in very fresh at south-south-east. Several of the British ships were taken aback, and came round with their heads to the westward; whilst the others paid off, and continued on their former tack. The effect was somewhat the same on the enemy's squadron; and both admirals collected their ships as well as their disabled condition would permit. As the *Monarca* and *Hero* were so much damaged as to be incapable of taking their station, Sir Edward Hughes wore round, and steered to the westward with his squadron, whilst the engagement still continued to be partially maintained. At 2 p.m. the French ships stood in shore, and at 6 p.m. came to an anchor. The British squadron anchored about three leagues to windward, in so shattered a condition as to be incapable of pursuing the enemy, who reached Cuddalore without further molestation.

The following is a statement of the killed and wounded in the British squadron on the 6th of July, 1782, with the names of the officers of marines on board the respective ships:

*Hero*, 74 guns, Captain C. Wood, 12 killed, 23 wounded. Captain Thomas Lewis, Second-Lieutenant George Thompson.

*Exeter*, 64 guns, Commodore Richard King, Captain C. Hughes, 11 killed, 24 wounded. Lieutenants Thomas Corbyn, and George Palmer.

*Isis*, 50 guns, Captain Hon. T. Lumley, 9 killed, 19 wounded. Captain Robert Carter, Lieutenant Richard Lee.

*Burford*, 70 guns, Captain P. Rainier, 7 killed, 34 wounded. Captain Jenkinson, 98th regiment (killed).

*Sultan*, 74 guns, Captain James Watts, 16 killed, 21 wounded. Captain William Hamilton Gibbons, Lieutenant Richard Williams (wounded).

*Superb*, 74 guns, Vice-Admiral Sir Edward Hughes, Captain D. McLellan (killed), 7 killed, 19 wounded. Lieutenant Samuel Orr, (wounded 3rd of September).

*Monarca*, 70 guns, Captain J. Gell, 8 killed, 46 wounded. Captain Robert Clugston, Lieutenant A. D. Barrett, (both killed on the 3rd of September).

*Worcester*, 64 guns, Captain George Talbot, 1 killed, 9 wounded. Lieutenant Johnston (wounded), Second-Lieutenant Devreux Edwards, (killed 3rd September).

*Monmouth*, Captain James Alms, 12 wounded. Captain Thomas Pearce, Lieutenant Benjamin Mounier.

*Eagle*, 64 guns, Captain John Reddal, 4 killed, 9 wounded. Lieutenants Joseph Lambrecht, John Norman.

*Magnanime*, 64 guns, Captain Charles Wolsely, 2 killed, 17 wounded. Captain William Adlam, Lieutenant Thomas Rolf.

Total,—77 killed, and 233 wounded.

After refitting in Madras roads, Sir Edward put to sea on the 20th of August, with the addition to his squadron of the *Sceptre* 64 guns, Captain Samuel Graves. The admiral's first design was to protect our garrison at Trincomalé, and cover the squadron of Sir Richard Bickerton, whose arrival from England was hourly expected; but M. de Suffren having united his force to the ships under M. d Aymar, they proceeded to the attack of the British posts at Trincomalé, which surrendered to the French, after a short defence, on the 30th of August.

On account of the southerly winds, Sir Edward Hughes did not arrive off Trincomalé until the 2nd of September, where he found the enemy's squadron of fourteen ships of the line, a 50-gun ship, and three frigates anchored in the bay. Early on the 3rd they put out to sea, with a strong breeze at S.W. which placed them to windward of the British, who, formed in line of battle ahead, received the attack of the enemy at 10 h. 30 m. a.m.; but it was not until 2 p.m. that the action commenced

The superiority in numbers of the French enabled them to place additional ships against the extremities of our line, and by these means the *Worcester* and *Monmouth*, the rearmost ships, were furiously assailed; as were the *Exeter* and *Isis* in the van. The cannonade was kept up with great vigour until 5 h. 30 m. p.m., when the wind shifting suddenly from S.W. to E. S. E., Sir Edward Hughes made the signal to wear, which evolution was performed in the most admirable order, whilst the French also came round on the other tack. The engagement was renewed with great spirit, and with such effect on the part of the British, that at 6 h. 30 m. p.m. the main and mizenmasts of the *Héros*, the ship of M. de Suffren, were shot away, and about the same time the *Worcester's* main top-mast came down: about 7 h. p.m. the body of the French squadron hauled their wind to the southward, exposed for some time to the fire of the British ships in the rear.

Considering how closely the ships were engaged, it is surprising that the loss on the part of the British amounted to no more than 51 killed, and 283 wounded; but the number of officers was great beyond example. Captains Wood of the *Worcester*, Watt of the *Sultan*, were mortally wounded; and Lumley of the *Isis* fell during the action. On board the:

*Superb*, 4 men were killed; Lieutenant Samuel Orr of the marines, wounded, Lieutenant Thompson of the 98th regiment, and 49 men wounded.

*Sultan*, 4 killed; Lieutenant Stewart of the 78th regiment, and 43 wounded.

*Monarca*, Captain Robert Clugstone, with Lieutenant Barrett of the marines, and 4 men were killed; the Hon. Captain Maitland of the 78th regiment, and 12 wounded.

*Worcester*, Lieutenant Edwards of the marines and 4 men killed, and 16 wounded.

The great object of the French and Spanish forces in the West Indies was the reduction of Jamaica; and in order to frustrate their design, Admiral Rodney resumed his command on that station, and arrived off Barbadoes from England on the 19th of January, with a reinforcement of twelve sail of the line. The admiral learning that St. Christopher's had fallen, proceeded to St. Lucia, where he was lying at anchor on the 8th of April, when information reached him of the sailing of the French fleet under the Comte de Grasse from Port Royal, consisting of thirty-three ships of the line and two ships of 50 guns, having a large body of troops on board. The British fleet, consisting of thirty-six sail of the line and three ships of 50 guns, immediately got under weigh; and at daylight on the morning of the 9th, part of the enemy was seen between Dominica and the Saintes; whilst the remainder, with a numerous fleet of transports, were lying becalmed in Prince Rupert's bay. As soon as the breeze sprang up, the enemy stood away towards Guadaloupe, followed by the van of the English under sir Samuel Hood, whilst the body of the fleet was still lying becalmed.

The Comte de Grasse, perceiving the separation of the van division of the British from their centre and rear, bore down upon it, and for some time those eight ships were engaged with fifteen of the enemy. About noon the breeze reached the ships under Sir George Rodney, when they immediately tacked and closed with those under Sir Samuel Hood, who was again engaged with the enemy; but the Comte de Grasse, on the approach of the British line, hauled his wind, and at 1 p.m. his ships tacked in succession.

During the 10th the French continued in sight, but at a considerable distance to windward. At daylight on the 11th two of the enemy's ships were so far to leeward of their fleet, that Admiral Rodney, in order to cut them off, made a signal for a general chase; upon which the Comte de Grasse bore down to their support. At 6 p. m. the British, were about three leagues to leeward of the French fleet, which then consisted of thirty-one ships of the line; its number having been diminished by two ships, which were so disabled on the 9th as to put into Basseterre to refit.

At daybreak on the 12th of April, the enemy's fleet was to windward of the Saintes, steering to the northward with a fresh breeze; and one of their ships with loss of foremast and bowsprit, in tow of a frigate, was standing in for Guadaloupe. After an attempt to cut off this disabled ship, which the French admiral supported by bearing away to her assistance, the two fleets formed their lines upon opposite tacks, and the French van was a little to windward of the British.

About eight o clock the action commenced, by the centre and rear of the enemy with the van and centre of the English, and it continued until 10 a. m., at which time Rear-Admiral Drake's division had passed their rear. At this period the van of the French, and the centre and rear of the British, had but little wind from the southward, which occasioned an alteration in the course of that part of the enemy's fleet; and by compelling its van to steer to the westward, whilst the rear continued its course to the southward, it completely deranged the French line of battle, and formed the opening in which Admiral Rodney found his ship and some part of his division, when the firing ceased, and the smoke cleared away about noon.

The van of the French, by steering to the westward in consequence of the southerly breeze, was forced into action with the British rear; whilst the centre of the latter, by changing its course with the alteration of the wind, steered to the eastward, instead of the northerly course it had been pursuing. This also occasioned a division in the British line, whilst thirteen ships of the French rear were between the British van of seventeen, and Admiral Rodney with six of the centre division. These six ships had also five of the enemy under Comte de Grasse on the other side of them, and the French admiral was completely cut off from the rest of his fleet by Rear-Admiral Hood's division, then engaged with the van of the French. Thus, by a fortuitous circumstance, the fleets became divided into three different parts, entirely separated by ships of the opposing fleet intervening.

About noon all firing had ceased, and the French, endeavouring to unite, bore up together, pursued by the British, who attacking the disabled ships of the enemy, soon compelled them to yield. At about a quarter past noon, the *Glorieux* of 74 guns struck her colours on the approach of British ships. The *Cesar*, 74, was next taken possession of by the *Centaur*, after a gallant resistance; whilst the *Hector*, 74, struck to the *Alcide*. The *Canada* was engaged with the *Ville de Paris* of 110 guns, bearing the flag of Admiral de Grasse, until Sir Samuel Hood in the *Barfleur* came up, when the French admiral struck his colours, after sustaining a severe loss in killed and wounded. About this time, just as the sun was sinking below the horizon, the *Ardent* of 64 guns (which had been captured off Plymouth by the combined fleet), struck to the *Belliqueux*; and the British admiral, considering the French fleet completely defeated, gave over the pursuit.

As there was a probability that the disabled ships might be fallen in with, the admiral detached Sir Samuel Hood with his division, who on the 19th discovered five sail in the Mona passage, which separates Porto Rico from Hispaniola, After a pursuit of several hours, the *Valiant* and *Magnificent*, being considerably ahead of the squadron, captured the *Caton* and the *Jason* of 64 guns. Those ships made a gallant resistance, and sustained a heavy loss, whilst their opponents had only 8 killed, and 14 wounded.

The total loss of the British was 240 men killed, and 797 men wounded. The officers of marines included in this return were as follow:—

*Royal Oak*, Captain William Bird, wounded; *Magnificent*, Captain Baggs, wounded; *Repulse*, Captain Henry Bell, wounded; *Torbay*, Lieutenant Mounier, killed; *Princessa*, Lieutenant Laban, wounded; *Montagu*, Lieutenant Buchan, wounded.

In the early part of the year, vast preparations were made by the King of Spain for the reduction of Gibraltar, in forming floating batteries, supported by the combined fleet of France and Spain; and 12,000 French troops, under the Duc de Crillon, joined the Spanish Army.

On the 8th of September, General Elliot ordered a powerful fire to be opened on the enemy's works on the land side; and on the following day a new battery, mounting 64 heavy guns, added to the other cannon and 60 mortars on the Spanish lines, continued to pour an incessant fire against the garrison, whilst a squadron of nine sail of the line and some frigates attacked the sea defences of the rock.

At length the combined fleets, consisting of twenty-seven Spanish and twelve French ships of the line, arrived in Algesiras from Cadiz; and having joined those already before Gibraltar, this powerful armament amounted to forty-eight ships of the line, added to the ten floating batteries, mounting 154 pieces of heavy brass cannon; and their crews, with the artillery on board those formidable vessels, were not less than six thousand men.

On the 13th of September, the battering ships took their stations between the new and old mole, parallel with the rock, and about half a mile distant from it. The attention of General Elliot was principally directed to the effect of the red-hot shot upon the battering ships, but at the same time the whole peninsula seemed to be overwhelmed by the torrents of fire which poured upon it. About two o clock in the morning, the admiral's ship was observed to be on fire, and shortly afterwards a second ship was in flames. Through the whole night of the 13th the fire was continued by the garrison without intermission, and when daylight appeared, a dreadful scene presented itself; the flames continued to rage on board the battering ships, and the men were seen imploring pity and assistance.

The governor having humanely ordered a cessation of the cannonade, the boats from the rock assisted in rescuing the Spaniards from the destruction which was at hand; and by the intrepidity of Captain Curtis of the navy, and his gallant followers, above 400 of the enemy were extricated from their perilous situation. Nine battering ships blew up, and the tenth was destroyed by the British. The impression made on the enemy by the resistance of the garrison is strongly depicted in the following extract of a letter from a French officer:—

The eye is fatigued with the sight, and the heart, is rent with the groans of the dying and wounded. Their number makes me thrill with horror; and I am told that in other parts of the lines, not within my view, the number is still greater.

The loss of the garrison was comparatively small: the whole number between the 9th of August to the 17th of October, being 65 slain, and the wounded 388; nor was the danger done to the works very considerable.

About the time of the attack, Lord Howe sailed from England with thirty-four ships of the line, escorting a fleet of transports laden with troops and supplies for the garrison; but owing to contrary winds they did not reach the straits until the 11th of October, and on the 18th this powerful armament entered the bay, in presence of the combined fleets of France and Spain.

On the 14th of September the *Rainbow* of 44 guns, Captain Trollope, cruising off the Isle of Bas, captured the French 40 gun frigate *Hebe*, after a short action, in which the French ship had 5 killed, and several wounded; but the *Rainbow* sustained no injury, and had only one man killed.

The *Santa Margarita*, Captain Elliot Salter, being on a cruise near Cape Henry, on the 29th of July brought to action the French 36-gun frigate *Amazone*. At 5 h. p. m., when within musket-shot, the enemy's ship opened her fire, and wore round on the same tack as the *Santa Margarita*: both then gradually closed until within pistol-shot of each other, in which position the action was maintained for an hour and a quarter; when the *Amazone* surrendered, with loss of main and mizen-masts, her captain, the Vicomte de Montguiote, and 70 men killed, and more than that number wounded. The *Santa Margarita* had 5 men killed, and 17 wounded.

Lieutenant Frederick Hill Flight, and Second-Lieutenant Thomas Dyne, were the Officer of Marines on board the *Santa Margarita*.

On the 6th of December the *Ruby* of 64 guns, Captain John Collins, having chased from the squadron under sir Richard Hughes, near Barbadoes, captured the French 64-gun ship *Solitaire*, commanded by the *chevalier,* De Borda, after a close action of forty minutes, during which the enemy lost her mizen-mast, and had 20 men killed, and 35 wounded. The *Ruby* had only 2 men slightly wounded, but her masts, sails, and rigging were much injured. Captain Collins was honoured with knighthood for his gallant conduct in this action. The officers of marines in the *Ruby* were, Captain Jonas Matthews, Lieutenant Solomon Debrisay, and Second-Lieutenant Mark Oates.

While the fleet under Earl Howe was equipping at Spithead to proceed to the relief of Gibraltar, the *Royal George* of 108 guns was careened, that some defects under water might be repaired. The ship, as usual on coming into port, was crowded with people from the shore; and among these were many wives and families resident in the neighbourhood of Portsmouth. In this situation, about ten in the morning on the 29th of August, while Rear-Admiral Kempenfelt was writing in his cabin, a sudden squall of wind threw the ship upon her broadside: the ports being open, and the sudden motion of the cannon probably increasing the shock, she almost instantly filled with water and sank.

Rear-Admiral Mr. Saunders, First-Lieutenant Mr. Waghorne, 5th

Lieutenant Major John Graham, First-Lieutenants Richard Graham and Adam Currie, and Second-Lieutenant William Smith of the marines, the master, carpenter, surgeon, three master's mates, and all the midshipmen except four, with above 800 persons, are supposed to have perished. Upwards of 300 persons, including Captain Waghorne, were saved. The *Royal George* was launched in 1755, and was a favourite ship, having carried the flag of Admiral Boscawen; and of Lord Hawke on the 20th of November, 1759, when he defeated the French fleet under Conflans in Quiberon bay.

The Honourable Captain James Luttrell, in the *Mediator* of 44 guns, when cruising off Ferrol, on the 12th of December fell in with a squadron of five ships of war bound to Port-au-Prince, consisting of *L'Eugène* of 36 guns, an American brig of 14 guns, the *Ménagère*, a large ship *en flute*, mounting 30 guns, laden with stores and ammunition; next to this ship was placed the *Alexander*, 24 guns, under American colours, and the nearmost of their line was the *Dauphin Royal* of 28 guns. At 10 a. m. the enemy opened their fire, as the *Mediator* bore down upon them; and on their being obliged to tack and wear, the British ship was enabled to close with her opponents; upon which the brig and the *Dauphin Royal* stood away under a crowd of sail. At eleven the *Mediator* cut off the *Alexander* from her consorts, and pouring in her broadside, compelled the enemy to strike her colours. The other two ships, after firing a few guns, made off before the wind. About noon, as soon as the prisoners were exchanged, Captain Luttrell went in pursuit of the and *Eugène*; but the latter having separated, her consort was pursued until 9 p. m., when the *Menagere*, being within gunshot, hauled down her colours.

The *Mediator* was much cut up in her masts and rigging, but suffered no loss. The *Alexander* had 6 killed and 9 wounded, and the *Ménagère* 3 killed and 7 wounded. Lieutenant Rankine of the marines was serving on board the *Mediator*.

On the 2nd of January, 1783, the 32-gun frigate *Magicienne*, Captain Thomas Graves, in company with the *Endymion* frigate, escorting a convoy to the West Indies, chased two suspicious sail. At 12 h. 30 m. a. m., the *Magicienne* opened her fire, and after a few broadsides her opponent surrendered. The *Magicienne* then stood on, and brought the headmost ship to action, which continued until 2 h. 30 m. p. m., when the British ship's mizen-mast and main-topmast came down, and in another five minutes the fore and main-masts followed. The *Endymion* soon arrived up, cheered, and passed on in pursuit of the enemy, which was the *Sybille* of 40 guns, having about 300 supernumerary seamen on board, bound to the Chesapeake. The *Magicienne* lost 3 officers, and 16 seamen and marines killed; her first-lieutenant, 1 midshipman, her boatswain, Lieutenants Henry Reddish Furzer and William Minto, of the marines, and 29 wounded, out of a crew of 189 men.

The fleet under Vice-Admiral Barrington, consisting of twelve sail of the line, had nearly reached Ushant on their way down Channel on the 5th of April, when several vessels hove in sight, and the signal was immediately made for a general chase. About sunset the strangers were discovered to be three or four ships of war, and seventeen sail of convoy. At half-past nine the sternmost ship, on perceiving that the *Foudroyant* of 80 guns, Captain Jervis (afterwards Earl St. Vincent), was gaining fast upon her, bore away, and was pursued by the British fleet. It came on to blow fresh, which occasioned the *Foudroyant* to separate from the squadron, and at 12 h. 47m. a.m. on the 6th she brought the French 74-gun ship *Pégase* to close action, and continued to engage her until 1 h. 30 m. a. m., when she laid her on board on the larboard quarter, and compelled the French ship to surrender, having 80 men killed and 40 wounded, whilst the *Foudroyant* had only 3 men wounded. The Officers of Marines of the *Foudroyant* were, First-Lieutenant John Hobbs, Second-Lieutenant Richard Murphy.

At daylight on the 16th of March, the *Success* of 32 guns, Captain Maurice Pole, when off Cape Spartel, in company with the Vernon store-ship, captured the Spanish 32-gun frigate *Santa Catalina*, of 34 guns, after an action of two hours, in which the *Vernon* took but little part. The Spanish ship had 25 men killed, and only 8 wounded; and her masts were so disabled, that the fore and main-masts fell soon after she surrendered. The *Success* had only 1 man killed, and 4 wounded. Lieutenant Pownal was the officer of marines on board the *Success*.

The year closed with negotiations for a general peace, the provisionary articles of which were mutually signed at Paris, by commissioners from Great Britain and America, on the 22nd of November. These arrangements were shortly followed by the exchange of preliminary articles with France and Spain, on the 20th of January, 1783.

The establishment of the corps was now reduced to 4495 men, but in 1784 four companies were added to provide for the expedition to Botany Bay. Nothing of importance occurred until the period of the French revolution in 1792, which event produced a renewal of hostilities, and consequently a considerable augmentation in the marines.

## Chapter 4

# From the Year 1792 to 1796

The most important matter that employed the attention of the House of Commons in the early part of the year 1792, was a message from His Majesty, presented by Mr. Pitt on the 28th of January, which in fact announced the commencement of hostilities against France.

In almost every war between Great Britain and France, the West India islands have been among the first and principal scenes of contest, and the efforts of the British minister were again directed to that quarter of the world, with considerable hope of success; for these islands, generally, were badly defended, and the French were too much occupied in preserving their own territories in Europe, to provide adequate means of protection for their distant possessions; and as the black population of the colonies was strongly incensed against their employers, the British Government confidently anticipated a speedy and easy reduction of the French West India islands.

On the 12th of April, 1793, an attack was made upon the island of Tobago by Vice-Admiral Laforey in the *Trusty* of 50 guns, and some small craft, conveying 470 troops, including 32 marines under Major Richard Bright, from Barbadoes. The landing was effected on the 14th; and on the 15th, after assaulting the fort of Scarborough, which was garrisoned by 200 men under a lieutenant-colonel of the French 32nd regiment, the island became again a dependency of Great Britain.

An attempt was next made on Martinique by Rear-Admiral Gardner with three ships of the line and a fleet of transports, having on board 1100 British, and 800 French-Royalist troops, who were landed on the 16th and 17th; and on the 18th the united forces moved forward in two columns to the attack, the two batteries defending the town of St. Pierre. Owing to some confusion among the Royalists they fired upon each other, and then retreated to the place of debarkation, followed by the English; and the admiral was compelled to re-embark in great haste, whilst many hundreds, who had espoused the royalist cause, took refuge on board the ships, to avoid the cruel vengeance of their adversaries.

The revolted state of the inhabitants in St. Domingo induced the better disposed to seek for British protection; and in consequence of information brought to Commodore Ford, commanding the naval forces at Jamaica in the 50-gun ship *Europa*, and some small frigates, that officer arrived near the harbour of Cape Nicolas Mole on the 21st of September; and finding that the inhabitants were apprehensive of an attack from the *mulattoes* and blacks, the commodore sent on shore terms of capitulation similar to those agreed upon at the surrender of Jeremie. Soon after daylight the next morning this proposal was returned, duly executed; and the *Europa* having proceeded to the anchorage, the town and its extensive dependencies surrendered to His Britannic Majesty.

The marines of the *Europa*, under Major Robinson, were the only British force on shore for several days in this important service; and they continued there until the arrival of troops from Jamaica.

The first encounter since the commencement of the war was on the 13th of May, when the 32-gun frigate *Iris* fell in with the French frigate *Citoyenne Française* of 32 guns, off Bordeaux, and after engaging her from 6h. 30m. p.m. until 8 a.m., the stranger hauled her tacks on board, and shot ahead. At this moment, when the *Iris* was preparing to make sail in pursuit, her foremast, main top-mast, and mizen-mast went over the side. The *Iris* had 4 men killed, and 32 wounded; whilst the enemy sustained a loss of 15 killed, and 37 wounded.

On the 27th of May, the *Venus* of 32 guns, Captain J. Faulknor, when one hundred and twenty-five leagues to the westward of Cape Finisterre, discovered the French 36-gun frigate *Semillante*. At 8 a.m. the *Venus* opened her fire, and a warm action was maintained on both sides, as the ships gradually approached, until 10 a.m., when they were scarcely half a cable's length asunder.

By this time the *Semillante* had suffered severely in her masts and rigging, with a loss of 12 men killed, and 20 wounded; and when the *Venus* was endeavouring to run her alongside, a stranger, under French colours, hove in sight to leeward, on which the *Semillante* bore up to join her. This terminated the action, and the *Venus* hauled to the wind as well as her crippled state would permit, having sustained a loss of

2 killed, and 20 wounded. A party of the 2nd regiment of Foot was serving as marines on board the *Venus*.

The consort of the *Semillante* was the twelve-pounder 36-gun frigate *Cléopâtre*, Captain Mullon, of which we have to give a further account, by relating her proceedings in the ensuing month, when cruising off the Start. On the 18th of June, at 4 a.m., the *Cléopâtre* was discovered by the *Nymphe* of 36 guns, eighteen-pounders, Captain Edward Pellew, and immediately chased; but at 5 a. m., finding her adversary closing with her fast, the *Cléopâtre* hauled to the wind and, under top-sails, resolutely awaited her approach. At 6h. 15m. a.m., when within hail, both ships opened their fire, and the action continued with great fury until 7 a.m., both frigates running before the wind. The wheel and mizen-mast of the *Cléopâtre* having been shot away, she fell on board of her antagonist's head and stern; and at 7h. 10m. a.m. was boarded by a party from the *Nymphe*, who struck the French national colours. The *Cléopâtre* had her captain killed, and her total loss amounted to 63 killed and wounded. On board the *Nymphe* 23 men were killed; Lieutenant John Whitaker of the marines, and 26 men wounded.

The assemblage of a powerful fleet in the harbour of Toulon, made it necessary that a British naval force should be despatched to the Mediterranean. Accordingly, a fleet in several divisions proceeded to that station; and on the 15th of August Vice-Admiral Lord Hood arrived before Toulon, with twenty-one sail of the line and several frigates. The French had in that port, ready for sea, seventeen ships of the line, four refitting, nine repairing, and one on the stocks; making a total of thirty sail of the line. The fleet was commanded by Rear-Admiral the Comte de Tregoff, whose attachment to the ancient monarchy was in accordance with the sentiments of a great portion of the inhabitants of the southern provinces.

In order to encourage the loyalists to declare their sentiments, Lord Hood issued a preliminary declaration, in which he pledged himself to support the people of Provence, provided the standard of royalty were hoisted, the ships in the harbour dismantled, and free egress and regress allowed to the British fleet. In that case, no private property of any individual, whatever his previous principles or conduct might have been, should be injured; and as England had no object in view but a firm and lasting peace on liberal and honourable terms, his lordship solemnly promised them, that the port, with all the ships and the forts of Toulon, should be restored to France, when that object was accomplished.

He next addressed an animated proclamation to the towns and provinces in the south of France, assuring them of the determination of the coalesced powers to co-operate with the well disposed, in putting down the tyrannous faction that governed the country. The reply to this proclamation was favourable to the admiral's wishes, and on the 27th of August Lord Hood landed 1500 troops, with 200 marines and seamen, near Fort la Malgue, of which they immediately took possession, and Captain Elphinstone of the *Robust* was appointed governor. On a message being conveyed from the fort to the French Rear-Admiral Julien, that such ships as did not proceed into the harbour would be treated as enemies, the crews abandoned their ships, and about 5000 men and officers escaped into the interior. In the morning the ships moved into the harbour, and in the afternoon the British and Spanish fleets (the latter, composed of seventeen sail of the line, having recently arrived) anchored together in the outer harbour of Toulon. A reinforcement of 1000 men from the Spanish fleet having been sent into Fort la Malgue, Rear-Admiral Gravina took the command of the troops, and Rear-Admiral Goodall was appointed Governor of Toulon and its dependencies.

On the 31st, Captain Elphinstone, with 300 British and the same number of Spanish troops, made a successful attack on a French body of 800 infantry, with two pieces of cannon, near Ollioules; and after a slight resistance the enemy abandoned the position, leaving their cannon and ammunition in the hands of the British. In this affair Captain Douglas of the 11th regiment was killed, and 13 wounded; and the Spaniards lost 2 killed, and 3 wounded.

During the night of the 30th of September the republicans, availing themselves of a thick fog, surprised a detachment of Spanish troops, and took possession of the heights of Pharon, immediately over Toulon; but on the following day they were driven from their new possession with great slaughter by the allied troops under the command of Brigadier-General Mulgrave, assisted by Rear-Admiral Gravina and Captain Elphinstone. Out of 2000 men the republicans lost 1 500 in killed, wounded, and missing. Of the combined forces 8 were killed, 72 wounded and missing, and 48 prisoners. Buonaparte assisted in defending a battery on the Pharon heights; and for his skill and bravery on that day he became so much noticed, that he was shortly afterwards made a brigadier-general.

On the night of the 5th of October, a detachment of 50 Spaniards,

100 Piedmontese, 50 Neapolitans, and 408 British, including 50 marines and a party of seamen,—the whole under Lieutenant-Colonel Nugent, proceeded to the attack of three batteries recently erected on the heights Des Moulins, and two to the southward on the height De Regnier; all of which menaced the shipping in the road: the force on these heights consisted of more than 1200 men, besides 300 in the batteries. The British, having gallantly marched up the difficult ascent, stormed and carried the batteries with very little loss; and after destroying the guns, they returned to their quarters without molestation.

Towards the end of October, the third and last division of Neapolitan troops arrived at Toulon, and the combined forces were then as follows:—French Royalists, 1542; Piedmontese, 1584; Neapolitans, 4,832; Spaniards, 6,840; British, 2,114; making a total of 16,912 rank and file. Of this number not more than 12,000 were effective, the remainder being sick in the hospitals; and of those fit for duty, three-fourths were necessarily distributed among the different posts, extending at least fifteen miles, including several intermediate points; between most of which there was only a water communication.

The army of Kellerman had directed its march on Toulon, and supposing that half of his force had arrived by the 9th of October, there would then have been before the place 33,000 troops. General Dugommier had taken charge of the besieging army, having under him the Generals Laharpe, Garnier, Lapoype, Monnet, and though last, not least, Napoleon Buonaparte.

On the evening of the 15th of November the republican troops made a vigorous attack on Fort Mulgrave, situated on the heights of Balaguier: the first assault was directed against the right, where the Spaniards were stationed, who retreated in disorder, firing their muskets to create alarm. Major-General O'Hara fortunately arriving at this moment from on board the *Victory*, directed a company of the Royals to advance; and these gallant fellows instantly leaped the works, and routed the enemy with the bayonet. The loss of the allies amounted to 61 in killed and wounded, including among the latter captain Duncan Campbell of the Royals, who had commanded the detachment, and Lieutenant Lemoine of the Royal Artillery. The loss of the French was supposed to amount to 600 in killed and wounded.

General Dugommier, having erected works on the heights of Arènes, directly opposite to the fort of Malbousquet, on which were mounted twenty pieces of cannon, established his camp on the crest of another eminence, at a short distance in its rear; and as these guns greatly annoyed the garrison and endangered the arsenal, which was contiguous to it, it was determined to attack the enemy's position.

For this service a corps of 400 French Royalists, 600 Spaniards, 600 Neapolitans, 300 Sardinians, and 300 British, forming a total of 2200 men, under Major-General Dundas, marched from Toulon on the morning of the 30th of November. They ascended the heights with great difficulty, and succeeded at once in driving the enemy from their guns; but the troops, misled by their impetuosity, descended to the hollow in its rear in their endeavour to carry the next eminence, to which the retreating enemy had fled. Here the main body of Dugommier's army attacked them, and not only compelled them to make a rapid retreat, but to relinquish the battery which their valour had won, and which they could have held, and carried off the guns, had they remained in that position. The loss in this unfortunate attack was severe on the part of the British, who had 20 killed, 90 wounded, and 98 missing. General O'Hara, in endeavouring to rally the troops, was wounded and taken prisoner, and General Dugommier received a wound in the knee, when repelling our attack.

By the early part of December the republican forces had received such considerable reinforcements, that a council of war decided on an immediate attack on the fortifications and town of Toulon; but whilst these measures were under consideration, on the night of the 14th of December, in the midst of a heavy storm, the French marched from their encampments in three columns, each taking a route leading towards a different point, so that their attack might be simultaneous. By two a. m. on the 16th, the besiegers had erected five batteries in front of Fort Mulgrave, and continued to cannonade the works with considerable effect until two a.m. on the 17th; when, under cover of the dark and tempestuous weather, the enemy succeeded in entering the fort by the Spanish side; and although resisted by the few remaining British under Captain Conolly of the 18th regiment, they compelled the remnant of the garrison (originally not more than 700) to retire towards the shore of Balaguier. During these operations, the column under General Lapoype having succeeded in carrying all the posts upon the heights of Pharon, the line of defence was broken upon in two of its essential points, and the position was so commanding, that the ships were compelled to retire to a place of greater safety.

Under these circumstances a council of war was held by the British, when it was determined to evacuate Toulon, as soon as proper arrangements could be made for that purpose. The troops occupying the redoubt and the lunette of Pharon were ordered to retire to the posts of Artigues and St. Catherine's, whilst those of St. Antoine, St. André, Pomet, and the Mills might be withdrawn; but that of Malbousquet and Mississi to be retained as long as possible. The French ships of war, being armed, were to proceed to sea with the fleet, while those in the harbour, together with the arsenal and magazines, were to be destroyed.

The troops were withdrawn from the heights of Balaguier without much interruption from the enemy, as were those of the other posts deemed necessary to be evacuated. The purposed retention of the forts of Malbousquet and Mississi was prevented by the indiscretion of the Neapolitans, who abandoned them without orders, and deserting their posts, hastened on board the ships in the utmost confusion and disorder. In the course of the 18th, the remaining troops were concentrated in the town and in the fort of La Malgue, ready to embark when the conflagration of the shipping should take place.

The important service of destroying the ships and magazines was entrusted to Sir Sidney Smith, at his own particular request and on the same afternoon, taking with him a small lateen vessel, in which he had recently arrived from Malta, and three English and three Spanish gunboats, Sir Sidney proceeded to the arsenal to prepare the combustibles required for the occasion. The dockyard gates had been judiciously closed and secured, and the galley-slaves, amounting to about 800, for the most part unchained, seemed to view these preparations with vindictive satisfaction; and as the guns of the tender and of a gun-boat were pointed towards them, they remained quiet spectators of the impressive scene. All this while the party of Sir Sidney Smith was exposed to a fire of shot and shell from Malbousquet and the neighbouring hills, which tended to keep the slaves, as well as the republicans in the town, in entire subjection.

At 8 p.m. the *Vulcan* fire-ship, Captain Charles Hare, was towed into the basin; and at 10 p.m., on a preconcerted signal, the trains leading to the different magazines and storehouses were set fire to, as well as the fire-ship. The flames ascended in terrific grandeur, and the rapid spread of the fire, almost overpowering by its heat, laid open to view all who were aiding in this perilous service; whilst the enemy, having distinct objects to point at, opened their batteries from every quarter. At this juncture an unexpected and awful explosion took place: the Spaniards, instead of scuttling, set fire to the *Iris* frigate, containing several thousand barrels of powder, and its effect shook one gunboat to

125

pieces, while another was blown into the air; but, providentially, only three of the crew were killed.

The business of the arsenal completed, Sir Sidney Smith and his brave followers proceeded to the destruction of two 74 gunships, filled with French prisoners, who being landed in a place of safety, the *Héros* and *Themistocle* were set on fire. The gallant officer and his party, having effected all that could be done, were returning to the fleet, when another powder-vessel exploded close to them; but, extraordinary as it must appear, without doing any injury. The British were now so exhausted, that they stood slowly out towards their friends, heeding little, after their last narrow escape, the few ill-directed shots that were fired from forts Balaguier and Aiguillette.

The commencement of the conflagration had been the signal for evacuating the town, and under the direction of Captain Elphinstone, late governor of Fort la Malgue, the whole of the troops embarked, and were on board the fleet by daylight on the morning of the 19th, without sustaining any loss. The fugitives from Toulon, to the amount of 14,877, men, women, and children, received an asylum on board the British ships, where they crowded to such an extent, that the *Princess Royal* had 4000, and the *Robust* 3000 of those unhappy people. Of the unfortunate who were left to the mercy of the enraged republicans, above 5000 perished by the sword or the guillotine, or were drowned in their endeavours to escape from the infuriated soldiery. Twenty sail of the line were lost to France: three ships of 80 guns, and fourteen of 74 guns, were destroyed, and the *Commerce de Marseilles* of 120 guns, with the *Pompée* and *Puissant* of 74 guns, were brought to England.

In the latter part of July, the 32-gun frigate *Boston*, Captain George W. A. Courtenay, was cruising off New York, watching the French 36-gun frigate *Embuscade*, Captain J. B. F. Bompart, lying in that harbour. In consequence of a hostile message sent by Captain Courtenay, the French frigate put to sea, and on the morning of the 31st was seen coming down before the wind, to accept the challenge. After some preparation, the *Embuscade*, at 5h. 5 m. a.m., ranged along the weather side of the Boston, and a furious action was maintained on both sides. At 6 h. 20 m. a. m., Captain Courtenay and Lieutenant James Edward Butler of the marines, while standing at the fore-part of the quarter-deck, were killed by the same shot. By this time the *Boston* had lost her main and mizen top-masts, and was much disabled in her sails and rigging. Thus circumstanced, with two of her lieutenants wounded, the British frigate bore up and made sail, followed by the *Embuscade* until eight a.m., when the French frigate hauled to the wind. The *Boston* sustained a loss of 10 killed, and 24 wounded: the *Embuscade* 50 killed and wounded.

During the time that Toulon remained in possession of the allies, a formidable insurrection existed in Corsica, and General Paoli, the leader of the insurgents, having sought the aid of the English; Commodore R. Linzee, with the *Alcide* and *Courageux* of 74, *Ardent* 64, *Lowestoffe* 32, and *Nemesis* 28, sailed from Toulon for Villa Franca in the month of September. Owing to some unexplained cause, the commodore delayed the attack on the redoubt of Fornelli, which is situated about two miles in advance of the town of San Fiorenzo, until the garrison had made such preparations as enabled them to defeat the attempt. On the night of the 30th of September, the *Ardent* was led into a situation to annoy the redoubt, and at the same time covering the approach of the other ships.

At 3 h. 30 m. a.m. on the 12th of October, having opened her fire, she was soon joined by the *Alcide* and *Courageux*, and the three ships maintained a warm cannonade until 8 h. 15 m. a.m., without any visible effect on the redoubt; but the *Courageux* and *Ardent* had been unexpectedly opposed to a raking fire from the town of San Fiorenzo, by which they were considerably damaged; the *Courageux* having 2 killed and 13 wounded, the *Ardent* 14 killed and 17 wounded, and the *Alcide* 9 men wounded. The failure was attributable to a want of co-operation on the part of Paoli's adherents, who had undertaken, simultaneously with the naval operations, to storm the forts on the land side; but it is probable that the ill success was in great measure occasioned by the tardiness of the commodore in making the attack.

The great importance of the harbour of San Fiorenzo to Great Britain, as a point of rendezvous for her Mediterranean squadrons, suggested to Lord Hood the propriety of assisting the loyal part of the inhabitants in their attempt to expel the French from the island. On the 24th of January the fleet and transports with the troops, amounting to sixty sail, quitted the bay of Hyères, and proceeded to that of San Fiorenzo; but the armament was driven to leeward by a heavy gale, and did not reach Porto Ferrajo, in the island of Elba, until the 29th. On the 5th of February the *Alcide*, *Egmont*, and *Fortitude*, of 74 guns, with *Lowestoffe* and *Juno* frigates, were detached to a bay to the westward of Cape Mortella; and on the evening of the 7th, 1400 troops under Major-General Dundas having landed and taken possession of a height which commanded the tower of Mortella, an attack was made upon it on the following day. The *Fortitude* and *Juno*, after engaging two hours and a half, were compelled to withdraw, with a loss on board the former of 6 men killed, and 56 wounded; nor was the battering from the height attended with better success until some additional guns were mounted, and then the brave garrison of thirty-three men, commanded by Enseigne le Tellier, was compelled to surrender.

The post next attacked was the Convention redoubt, mounting twenty-one pieces of heavy ordnance, and considered as the key of San Fiorenzo. By surprising exertions, several eighteen-pounders were placed on an eminence of very difficult ascent, 700 feet above the level of the sea: this rocky elevation was deemed inaccessible, but the seamen, by means of blocks and tackles, contrived to haul up the guns, and a cannonade was unremittingly kept up during the 16th and 17th, when the works were stormed; but the greater part of the garrison had retreated, and during the night passed over to the town of San Fiorenzo, with their two frigates. On the 19th, after sinking one of their frigates and burning the other, the French evacuated the town of San Fiorenzo, and retreated towards Bastia, leaving the British in possession of the former place, as well as of the tower and batteries of Fornelli; and the seamen soon found means to weigh, and carry off the *Minerve*, a fine frigate of 40 guns.

On the 4th of April, Lord Hood arrived at the anchorage before Bastia, and on the same evening the troops, guns, and stores were landed; and a detachment of seamen, commanded by Captain Horatio Nelson of the *Agamemnon*, disembarked to the northward of the town. The total of the combined forces, when landed, amounted to 1248 officers and men, exclusive of about the same number of Corsicans under general Paoli; whilst the French and Corsican troops in the garrison of Bastia were about 3000. Lord Hood moored the fleet in the form of a crescent, just out of the reach of the enemy's guns, and the entrance to the harbour was effectually guarded by gun-boats and armed launches.

After a siege of thirty-seven days, and four of negotiation, the town and citadel of Bastia, with the several outposts, surrendered. The loss sustained by the army was only 7 killed and 21 wounded; and that of the navy, Lieutenant Carey Tupper of the *Victory*, and 6 men killed; Lieutenant Andrews, and 12 men wounded. On the 19th, Captain Nelson, the senior officer in the absence of Lord Hood, (who with the fleet had sailed to look after the Toulon squadron,) disembarked the troops at Port Agra, situated about three miles from Calvi; and on the same day Lord Hood, arriving in Mortella Bay, sent on shore a detachment of seamen under Captains Hallowell and Serecold. On the 27th, the *Victory* having arrived before Calvi, seven of her lower-deck guns were landed, and the batteries were soon opened; but it was not until the siege had lasted fifty-one days that General Casa-Bianca could be induced to capitulate; and on the 10th of August the garrison of Calvi surrendered.

The loss on the part of the British Army was 1 field-officer, 2 lieutenants, and 20 men killed; 3 captains, 4 lieutenants, and 46 wounded. Of the navy, Captain W. Serecold, 1 midshipman, and 5 seamen were killed, and 6 seamen wounded. Captain Nelson was not reported wounded, although he lost the sight of his right eye, from some particles of sand which had been driven into it, by a shot striking the battery near him.

On the 20th of October the 36-gun frigate *Crescent*, Captain James Saumarez, was standing close along shore, off Cape Barfleur; and just as the day dawned, she discovered to leeward the French 36-gun frigate *Reunion*, Captain F. A. Denian. The *Crescent* immediately bore away, and in a short time ranged up alongside the French frigate. In the early part of the action which ensued, the *Crescent*, after losing her fore-topsail yard and then her fore-topmast, came round on the opposite tack, and brought her larboard guns to bear. The *Reunion*, having lost her fore-yard and mizen topmast, was exposed to several raking broadsides from her opponent; and after a gallant defence of two hours and ten minutes, in which she had 33 killed and 48 severely wounded, the French frigate struck her colours, just as the British 32-gun frigate *Circé* was perceptible to leeward, using every exertion to close. Lieutenant Henry Hodge was serving on board the *Crescent*, which ship had only one man wounded.

On the 4th of October, the 32-gun frigate *Thames*, Captain James Cotes, being some degrees to the westward of Ushant, engaged the French 40-gun frigate *Uranie* from 10 h. 30 m. a.m., until 2 h. 20 m. p.m., when the latter made off, leaving the British frigate so much crippled as to be incapable of pursuit, having 11 men killed, and 23 wounded. Whilst repairing her damages, three French frigates and a brig hove in sight, and the *Thames* was captured and carried into Brest. Lieutenant Anthony Stransham was serving on board the *Thames*.

In the latter part of the month of January, 1794, Vice-Admiral Sir John Jervis, K.B. arrived at Barbadoes as the commander-in-chief on that station, accompanied by Lieutenant-General Sir George Grey with 7000 troops; and on the 5th of February, the expedition arrived off Martinique, consisting of the following ships of war:—*Boyne* 98 guns, *Vengeance* and *Irresistible* of 74 guns, *Asia* and *Veteran* of 64, with several frigates and sloops. The troops were disembarked at three different points, and the respective divisions overcame all opposition.

By the 16th of March the whole island, except Forts Bourbon and Royal, was in possession of the British; but this was not effected without the loss of 71 killed and 193 wounded. Lieutenant W. Tremenheere, with a small party of marines and 200 seamen under Captain E. Harvey, were landed, and having conveyed a twenty-four pounder gun and two mortars to the heights of Sourière, a fire was opened upon Fort Bourbon, and the island soon surrendered. Guadaloupe was the next object of attack, and a detachment of seamen and marines having assisted in the reduction of the strong post of Fleur d'Epée, the whole colony surrendered on the 20th; but a French squadron appearing off the island on the 3rd of June, disembarked 1400 troops, who regained possession of Fleur d'Epée Sir John Jervis being apprised of this reverse, quickly repaired off Guadaloupe with four ships of the line, and on the 19th two battalions of seamen were landed, and took possession of the village of Gosier.

From the 25th to the end of June several skirmishes took place; and on the morning of the 2nd of July an unsuccessful attempt was made upon the town of Pointe-à-Pitre, which failure led to the abandonment of Grand-terre by the British forces. Between the 10th, and the 3rd of July, the army had 105 killed, 330 wounded, and 56 missing. On the part of the navy, Captain Lewis Robertson, 4 seamen, and 2 marines were killed; Lieutenant Isaac Woolley, Lieutenant of Marines John Mercer, 24 seamen, and 3 marines wounded; and 16 seamen missing.

On the 3rd of February the important post of Cape Tiburon, St. Domingo, mounting twenty-two pieces of cannon, was taken by the British; and on the 18th, the port of Aoul was carried, after a sharp resistance, by a body of troops under Lieutenant-Colonel Dansey. Fort Brissoton surrendered on the 2nd of June, and on the morning of the 4th the British colours were hoisted at Port-au-Prince. Throughout the operations which led to the capture of the West India islands, the navy and marines took part with the troops; and Sir John Jervis observes:

The unabated exertions of the officers and men under his command could never be surpassed; and that, keeping constant pace with the troops, no difficulty or danger arrested, for an instant, their career of glory."

In the course of this year several French frigates, chiefly in squadrons of three or four, cruised in and near the British Channel, and were so successful in their attempts to capture or destroy our merchant shipping, that three British squadrons were ordered to sea to intercept them. One of these, under command of Commodore Sir John Borlase Warren, consisting of five frigates, fell in with three French frigates and a corvette on the 23rd of April, near Guernsey. At 6 h. 30 m., the *Flora* being abreast of the rearmost ship, opened her fire, and continued engaging as she passed the three sternmost of the enemy; but having her main-topmast shot away, and otherwise crippled, she dropped astern, and was succeeded by the *Arethusa*.

The French now made all sail to escape, but the *Arethusa*, *Melampus*, and *Concorde* soon approached the *Pomone* of 40, and *Babet* of 20 guns, and both these ships surrendered, after a gallant resistance, at 9 h. 30 m. p. m. The pursuit of the other two frigates was continued by the *Concorde* and *Melampus*, and the *Engageante* of 36 guns was captured by the *Concorde*, after a close engagement of more than an hour, in which the French ship suffered severely. The *Résolue* effected her escape into Morlaix.

The following is a statement of the killed and wounded, with the names of the officers of marines serving on board the squadron:—

*Arethusa*, 38 guns, Captain Sir Edward Pellew, 3 killed, 5 wounded. First-Lieutenant Richard Williams.

*Flora*, 36 guns, Commander Sir John B. Warren, bart., 1 killed, 3 wounded. First-Lieutenant John Richardson.

*Melampus*, 36 guns, Captain Thomas Wells, 5 killed, 5 wounded. Second-Lieutenant John Campbell.

*Concorde*, 36 guns, Captain Sir Richard Strachan, 1 killed, 12 wounded.

*Nymphe*, 36 guns, Captain George Murray. First-Lieutenant Solomon Desbrisay.

Total,—10 killed, 25 wounded.

The *Pomone* lost her main and mizen-masts, and had above 100 men killed and wounded.

A very determined defence was made by the French 36-gun frigate *Atalante*, Captain C. A. L. D. Linois, when captured by the *Swiftsure* of 74 guns, Captain Charles Boyles, on the 7th of May, after a running fight of an hour, in which she lost 10 men killed, and 32 wounded. The *Swiftsure* had one man killed.

On the 29th of May the 28-gun frigate *Carysfort*, Captain Francis Laforey, cruising to the westward of Ushant, captured the French 32-gun frigate *Castor*, after an action of one hour and fifteen minutes; in which the latter had 16 killed, and 9 wounded. The *Carysfort* had 1 man killed, and 4 wounded. Lieutenant James Fynmore was serving on board the *Carysfort*.

On the 17th of June, as the *Romney*, 50 guns, Captain the Hon. William Paget, having a convoy under her charge from Naples to Smyrna, was passing the island of Miconi, in the *Archipelago*, a French frigate was discovered at anchor. Captain Paget directed the convoy to proceed on, and the *Romney* was presently at an anchor within a little more than a cable's length of the 40-gun frigate *Sibylle*, Commodore J. M. Rondeau. At one p.m. the *Romney*, having taken her position with springs on her cables, opened her fire, and the action continued without intermission for an hour and ten minutes; when the *Sibylle*, being in a defenceless state, and having 46 men killed, and 112 wounded, struck her colours. The *Romney* had only 266 men and boys on board; and of these, 8 were killed and 30 wounded. Lieutenant W. H. Allen was the officer of marines on board the *Romney*.

On the 21st of October a squadron of four frigates under Sir Edward Pellew, when a few leagues to the westward of Ushant, chased the French 40-gun frigate *Révolutionaire*, Captain H. A. Thevenard. The superior sailing of the *Artois* of 38 guns, enabled her to bring the French frigate to action, and the latter defended herself with great spirit for forty minutes; when the *Diamond* having approached within gunshot, and the other two ships coming up fast, the *Révolutionaire* struck her colours, with a loss of 8 killed, and 4 wounded. The *Artois* had 2 killed; Lieutenant Peter Craigie of the marines (who died after suffering amputation), and 5 wounded.

On the 2nd of May a fleet under Earl Howe, consisting of thirty-four ships of the line, with a number of smaller vessels of war, and nearly a hundred sail of merchant-men, sailed from Spithead. When off the Lizard, Rear-Admiral Montagu was detached with eight ships of the line, to protect the East and West India convoys; leaving twenty-six sail of the line and seven frigates cruising off Ushant.

On the 16th of May the French fleet, consisting of twenty-five ships of the line and several frigates, under Rear-Admiral Villaret de Joyeuse, and the Conventional Deputy Jean Bon Saint-Andre, sailed from Brest, with the wind at north-east; and on the 28th the enemy was seen to windward, bearing down towards the English fleet; but they hauled to the wind when they had reached within nine miles; and, after some delay, formed an indifferent line ahead. In the afternoon the rear division, under Rear-Admiral Pasley, was partially engaged with the enemy, and the *Révolutionaire* of 120 guns suffered so severely that she bore away from the fleet, and was taken into Rochefort in a disabled state.

During the night of the 28th the two fleets continued in sight of each other; and on the morning of the 29th Earl Howe, with the intention of making some further impression on the rear of the enemy, ordered the fleet to tack, and then cut through the enemy's line in order to obtain the weather-gage. At 8 a.m. the van of the French wore round to support their rear, and then hauled to the wind. At 9 a.m., when on the larboard and same tack as the British fleet, the French bore away, and at 10 a. m. opened an ineffectual fire upon our van; but some of that division were enabled to get sufficiently near to make an impression on several of the French ships, nor did the British escape with impunity. At 11 h. 30 m. the signal was made to tack in succession, with the intention of passing through the enemy's line; but the *Caesar*, the leading ship, wore round, and then ran past the eighth ship of the enemy, before she hauled to starboard and cut through.

About 1 p. m. the *Queen* wore, and passing under the lee of the *Terrible* of 110 guns, ran along the French line, and became so much crippled, that she could not haul up and pass through as intended. On perceiving the disabled condition of the *Queen*, Lord Howe resolved to set the example of cutting the enemy's line, and at 1h. 30 m. p.m. the *Queen Charlotte* tacked, and then passed close under the stern of the *Eole*, the sixth ship from their rear; and the two seconds to the British admiral, the *Bellerophon* and the *Leviathan*, passed respectively under the sterns of the *Tyrannicide* and *Indomptable*. Lord Howe then came round again on the larboard tack, and hoisting the signal for a general chase, the *Queen Charlotte* pursued the *Terrible*.

At 4 p. m. the *Queen Charlotte*, with several ships, ran down to cover the *Queen* and *Royal George*, who were much disabled, from the attack of the French admiral. This movement again brought the two vans within random shot, and afforded an opportunity for the *Glory* to distinguish herself. At 5 p.m. the French commander-in-chief, having

133

recovered his two disabled ships, wore round, and rejoined the rear of his fleet; and the British, by wearing in the same direction, kept the weather-gage. During the two following days the weather was so foggy, that the enemy could only be seen at times; but on the 31st, at 9 a.m., the French fleet was descried to the northward, and plainly seen to consist of twenty-six of the line. At 2 p.m. Lord Howe bore up, and ran down towards the enemy until 3 h. 30 m., when the British hauled to the wind on the larboard tack. At 5 p.m., having formed the larboard line of bearing, they edged away towards the enemy; but the admiral preferring a daylight contest, again brought the fleet to the wind at 7 p.m., and kept under commanding sail during the night, to preserve the weather-gage.

On the 1st of June, latitude 47° 48 north, longitude 18° 30 west, the wind moderate from south and by west, the enemy were seen about six miles on the lee bow of the British, in line of battle upon the larboard tack. At 5 a.m. the British fleet bore up, but at 7 h. 10 m. hauled to the wind on the same tack as the enemy; and as soon as the crews had taken their breakfast, at 8 h. 12 m. a.m. they filled, and bore down upon their opponents. About a quarter past nine the French opened their fire upon the van of the British, who were steering in a lasking direction towards the enemy. Soon after 10 a.m. the *Queen Charlotte* passed under the stern of the *Montague* of 120 guns, and ranged close up on her lee bow, where she became exposed to the fire of the 80 gun ships *Juste* and *Jacobin*. A few of the British ships following the example which had been set them by their noble and gallant chief, cut through the French line, and engaged their opponents to leeward; but the remainder hauled up to windward, some at a great distance, whilst others were sufficiently near to engage with effect.

At half past ten, when the action was at its height, the French admiral in the *Montagne* made sail ahead, followed by his second in the line, and afterwards by such ships as had suffered but little in the contest. By 11 h. 30 m. a.m. the firing had nearly ceased, when the British were left with eleven, and the French with twelve, more or less dismasted ships: at this time none of the enemy had struck their colours, and many of the crippled ships were striving to escape under a spritsail, or some small sail set on the stump of their masts. Admiral Villaret, having failed in his attempt to cut off the *Queen*, which lay disabled at some distance from the body of her fleet, stood on, and contrary to all expectation, was enabled to cover and rescue four of his dismasted ships, the *Republican* 110, *Muscius* 74, *Scipion* 80, and *Jemappes* 74; a fifth, the

*Terrible* 110, having previously joined him, by gallantly fighting her way through the British fleet.

At about 1h. 15 m. p.m. the action had nearly ceased; but it was not until 2 h. 30 m. p.m. that the six dismasted French ships nearest at hand, the *Sans Pareil* 80, *Juste* 80, *Amérique, Impétueux, Northumberland,* and *Achille,* of 74 guns, were secured. At a little after 6 p.m. a seventh French ship, the *Vengeur* of 74 guns, was taken possession of, but in so shattered a state that in ten minutes afterwards she went down, with upwards of 200 of her crew on board, composed chiefly of wounded men.

Admiral Villaret, after recovering his four disabled ships, two of them without a stick standing except their bowsprit, stood away to the northward; and before 7 p.m. the whole of his nineteen remaining line of battle ships were out of sight of the British fleet. It was not until the 3rd that Lord Howe had sufficiently repaired his ships to proceed to Spithead; where he anchored with his prizes and the whole of his fleet, except thirteen ships, which he had ordered to Plymouth.

As our limited space will not admit of a detailed account of this glorious contest, we merely subjoin a list of the ships and their commanders, with the killed and wounded on the 29th of May, and on the 1st of June; together with the names of the officers of marines serving in the fleet:—

*Queen Charlotte,* 100 guns, Admiral Earl Howe, Captains Sir R. Curtis and Sir A. Douglas, May 29, 1 killed; June 1, 13 killed, 29 wounded. 2nd regiment of Foot.

*Royal George,* 100 guns, Vice-Admiral Sir A. Hood, Captain W. Domett, May 29, 15 killed, 23 wounded; June 1, 5 killed, 49 wounded. Captain L. P. Jones, First-Lieutenant Andrew Polkington, Second-Lieutenant Samuel Claperton.

*Royal Sovereign,* 100 guns, Vice-Admiral T. Graves, Captain H. Nicholls, May 29, 8 killed, 22 wounded; June 1, 6 killed, 22 wounded. Captain C. B. Money, First-Lieutenant Charles Allen, First-Lieutenant Stephen Mitchell.

*Barfleur,* 98 guns, Rear-Admiral G. Bowyer (wounded), Captain C. Collingwood, June 1, 9 killed, 25 wounded. 69th regiment of Foot.

*Impregnable,* 98 guns, Rear-Admiral B. Caldwell, Captain G. B. Westcott, June 1, 7 killed, 24 wounded. Captain-Lieutenant George James Prosser, First-Lieutenant Nicholas Croad, Second-Lieutenant John Hebrington.

*Queen,* 98, Rear-Admiral A. Gardner, Captain J. Hutt (wounded),

May 29, 22 killed, 27 wounded; June 1, 14 killed, 40 wounded. Captain-Lieutenant Thomas Solby, Second-Lieutenant Frederic Liardet.

*Bellerephon*, 74 guns, Rear-Admiral T. Pasley (wounded), Captain W. Hope, June 1, 4 killed, 27 wounded. Captain Walter Smith, First-Lieutenant Samuel Foreshall, Second-Lieutenant Richard Gamble.

*Glory*, 98 guns, Captain J. Elphinstone, June 1, 13 killed, 39 wounded.

*Gibraltar*, 80 guns, Captain J. McKenzie, June 1, 2 killed, 12 wounded. 25th regiment of Foot.

*Caesar*, 80 guns, Captain A. J. Pye Molloy, May 29, 3 killed, 19 wounded; June 1, 15 killed, 52 wounded. Captain James Driffield, First-Lieutenant Benjamin Dickenson, Second-Lieutenant Thomas Hopper.

*Brunswick*, 74 guns, Captain J. Harvey (killed), June 1, 44 killed, 114 wounded. 29th regiment of Foot.

*Valiant*, 74 guns, Captain T. Pringle, June 1, 2 killed, 9 wounded. Captain Robert Moncrieffe, First-Lieutenant Henry Cox, Second-Lieutenant George Jones.

*Leviathan*, 74 guns, Captain Lord H. Seymour, June 1, 10 killed, 33 wounded. Captain Theophilus Lewis, First-Lieutenant Thomas Maxwell, First-Lieutenant Richard Stephens.

*Alfred*, 74 guns, Captain J. Bazeley, June 1, 8 wounded.

*Culloden*, 74 guns, Captain J. Schomberg, June 1, 2 killed, 5 wounded. Captain W. Henville, First-Lieutenant Hugh Holland, Second-Lieutenant G, A. Livingstone.

*Defence*, 74 guns, Captain J. Gambier, May 29, 1 killed, 3 wounded; June 1, 17 killed, 36 wounded. Second-Lieutenant Samuel Brother.

*Invincible*, 74 guns, Captain Hon. T. Pakenham, May 29, 10 killed, 21 wounded; June 1, 4 killed, 10 wounded. Captain-Lieutenant James Cassell, First-Lieutenant Alexander Mackenzie, First-Lieutenant Thomas Piers.

*Majestic*, 74 guns, Captain C. Cotton, May 29, 1 killed, 13 wounded; June 1, 2 killed, 5 wounded. 2nd regiment of Foot.

*Marlborough*, 74 guns, Captain Hon. C. C. Berkeley, June 1, 29 killed, 90 wounded. Lieutenant Charles Lyon, 25th regiment of Foot.

*Montagu*, 74 guns, Captain J. J. Montagu, June 1, 4 killed, 13 wounded. Captain Robert Henderson, Second-Lieutenant Charles Lewis, Second-Lieutenant William Ratton.

*Orion*, 74 guns, Captain J. T. Duckworth, May 29, 3 killed; June 1, 2 killed, 24 wounded. Captain George Dyer, First-Lieutenant Palms Westropp, Second-Lieutenant William B ransom.

*Ramilies*, 74 guns, Captain H. Harvey, May 29, 3 killed; June 1, 2 killed, 7 wounded. 29th regiment of Foot.

*Russell*, 74 guns, Captain J. W. Payne, June 1, 8 killed, 26 wounded. 2nd regiment of Foot.

*Thunderer*, 74 guns, Captain A. Bertie. 29th regiment of Foot.

*Tremendous*, 74 guns, Captain J. Pigott, June 1, 3 killed, 8 wounded. Lieutenant-Colonel Duncan Campbell, First-Lieutenant John Simpson.

*Phaeton*, 38 guns, Captain W. Bentinck, June 1, 3 killed, 5 wounded. First-lieutenant A. J. Trigent.

| | | | |
|---|---|---|---|
| 67 killed, | 128 wounded, | | on the 29th of May. |
| 220 ,, | 712 | ,, | on the 1st of June. |
| Total,— 287 | 840 | | |

The thanks of both houses of Parliament were voted to the flag-officers, captains, and other officers of the fleet for their bravery and gallant conduct, with their approval and acknowledgment of the services of the seamen, marines, and soldiers. The city of London voted the sum of £500 for the relief of the wounded warrant-officers, petty-officers, seamen, and marines, and also for the widows and children of those who so gloriously fell in the action.

Notwithstanding this proud mark of approval, it was so apparent that several captains in the fleet had not done as much as was expected by their country, that the lords commissioners of the Admiralty restricted the distribution of medals to certain officers, excluding the commanders of eight ships in the fleet; and the sentence of a court-martial held on Captain Anthony Pye Molloy, at his own request, in consequence of some observations made by the commander-in-chief reflecting on his conduct, dismissed him from the command of the *Caesar*.

Early on the morning of the 6th of November, at 5 a.m., the 74-gun ships *Alexander*, Captain Rodney Bligh, and *Canada*, Captain Hamilton, fell in with a French squadron of five sail of the line and two frigates, under Rear-Admiral Nielly, who bore up in chase of the British ships. A running fight was continued until 1 p.m., when the *Alexander*, having suffered considerably, her main-yard, spanker-boom, and her three top-gallant masts shot away, and having sustained a loss of 40 men killed and wounded, including among the latter a lieutenant of marines, struck her colours and was taken into Brest.

The Officers of Marines were Major W. Tench, with Lieutenants

Oliver, Fitzgerald, and William Brown. The *Canada* arrived at Plymouth in safety.

In the early part of December, while the 64-gun ship *Ardent*, Captain Robert Manners Sutton, was stationed off Villa Franca, she took fire and blew up, and everyone on board perished.

The revolutionary spirit which prevailed in Holland, rendered that country an easy conquest for the armies of France; whilst she retained the nominal dignity of an independent state, under the style of the Batavian republic, it gave to the conquerors every advantage which they could have derived from possessing Holland as a province, without incurring the expense of maintaining her as an integral part of the French empire.

England took the earliest opportunity of weakening the maritime power of the new ally of France; and on the 19th of January, 1795, orders were issued for seizing all Dutch vessels in the British ports.

On the 5th of January the 32-gun frigate *Blanche*, Captain Robert Faulknor, cruising off Grande-terre, Guadaloupe, sustained a very severe action with the French 36-gun frigate *Pique*. At 1 a.m. the two frigates became closely engaged, and at 2 h. 30 m. the main and mizen-masts of the *Blanche* fell over the side; the *Pique*, having shortly afterwards ran foul of her antagonist on the larboard quarter, made several ineffectual attempts to board. About 3 a.m. Captain Faulknor was killed by a musket-ball, whilst assisting Lieutenant David Milne in lashing the bowsprit of the *Pique* to the capstan of the British frigate; but the lashings soon afterwards broke loose, and the *Pique* crossing the stern of the *Blanche*, fell on board of the latter's starboard quarter.

Her bowsprit was immediately lashed by the British crew to the stump of the *Blanche's* mainmast; and in this position, towed before the wind, the enemy were defeated in their attempts to cut the lashings, by the rapid and well-directed fire of the marines under Lieutenant Thomas Richardson. Although exposed to a galling and raking fire, with her three masts over the side, the *Pique* continued to defend herself until 5 h. 15 m. a.m., when, having sustained a loss of 76 killed and 110 wounded, out of a crew of 279 men and boys, the French hailed that they had surrendered. The *Blanche* lost her commander and 7 killed, and 21 wounded.

On the 13th of March the 32-gun frigate *Lively*, Captain George Burlton, when about thirteen leagues to the westward of Ushant, captured the 28-gun corvette *Tourterelle*, after a gallant defence, which lasted from 10 b. 40 m. a.m. until 1 h. 30 m. p.m., when, being much disabled, with 16 men killed and 25 wounded, she struck her colours. The *Lively* had only two men wounded. The Officer of Marines of the *Lively* was Lieutenant B. Burke.

The *Astrea* of 32 guns, Captain Lord Harry Paulet, having chased from a squadron under Rear-Admiral Colpoys cruising to the westward, on the 10th of April, at 10 h. 30 m. p.m., brought to close action the French 36-gun frigate *Gloire*, Captain Beens, and after a defence of fifty-eight minutes, compelled the enemy to haul down her colours. The *Astrea* did not lose a man, and had only 8 wounded. The *Gloire* lost 40 in killed and wounded. Second-Lieutenant William Johnstone was the officer of marines on board the *Astrea*.

On the 17th of May the 36-gun frigate *Thetis*, Captain the Hon. A. F. Cochrane, and 28-gun frigate *Hussar*, Captain J. P. Beresford, when twenty leagues from Cape Henry, attacked five French frigates, armed *en flute*; and after an action of an hour, captured the *Prévoyante* mounting 24 guns, and *Raison* 18 guns. The *Thetis* had 8 men killed, and 9 wounded; the *Hussar* 3 men wounded. Lieutenant Paul Crebbin of the marines was serving on board the *Thetis*; and on board the *Hussar*, Lieutenant James Atcherly.

Vice-Admiral Hotham was lying in Leghorn roads, with a fleet of fifteen sail of the line and several frigates, when he received intelligence, on the 8th of March, that the French fleet had been seen off the island of Sainte Marguerite. On the 9th the British fleet put to sea, and the 10th the look-out ships got sight of the enemy. On the 13th the French fleet, consisting of thirteen ships of the line, was seen to windward, and the admiral made the signal for a general chase. The *Inconstant* being far in advance, Captain F. T. Freemantle had the opportunity of distinguishing himself, by ranging up within musket-shot of the 80-gun ship *Ça-Ira* (who had lost her fore and main topmasts), and engaging her for some time. During the day the *Agamemnon*, *Bedford*, and *Egmont* became engaged with the rearmost ships, but nothing of importance occurred.

On the 14th, at 5 h. 30 m. a.m., when about seven leagues to the south-west of Genoa, the British finding themselves to windward of the enemy, the *Bedford* and *Captain* were ordered to attack the dismasted *Ça-Ira*, then in tow of the *Censeur* of 74 guns, and at some distance from the body of their fleet. Both the British ships were so roughly handled in their attempt, as to be compelled to withdraw from the contest, and the *Captain* was rendered so unmanageable that she was towed clear of her opponents. The wind having died away, it was with difficulty that the enemy's fleet wore round at 8 a. m.; and then passing to leeward of the British, they became engaged with the *Illustrious* and *Courageux*, both which ships suffered severely; the former losing her main, mizen-mast, and fore-topmast, and the *Courageux* her main and mizen-masts. The French line then stood on, abandoning the *Ça-Ira* and *Censeur* to their fate; but neither of these ships surrendered until they were dismasted and incapable of further resistance, and sustained a loss of 400 men in killed and wounded. The troops serving in the fleet were principally from regiments of the line: the only Officers of Marines were Captain Hugh Dawes, Lieutenants Henry Johnstone, Francis Lynn, and William Allen.

Vice-Admiral Hotham was lying in San-Fiorenzo bay on the 8th of July, with the fleet as stated above, to which must be added the *Victory* 100 guns, *Barfleur* 98, *Gibraltar* 80, *Bombay Castle, Saturn, Cumberland, Culloden,* and *Audacious,* of 74 guns, making a total of twenty-three sail of the line and two frigates, when the French fleet, consisting of seventeen sail of the line with several frigates, appeared off that harbour. Admiral Hotham immediately put to sea, and the British, before noon, were under all sail, steering westward in pursuit of the enemy.

On the 13th, at daybreak, when off Hyères, the French fleet was discovered about five miles to leeward; upon which Vice-Admiral Hotham formed his ships in line of battle, and edged away, so as to cut off the enemy from the shore, then about five leagues distant. At 12 h. 30 m. p.m. a shift of wind brought the leading ships, which were the *Victory, Culloden,* and *Cumberland,* in a position to engage; and at 2 p.m. the *Alcide* 74, struck her colours. Shortly afterwards several other British ships had been distantly engaged, and were coming up fast with the enemy, when the signal was made to discontinue the action. The *Victory* had 2 midshipmen and 3 marines killed; 1 lieutenant, 1 midshipman, Major Frederick Hill Flight and Lieutenant William Darley, of the marines, and 11 men wounded; *Culloden,* 2 killed, and 5 wounded; *Blenheim,* 2 killed, 2 wounded; *Captain,* 1 killed; and *Defence,* 1 killed and 6 wounded: making a total of 11 killed, and 27 wounded.

On the 8th of June a squadron of five sail of the line and two frigates, under Vice-Admiral William Cornwallis, when off the Penmarcks, was chased and brought to action by a French fleet of twelve sail of the line and eleven frigates. The *Mars* and *Triumph* bore the brunt of the action, which lasted from 9 a.m. until 6 h. 10 m. p.m., when the enemy gave over the pursuit. The *Mars* was the only ship that sustained any loss, and that was confined to 12 men wounded.

On the 22nd Lord Bridport, with fourteen sail of the line and several frigates, when to the westward of Belleisle, and returning to his station off Ushant from escorting the expedition under Sir J. B. Warren to Quiberon, discovered the French fleet under Admiral Villaret, which had chased Admiral Cornwallis, standing towards the land: all sail was made in pursuit, but in the afternoon it fell nearly calm. At 3 a. m. on the 23rd, a light breeze sprang up from the south-west, and as the daylight appeared, the French fleet were seen right ahead in a cluster, except three or four ships, who were somewhat astern of their companions. At 6 a.m. the sternmost of the enemy opened their fire, and at 6 h. 15 m. the *Queen Charlotte* and *Orion* commenced action with the *Alexandre* and *Formidable.* The breeze freshening, brought up the remainder of the British ships, and the cannonade continued until 7 h. 57 m. a.m., when lord Bridport made the signal to discontinue the action; having taken possession of the *Alexandre* 74 guns (formerly British), *Formidable* 74, and *Tigre* 74. The loss sustained by the British fleet amounted to 31 killed, and 113 wounded. Lieutenant William Jephcott of the marines was killed on board the *Sans Pareil.*

On the 24th of June the 28-gun frigate *Dido*, Captain George Henry Towry, and 32-gun frigate *Lowestoffe*, Captain Robert Gambier Middleton, when near Toulon, discovered the French 40-gun frigate *Minerve*, and 36-gun frigate *Artémise*. At 8 h. 30 m. a.m. the *Minerve* wore round on the same tack as the *Dido*, and opened her fire; shortly afterwards the *Minerve* bore up and ran the *Dido* on board, with her bowsprit locked in the mizen rigging of her little opponent; and after several attempts to board, which were defeated by the marines and pikemen of the *Dido*, the bowsprit of the *Minerve* snapped in two, carrying with it the wounded mizen-mast of the British frigate.

The *Minerve* then passing ahead, received the fire of the *Lowestoffe*, which brought down the French ship's fore-mast, also her main and mizen top-masts. About this time the *Artémise* fired an ineffectual broadside, and hauled her wind under all sail. At 11 h. 45 m. a.m. the *Minerve*, on the fail of her mizen-mast, hailed to say they had surrendered. The *Dido* had 6 men killed; her First-Lieutenant Richard Buckoll, and 14 wounded. The *Lowestoffe* had only 3 men wounded.

In the early part of August a squadron, consisting of the *Monarch*, *Victorious*, and *Arrogant*, of 74 guns, *America* and *Stately*, of 64 guns, with two brigs, having on board a detachment of the 78th regiment commanded by Major-General Craig, anchored in Simon's Bay, Cape of Good Hope. The governor-general, Sluysken, refusing to place the colony under the protection of His Britannic Majesty, a debarkation took place of 450 men of the 78th regiment, with 300 marines, commanded by Major Hill, having under him Majors Ballinghall, Douglas, and Wingrove; Captains Samuel Baldwin and Gilbert Gardner, and Lieutenants C. W. Adair (adjutant), Wingrove, Burn, Clapperton, Glaze, Templeton, and Thomas Mould. Meanwhile the Dutch militia had taken post on the adjacent heights, and occupied a pass about six miles distant from the town, which they had well fortified. A thousand seamen were also landed, and formed into battalions under Captains Hardy of the *Echo*, and Spranger of the *Rattlesnake*.

On the 7th of August the lighter ships of the squadron stood in shore, and with the gunboats and launches covered the advance of the troops so effectually, that at 4 p.m. Major-General Craig, after a fatiguing march over heavy sandy ground, arrived at and took possession of the abandoned Dutch camp.

The advanced guard of the 78th, supported by the battalion, drove the Dutch from an advantageous post on a rocky eminence, and on the following day, the 8th, the enemy having augmented his force from Cape Town, and having several fieldpieces, advanced to regain the position they had lost; but after some skirmishing the Dutch were compelled to retire. The battalion of marines under Major Hill obtained the commendation of Major-General Craig, "for their steadiness and resolution" on this occasion.

Some partial successes gained by the Dutch on the 1st and 2nd of September, encouraged them to meditate a general attack on the British camp; and in the night they advanced with all their force, accompanied by eighteen field-pieces. At this anxious moment the long-expected English fleet, with reinforcements, opportunely appeared in the offing; and on the following morning fourteen sail of East India ships, conveying a large body of troops, with artillery and stores, under the command of General Alured Clarke, came to an anchor in Simon's Bay. The disembarkation was completed on the 14th, and the troops having immediately commenced their march, the Dutch governor became so alarmed, that he proposed terms of capitulation: and on the 16th the colony surrendered, when about 1000 regular troops were made prisoners.

On the 28th of September the 32-gun frigate *Southampton*, Captain James Macnamara, when cruising off Genoa, chased several suspicious sail, and at 10 p.m. brought to action the French 36-gun frigate *Vestale*. After exchanging several broadsides, the enemy's ship made oft under all sail, closely pursued by the *Southampton*, until the mizen of the latter fell over the side; and although great exertion was made to clear the wreck, and in erecting a jury-mast, the *Vestale* effected her escape, having 8 men killed, and 9 wounded. Lieutenant Archibald Campbell of the marines was serving on board the *Southampton*.

On the 5th of December, as the 74-gun ship *Culloden*, Captain Thomas Troubridge, lay at Spithead, the crew, bursting into open mutiny, unshipped the ladders; and having broken into the magazine, they raised a barricade of hammocks across the deck between the bits, loaded the two second guns from forward with canister and grape, and pointed them towards the hatchway. The marines, with the exception of six, were immediately under arms, commanded by Captain Thomas Currie, with First-Lieutenant Hugh Holland, and Second-Lieutenant G. A. Livingstone. The seamen continued below during the night, arming themselves and preparing for defence; but on the morning of the 17th the petty-officers and some of the seamen were allowed to come upon deck. Notwithstanding the endeavours of Admirals Lord Bridport, Cornwallis, and Colpoys to induce the men to return to their allegiance, they continued to act in defiance of their officers until the 10th, when Captain the Hon. Thomas Pakenham succeeded in persuading them to return to their duty.

On the 15th the ten ringleaders were tried by a court-martial, and on the 13th of January five of them suffered on board the *Culloden* at Spithead, and the others received the king's pardon.

On the 16th of February, 1796, a small squadron, under Rear-Admiral Peter Rainier, with three transports conveying troops, arrived off the Dutch island of Amboyna, the capital of the Molucca islands; and the troops having landed on the same afternoon, possession was taken of the colony without resistance. The squadron sailed for the islands of Banda on the 5th of March, and on the evening of the 7th the expedition arrived off Banda Neira. Early on the afternoon of the 8th the troops, with the marines from the squadron, were disembarked on the north side of the island, covered by the *Orpheus* frigate, whose fire having silenced the batteries, they were soon occupied by the troops; and on the same evening these islands surrendered to the British arms.

In the early part of August a Dutch squadron, consisting of three small ships of the line, with three frigates and two smaller vessels, arrived off Saldanha bay, with the intention of making an attempt to regain possession of the Cape of Good Hope. Eight ships of the line, under the command of Vice-Admiral Sir George Keith Elphinstone, were lying in Simon's Bay when the intelligence was received of the arrival of the Dutch force, and on the 6th the British squadron put to sea; but the violence of the weather compelled them to return to their former anchorage on the 12th. On the 15th the vice-admiral again sailed, and on the following evening discovered the enemy's ships as before described, lying at anchor in Saldanha bay. The British ships soon afterwards anchored within gunshot of the hostile squadron, and a message was sent by Sir George Elphinstone, inviting the Dutch officer to surrender without attempting any resistance. On the 17th a capitulation was agreed to, and Rear-Admiral Lucas surrendered his nine ships.

On the 27th of April Rear-Admiral Sir Hugh C. Christian arrived off Saint Lucie, with a squadron and several transports, having a large body of troops on board under the command of Lieutenant-General Sir Ralph Abercromby, which were landed at several points, under cover of the ships of war; and 800 seamen were also disembarked, to co-operate in the intended attack on Morne Fortunée. Morne Chabot, the first post attacked, was carried by one division of the force on the 28th, with the loss of 13 killed, and 49 wounded; but the attempt on the batteries near the grand *cul-de-sac* on the 3rd of May, and on the post of the Vigie on the night of the 17th, although conducted with the greatest bravery, were both unsuccessful, and was attended with a loss of 12 killed, 56 wounded, and 34 missing at the first of these assaults; and of one officer killed, 114 men wounded, and 65 missing at the latter. After a few attacks of outposts, the enemy retired to the fortress of Morne Fortunée, and having obtained a suspension of arms, the garrison, amounting to 2000 men, marched out with the honours of war, and laid down their arms. The total loss sustained in the reduction of this valuable colony amounted to 66 killed, 378 wounded, and 122 missing. The marines of the squadron, amounting to 320 men, assisted in these operations, and their promptitude and gallantry was acknowledged by Lieutenant-General Sir Ralph Abercromby in the handsomest terms.

The island of St. Vincent was taken possession of on the 11th, after an obstinate resistance; on which occasion the British lost 38 killed, and 145 wounded. A few days afterwards Grenada also submitted; but not without a determined opposition, and a loss to the British of 9 killed, and 60 wounded.

On the 21st of March the town and fort of Léogane, in the island of San Domingo, was attacked by a detachment of colonial and British troops under Major-General Forbes, in two divisions, supported by the squadron, which consisted of the three ships of the line *Leviathan*, *Swiftsure*, and *Africa*, with the *Ceres* and *Iphigenia* frigates; but the fort proving better capable of defence than was anticipated, the troops were withdrawn on the following day and night, without sustaining much loss. The *Leviathan* had 5 men killed, and 12 wounded; and the *Africa* one killed, and 7 wounded; and both ships were so seriously damaged, that they were under the necessity of going to Jamaica to refit.

A more successful attack was afterwards made on the fort and parish of Bombarde, at a distance of fifteen miles. The only road leading to it, by which cannon could be conveyed, had been effectually blockaded by the enemy; nevertheless the troops, after some difficulty and opposition, surrounded the fort and compelled the garrison, consisting of 300 whites, to surrender; but the possession of the place cost the British 8 killed, and 18 wounded.

On the 18th of March the 38-gun frigate *Diamond*, Captain Sir William Sidney Smith, proceeded to attack a trench corvette and convoy in the port of Herqui, near Cape Fréhel, which was defended by two batteries mounting 3 twenty-four pounders, situated on a high promontory. Lieutenant H. Pine and Lieutenant Edmund Carter, of the marines, landed with a detachment and stormed the battery. The only loss sustained by the British in this gallant affair was Lieutenant Carter, mortally wounded.

Lieutenant George Jones, of the marines, was serving on board the 38-gun frigate *Révolutionaire*, Captain Francis Cole, when that ship, having chased from a squadron cruising off Ushant on the 13th of April, captured the French 36-gun frigate *Unite*, after a short resistance, in which the enemy had 9 men killed and 11 wounded; but the *Révolutionaire* did not sustain any loss.

On the 20th of April the 44-gun frigate *Indefatigable*, Captain Sir Edward Pellew, after a chase of fifteen hours, brought to action, at about midnight, the French 40-gun frigate *Virginie*; and the contest was continued under all sail during one hour and forty-five minutes, by which time the French frigate had lost her mizen-mast and main top-mast; nor was the *Indefatigable* much less disabled, having had her mizen top-mast and gaff shot away. The *Amazon* and *Concorde* arriving up, compelled the *Virginie* to surrender, having 15 men killed and 27 wounded. First-Lieutenant Samuel Williams was serving on board the *Indefatigable*, which ship did not lose a man in the action.

On the 8th of June, when cruising at the entrance of the Channel, the 32-gun frigate *Unicorn*, Captain Thomas Williams, and 36-gun frigate *Santa Margarita*, Captain Thomas Byam Martin, chased the French 36-gun frigates *Tamise* (late Thames) and *Tribune*, with the *Légère* corvette. At one p. m. the enemy opened a fire from their stern chasers with such destructive effect upon the sails and rigging of their opponents, that it was not until 4 p.m. that the *Santa Margarita* was enabled to close with the *Tamise*; and after a resistance of twenty minutes, compelled her to strike her colours, having 32 men killed, and 19 wounded. The *Santa Margarita*, on board which ship was Second-Lieutenant James Dyson of the marines, had only 2 men killed, and 3 wounded.

Seeing the fate of her companion, the *Tribune* endeavoured to make her escape; but the *Unicorn*, at 10 h. 30 m. p.m., after having ran above 200 miles in the pursuit, ranged up alongside her antagonist, and a close action continued for thirty-five minutes, when the *Tribune* dropped astern, and endeavoured to gain the wind of the *Unicorn*; but by throwing all aback, the latter placed herself on the *Tribune's* weather bow, and after a few broadsides brought down her fore and main-masts, also her mizen top-mast, and compelled her to strike her colours, having sustained a loss of 37 killed, and 15 wounded. Second-Lieutenant George Hart was serving on board the *Unicorn*, which ship, like the *Indefatigable*, had the good fortune to escape without any loss.

On the 13th of June, at 1 a.m., the 36-gun frigate *Dryad*, Captain Lord Amelius Beauclerk, cruising off Cape Clear, discovered the French 40-gun frigate *Proserpine*, and pursued her until 9 p.m., when she closed on the lee and larboard quarter of her opponent. After a resistance of forty minutes, the *Proserpine* having sustained a loss of 30 men killed, and 45 wounded, struck her colours. Lieutenant Thomas Shearman was serving on board the *Dryad*, whose loss amounted to 2 men killed, and 7 wounded.

On the 9th of June the British fleet was cruising off Toulon, when a French corvette was descried working up towards the road of Hyères; upon which, Captain Macnamara of the 32 gun frigate *Southampton*, was directed by Sir John Jervis to endeavour to bring her out, and with this intent the British frigate steered for the Grande Passe, between the islands of Porquerolles and Posteros. At 6 p.m., the corvette having been discovered lying close to the shore, the *Southampton* stood boldly across Hyères road, and at 8 h. 30 m. p.m. got within pistol-shot of the French ship-corvette *Utile*, of 24 guns, with a crew of 130 men. Captain Macnamara hailed, and cautioned the commander not to make a fruitless resistance; but the latter instantly snapped his pistol at the speaker as the *Utile* fired her broadside, which was quickly returned by the guns of the *Southampton*. After the third broadside, Captain Macnamara hauled athwart the hawse of the *Utile*, and having lashed the corvette's bowsprit to the main rigging of the British frigate, Lieutenant Lydiard, heading the boarders, sprang upon the Frenchman's decks, and after a determined resistance of ten minutes, during which the French captain gallantly fell at his post, the corvette surrendered. Lieutenant Archibald Campbell of the marines was serving on board the *Southampton*, whose loss on this occasion was confined to 1 marine wounded. The *Utile's* loss amounted to 8 men killed, and 17 wounded.

On the 17th of July the 50-gun ship *Glatton*, Captain Henry Trollope, mounting 28 long eighteen-pounders on the main-deck, and 28 carronade sixty-eight pounders on the lower deck, being then on the coast of Flanders, discovered several ships under the land, which proved to be four frigates: one mounting 46 guns, one of 44 guns, one of 40, one of 28, with two corvettes of 22 guns each, and two brigs. At 8 p.m. the four frigates formed in line to await the attack; and at 10 p.m. the *Glatton* ranged up alongside of the commodore, the second from the van, who, on displaying the French colours, opened a brisk fire, and was immediately seconded by the other ships. Shortly afterwards the leading ship tacked, and after receiving a destructive broadside from the *Glatton*, stood away to the southward.

In about twenty minutes after the commencement of the action, the French commodore tacked, to avoid running on the Brill shoal; and while in stays, received a heavy raking fire, which did considerable damage: the other French ships had previously gone on the other tack. After the *Glatton* got round, which was attended with some difficulty owing to the disabled state of her sails and rigging, she exchanged a few shot with one of the three ships to leeward; but before 11 p.m. the enemy withdrew from the contest, leaving the *Glatton* so much dismantled as to be incapable of pursuit. No men were killed on board the *Glatton*, and the only wounded were Captain Henry Strangeways of the marines, and a corporal. This gallant officer, although mortally wounded by a musket-ball in the thigh, and compelled to quit the deck to have a tourniquet applied, insisted on returning to his quarters, where he continued to animate his men, until, being faint from loss of blood, he was carried below.

On the 22nd of July the 32-gun frigate *Aimable*, Captain Jemmet Mainwaring, when cruising off the island of Guadaloupe, sustained a gallant action with the French 36-gun frigate *Pensée*, which, after some manoeuvring, commenced at 8 h. 35 m. a.m., and continued until 9 a.m., when the enemy bore away, firing her stern chase-guns until out of range of her dull sailing opponent. The *Aimable* had only two men wounded, but the *Pensée* is reported to have sustained a loss of 90 men in killed and wounded.

On the morning of the 22nd of July, the 32-gun frigate *Mermaid*, Captain Robert W. Otway, left the Saintes, near Guadaloupe, in pursuit of the French 40-gun frigate *Vengeance*, then under the land of Basseterre. At 11 h. 45 m. a.m., the batteries on shore fired several shot over the *Mermaid*, who about noon got within gunshot of her opponent. The action continued until 3 p.m., when the *Mermaid* had her foretop-gallant mast shot away; upon which the *Vengeance*, setting her courses, ran under the batteries, and shortly afterwards anchored in the road of Basseterre. The *Mermaid* sustained no loss, but the *Vengeance* had 12 men killed and 26 wounded. Second-Lieutenant Richard Cox of the marines was serving on board the *Mermaid*.

On the 9th of September the *Arrogant* of 74 guns, Captain Richard Lucas, on board of which ship were, Captain George Ball and First-Lieutenant Robert Johnston, of the marines; with the *Victorious* 74, Captain William Clark; Captain of Marines, Major Frederick H. Flight, First-Lieutenant William Darley, and Lieutenant Thomas Buck; when off Pulo Way, isle of Sumatra, sustained an action with six French frigates under Rear-Admiral Sercey. The firing commenced at 7 h. 25 m. a.m., and lasted until 10 h. 55 m., at which time the enemy's squadron bore up to the westward under a crowd of sail. The *Arrogant* was very seriously cut up, and lost 7 killed and 27 wounded. The *Victorious*, who had only 485 men at quarters, having a lieutenant and 90 men away in prizes, lost 17 men killed, her captain and 55 wounded.

On the morning of the 13th of October, the 32-gun frigate *Terpsichore*, Captain Richard Bowen, when cruising off the port of Carthagena, observed the Spanish 34-gun frigate *Mahonesa* running down towards her. Having approached within hail at 9 h. 30 m. a.m., the Spanish frigate rounded to on the weather-beam of the *Terpsichore*, and commenced an action which continued with great spirit for an hour and twenty minutes, when the enemy endeavoured to make off. At this time the *Terpsichore* was much disabled in her masts, spars, and rigging; but in less than twenty minutes the British frigate had refitted, was again alongside her opponent, and ready to recommence the contest; when the *Mahonesa* struck her colours, having lost 30 men killed, and as many wounded. Second-Lieutenant John Orton of the marines was serving on board the *Terpsichore*, which ship had none killed, and but four men wounded.

Having repaired her damages at Gibraltar, the *Terpsichore* was again at sea in search of an opponent, when on the 12th of December, at daybreak, being twenty leagues to the westward of Cadiz, an enemy's frigate was discerned lying to, about four miles on the weather-quarter. Sail was immediately made in chase, which continued until 9 h. 30 m. p.m. on the 13th, when the enemy's ship, (which was the French 36-gun frigate *Vestale*), hauled up her courses and hove to. At 10 p.m. the *Terpsichore* ranged close up on her weather-quarter, and both ships opened their fire, which continued until 11 h. 4 m. p.m., when the *Vestale* struck her colours, having lost her captain and 27 killed, and 37 men wounded. The *Terpsichore* could only muster at quarters 166 men and boys, having away in prizes two lieutenants, three midshipmen, and 41 men: her loss in the action amounted to four seamen killed, Lieutenant George Bowen and 17 men wounded. During the night of the 13th, the French crew rose on the small party in possession of the prize, and carried her into Cadiz.

On the 19th of December Commodore Nelson, in the 38-gun frigate *Minerve*, Captain George Cockburn, with the 32-gun frigate *Blanche*, Captain d'Arcy Preston, when near Porto Ferrajo, fell in with two large Spanish frigates; and whilst the *Blanche* wore and attacked the one to leeward, the *Minerve* hauled up, and at 10 h. 40 m. brought to close action the 40-gun frigate *Sabina*. After a brave resistance of two hours and fifty minutes, the Spanish ship struck her colours, with the loss of her mizen-mast, and having 10 men killed, and 45 wounded. The *Minerve* had 7 killed; Lieutenant Noble and 32 wounded. Shortly afterwards, another Spanish frigate was seen approaching; upon which the *Minerve*, casting off her prize, brought the stranger to action, and after engaging for half an hour, compelled her to haul off: at this moment the approach of the *Principe de Asturias* and two frigates, induced the British frigate to look to her own safety, whilst her prize, the *Sabina*, fell into the enemy's hands. In a few minutes after the *Minerve* poured her first broadside into the *Sabina*, the *Blanche* was close alongside the frigate to leeward, and after some sharp firing, the *Ceres* hauled down the Spanish colours, with the loss of 7 men killed, and 15 wounded; but like her consort, she was recaptured by the Spanish squadron. The *Blanche* sustained neither damage nor loss in the action.

CHAPTER 5

# From the Year 1797 to 1799

An expedition had been for some time in preparation in the different French ports for the invasion of Ireland, and the fleet was finally to assemble at Brest; from which anchorage they were to proceed to Bantry Bay. On the 16th of December this armament put to sea, consisting of seventeen ships of the line, thirteen frigates, six corvettes, with transports—in all forty-four sail, having 600 troops on board of each line of battle ship, and in each frigate 250; so that with the number on board the other vessels, the army amounted to 18,000 men; and in addition to the troops, which consisted of both cavalry and infantry, the fleet carried a quantity of field artillery, with stores and ammunition. It blew hard from the eastward, and during the night the *Séduisant* of 74 guns was wrecked on the Stevenet rock in the passage Du Raz, when about 700 men perished.

The remainder of the fleet arrived off Dursey Island on the 21st, and part of the ships anchored at the eastern extremity of Bear island, where they continued until the 25th; when a heavy gale drove them from their anchors, and compelled them to put to sea. They remained scattered on the coast for some days, and then made the best of their way back to Brest; as did the remainder of their men-of-war, with the exception of the *Droits de l'Homme* and some frigates, of which we shall have presently to give a favourable account. The *Droits de l'Homme* of 74 guns, Commodore La Crosse, having separated from her companions, steered for l'Orient; and on the 13th of January, 1797, when off the Penmarcks, was discovered through the thick weather which prevailed by the *Indefatigable* 44, Captain Sir Edward Pellew, and the *Amazon* 38, Captain Robert Carthew Reynolds.

At 4 h. 15 m. p.m. a squall carried away the fore and main topmasts of the French ship, and she continued steering towards the shore under her courses and mizen top-sail; whilst the *Indefatigable* and *Amazon* took positions upon either bow, pouring in an occasional raking fire until 4 h. 30 m. a.m. on the 14th, when the appearance of land close to leeward caused the frigates to haul off from the threatened danger, and the *Droits de l'Homme* to make a similar effort. During the whole of this long engagement the sea ran extremely high; the *Indefatigable* had four feet water in the hold, and all her masts were in a wounded state. The *Amazon* had also suffered severely from the enemy's fire in her masts and rigging, and she had 3 men killed and 15 badly wounded. On board the *Indefatigable* there were none killed, but 18 men were wounded. As daylight appeared, the French 74 was seen lying on her broadside in Audieone Bay, with the sea beating over her. The *Amazon*, on perceiving the danger, wore to the northward, and soon afterwards struck the ground and was wrecked; but her crew, with the exception of six persons, got safe to the shore. Lieutenants O'Connor and Wilson of the marines were favourably mentioned by Sir Edward Pellew, for their exertions on this trying occasion.

At this period the navy was so much augmented, that the supplies voted were for 120,000 men for the sea service, including 20,000 marines. On the 13th of February Admiral Sir John Jervis, with fifteen sail of the line, was steering towards Cadiz; when the *Minerve* frigate, Captain George Cockburn, bearing the broad pendant of Commodore Nelson, brought intelligence that the Spanish fleet had been seen at the mouth of the Straits, consisting of twenty-seven ships of the line and twelve frigates, under the command of Don Josef de Cordova, having sailed from Carthagena on the 12th of February. On the 14th, at daylight, several ships were discovered through the haze to windward of the fleet, and before 9 a.m. twenty sail of the line were visible from the *Victory's* mast-head. About 11 a.m. the fog had cleared away, and the Spaniards were seen grouped together under all sail, with the wind on the starboard quarter, running down to form a junction with six ships of the line to leeward, who were close hauled on the same tack, striving hard to close with the main body of their fleet.

With the intention of cutting off the lee division of the enemy, and at the same time to be prepared to receive the nineteen bearing down to windward, who at 11 a.m. began trimming in succession on the larboard tack, the British admiral formed his fleet in line of battle astern of the *Victory*, and steered to the south-west, keeping the six detached ships of the enemy on the lee or larboard bow, directing his course for the opening between the two divisions of the enemy, whilst the latter were still endeavouring to form a junction. At 11 h. 30 m. the van ships were distantly engaged, and about this time two Spanish three-deckers and a two-decker stood across the head of the British line, and joined the ships to leeward; thus augmenting the Spanish lee division to eight, and reducing their force to windward to sixteen sail of the line.

At 8 m. past noon, after passing the sternmost of the enemy's weather-ships, the leading British ship, the *Culloden*, tacked; and about the same time the Spanish lee division also went about, and stood towards the head of the British line, still on the starboard tack. The Spanish vice-admiral steered to cut the British line ahead of the *Victory*, but the latter was too rapid in her advance, and compelled the Spanish three-decker to tack close under her lee, raking her whilst in stays with such destructive effect, as induced her to bear away in great confusion, followed by the second three-decker and five other ships; but the *Oriente* gallantly kept upon the larboard tack, and passing along the British line, succeeded in joining her van. At 1 p.m., just as the rear ship of the British, still on the starboard tack, had reached beyond the leading ships of the Spanish weather-division, then passing in the contrary direction, the advanced ships of the enemy bore up together, as a last effort to join their friends to leeward.

Commodore Nelson in the *Captain*, the third ship from the rear of the British line, apprehensive that the weather-division of the enemy would form a junction with those to leeward before the ships in the British van could possibly reach them, immediately wore round, and passing between the *Diadem* and *Excellent*, ran athwart the bows of the Spanish ships as far as the sixth from the rear; and at 1 h. 30m. p.m., when the *Culloden* had arrived up from the British van and commenced firing, the *Captain* was engaged with the *Santissima Trinidada*; for the Spanish admiral, frustrated in his attempt of running to leeward, had with his fleet hauled up on the larboard tack. The *Blenheim, Prince George*, and *Orion*, had now taken part in the action, and at 2 h. 26 in. p.m. the *Excellent* opened her fire on the *Salvador del Mundo*, as she passed on the latter's weather bow; and then having stood on to the *San Ysidro*, ranged up on her lee-beam and engaged her until 2 h. 53 m. p.m., when the Spanish colours were hauled down.

The *Excellent* then passed on ahead and engaged the 80-gun ship *San Nicolas*, who had been contending with the *Captain*; and in hauling up to avoid her new antagonist, the *San Nicolas* ran foul of the *San Josef*, whose mizenmast had been shot away. The *Captain* now re-opened her fire upon the *San Nicolas*, and then laid her on board, hooking with her larboard cathead the starboard quarter-gallery of the Spanish 80, and with her spritsail yard, the latter's mizen-rigging. Commodore Nelson immediately boarded, and following a soldier of the 69th regiment, entered the upper gallery window; but by the time he reached the quarter-deck, Captain Berry was in possession of the poop, and the Spanish ensign was hauling down. At this time the *San Nicolas* was foul of the *San Josef*, and had opened a fire of small arms from her stern at the British on the forecastle of the captured ship; upon which Commodore Nelson directed his men to board the first-rate, and they were preparing for the assault, when a Spanish officer looked over the quarter-deck rail, and said they had surrendered.

The *Excellent*, on quitting the *San Nicolas*, took a position under the lee of the *Santissima Trinidada*, who was then warmly engaged by the *Orion* and *Irresistible*. After losing her fore and mizen-masts, the fire of this formidable ship ceased, and the Spanish colours disappeared; but the opportune arrival of eleven ships saved the crippled four-decker from further molestation. This was at about 4 p.m., and shortly afterwards the British admiral, observing the approach of these ships, ordered the frigates to take the prizes in tow, and for the ships of the fleet to form in close line ahead in the wake of the *Victory*. All firing had ceased before 5 p.m., when the British found themselves in possession of the *San Josef* and *Salvador del Mundo* of 112 guns, the *San Nicolas* of 80, and the *San Ysidro* of 74 guns. This conquest had been accomplished by fifteen ships of the line against twenty-six Spaniards, with the trifling loss on the part of the British of 73 killed and 227 wounded; and the only ship that lost a spar was the *Captain*, whose fore top-mast had fallen over the side.

The names of the officers of marines serving in the fleet are stated in the following order of battle, giving the killed and wounded on board of the respective ships:—

*Culloden*, 74 guns, Captain T. Troubridge, 10 killed, 47 wounded. Captain Thomas Carrie, Lieutenant G. A. Livingstone (killed), Lieutenant Richard Barford.

*Blenheim*, 98 guns, Captain T. L. Frederic, 12 killed, 49 wounded. Major James Berkeley, with a subaltern of the 51st, one of the 18th, and one of the 90th regiments.

*Prince George*, 98 guns, Rear-Admiral W. Parker, Captain John Irwin, 8 killed, 7 wounded. Captain Oliver Naylor, Second-Lieutenant

Robert Miles, Second-Lieutenant W. T. J. Matthews.

*Orion*, 74 guns, Captain Sir James Saumarez, 9 wounded. Captain J. B. Savage, First-Lieutenant Henry Hodge, Second-Lieutenant Thomas Weaver.

*Colossus*, 74 guns, Captain George Murray, 5 wounded. Captain Acheson Crozier, First-Lieutenant John Crane, Second-Lieutenant Jacob Harrison.

*Irresistible*, 74 guns, Captain George Martin, 5 killed, 14 wounded. Captain James E. Gordon, First-Lieutenant John Kendall, First-Lieutenant Charles Tyldesley.

*Victory*, 100 guns, Admiral Sir John Jervis, K.B., Captains Robert Calder and George Grey, 1 killed, 5 wounded. Major F. H. Flight, First-Lieutenant William Darley, Second-Lieutenant John Williams.

*Egmont*, 74 guns, Captain John Sutton. Major G. Whiting, Lieutenant W. H. Duer.

*Goliath*, 74 guns, Captain Sir C. H. Knowles, bart., 8 wounded. Major Andrew Burn, Lieutenant W. H. Young, Second-Lieutenant Charles Harvey.

*Barfleur*, 98 guns, Vice-Admiral Hon. William Waldegrave, Captain James R. Dacres, 7 wounded. Major James Young, first-Lieut. William Johnstone, Second-Lieut. Edward Cox.

*Britannia*, 100 guns, Vice-Admiral Charles Thompson, Captain Thomas Foley, 1 wounded. 69th regiment.

*Namur*, 90 guns, Captain J. H. Whitshed, 2 killed, 5 wounded. Captain N. Croad, First-Lieutenant Henry A. Durrie, Second-Lieutenant Thomas Henderson.

*Captain*, 74 guns, Commodore Horatio Nelson, Captain R. W. Miller, 24 killed, 56 wounded. Major William Norris (killed), Lieutenant John Graham, and Lieutenant Charles Pearson, 69th regiment.

*Diadem*, 64 guns, Captain G. H. Towry, 2 wounded. 11th regiment.

*Excellent*, 74 guns, Captain Cuthbert Collingwood, 11 killed, 12 wounded. Captain Arthur Ball, Lieutenants William Cottell, William Connolly.

Total,—73 killed, and 227 wounded.

Major Andrew Burn, being the senior Officer of Marines in the fleet, was promoted to the rank of lieutenant-colonel.

On the 6th of April, in the night, the boats of the 32-gun frigate *Magicienne*, and 44-gun frigate (*en flute*) *Regulus*, commanded by the lieutenants of those ships, on which Service Lieutenants Philip Luscombe Perry and George Frazer of the marines assisted, entered the harbour of Cape Roxo, in the island of San Domingo, where they captured, sank, and burnt, thirteen sail of square-rigged vessels; and they destroyed two batteries of two guns each at the entrance of the harbour.

On the 9th of March the 36-gun frigate *San Fiorenzo*, Captain Sir Harry Neale, and 36-gun frigate *Nymphe*, Captain John Cooke, being the inshore squadron off Brest, bore down and attacked the French 40-gun frigate *Résistance*, and 22-gun corvette *Constance*, and after a slight opposition, both the latter ships surrendered. Neither of the British ships suffered any loss, whilst the *Résistance* had 10 killed and 9 wounded; and the *Constance* 8 killed and 6 wounded. First-Lieutenant John Campbell was serving on board the *Nymphe*, and First-Lieutenant R. Carruthers on board the *San Fiorenzo*.

On the 28th of May the *Lively* and *Minerve* frigates, Captains Benjamin Hallowell and George Cockburn, discovered an armed brig anchored in the road of Santa Cruz. On the following day it was determined to attempt her capture by the boats, under the orders of Lieutenant Thomas Masterman Hardy, on which Service Lieutenant Robert Bulkley of the marines was a volunteer. At 2h. 30 m. p.m. the boats made a resolute attack upon the brig as she lay at anchor, and although opposed by a sharp fire of musketry, they boarded and carried her; and under a heavy fire from the batteries on shore, as well as from a large ship lying in the roads, the French brig *Mutine*, mounting 14 guns, was safely brought alongside the frigates by 4 p.m. The British had none killed, but Lieutenant Hardy and 15 men were wounded.

In the early part of July, a British fleet of twenty-one sail of the line, under Admiral Sir John Jervis, blockaded the Spanish fleet of twenty-six ships of the line in the harbour of Cadiz. On the 3rd of that month the town was bombarded by the *Thunder*, supported by the armed boats of the fleet, who were attacked by the Spanish gun-boats; but these were driven back under the guns of Cadiz, with the loss of two mortar boats and the commandant of the flotilla, who was captured after a personal conflict with Rear-Admiral Nelson. A second bombardment took place on the 5th by three bomb-vessels, covered by the *Theseus*, *Emerald*, and *Terpsichore*. The cannonade produced considerable effect both on the town and the shipping, and the British and Spanish gun-boats again encountered each other. The loss did not exceed 3 killed; Captain Thomas Oldfield of the marines, and 15 men wounded.

155

In the early part of July, the Earl of St. Vincent detached from the fleet cruising before Cadiz a squadron consisting of three sail of the line, three frigates, and a cutter, to make an attack on the town of Santa Cruz, in the island of Teneriffe, and attempt the capture of a galleon anchored in the bay. This service was entrusted to Rear-Admiral Horatio Nelson, who arrived there with the ships under his command on the 15th, and made immediate preparation for landing the seamen and marines.

On the 20th the three frigates, with the cutter and mortar-boat, together with the boats of the squadron, stood towards the shore; but a gale of wind coming on, they were prevented from landing. On the 22nd, it having been determined to make an attack on the heights on the north side of the bay, and then carry the fort by storm, at 9 p.m. the frigates anchored inshore off the east end of the town, and landed their men; but finding the heights too strongly guarded, the British re-embarked in the course of the night, and without loss. On the 24th the *Leander* joined the squadron, and at 5 p.m. the line of battle ships anchored about seven miles to the north-eastward of the town, and the frigates within two of the shore, as if intending to land in that direction; but this was a feint, and the mole-head was to be the rendezvous for the boats. At 11 p.m. about 700 men embarked in the boats, 180 in the *Fox* cutter, and 75 on board a large boat which had been captured, numbering, with a small detachment of artillery under Lieutenant Baynes, about 1100 men: the detachments of seamen were under their respective captains, and the whole commanded by the rear-admiral in person. Every precaution had been taken to keep the boats together, but the rough state of the weather, and the extreme darkness of the night, rendered this arrangement impracticable.

The following are the names of the ships composing the squadron, and the officers of marines who assisted in this expedition:—

*Theseus*, 74 guns, Rear-Admiral Sir Horatio Nelson, K.B., Captain R. W. Miller. Captain Thomas Oldfield, Lieutenant George Beatty, Arthur Hull.

*Culloden*, 74 guns, Captain Thomas Troubridge. Lieutenant Barford.

*Zealous*, 74 guns, Captain Samuel Hood. Captain James Home, Lieutenants William Vivion, William Judson.

*Leander*, 50 guns, Captain T. B. Thompson. Lieutenant Raby Robinson, (killed).

*Seahorse*, 38 guns, Captain T. F. Freemantle. Lieutenant Francis Wemyss.

*Emerald*, 36 guns, Captain John Waller. Lieutenant William Basham, (killed).

*Terpsichore*, 32 guns, Captain Richard Bowen. Lieutenant John Orton.

*Fox* cutter, Lieutenant John Gibson; and a mortar boat

About 1 h. 30 m. a.m. on the 25th, the *Fox* cutter, attended by the rear-admiral's boat and some others, had reached within half gun-shot of the mole head, undiscovered; when, on the alarm being given, a fire was opened from more than 30 pieces of cannon and a body of troops stationed along the shore, which so injured the *Fox*, that she immediately went down with 97 brave fellows, including Lieutenant Gibson. A shot struck the rear-admiral on the right elbow, just as he was in the act of drawing his sword, and so disabled him, that he was conveyed back to his ship: another shot sank the boat in which Captain Bowen had embarked, whereby 8 seamen perished. In spite of all this opposition the British effected a landing, and immediately stormed and carried the mole-head, defended by 300 men and 6 twenty-four pounders. Having spiked these guns our men were about to advance, when a destructive fire was opened upon them from the citadel and the houses near the mole-head, which occasioned the principal part of the loss sustained in this unfortunate enterprise.

Captain Troubridge with his division not being able to reach the mole, had pushed on shore under a battery close to the southward of the citadel, as did Captain Waller and a few other boats; but the surf ran so high that many of the boats put back, while those that did not return were instantly filled with water, which destroyed the men's ammunition. Captain Troubridge having collected a few men, advanced with Captain Waller to the principal square of the town, the appointed place of rendezvous; and not meeting the other officers with their detachments, he sent a sergeant with two of the inhabitants to summon the citadel. After waiting an hour, without receiving an answer to his message, Captain Troubridge marched to join Captains Hood and Miller, who with a small body of men had made good their landing to the southwest of the spot where he had disembarked.

By daybreak, Captain Troubridge's party consisted of no more than 180 seamen with small arms, 80 pikemen, and 80 marines, making a total of 340; and with this force he was meditating an assault. But as they soon found that the streets were commanded by field-pieces, and that 8000 armed Spaniards, with 100 Frenchmen, were approaching them from every point, and considering that the boats were all stove, and that no possibility existed of receiving a reinforcement, Captain Troubridge sent Captain Hood with a flag of truce to the governor, offering to capitulate on terms, that the British troops should be allowed to re-embark with their arms, take their boats, if saved, or to be provided with others; and in case of compliance, he engaged that the ships should no further molest the town, nor attack any one of the Canary islands.

Notwithstanding the surprise which the governor expressed on receiving such a proposal, and under such desperate circumstances, he nevertheless acceded to these conditions: Captain Troubridge accordingly marched his men to the mole-head, and embarked them in boats furnished by the Spaniards. The governor liberally supplied the retreating invaders with a ration of biscuit and wine, and removed the British wounded into the hospital; moreover, he intimated to Rear-Admiral Nelson that he was at liberty to send on shore and purchase such refreshments as his squadron might require.

Thus terminated an expedition, which although so fatal and unsuccessful, furnished abundant proof of the valour and intrepidity of British seamen and marines. The melancholy loss sustained included Captain Richard Bowen, Lieutenants John Weatherhead, *Theseus*; George Thorpe, *Terpsichore*; William Earnshaw, Leander; and John Gibson, Fox; Lieutenants of Marines Raby Robinson and William Basham; 23 seamen, and 14 marines killed: the rear-admiral (right arm amputated), Captains Freemantle and Thompson, Lieutenant Douglas, 1 midshipman, 85 seamen, and 15 marines wounded; 97 seamen and marines drowned, and 5 missing: total, 114 killed and drowned, 105 wounded, and 5 missing,—a loss exceeding the killed, and not far short of the total of the killed and wounded in the battle which obtained the glorious victory off Cape St. Vincent.

## BATTLE OF CAMPERDOWN.

In the early part of October, 1797, Admiral Duncan, with the major part of his ships, were refitting in Yarmouth roads, leaving a small squadron, under Captain Trollope, to watch the Dutch fleet in the Texel. On the 9th, the *Active* cutter appeared at the back of Yarmouth sands, with the signal flying for an enemy: all was bustle and confusion, and before noon Admiral Duncan, with eleven sail of the line, put to sea, directing his course with a fair wind straight across to his old station, and was joined on the next day by the remaining ships belonging to his fleet. On the afternoon of the 10th, the advanced ships were sufficiently near to count twenty-two sail of vessels at anchor in the Texel, but these were chiefly merchant-men; and on receiving information from Captain Trollope of the course of the enemy, the admiral stood along shore to the southward. On the 11th, at 7 a.m., the look-out ships made the signal for the enemy in sight to leeward; and at 8 h. 30 m. a.m. the Dutch squadron was discernible in the quarter pointed out, consisting of four ships of 74 guns, seven of 64 guns, four of 50 guns, one of 44 guns, one of 40 guns, and two ships of 32 guns; making fifteen ships of the line and four frigates, commanded by Vice-Admiral De Winter, who hauled to the wind on the larboard tack on discovering the British fleet; and squaring their main-yards, the Dutch resolutely awaited the approach of their opponents. The British ships were so scattered, that Admiral Duncan, at 11 h. 10 m., brought to on the starboard tack, to enable the dull sailers to take their allotted stations; but finding that the enemy were drawing fast inshore, he made the following signals:

Each ship to engage her opponent—to bear up—and, for the van to attack the enemy's rear.

At 11 a.m. Admiral Duncan made the signal to pass through the enemy's line and engage to leeward, which was replaced by the signal for close action. At about half-past noon the *Monarch*, bearing the flag of Vice-Admiral Onslow, passed under the stern of the *Jupiter*, the fourth ship from the rear, and then ranged close up to leeward, leaving the *Haerlem* to the *Powerful*. The *Monmouth* and *Russell* were soon in action, followed by the remaining ships of the larboard division.

It was about a quarter of an hour after the *Monarch* had broken the Dutch line, that the *Venerable*, frustrated in her attempt to pass astern of the *Vryheid* by the advance of the *States-General*, ran under the stern of the latter, whilst the *Triumph* closed with the next ship in the line, the *Wassanaer*. Meanwhile, the *Venerable* had ranged close on the lee side of the *Vryheid*, with whom the *Ardent* was warmly engaged on the opposite side, and ahead by the *Bedford*, as the latter cut through the line astern of the *Devries*.

The ships in the centre of the enemy's line, not being immediately engaged, advanced to the succour of their admiral; and from their fire, the *Venerable* and *Ardent*, as well as the other ships of the British van, received considerable injury. The *Hercules* having caught fire on the poop, bore up out of the line, and shortly after the flames were extinguished she surrendered, for it was stated that in their alarm they had thrown their powder overboard.

The *Venerable* had received so much damage as to be obliged to haul off; upon which the *Triumph*, after compelling the *Wassanaer* to surrender, closed with the *Vryheid*, and this nobly defended ship, after being engaged by four powerful opponents, with her three masts over the side, dropped out of the line and struck her colours. The action ceased with the surrender of Admiral De Winter's ship, at which time the British were in possession of the *Vryheid* and *Jupiter*, of 74 guns; *Devries, Gelykheid, Haerlem, Hercules*, and *Wassanaer*, of 64 guns; *Alkmaar* and *Delft*, of 50 guns, and the frigates *Monnikendam* and *Ambuscade*. The remainder of the Dutch ships bore away towards the land, then only five miles distant; and as the British fleet was in nine fathoms water, they hastened to secure their prizes, to enable them to get clear of the shore, which was the land between Camperdown and the village of Egmont.

The British fleet consisted of the following ships, which sustained the casualties severally enumerated:

*Venerable*, 74 guns, Admiral A. Duncan, Captain W. G. Fairfax, 15 killed, 62 wounded. Brevet-Major Thomas Trollope, Second-Lieutenant Patrick O'Malley, and Second-Lieutenant George Chambers (Wounded).

*Monarch*, 74 guns, Vice-Admiral R. Onslow, Captain E. O Brien, 36 killed, 100 wounded. Captain Thomas Abernethy, Second-Lieutenant Richard R. Trotter, Second-Lieutenant J. J. Smith (wounded).

*Russell*, 74 guns, Captain H. Trollope, 7 wounded. Second-Lieutenant John Jennings, Second-Lieutenant Robert Stevens.

*Montagu*, 74 guns, Captain John Knight, 3 killed, 5 wounded. Captain John Williams, Second-Lieutenant Thomas Aslett, Second-Lieutenant Robert Miles.

*Bedford*, 74 guns, Captain Sir T. Byard, 30 killed, 41 wounded. Captain John Victor, First-Lieutenant Richard Bunce, Second-Lieutenant James Collins.

*Powerful*, 74 guns, Captain W. O. B. Drury, 10 killed, 78 wounded. Captain Thomas Strickland, Lieutenant Francis Black, Second-Lieutenant R. G. W. Walker (wounded).

*Triumph*, 74 guns, Captain W. Essington (wounded), 29 killed,

55 wounded. First-Lieutenant Thomas A. Parke, Second-Lieutenant Henry Steele.

*Belliqueux*, 64 guns, Captain J. Inglis, 25 killed, 78 wounded. Captain James Cassel (wounded), Second-Lieutenant Robert Pinkerton.

*Agincourt*, 64 guns, Captain J. Williamson. Captain T. Hopper.

*Lancaster*, 64 guns, Captain J. Wells, 3 killed, 18 wounded. Captain Walter Smith, Second-Lieutenant John Sandys, (wounded).

*Ardent*, 64 guns, Captain R. R. Burgess, 41 killed, 107 wounded. Captain Richard Cuthbert (wounded), Second-Lieutenant James Marrie.

*Veteran*, 64 guns, Captain G. Gregory, 4 killed, 21 wounded. Captain-Lieutenant Henry Elliott, Second-Lieutenant R. J. Mapowder.

*Director*, 64 guns, Captain W. Bligh, 7 wounded. Captain Thomas Davy, First-Lieutenant David Weir.

*Monmouth*, 64 guns, Captain J. Walker, 5 killed, 22 wounded. Captain John Clarke, Second-Lieutenant Robert Phillips.

*Isis*, 50 guns, Captain W. Mitchell, 2 killed, 21 wounded. First-Lieutenant J. N. N. D'Esterre, Second-Lieutenant Charles Rea (wounded).

*Adamant*, 50 guns, Captain W. Hotham, Second-Lieutenant John Owen, Second-Lieutenant John Maughan.

Total,—203 killed, and 622 wounded.

The Dutch were formed in line of battle thus: *Beschermer* 50, *Gelykheid* 64, *Hercules* 64, *Devries* 64, *Vryheid* 74 *States-General* 74, *Wassenaer* 64, *Batavier* 50, *Brutus* 74 *Leyden* 64, *Mars* 64, *Cerberus* 64, *Jupiter* 74, *Haerlem* 64, *Alkmaar* 50, and *Delft* 50 guns.

The appearance of the British ships at the close of the action was very unlike what it generally bad been, when opposed to the navies of France or Spain: not a single lower mast, nor even a top-mast, was shot away; nor were the sails and rigging in their usual injured state, for the shot of the Dutch ships were all directed at the hulls of their opponents.

The loss sustained by the British amounted to 203 killed, and 622 wounded. Amongst the latter were Captains of Marines Richard Cuthbert and James Cassel; Second-Lieutenants Chambers (both feet shot off), J. J. Smith, R. G. W. Walker, John Sandys, and Charles Rea.

The captured ships were mostly dismasted, and their hulls had suffered proportionately with their loss of men, wh.ch amounted to 540 killed, and 620 wounded.

Notwithstanding the glorious issue of this battle much censure was cast upon several captains of the British fleet, for not following the noble example of their gallant chief in closing with the enemy as they might have done; and, in consequence of their keeping aloof, the slaughter fell severely upon those that so nobly did their duty. Justice required that at least one captain should be tried by a court-martial upon two charges: one for disobedience of signals in not going into action, the other for cowardice and disaffection. The court considered the first charge proved, but not the second; and sentenced Captain Williamson, of the *Agincourt*, to be placed at the bottom of the list of post-captains, and to be rendered incapable of again serving in the navy. The prosecution of this officer sprang out of the spirited remonstrance of Captain Thomas Hopper of the marines, who, mortified at the reluctance of his captain to close with the enemy, exclaimed, "This is the second time that I have seen the British flag disgraced by the cowardice of my captain."

On the 20th of December, at 10 a.m., the 36-gun frigate *Phoebe*, Captain Robert Barlow, being in latitude 50° north, longitude 8° west, discovered and chased the French 36-gun frigate *Néréide* on her weather bow. The pursuit continued all the day, and at 6 p.m. both ships having been taken aback, bore up; and at 9 p.m. the *Néréide* commenced firing her stern chasers, which did considerable damage to the *Phoebe's* sails and rigging. At 9h. 10m. p.m., just as the *Phoebe* was in a situation to commence the attack, the *Néréide* hove in stays, and as soon as the *Phoebe* could reduce her sails she came round, and the two frigates exchanged broadsides in passing on opposite tacks. At 10 p.m. the *Phoebe* got alongside her opponent, and both ships having backed their main top-sails, commenced the action in right earnest, the *Néréide* placing herself within musket-shot to windward of her opponent.

In a short time the French frigate fell on board of the *Phoebe*, but the latter bore away clear of her; having again hauled up, she renewed her fire, and both ships continued to engage until 10 h. 45 m. p.m., when the *Néréide* hauled down her light, and hailed that she surrendered. Out of a crew of 330 men, she had 20 killed and 55 wounded; whilst the *Phoebe*, out of 261 men and boys, had only 3 killed and 10 wounded. Lieutenant Robert D. Stuart, and his detachment of marines, obtained the favourable report of Captain Barlow.

On the occasion of the public thanksgiving in St. Paul's Cathedral, the following order was issued:—

Admiralty Office, 11th of December, 1797.

Sir,

I am commanded by My Lords the Commissioners of the Admiralty, to signify their direction to you to order a captain's guard of marines, together with the band of the division under your command, to march from Chatham to be in town on the 18th instant, (which, if possible, is to be commanded by officers who were in the actions of 1st of June, 1794, 14th of February, or 11th of October last,) in order to attend His Majesty to St. Paul's Cathedral on the 19th instant, to offer thanksgiving for the many victories obtained by His Majesty's navy in the course of the present war. This being a King's Guard, the colours must of course accompany it, and Their Lordships desire it may be selected from the best and most orderly men at quarters.

I am, sir, &c &c.

(Signed)      William Marsden.

To Major-General Innes, Chatham.

Chatham, 13th December, 1797.

Agreeable to the orders of My Lords Commissioners of the Admiralty, a captain's guard, consisting of 1 captain, 4 subalterns, 8 sergeants, 8 corporals, 3 drummers, and 120 privates, with the divisional colours and band, are to march on Friday morning next to London, to be in readiness to attend His Majesty to St. Paul's Cathedral on the 19th instant, to offer thanksgiving for the many signal victories obtained by His Majesty's navy in the course of the present war. The officers for this duty are Major Andrew Burn, First-Lieutenants Thomas Piers, Templeton, M'Leod, and Woodmeston: Second-Lieutenants Robert Phillips, Charles Rea, and —— Merry.

D. O., 14th of December, 1797.

To the non-commissioned officers and privates of the detachment under orders to march tomorrow.

From your characters as men and soldiers, you have been selected from the whole of the division to compose a guard of honour to attend your sovereign to St. Paul's on the day of general thanksgiving for the signal victories obtained over the enemies of your country by His Majesty's naval forces, in which the corps to which you belong has ever borne a part.

Upon so solemn an occasion you need not be told, that not only the eyes of your king, but those of your country will be fixed upon your conduct on that day. To add further to the honour of your situation, the officers by whom you will be conducted are such as have distinguished themselves in the different actions with the enemy's fleets.

You will not fail to recollect, that the division to which you belong has well earned the honour of being styled the first division, from the eminent loyalty it displayed in its answer to the infamous hand-bill, and which conduct was followed by every other corps. And although but a small part, you are to consider yourselves as the representatives of the whole, being entrusted with the most sacred pledge for your good behaviour,—the colours of your division.

Firmly relying upon your correctness in all points, I look forward with impatience for your return, to receive my public thanks.

In the early part of this year a spirit of mutinous dissatisfaction prevailed in the fleet, which has been attributed by some to the machinations of traitors and corresponding societies, and the secret influence of foreign enemies; and by others its origin has been imputed to the severity of the officers. These may possibly have conduced to the unhappy measures which followed; but we do not apprehend that a rigid discipline was at that period a source of complaint in the navy. It arose more probably from a sense of their neglected situation; for they had long complained of the smallness of their pay, and the insufficiency of their provisions, which continued in the same proportion as in the reign of Charles the Second, notwithstanding the great increase in the price of every article of subsistence.

The striking disproportion in the distribution of prize-money was considered, both by the seamen and marines, as not only inequitable, but as a proof of their inferiority in the estimation of the officers, although it was to their own gallant exertions that the success in our engagements with the enemy was mainly to be attributed. These causes of discontent extended throughout the fleet, and the plan of operations was so well arranged, and conducted with so much spirit and ability, that it evidently must have been concerted by persons of no mean capacity; who, taking advantage of the neglect the sailors and marines had so much reason to complain of, instilled in their minds a spirit of insubordination, which spread through the whole fleet.

The first intimation of this dissatisfied spirit in the navy, was by some letters addressed to Earl Howe, in the months of February and March; but no serious outbreak took place until the return of the Channel fleet to Spithead, when a secret correspondence was arranged between all the ships, and a determination entered into that no ship should proceed to sea until their grievances were redressed.

On the 15th of April (Easter Sunday), Lord Bridport made the signal to prepare for sailing: whereupon the crew of the *Queen Charlotte* manned the rigging, and gave three cheers; and this expression of their mutinous determination was followed by every other ship in the fleet.

After this open demonstration, the seamen resolved not to weigh anchor until their just demands were complied with, *unless the enemy's fleet should put to sea*; in which case they would go out, fight them, and then return and renew their complaints. Every man took an oath to support the cause in which he had engaged, and ropes were rove at the yard-arm in every ship, as an indication of the punishment which awaited those who might betray it. Several officers who were considered obnoxious, were sent on shore from various ships; nevertheless the strictest discipline was maintained, and the admiral retained the command of the fleet.

On the 18th two petitions, one to the Admiralty and the other to the House of Commons, were signed by the delegates, worded in very respectful language. In their address to the Parliament they stated, that as all the articles necessary for subsistence had advanced in price full thirty *per cent*, since the reign of Charles II., they requested that a proportionate relief should be granted to them; and they also expressed their dissatisfaction that the pensions of Chelsea had been augmented to thirteen pounds a-year, whilst those of Greenwich still remained at seven. In their appeal to the Admiralty, they recalled Their Lordships' recollection to the services done by the petitioners, and expressed their determination to uphold the honour of their country. They then directed the attention of the commissioners to the inadequacy of the seamen's pay, and the insufficiency of their provisions; demanding an increase of both, the continuance of pay to wounded seamen until cured or discharged, and the liberty of going on shore when in harbour.

The government now became alarmed, and the Board of Admiralty was transferred to Portsmouth, in order to watch the transactions in the fleet, and to consult on the readiest and most effectual means of quelling this mutinous combination.

Earl Spencer authorised Lord Bridport to inform the ships companies that the Lords Commissioners would recommend it to the king to propose to Parliament an augmentation of pay of four shillings a-month to petty-officers and able seamen, three to ordinary seamen, and two to landsmen; and that the wounded seamen should continue in receipt of their pay until cured or declared unserviceable, and then be allowed a pension, or admitted into Greenwich Hospital.

To this notification the seamen requested that the long established distinctions in the navy of able and ordinary seamen should be retained, the pay of the former to be raised to one shilling a-day, and that of the petty-officers and seamen in the usual proportion; they also requested that the pay of the marines, while on board, should be the same as that of ordinary seamen, and that the pensions of Greenwich Hospital should be increased to ten pounds.

On the 20th of April a notification was made to Lord Bridport from the Admiralty, signifying Their Lordships compliance with the demands of the seamen; and requiring the crews to return to their duty on pain of forfeiting their right to smart money, their claims for pension, and admittance to Greenwich Hospital; and they were to be held responsible for the consequences that might ensue from their disobedience. At the same time an offer was proposed of an unqualified pardon for all that had passed, provided they submitted to the authority of their officers, and ceased to hold communication with those who remained in a state of mutiny.

On the 21st Vice-Admirals Gardner and Colpoys, and Rear-Admiral Pole, went on board the *Queen Charlotte* to confer with the delegates, who explicitly informed those officers that it was the determination of the crews not to agree to anything which had not the sanction of Parliament, and guaranteed by the king's proclamation. Admiral Gardner was so irritated by this declaration, that he seized one of the delegates by the collar and swore he would have them all hanged, with every fifth man throughout the fleet. This inconsiderate violence of the admiral so exasperated the crew of the *Queen Charlotte*, that it was with difficulty they could be restrained from an attempt on the admiral's life.

The delegates from the *Royal George* having returned to their ship, and communicated what had happened, the crew resolved to summon all the delegates, and immediately hoisted the red, usually called the bloody flag, which, from its sanguinary import, struck terror through the fleet. The crews then proceeded to load their guns, and the ships were put in the same state of defence as when at sea.

On the following day they addressed a letter to the Admiralty explaining the motives of their conduct, and another to Lord Bridport, in which they styled him their father and friend, and assuring him of their respect and attachment. This induced His Lordship to re-hoist his flag on the 23rd, which he had ordered to be struck during the disturbance on the 21st. He then, in a short and pathetic address, informed the crew that he brought with him a redress to all their grievances, and the king's pardon for all that had passed. After some deliberation the offer was accepted, and the men returned to their duty. It was now generally supposed that all disputes were finally settled, and the fleet dropped down to St. Helen's, preparatory to sailing; but on the 7th of May the crews refused to put to sea, and the delegates resolved on holding what they termed a convention on board the 98-gun ship *London*, bearing the flag of Vice-Admiral Colpoys. But the vice-admiral told them that if they attempted to meet in convention, he should order the marines to fire upon them; and as they persisted, the marines were immediately under arms. A scuffle then ensued, and one of the delegates fired at and wounded Lieutenant Simms, of the marines.

The seamen of the *London* now gained the command of the decks, in defiance of their officers and the marines; and turning the muzzles of the foremost guns aft, threatened to fire if any resistance were made. They at the same time made every preparation for hanging Lieutenant Bover, who had shot a man in attempting to turn the muzzle of the gun towards the quarterdeck; but the life of this spirited officer was spared, by the vice-admiral explaining to them that the lieutenant, as well as himself, acted under the orders of the Admiralty. The crew then confined the admiral and all the officers to their cabins, and made the marines prisoners. On the 11th the vice-admiral, the captain, several other captains in the fleet, together with Vice-Admiral Gardner and three of his lieutenants, were sent on shore.

During the early part of these disturbances, the late Sir Richard Williams, who was serving on board the *Robust* as Captain of Marines, applied to the captain of the ship for authority to act, assuring him of the good disposition of the men under his command, and pledging himself by their efforts to save the ship. But Captain Thornborough shrunk from committing the marines to a possible conflict with the sailors, and recommended a little delay. In a few minutes the marine officer returned: it was not yet too late, but not another moment could be spared. The humane feelings of the commander impelled him still to temporise; and when Captain Williams returned, it was to say that his men must now save themselves, and the ship was lost. The loyalty and determination of this gallant officer so exasperated the seamen, that he, in company with some other officers, was sent out of the ship, and landed on South-sea beach in the night.

From some mistrust of the government, the seamen renewed their former menaces of resistance, and Lord Howe was selected by the Admiralty to quell this unexpected insubordination. His Lordship, from his humane disposition and many great qualities, was held in high esteem by those who had served under him; and his presence and exhortation happily dissipated the serious apprehensions that were beginning to prevail. Good order was restored by the confidence the seamen reposed in the assurance of their noble chief, and the ships crews at Plymouth followed the example, by returning to their duty.

On the 8th of May, Mr. Pitt made an application to Parliament for a sum of money sufficient for augmenting the pay of the seamen, and moved that the sum of £436,000 be granted to answer the additional pay and allowance to the seamen and marines in the navy. After some expression of censure on the part of the opposition for the delay of the minister in meeting the demands of the aggrieved, the bill passed the house, and immediately received the royal assent by commission.

The suppression of the disturbances in the fleet, without recurring to violent measures, but by compliance with their just demands, produced universal satisfaction; and it was hoped that no further disturbance would arise to spread alarm throughout the nation; but these reasonable expectations were soon disappointed by a fresh outbreak in the fleet at the Nore.

On Sunday the 27th of May, the fleet under the command of Admiral Duncan, consisting of fifteen sail of the line, was lying in Yarmouth roads, when about 4 p.m. the crew of the 74-gun ship *Venerable*, bearing the admiral's flag, mounted the rigging and gave three cheers. Major Trollope, commanding the detachment of marines on board, instantly got his men under arms, accompanied by the officers of the ship; and as the men descended from the rigging, the ringleaders, to the number of six, were confined in irons. Had an exemplary punishment been immediately inflicted, the result might probably have prevented the fatal occurrences which soon followed; but the admiral, remarkable for uniting in his own person the most undaunted courage with the most benevolent heart, forgave the offence, upon a promise of their never being again guilty of insubordination. Although the crew of the *Venerable*, by their subsequent conduct, amply redeemed their character, yet the outrage which they had perpetrated had infected the surrounding ships, and in several instances there was a determination to obtain redress of their grievances.

On the morning of the 29th of May, when the signal was made for the fleet to weigh, it was reluctantly complied with, and such ships as did get under sail soon returned to Yarmouth roads. Soon afterwards, but in the course of the day, with the exception of the *Venerable* and *Adamant*, who proceeded off the Texel, the whole returned to Yarmouth roads. Admiral Duncan, on finding himself deserted by his squadron, turned the hands up on board the *Venerable*, and thus addressed his crew:

My Lads,

I once more call you together with a sorrowful heart from what I have lately seen, the disaffection of the fleets: I call it disaffection, for the crews have no grievances. To be deserted by my fleet in the face of an enemy, is a crime which, I believe, never before happened to a British admiral; nor could I have supposed it possible. My greatest comfort, under God, is, that I have been supported by the officers, seamen, and marines of this ship; for which, with a heart overflowing with gratitude, I request you to accept my sincere thanks. I flatter myself, much good will result from your example, by bringing those deluded people to a sense of that duty which they owe, not only to their king and country, but to themselves.

The British navy has ever been the support of that liberty which has been handed down to us by our ancestors, and which I trust we shall maintain to the latest posterity; and that can only be done by unanimity and obedience. This ship's company, and others who have distinguished themselves by their loyalty and good order, deserve to be, and doubtless will be, the favourites of a grateful country. They will also have, from their inward feelings, a comfort which will be lasting, and not like the floating and false confidence of those who have swerved from their duty.

It has often been my pride, with you, to look into the Texel,

169

and see a foe which dreaded coming out to meet us: my pride is now humbled indeed! My feelings are not easily to be expressed; our cup has overflowed, and made us wanton. The all-wise Providence has given us this check as a warning, and I hope we shall improve by it: on him, then, let us trust, where our only security can be found. I find there are many good men among us; for my own part, I have had full confidence in all of this ship, and once more beg to express my approbation of your conduct. May God, who has thus far conducted you, continue to do so; and may the British navy, the glory and support of our country, be restored to its wonted splendour, and be, not only the bulwark of Britain, but the terror of the world. But this can only be effected by a strict adherence to our duty and obedience; and let us pray that the Almighty God may keep us in the right way of thinking.

God bless you all!

This unassuming and impressive appeal to the generous character of English seamen, roused them to a proper sense of their duty, and they declared their resolution to support their admiral under all circumstances. Their example was followed by the other ships which had remained with the *Venerable* in Yarmouth roads, and notwithstanding the defection of so considerable a part of his squadron, Admiral Duncan repaired to his station, to watch the motions of the Dutch fleet.

The principal subject of complaint, on the part of the mutineers, was the unequal distribution of prize-money, for which they blamed their fellow-seamen at Portsmouth. Emboldened by the strength of their position, they resolved to persevere in, their demands; and they proceeded to secure sufficiency of provisions by seizing vessels laden with stores; and they cut off all communication with London by placing four of their ships across the entrance of the Thames.

These transactions were warmly reprobated by the seamen at Portsmouth and Plymouth; who, admonishing their fellow-seamen at the Nore, condemned their proceedings as a scandal to the name of the British sailor; and they exhorted them to turn to their duty, and to be satisfied with the concession already obtained. But this warning proved ineffectual: the committee of delegates on board the *Sandwich* commissioned Captain the Earl of Northesk, whom they had in confinement on board the *Montague*, to lay their petition before the king in the name of the fleet. This address was loyal and respectful to His

Majesty, but reflecting severely on his ministers; and they threatened, in case of a refusal of their demands, to put immediately to sea. Not receiving an answer to their message, and learning that their proceedings were highly disapproved of by the nation at large, the mutineers, despairing of success, struck the red flag, and restored a free passage of the trade to the metropolis. Every ship was now left at its own command, and they all gradually returned to obedience; although on board of some, violent struggles took place between the loyal and the disaffected parties.

The principal ringleader of the mutiny, Richard Parker, was imprisoned, and after a trial on board the *Neptune* which lasted three days, he was sentenced to death. He suffered with great intrepidity, acknowledging the justice of his sentence, and expressing his hope that mercy might be extended to his associates; but it was considered necessary to make public examples of the most guilty, who were accordingly tried, condemned, and executed. Others were sentenced to be severely flogged, whilst several remained under sentence of death until after the victory obtained by Admiral Duncan off Camperdown, when His Majesty sent a general pardon to those unhappy men. The mutiny at Portsmouth and Plymouth may be attributed to the popular maxim, of the inherent right of all men to require an equitable treatment; and if denied them, to obtain it by force if other means proved insufficient. The unjust treatment of sailors in the navy was undeniable: it was a subject of ordinary discourse, and the impartial public loudly participated in their claims for redress.

There certainly was a reasonable pretext for the combinations at Portsmouth and Plymouth, but the formidable revolt at the Nore was not impelled by necessity, nor provoked by unjust aggression or neglect. It was impatience of authority, progressive in its demands, intent on civil discord and convulsion; and was rather the influence of malcontent incendiaries, than the genuine spirit of the English sailor. As soon as the determination of taking the ships to the Nore was made known, the officers of the *Agamemnon* declined doing duty, and retired to the ward-room, where they remained unmolested.

When the mutineers applied to Captain David Wilson of the marines for the keys of the arm-chest, the gallant veteran, finding himself unsupported by Captain Fancourt, threw the keys overboard, telling the delegates to go after them. On board this ship, as in many others, if the captain had shown a determination to resist the demands of the seamen, there is little doubt but the spirit of insubordination would have been crushed. Unhappily, there was a yielding timidity, that was soon taken advantage of by the daring leaders of this combination. Captain Fancourt declined calling on the marines to act; for the late Captain Edward Pelham Brenton of the navy, who was then a lieutenant of the *Agamemnon*, states:

> The captain, when urged to avail himself of the assistance of the marines, refused to do so, because some of the men would be shot, and he could not endure seeing them lying suffering on the deck; but with a little patience, there would be unanimity again!

The marines would as zealously have obeyed their officers as they did on board the *Venerable* and *Adamant*, had the opportunity been afforded them; and we find that, in the sequel, when there was some disaffection among the mutineers, the marines again showed their readiness to support the officers in regaining the command of their ships.

In the reply of the seamen to the Lords Commissioners of the Admiralty there is a passage referring to the claims of the marines, to this effect:—

> And as a further proof of our moderation, and that we are actuated by a true spirit of benevolence towards our brethren the marines, who are not noticed in Your Lordships answer, we humbly propose that their pay be augmented, while serving on board, in the same proportion as ordinary seamen.

The commissioners, in their consideration of this representation, resolved to recommend to His Majesty:

> None of the allowance made to the marines, when on shore, shall be stopped on their being embarked on board His Majesty's ships. We have also resolved, that all seamen, marines, and others serving in His Majesty's ships shall have the full allowance of provisions, without any deduction for leakage or waste.

The contaminating effect of insubordination extended beyond the discontented crews of the fleet, and evil-disposed persons on shore contrived to disseminate a spirit of disaffection among the troops; but their treacherous designs were overthrown by a firm and vigorous resistance. Sergeant Andrew Gilborn, for his loyalty on the occasion, was promoted to the rank of second-lieutenant; and in the ensuing year Sergeant O'Neal obtained a similar reward for conduct equally praiseworthy, in detecting a conspiracy on board the 80-gun ship *Caesar*.

The following are copies of letters detailing these circumstances:—

Marine Barracks, Plymouth, 9th of July, 1797.

Sir,

I have to request you will represent to My Lords Commissioners of the Admiralty, that Sergeant Andrew Gilborn of this division was the man who was instrumental in discovering the late mutiny, and whose activity after the discovery enabled me to bring the charges home to the individuals who have suffered for it. His conduct appears to me to deserve some marked approbation; and I think if a commission was given him, in which opinion I am joined by Major-General Campbell, the president of the court-martial, it would be a very strong incitement to the non-commissioned officers for similar exertions: his services have been in his situation various and meritorious, and he is a child of the service, his father for many years serving with credit here as a sergeant-major.

If Their Lordships should not think it right to give him a commission, I trust they will find it necessary to order him some other reward, to show good conduct does not pass unnoticed.

(Signed)         J. Bowater.

E. Nepean, Esq.

Admiralty Office, 11th July, 1797.

Sir,

I have received and read to My Lords Commissioners of the Admiralty your letter of the 9th instant, recommending Sergeant Andrew Gilborn to Their Lordships as deserving some marked approbation of his conduct in discovering the late mutiny, and whose activity afterwards enabled you to bring the charges home to the individuals who have suffered for it: and in return, I am commanded by Their Lordships to acquaint you, that in consequence of what has been stated of his good conduct, he has been promoted to the rank of second-lieutenant.

(Signed)         E. Nepean.

M. G. Bowater.

Marine Barracks, Plymouth, 26th August, 1798.

Sir,

I beg you will lay the enclosed letter from Captain Home before my lords commissioners of the Admiralty, and I have in justice to Sergeant O'Neal to state, that he was also very active in bringing forward evidence on the marines who mutinied, and were shot here the 6th of July, 1797. His family is also good, and his appearance much above his present situation; I therefore think it a part of my duty to say, if Their Lordships should be pleased to honour him with a commission, I think it would be rewarding merit.

(Signed)                                                         J. Bowater.

E. Nepean, Esq

Admiralty Office, 28th August, 1798.

Sir,

I have received and read to my lords commissioners of the Admiralty your letter of the 26th instant, inclosing one you had received from Captain Home, stating the meritorious behaviour of Sergeant O'Neal in detecting the late conspiracy of the united Irishmen belonging to His Majesty's ship *Caesar*, and strongly recommending him to Their Lordships for promotion; at the same time informing Their Lordships, that Sergeant O'Neal was also very active in bringing forward evidence on the marines who mutinied, and were shot at Plymouth in July 1797, and recommending him to Their Lordships as meriting the reward of a commission; and in return, I am commanded by their lordships to acquaint you, that in consequence of the good conduct of Sergeant O'Neal on the occasions above stated, Their Lordships have been pleased to recommend him to His Majesty for a commission of second-lieutenant of marines, and that you should take care to let the cause of his promotion be generally known, as an inducement to other persons who may be placed under similar circumstances to follow so laudable an example.

(Signed)                                                       E. Nepean.

M. G. Bowater

On the night of the 22nd of September, the 32-gun frigate *Hermione*, Captain Hugh Pigot, was cruising off the west end of Porto Rico, when a most daring and unexampled mutiny broke out on board of her. It appears that Captain Pigot had threatened to flog the last man off the mizen top-sailyard, after reefing top-sails; and the men well knowing from his determined character that he would keep his word, each hastened to get into the top, and in their eagerness to escape punishment, two poor fellows, missing their hold, fell on the quarter-deck, when both were killed. The circumstance being reported to the captain, he brutally replied, "Throw the lubbers overboard."

This tyrannical conduct, coupled with a succession of acts of oppression, produced such increasing discontent, that on the following night the men loudly expressed their dissatisfaction; and on the first-lieutenant going among them to inquire the cause of the disturbance, the wretches cut his throat with a tomahawk, and then threw him overboard. The captain, hearing a noise, ran on deck, but was driven back with repeated wounds; and his coxswain and three other seamen, having followed him into his cabin, forced him out of the windows. In a similar manner the mutineers proceeded with eight other officers, cutting and mangling their victims in the most cruel manner; and the only officers that escaped were the master, gunner, carpenter, and one midshipman (David O'Brien Casey).

We have gone somewhat into the details of this revolting act of cruelty to show, that although the tyrannous conduct of Captain Pigot had driven the men to desperation, yet the marines were not unmindful of the trust reposed in them; and the following evidence of the captain's steward, extracted from the minutes of the court-martial, testify that, even under such aggravating circumstances, a marine was still faithful to the trust reposed in him.

On the 21st of September, about 11 p.m., I left the cabin, after extinguishing the light, and went to my hammock under the half-deck, where I had lain but a few minutes, when I heard a confused noise of people round the main-mast. The next thing I heard was, the bulk-head of the cabin burst through, and a number of people rushing in. I immediately jumped out of my hammock, and saw the sentinel at the cabin door, bleeding. I entreated him, for God's sake, to tell me what was the matter: he said that some of the people had broke into the cabin, and were murdering Captain Pigot, begging me at the same time to keep out of the way, as they had been asking for me.

This clearly proves that the marine was firm to his duty, and by resisting the mutineers in their attempt to enter the cabin, he probably fell a victim to his loyalty. The captain, three lieutenants, purser, surgeon, captain's clerk, one midshipman and lieutenant of marines, were murdered. The ship was carried into La Guyra, a port of the Spanish main; and was recaptured by the boats of the *Surprise*, as related in our account of the transactions of 1799.

During the early part of the year, 1798, the French Government kept England in a state of alarm by the threat of an invasion; but while troops were assembling on the northern shores of France for the purpose of putting this plan into execution, a more serious and secret expedition was preparing at Toulon, which sailed from that port on the 19th of May under the command of General Buonaparte, as we shall presently relate.

Lord Bridport, while cruising off Brest on the 21st of April with the Channel fleet, consisting of ten sail of the line, detached the *Mars* and *Ramillies*, of 74 guns, with the *Jason* frigate, in chase of some suspicious vessels. The *Mars*, Captain Alexander Hood, having distanced her companions, continued the pursuit of a ship of the line, which at 7 h. 30 m. p. m. evinced an intention to escape through the passage Du Raz. At 8h. 30 m. p.m., the Bee du Raz bearing north by east two or three miles, the French 74-gun ship *Hercule*, Captain L'Héritiér, finding it impossible to work up against the strong current, came, to an anchor, and furled sails. At 9h. 15 m., the *Mars* having closed with the *Hercule*, both ships commenced the action at the same time, and Captain Hood finding that the current would not admit of remaining under weigh, the *Mars* ranged ahead, let go her anchor, and then dropped alongside of her opponent at 9 h. 30 m. p.m.

The cannonade continued until 10 h. 30 m., at which time, the *Hercule* having failed in two attempts to board, and being very much shattered, a French officer hailed that they had surrendered. The loss sustained by the *Mars*, out of a crew of 634 men and boys, amounted to her commander, Captain Joseph White of the marines, and 20 killed, and 8 missing; 2 lieutenants, 1 midshipman, and 57 wounded. The *Hercule* had 290 men killed and wounded. The subalterns of marines on board the *Mars*, were First-Lieutenant Christopher Epworth, Second-Lieutenants J. H. Hawkins and Walter Taite.

On the 26th of June the 36-gun frigate *Sensible*, on her passage from Malta to Toulon with despatches, was fallen in with by the 38-gun frigate *Seahorse*, Captain Edward James Foote, who, after a chase which continued from 4 p. m. until 4 a.m. on the 27th, came up with the trench frigate, and a close action was maintained for about eight minutes; when the *Sensible*, having lost 18 men killed, her captain and 36 wounded, hauled down her colours. Lieutenant Francis Wemyss was serving on board the *Seahorse*.

On the 13th of May the 36-gun frigate *Flora*, Captain R. G. Middleton, chased the French brig-corvette *Mondovi*, mounting 16 guns with a crew of 68 men, into the harbour of Cerigo, in the island of that name in the Archipelago; and on the same evening the boats of the frigate, under the orders of Lieutenant William Russell, attacked the *Mondovi*, in face of a heavy fire from the brig and the boats which commanded the entrance of the harbour. She was nevertheless gallantly boarded, and brought out with no greater loss on the part of the British than one marine killed; Lieutenant Richard Parry of the marines (who was a volunteer on this service), and seven wounded. The *Mondovi* lost 1 killed, 4 drowned, and 8 wounded.

On the 15th of July, at 9 a.m., the *Lion* of 64 guns, Captain Manley Dixon, when near Carthagena, fell in with four Spanish 34-gun frigates, who were formed close in order of battle, on the larboard line of bearing. The third from their van, the *Dorotea*, having her fore topmast gone, the *Lion* bore down and made this ship her principal object of attack. The other three frigates tacked in succession, and passed the *Lion* very gallantly within musket-shot, receiving the broadside of the British ship as they passed. Captain Dixon continued to pursue the *Dorotea*, who kept up a galling fire from her chase guns.

The three frigates having again tacked, made a second attempt to support their friend; but they were repulsed by a broadside from the *Lion* as she closed with the *Dorotea*, who still nobly defended herself, whilst her consorts made a third and ineffectual attempt to rescue her. The *Lion* now wore round on the same tack as the *Dorotea*, who, being abandoned by her friends, with her mizen-mast over the side, and having sustained a loss of 20 men killed and 23 wounded, hauled down the Spanish colours. The *Lion* suffered considerably in her masts and rigging, but she had only 2 men wounded. The Officers of Marines were Lieutenants Philip Patriarche and John C. Hoskins.

For some months past great exertions were made in the southern ports of France in equipping the expedition intended for the invasion of Egypt, and on the 19th of May this formidable armament sailed from Toulon. It consisted of thirteen sail of the line, eight frigates, two Venetian sixty-fours, six frigates *en flute*, with various smaller vessels; numbering together seventy-two vessels of war, and when joined by vessels from other ports, a total of 400 transports. This immense fleet, whose crews amounted to 10,000 men, conveyed 36,000 troops, and the whole force was under the command of Napoleon Buonaparte.

The fleet first steered for Genoa, and having been joined by the transports in that port, stood across to Cape Corse, and remained in sight of the eastern coast of Corsica until the 30th. It then sailed along the island of Sardinia, in expectation of the convoy from Civita Vecchia; but after waiting until the 7th of June, the fleet proceeded without the looked-for reinforcement. On the 8th the expedition quitted the coast of Sicily, and on the 9th, when in sight of the islands of Goza and Malta, was joined by the Civita division of transports. The troops effected a landing on the 10th, and on the 12th the islands of Malta, Goza, and Comino surrendered by capitulation.

After a stay of four days, Buonaparte quitted Malta on the 19th of June, leaving General Vaubois with 4000 troops in possession of the island. The expedition steered a direct course to the eastward, the advanced frigates detaining and destroying every vessel they fell in with, to prevent the circulation of intelligence respecting the probable destination of the fleet; and on the morning of the 1st of July, the minarets of Alexandria were discerned by the leading ships. Learning that an English squadron had appeared on the coast, Buonaparte expedited the landing of part of the army; and on the 2nd, after an action in which the French had many killed and wounded, including General Kléber among the latter, they obtained possession of Alexandria. In the course of the next day the remainder of the troops were disembarked, and the ships of the line and four frigates proceeded to the bay of Aboukir; where we take leave of them for a short time, to introduce a subject of greater interest.

Rear-Admiral Sir Horatio Nelson having returned to England to recruit his health, after the unsuccessful and disastrous attack on Santa Cruz, arrived off Cadiz in the *Vanguard* on the 29th of April, and on the 2nd of May repaired to Gibraltar, where, being joined by the *Orion* and *Alexander*, seventy-fours, two frigates and a sloop, he sailed thence on the 9th. On the 22nd, in a heavy gale, the *Vanguard* carried away her main and mizen top-masts, and then her fore-mast, and consequently proceeded to the harbour of St. Pietro, in Sardinia, in company with the two other line of battle ships. Having got up a jury fore-mast, the *Vanguard* and her companions put to sea on the 27th, and steered for the rendezvous off Toulon, which they reached on the 31st. On the 5th of June the *Mutine* brig apprised Sir Horatio that ten ships of the line were on their way to join him; and on the evening of the 7th this reinforcement placed themselves on the orders of the rear-admiral, making his force thirteen sail of the line, one of 50 guns, and a brig.

The squadron, after being some days detained by a calm, steered towards the island of Corsica, where it arrived on the 12th, and then pursued its course along the shore of Tuscany, with a fine breeze at north-west. On the 17th they stood into the bay of Naples, and learning that the French had coasted the island of Sardinia, and probably proceeded to Malta, the rear-admiral again got under sail; but the light airs during the two succeeding days so retarded the progress of the squadron, that it was not until the morning of the 20th that it entered the straits of Messina. Receiving intelligence of the French being in possession of Malta and Goza, and that their fleet was lying at anchor at the latter place, the British were soon clear of the straits, and the island of Malta was now their destination. At daybreak on the 22nd it was ascertained from a Ragusian brig, which had the day before passed through the French fleet, that the enemy quitted Malta on the 18th, with the wind at northwest; it was therefore conjectured that Alexandria was their destination, and accordingly the British fleet immediately bore up, and steered south-east under all sail.

From the 22nd to the 28th only three vessels were spoken, and from these no intelligence could be obtained, nor was there any appearance of the enemy as the harbours of Alexandria opened to their view. A retrograde movement was now resolved upon, taking a more northerly course, and it was not until the 4th of July that the British made the coast of Natalia. The fleet continued beating to windward until the 16th, when the weather becoming more favourable, it anchored on the 19th in the harbour of Syracuse; and having obtained provisions and water, put to sea again on the 25th. It is remarkable that the two fleets crossed each other's track on the 22nd of June; but as the weather was hazy, and the British sailed in close order, having no frigates to spread as look-out ships, the enemy was not discovered. It is equally striking, that as the British squadron quitted the shore on its departure from Alexandria, it was actually seen from the Pharos tower on the morning of the 30th, the very day on which the French, in the evening, made their appearance on the coast of Egypt.

On leaving Syracuse, the rear-admiral directed his course to the Morea; for as the enemy had not been seen in the Archipelago, nor in the Adriatic, and not gone down the Mediterranean, no other conclusion remained but that Egypt had been their destination. On the 28th the *Culloden* was despatched to Coron, whence she brought intelligence that the French fleet had been seen about four weeks since on the coast of Candia, steering south-east. The British ships now pursued that course, and on the 1st of August, at 10 a.m., the minarets of Alexandria made their welcome appearance but although the French flag was flying on the walls of the city, the enemy's fleet was not discovered. This disappointment was of short duration, for at 1 p. m. the *Zealous* signalled that seventeen ships of war, thirteen or fourteen of them in line of battle, were at anchor in a bay upon her larboard bow. The British fleet instantly hauled up, steering to the eastward under top-gallant sails, with a fine breeze at north-north-west. The enemy's fleet, which had been signalled by the *Zealous*, consisted of one ship of 120 guns, three of 80 guns, nine of 74 guns, and four frigates.

On first taking up this anchorage, Vice-Admiral Brueys held a council of war, composed of the flag-officers and captains, to determine whether, in case of attack, the fleet should engage at anchor or under sail. All the officers, except Rear-Admiral Blanquet, approved of the fleet's remaining at anchor; but he maintained, that it was only when a fleet could be supported by strong forts crossing each other in their fire, that any advantage could be gained by anchoring; and as the majority was against his opinion, the rear-admiral requested that the Franklin might be placed as one of the seconds to the commander-in-chief. This request was complied with, and the ships were formed in line ahead in the following order:—*Guerrier* 74, *Conquérant* 74, *Spartiate* 74, *Aquilon* 74, *Peuple-Souverain* 74, *Franklin* 80, *Orient* 120, *Tonnant* 80, *Heureux* 74, *Mercure* 74, *Guillaume Tell* 80, *Généreux* 74, *Timoléon* 74, with the four frigates forming an inner line.

The van ship bore from Aboukir island south, distance a mile and three quarters, and between each line of battle ship the distance was about 160 yards; so that the line occupied a space of about a mile and five-eighths, but the line was not a straight one; from the *Orient*, the centre ship, the van bore north-west, the rear ship south-east by south, and the *Guerrier* and *Timoléon* from each other about north-west half north, and south-east half south; hence the line formed an obtuse angle, having its projecting centre towards the sea. Besides the bomb-vessels, which were stationed on the flanks of the line, a battery was erected on Aboukir Island, mounting 4 twelve-pounders, a few pieces of lighter calibre, and 2 thirteen-inch mortars. As soon as the French admiral was convinced that the British intended an immediate attack, he directed the necessary preparations for battle, and ordered each ship to lay out an anchor on the south-east, and to send a stream cable to the next ship astern of her, making a hawser fast to it, in order to spring her broadside towards the enemy.

The British ships at 4 p.m. were ordered to prepare to anchor by the stern, and shortly afterwards the admiral made the signal to attack the enemy's van and centre; thus occupying the attention of only one half their line, while it was intended to place a British ship on the bow and quarter of every French ship of the seven brought into action. At 5 h. 30 m., the fleet being nearly abreast of the shoal, the signal was made to form in line of battle ahead and astern of the admiral, as most convenient; and at 6 p.m. Captain Hood, in the *Zealous*, by careful sounding, led the fleet, which on rounding the shoal brought the wind on their starboard beam, in the following order:—*Goliath, Zealous, Orion, Audacious, Theseus, Vanguard, Minotaur, Defence, Bellerophon, Majestic, Leander*, with the *Culloden* at some distance to the northward, and beyond her the *Alexander* and *Swiftsure*, using every exertion to close with the squadron. Soon after the British ships had thus formed, they hoisted their colours, with jacks in various parts of the rigging.

At about 6h. 20 m. p.m., the French line having also hoisted their colours, the *Conquérant* and the *Guerrier* opened their fire upon the *Goliath* and *Zealous*, then in line close to each other, and at some distance ahead of the other ships. At 6h. 30 m. the *Goliath* crossed the head of the French line, and after pouring her broadside into the bows of the *Guerrier*, bore up for that ship's inner bow; but the anchor did not bring the ship up until abreast of the larboard quarter of the second ship, the *Conquérant*, and she then commenced a warm action with the latter. The *Zealous*, following the *Goliath*, brought up abreast of the inner and larboard-bow of the *Guerrier*, which was precisely the position Captain Foley intended the *Goliath* to have taken, and in less than five minutes her fire brought down the *Guerrier's* fore-mast, just at the moment the sun was sinking into the horizon; and this auspicious commencement of the battle was greeted with three cheers from the British fleet.

The *Orion*, after firing at the *Guerrier* in passing, rounded the *Zealous* on her starboard side, and passed the *Goliath* on the same side, intending to bring up abreast of the fourth ship, the *Aquilon*; but the *Sérieuse* frigate having presumed to fire at the *Orion*, the latter opened upon her so effectually with her starboard guns, that the frigate, after being dismasted, drifted upon the shoal and sank: the *Orion* then dropped her anchor, and brought up, head to wind, abaft the *Peuple-Souverain*. Previous to the delay occasioned by the interruption of the *Sérieuse*, the *Theseus* and *Audacious* had previously anchored; the former, steeringclose ahead of the *Guerrier*, and passing between the *Zealous* and *Goliath*, into whose opponents she successively fired in passing, anchored by the stern in line ahead of the *Goliath*, and abreast of the *Spartiate*. In the meantime the *Audacious* had anchored on the outside of the line, and on the starboard bow of the *Conquérant*.

Having detailed the proceedings of the leading ships, and explained the manner in which they took up their respective positions, it must be evident that this advantageous manoeuvre arose from pure accident, and was never premeditated by the victorious leader of the attacking squadron: it was entirely owing to the circumstance of the *Goliath* not bringing up in the situation assigned to her, and which incident induced Captain Hood to place the *Zealous* in the position intended for the leading British ship. The two succeeding ships availed themselves of the opportunity which presented itself, of doubling in upon the van of the enemy; and by thus bringing their whole force upon the van and centre, the British were enabled to subdue a considerable portion of their opponents, and then fall upon the rear of the French line; which, until that moment, had been incapable of taking any part in the action.

The *Vanguard*, after receiving the fire of the van-ships as she edged away, anchored within eighty yards of the starboard beam of the *Spartiate*, at about 6 h. 40 m. p. m.; and a few minutes afterwards the *Minotaur*, placing herself ahead of the *Vanguard*, brought up abreast of the *Aquilon*. At about 7 p.m. the *Defence* anchored on the starboard side of the *Peuple Souverain*, whilst the *Bellerophon* and *Majestic* passed on with the intention of attacking the ships in the centre and rear; and shortly after 7 p. m. the *Bellerophon* dropped her stern anchor abreast of the *Orient*. Soon afterwards the *Majestic* brought up abreast of the *Tonnant*, from whose heavy fire the British ship suffered severely, and lost her gallant captain.

To return to the proceedings in the van: the *Guerrier* continued to defend herself until 9 p.m., although exposed to the constant fire of the *Zealous*, who had placed herself in a position of comparative safety; and after being assailed by the raking broadsides of three other ships, and having lost her three masts, with more than 350 men killed and wounded, the *Guerrier* was taken possession of by the *Zealous*, whilst the latter had only seven men wounded. The *Conquérant*, unable to contend against her three opponents, was the first ship that surrendered: her fore and mizen-masts were shot away, and her main-mast in a falling state; and she sustained a heavy loss in killed and wounded. Of her principal opponents, the *Goliath* had 21 killed and 41 wounded; whilst the *Audacious*, from her secure position on the larboard bow, had only 1 killed and 35 wounded.

The *Spartiate*, after sustaining the fire of the *Theseus, Vanguard*, and *Minotaur*, and from the quarter-guns of the *Audacious*, and having lost all her masts, struck her colours about the same time as the *Guerrier*. The *Vanguard* was exposed to the raicing fire of the *Aquilon* as she sprung her broadside, until the *Minotaur* gave the French ship full occupation; and from the united fire of the *Aquilon* and *Spartiate*, the *Vanguard* sustained a loss of 30 killed, and 76 wounded.

The *Aquilon*, assailed by the *Minotaur* on her starboard side, and by the *Theseus* on the inner side of the line, was soon reduced to the same dismasted state as her three companions ahead; and at 9 h. 25 m. p.m. she struck her colours. The *Minotaur* had 23 killed and 64 wounded: and the *Theseus* 5 killed and 30 wounded.

The *Peuple-Souverain* lost her fore and main-masts by the close fire of the *Defence* and raking broadsides of the *Orion*, as the latter lay on the French ship's larboard quarter. The cable of the *Defence* having been shot away, she re-anchored abreast of the *Orient*. The *Defence* had only 4 killed and 11 wounded; while the *Orion* sustained a loss of 13 killed and 29 wounded.

The *Bellerophon*, from being exposed to the formidable broadside of the *Orient*, lost her mizen-mast, and then her main-mast at about 8 p.m. At about 8 h. 20 m. p.m., being entirely disabled, she cut her stern cable, and setting her sprit-sail, wore clear of the fire of her powerful opponent: but she had scarcely filled her fore top-sail, than her shattered fore-mast fell over her larboard bow. In drifting along the French rear, she received a broadside from the *Tonnant*, and some distant shots from the *Heureux*. The loss sustained by the *Bellerophon* amounted to 49 killed, and 148 wounded.

The *Majestic* anchored so close to the *Tonnant*, that her captain was killed by a musket-ball, about half an hour after the firing commenced. About 8 h. 30 m., finding she was drifting athwart the hawse of the *Heureux*, the *Majestic* slipped her stern cable, and letting go her best bower, brought up head to wind, having the *Heureux* on her starboard quarter; and shortly afterwards the *Tonnant*, after slipping her cable in consequence of the fire on board the *Orient*, brought up on the larboard bow of the British ship.

When the *Alexander* and *Swiftsure* had reached the island of Aboukir, and expected soon to be round the reef that lies off its northern extremity, the wind shifted from north-north-west to north, which caused the *Alexander*, then on the lee bow of the *Swiftsure*, to tack, and consequently gave the lead to the latter ship. The *Culloden* having unfortunately grounded shortly after the commencement of the action, stuck fast on the reef off the island, and her signals enabled her two friends, as they successively came up, to round the shoal in safety.

About 8 p.m., just as the *Bellerophon* had withdrawn from the contest, the *Swiftsure* brought up by the stern, about half a ship's length from the spot the former had quitted, and opened a fire from her foremost guns at the starboard bow of the *Orient*, and her aftermost at the quarter of the *Franklin*; whilst the *Leander*, who had recently arrived, (on account of her detention in rendering the *Culloden* assistance,) kept under weigh in the vacant space left by the *Peuple-Souverain* when she quitted the line, and poured a raking fire into the bows of the *Franklin* with impunity. Shortly afterwards the *Alexander* came rapidly up, passed through the opening which the *Tonnant* had left, and dropped her bow anchor, so as to bring her broadside to bear on the larboard quarter of the three-decker.

About 9 p.m. a fire broke out on the poop of the *Orient*, which after spreading along the decks, and ascending the rigging with terrific rapidity, reached the magazine; and about 10 p.m. this superb ship blew up with a tremendous explosion. The vibration shook the ships severely, but the flaming mass very fortunately flew over the *Swiftsure*, whilst a few fragments fell on board the *Alexander*. This melancholy catastrophe was so impressive, that it was full ten minutes before the mighty strife was renewed. By this time the wind, as if just recovering from the trance into which all nature had been hushed, freshened up; and as the breeze ruffled the water's surface, it seemed to bring reanimation to the appalled senses of the combatants.

The *Franklin* was the first to recommence hostilities by firing her lower deck guns at the *Defence* and *Swiftsure*, who returned the fire with powerful effect, as they lay close on her starboard bow and quarter. This gallantly fought ship, without a second ahead or astern, continued to defend herself until her main and mizen-masts went by the board; and being incapable of further opposition, she struck her colours about midnight. At this time no other French ship but the *Tonnant* continued the cannonade, while the *Swiftsure*, owing to the position of the *Alexander*, could make little or no return to the *Tonnant's* galling fire. The *Majestic* was still the principal opponent of this formidable ship, whose heavy fire brought down her main and mizen-masts at 3 a.m. on the 2nd; and shortly afterwards the *Tonnant's* three lower masts were shot away, but even this circumstance did not compel her to strike her colours.

At 4 a.m., just as the day broke, the firing recommenced between the *Tonnant*, *Guillaume* Tell, *Généreux*, and *Timoléon* on one side, and the *Alexander* and *Majestic* on the other. This renewal of the action brought the *Theseus* and *Goliath* to the spot, when the *Artémise* frigate fired a broadside and struck her colours, but she shortly afterwards caught fire and blew up. In the meantime the four French ships had dropped so far to leeward, as to be almost out of gunshot of the British. The *Goliath*, *Theseus*, *Alexander*, and *Leander* stood towards the *Heureux* and *Mercure*, who had run themselves on shore to the southward of the bay, and compelled them to surrender; but whilst attending to these ships, the *Généreux* and *Guillaume Tell*, with the frigates *Justice* and *Diane*, took the opportunity of getting under weigh, and effected their escape; receiving the fire of the *Zealous* in passing, which they returned, without doing any injury except to the sails and rigging.

The *Tonnant* and *Timoléon* were lying ashore mere wrecks, but both kept their colours flying until the approach of the *Theseus* and *Leander* on the morning of the 3rd, when the *Tonnant* surrendered; and shortly afterwards the *Timoléon*, having been set on fire by her crew, exploded. Thus terminated this memorable battle, leaving in the hands of the British two ships of 80, and seven of 74 guns; whilst only two of the line and two frigates made their escape.

The following is a statement of the British ships, in the order in which they led into action on the 1st of August, 1798, showing the number of killed and wounded; also the names of the officers of marines serving on board the respective ships:—

*Goliath*, 74 guns, Captain T. Foley, 21 killed, 41 wounded. Lieutenants Charles Harvey and William Bulkley.

*Zealous*, 74 guns, Captain Samuel Hood, 1 killed, 7 wounded. First-Lieutenant William Vivion, Second-Lieutenant William Judson.

*Orion*, 74 guns, Captain Sir James Saumarez, 13 killed, 29 wounded. Captain John B. Savage, Second-Lieutenant Thomas Weaver.

*Audacious*, 74 guns, Captain Davidge Gould, 1 killed, 35 wounded. Captain James Weir, Lieutenants Richard McCarthy and Augustus Bozon.

*Theseus*, 74 guns, Captain R. W. Miller, 5 killed, 30 wounded. Captain Thomas Oldfield, First-Lieutenant George Beatty, Second-Lieutenant Arthur Hull.

*Vanguard*, 74 guns, Rear-Admiral Sir Horatio Nelson, K.B., Captain Edward Berry, 30 killed, 76 wounded. Captain-Lieutenant William Faddy (killed), First-Lieutenants Thomas Young and Christopher Noble, and Second-Lieutenant J. Hair.

*Minotaur*, 74 guns, Captain T. Louis, 23 killed, 64 wounded. Second-Lieutenant John S. Kirchner (killed), Second-Lieutenant John Jewell (wounded).

*Defence*, 74 guns, Captain J. Peyton, 4 killed, 11 wounded. Captain William Binks, Second-Lieutenant James Wheeler.

*Bellerophon*, 74 guns, Captain H. D'Esterre Darby, 49 killed, 148 wounded. Captain John Hopkins (mortally wounded), Second-Lieutenant John Wright.

*Majestic*, 74 guns, Captain G. B. Westcott (killed), 50 killed, 143 wounded. Captain George Dunsmuire, First-Lieutenant Robert Hart.

*Leander*, 50 guns, Captain T. B. Thompson, 14 wounded. No marine officer.

*Culloden*, 74 guns, Captain T. Troubridge. Captain-Lieutenant James Knox, Lieutenant Richard Barford.

*Alexander*, 74 guns, Captain A. J. Ball, 14 killed, 58 wounded. Captain John Creswell (wounded), First-Lieutenants Thomas B. Adair and John Scobell.

*Swiftsure*, 74 guns, Captain B. Hallowell, 7 killed, 22 wounded. Captain Charles Allen, First-Lieutenant James Short, Second-Lieutenant John Witts.

Total,—218 killed, and 678 wounded.

This glorious victory obtained rewards for the officers of every class. The rear-admiral was created a peer of Great Britain by the title of Baron Nelson of the Nile and of Burham Thorpe, with a pension of £2000 *per annum* from the Parliament of England, and £1000 from that of Ireland. The senior lieutenants of each ship, and many inferior officers, were promoted; but the only reward conferred upon the marines was the brevet rank of major on the senior officer serving in the squadron,—Captain Thomas Oldfield.

It is related of the late Sir John Savage, who was captain of marines on board the *Orion* in the eventful battle before us, that when the ship was approaching her station, he thus laconically addressed his men as they were drawn up on the poop:—

My lads, do you see these ships; and do you see that land? Well, the ships are those of the enemy, and that is the land of Egypt;

and if you don't give those Frenchmen a d—d good licking, you will very soon be in the house of bondage!

The 50-gun ship *Leander* sailed from before Alexandria on the 6th of August, with the despatches from Rear-Admiral Sir Horatio Nelson to the commander-in-chief on the Mediterranean station; and on the 18th, when within six miles of the west end of Goza de Candia, discovered a large ship coming towards her with a fine breeze from the southward, whilst the *Leander* lay becalmed. The stranger was the French 74-gun ship *Généreux*, which had escaped from the Battle of the Nile, mounting 80 guns, with a crew of 936 men and boys; while the *Leander* mounted 51 guns of smaller calibre, and had only 282 men and boys on board.

At 9 a.m. the *Généreux* ranged up within half gunshot on the *Leander's* larboard and weather quarter, both ships being under a press of sail; but finding an action inevitable, the *Leander* took in her canvas, and hauled up to bring her broadside to bear. On a shot being fired by the *Généreux*, a vigorous cannonade commenced on both sides, the ships nearing each other until 10 h. 30 m. a.m., when the French ship struck the *Leander* on her larboard bow, and dropped alongside. A spirited and well-directed fire from the marines on the poop of the Leander, commanded by Sergeant James Dair, (no officer having arrived on board since the death of Lieutenant Raby Robinson, who was killed at Teneriffe,) and from the small-arm men of the quarter-deck, prevented the enemy in their attempts to board.

A light air springing up, the *Généreux* forged ahead and disentangled herself from the *Leander*, now lying with her mizenmast over the starboard quarter, her fore top-mast over the larboard bow, and both her lower yards on the booms. In this crippled condition the Leander, by the aid of her sprit-sail, wore under the stern of her antagonist, and raked her with great effect. The cannonade continued without intermission until 3 h. 30 m. p.m., when the *Généreux*, by the aid of a light breeze, was enabled to station herself on the larboard bow of her opponent. The *Leander* was now totally ungovernable; not a stick standing, save the bowsprit and the shattered remains of the fore and main-masts, and the ship's hull was cut to pieces. In this defenceless state the *Leander*, on being hailed by her opponent, signified she had surrendered. Her loss amounted to 35 killed and 57 wounded, out of a reduced crew of 282 men and boys. Of this number Sergeant James Dair and 7 marines were killed, and 9 privates wounded.

The defence of this nobly-fought ship is so unparalleled, in contending six hours against an enemy of such superior force, that we give the comparative statement of their armament:—

|  | Leander. | Généreux |
|---|---|---|
| Broadside guns number | 26 | 40 |
| lbs. | 432 | 1024 |
| Crew number | 282 | 936 |
| Size tons | 1052 | 1926 |

In July 1795, Sir Sidney Smith, when in command of the *Diamond* frigate, took possession of the two islands of St. Marcouf, situated off the River Isigny, on the coast of Normandy, and about four miles from the shore. The islands, which are close to one another, and each about 200 yards in length and 120 in breadth, were mounted with several pieces of cannon, and garrisoned by a detachment of invalids and a party of marines, under Lieutenants J. Maughan, — Ensor, and — Lawrence, with a proportion of seamen; and the whole under the command of lieutenant Charles P. Price, of the navy.

On the night of the 7th of April an expedition, consisting of thirty-three flat-bottomed boats carrying troops, accompanied by some gun-brigs, sailed from Havre to attack these islands; but meeting with the *Diamond* and *Hydra* frigates, they were driven back and stood into Caen, where they were reinforced by seven heavy gun-brigs and forty sail of boats. After three weeks  blockade, this formidable flotilla reached the road of La Hogue, which is situated about halfway between Cape Barfleur and the islands, and they waited until the neap tides, when the current would offer less opposition to their progress.

On the 6th of May, at midnight, the guard-boat made the signal for the enemy's approach, and although the French officers were heard giving their orders, the night was so dark that none of the boats were visible. The attacking force consisted of fifty-two gun-brigs and flat-bottomed boats, having on board above 5000 men. At daybreak on the 7th, the flotilla was seen drawn up in line opposite to the south-west front of the western redoubt, and a fire was instantly opened upon them from seventeen pieces of cannon, consisting of 4 four-pounders, 2 six-pounders, and 6 twenty-four pounder long guns, and 2 thirty-two pounder carronades. The brigs remained at the distance of three hundred yards, in order to batter the redoubt with their long guns, while the boats rowed up until within musket-shot of the battery; but the discharge of round, grape, and canister, poured such destruction among them, that they were soon compelled to seek their safety in flight. Six or seven boats were seen to go down, and one small flat was afterwards towed in, bottom upwards, on board of which some papers were found, stating that she had a crew of 144 persons, including 129 men of the second Boulogne battalion.

The loss sustained by the British in this affair amounted to 1 marine killed, 2 marines and 2 seamen wounded; a loss much less in amount than might have been expected from the fire of upwards of 80 long guns, many of which were thirty-six, and none less than eighteen-pounders. According to the French account, their loss amounted to several hundred in killed and wounded. Owing to the calm state of the weather, the British squadron were unable to intercept the flotilla, and consequently they got back to the Hogue without further loss. A French squadron, consisting of the *Hoche* 74 guns, Commodore Bompart, with eight frigates, having on board 3000 troops with a large train of artillery, sailed from Brest on the evening of the 6th of September, with an intention of invading Ireland. On the following morning they were discovered by the *Ethalion*, who continued to watch their movements; and by the time the French ships arrived on the Irish coast, a considerable British force was in pursuit. On the 11th of October, when off Tory Island, the leading frigate got sight of the enemy; and on the 12th, at daybreak, the British found themselves in a situation to prevent their escape. The French ships were formed in an irregular line ahead, thus:—

*Semillante* 36, *Romaine* 40, *Bellone* 36, *Immortalité* 40, *Loire* 40, *Hoche* 74, *Coquille* 36, and *Embuscade* 36 guns.

The British squadron consisted of the following ships:—

*Canada*, 74 guns, Captain Sir J. B. Warren, 1 wounded. Captain William Patten, First-Lieutenant Mark Oates, Second-Lieutenants Thomas Moore and Richard Bagnold.

*Foudroyant*, 80 guns, Captain Sir J. T. Bayard, 9 wounded. Captain George Wolfe, First-Lieutenant Richard Bunce, Second-Lieutenants Joseph Collins and Zachaeus Miller.

*Robust*, 74 guns, Captain Edward Thornborough, 10 killed, 40 wounded. Captain Richard Williams, First-Lieutenant W. Cottle (mortally wounded), Second-Lieut. Charles Coleman.

*Melampus*, 36 guns, Captain Graham Moore, 1 wounded. Lieutenants Francis Hole and James Isherwood.

*Magnanime*, 44 guns, Captain the Hon. M. de Courcy, 7 wounded.

Lieutenant W. H. Snowe, Second-Lieutenant Thomas Patterson. *Ethalion*, 38 guns, Captain G. Countess, 1 killed, 4 wounded.

*Anson*, 44 guns, Captain P. C. Durham, 2 killed, 13 wounded. First-Lieutenants Thomas Deering and A. Bell (wounded).

*Amelia*, 38 guns, Captain the Hon. C. Herbert. First-Lieutenant James Coles.

At 7 a.m. on the 12th, the *Robust*, followed by the *Magnanime*, edged away, and at 7h. 20m. they became closely engaged with the *Embuscade* and *Coquille*, and then passed on to the *Hoche*. The *Foudroyant* coming up, and discharging a few broadsides at the *Loire, Immortalité*, and *Bellone*, who had been keeping up a galling fire upon the *Magnanime* as she ranged ahead, and to leeward of the *Robust*; the three French frigates ceased their annoyance, and made sail to the southwest. The *Hoche*, after sustaining the attack of the principal part of the British squadron, but more particularly of the *Robust* and *Foudroyant*, struck her colours at 10 h. 50 m. a.m.; and out of 1237 men and boys, the *Hoche* lost 270 in killed and wounded. The *Bellone*, after receiving the fire of several ships, defended herself against the *Ethalion* for nearly two hours; nor did she surrender until her rigging and sails were cut to pieces, and her loss, out of 519 men, amounted to 20 killed and 45 wounded. The *Embuscade*, out of 486, lost 15 killed and 26 wounded; and the *Coquille*, having 18 killed and 31 wounded out of 507, also surrendered to the British squadron. The remaining five frigates, as they stood away to the westward, successively engaged the *Anson*, who had 2 men killed and 11 wounded, and her masts and rigging much cut up.

On the 14th the *Resolue*, at 1 a.m., was fallen in with by the *Melampus*, and after a feeble resistance was captured. On the 17th the *Loire* was engaged by the 32-gun frigate *Mermaid*, Captain James N. Newman, and *Kangaroo* 18-gun brig, Captain Edward Brace. After a spirited action, in which the *Mermaid* had her mizen-mast and main top-mast shot away, and was otherwise much damaged, with loss of 3 killed and 13 wounded; and having also disabled the brig, the *Loire* put before the wind and was soon out of sight, although her mast, sails, and rigging gave evidence of the effect produced by the animated fire of her opponent. Lieutenant Mortimer Timson of the marines was serving on board the *Mermaid*.

The *Loire* had only escaped from one antagonist to fall into the hands of another, for at daylight on the 18th, having lost her main and fore top-mast, she was discovered by the 44-gun frigate *Anson*, Captain P. C. Durham; who had lost her mizenmast, main-yard, and main cross-trees in her previous action with the French ship and her four companions. The *Anson* commenced the action at 10 h. 30 m., and the two disabled ships continued the contest until 11 h. 45 m. a.m., when the *Kangaroo* bore up and fired her broadside. Shortly afterwards the *Loire's* mizen-mast came down, and she surrendered. The *Anson* had 2 men killed; First-Lieutenant Wm. A. Bell of the marines, and 12 wounded. The *Loire*, out of a complement of 624 men, had 46 killed and 71 wounded. Captain Durham speaks highly of First-Lieutenant Deering of the marines.

We have now disposed of five frigates of M. Bompart's squadron; a sixth, the *Immortalité*, when on her cruise to Brest on the 28th of October, was pursued by the 38-gun frigate *Fisgard*, Captain T. B. Martin, and brought to action at 11 h. 30 m. a.m. So effectual was the fire of the French frigate, that in less than half an hour the *Fisgard* was rendered ungovernable, having her sails and rigging cut to pieces; but by active exertion she was again alongside of the enemy at half-past one o clock. The firing was renewed with great fury, and continued until 3 p.m.; when the *Immortalité*, with her mizen-mast over her side, and having six feet water in the hold, her gallant captain with 54 killed and 61 wounded out of a complement of 580, was compelled to haul down her colours. The *Fisgard*, out of 281 men and boys, lost 10 killed; Lieutenant Mark Anthony Gerrard of the marines, and 23 wounded. The two remaining frigates, the *Semillante* and *Romaine*, reached the ports of l'Orient and Brest.

On the 29th of June the *Jason* and *Pique* frigates, Captains Charles Sterling and David Milne, when off the Penmarcks, at 7 p.m. chased the French 40-gun frigate *Seine*, which had sailed from the Isle of France, and was making for the first French port. The pursuit continued throughout the day, and at 9 p.m. the *Pique* commenced firing her bow guns. At 11 p.m. she ranged up alongside, and a running fight continued for two hours and thirty minutes, when the British frigate had her main top-mast shot away, and consequently dropped astern. The *Jason* now coming up, took the ground; and the *Pique*, when on the larboard side of her consort, also stuck fast.

Almost at the same instant the land near Pointe de la Trenche was seen ahead, and the French frigate was also aground, and totally dismasted. As the tide rose, the *Jason* swung with her stern towards the enemy's broadside, which cut up her rigging and sails, and she sustained the loss of her second-lieutenant and 6 men killed; her captain and 11 wounded. The *Jason* was soon able to bring her guns to bear; and on the approach of the *Mermaid* frigate, the *Seine* struck her colours, having sustained a loss of 170 killed and 100 wounded, out of a complement of 610 men. Every effort to get the *Pique* afloat proving unavailing, she was abandoned by her crew, whose loss amounted to 2 killed and 6 wounded. First-Lieutenant R. A. Symes was serving on board the *Jason*.

The 32-gun frigate *Ambuscade*, Captain Henry Jenkins, mounting 32 long twelve-pounders, and 8 carronade twelve-pounders—total 40 guns, with a reduced crew of 190 men and boys, was cruising off Bordeaux on the 14th of June at 7 a. m., when a sail was discovered running down before the wind. At 9 a.m., when the stranger had arrived nearly within gunshot, she hauled to the wind and made sail to get away; but the *Ambuscade* immediately went in pursuit, and at 11 h. 30 m. she was sufficiently near to exchange shots with the French corvette *Baïonnaise*, mounting 24 long eight-pounders, 6 long sixes, and 2 brass thirty-six pounders—total 32 guns, having a crew of 250 men and boys. The French ship, after shortening sail, commenced the action, which had continued an hour, when an unfortunate accident happened on board the *Ambuscade*: one of her main-deck guns burst, which did great damage, and wounded 11 men.

The corvette, on seeing the confusion on board the British ship, made sail; but the *Ambuscade* was presently alongside to leeward. At this time, the *Baïonnaise* being much cut up in her sails and rigging, and having sustained a considerable loss in officers and men, with no chance of escape, laid the *Ambuscade* on board, carrying away with her bowsprit the British ship's starboard quarter-deck barricade, mizzen-shrouds, and mizen-mast, which in its fall unshipped the wheel. The *Baïonnaise* then dropped under the *Ambuscade's* stern, but still remaining foul, by a grappling iron caught in the latter's rudder chain, the French troops from their bowsprit scoured the decks of the *Ambuscade*, whilst the British marines kept up a smart fire in return; but in a short time Lieutenant Dawson, Captain Jenkins and Lieutenant Sinclair of the marines, were severely wounded; and they were scarcely taken below when Mr. Brown, the master, was killed.

The only surviving lieutenant, Joseph Briggs, who had come from a sick cot to take part in the action, was wounded in the head, and the command of the ship now devolved on Mr. Wm. B. Murray, the purser. At this moment an explosion of some cartridges on the rudder-head, occasioned by firing a gun from the cabin windows into the bow of the *Baïonnaise*, produced a panic, which enabled the French crew from the bowsprit to reach the British quarter-deck, and after a short struggle the *Ambuscade* surrendered, with the loss of 10 killed and 36 wounded. The *Baïonnaise* had 30 killed; her commander, Captain Richer, and 30 men badly wounded.

## CHAPTER 6

# From the Year 1799 to 1801

Notwithstanding the losses which France had sustained during the past year, there were great preparations in the French arsenals for the equipment and increase of her navy; and measures were taken for the immediate construction of sixteen ships of the line, and eighteen heavy frigates.

The naval force of Great Britain continued on the same establishment as the preceding year; and the parliamentary vote was for 120,000 seamen, including 20,000 marines.

On the 9th of February the 32-gun frigate *Daedalus*, Captain Henry L. Ball, on the East India station, fell in with the French 36-gun frigate *Prudente*, (but mounting only 30 guns). At 10 minutes past noon the *Daedalus* bore up across the stern of the French frigate within pistol-shot, and after raking her, luffed up to leeward; and thus, close alongside, the two ships engaged with great spirit. In about a quarter of an hour the mizen-mast of the *Prudente* fell over her quarter; she nevertheless continued the action until 1 h. 21 m. p.m., when being much cut up in masts and sails, the French frigate hailed to say they had surrendered. Out of a crew of 301 men and boys, she lost 27 killed and 22 wounded. The *Daedalus* suffered but little, and had only 2 killed and 12 wounded, out of a crew of 212. Lieutenant Edward Jolliffe of the marines was serving on board the *Daedalus*.

On the 9th of June the 32-gun frigate *Success*, Captain Peard, chased a Spanish *polacre* into the harbour of La Seloa, near Cape Creux. Three boats were detached under the command of Lieutenant Facey, assisted by Lieutenant Stupart and Lieutenant John Davison of the marines, to bring out the *polacre*, which proved to be the *Bella Aurora*, mounting 10 carriage guns, with a crew of 110 men, surrounded by a boarding netting, and supported by a battery and a body of men at small árms on the shore. Notwithstanding this formidable preparation, she was gallantly boarded and brought out; but this bold enterprise was attended with a serious loss to the British, who had 4 seamen killed, and Lieutenant Stupart with 8 men badly wounded. For his services on this occasion Lieutenant Facey was promoted to the rank of commander.

On the 11th of December the French 40-gun frigate *Preneuse* was pursued by the *Tremendous* 74, and 50-gun ship *Adamant*, who were cruising off Port Louis, Isle of France; and finding it impossible to escape from the *Adamant*, she ran ashore on the west side of the River Tombeau, near to some batteries, and about three miles from Port Louis. The frigate cut away all her masts, and at 3 h. 30 m. p.m., in conjunction with the batteries, fired upon the *Adamant*, who was working up towards her. At 5h. 30 m. the *Adamant* commenced engaging, and after 15 minutes the *Preneuse* signified she had surrendered. At 7 p. m. three boats were sent to destroy the French frigate, under the orders of Lieutenant Edward Grey, accompanied by Lieutenants Walker and Symes, and by Lieutenant John Owen of the marines.

At 8 p.m. the French batteries opened their fire of shot and shell at the boats, and at the *Adamant* as she was working up towards the object of attack. About 9 p.m., just as the boats were getting alongside of the *Preneuse*, two launches filled with men pulled from her to the shore, whilst Lieutenant Grey and his party, under a heavy fire from the batteries, gallantly boarded the frigate; and having removed Captain L'Hermite, with 14 officers and the few men that remained on board, she was set on fire and destroyed, and the boats returned without sustaining any loss.

The appearance of a British squadron on the coast of Egypt in the latter part of October, assisted by some Russian and Turkish frigates, induced Buonaparte to strengthen Damietta, Rosetta, and particularly Alexandria; and having appointed General Marmont governor of the latter city, the general-in-chief busied himself in forming schemes that had for their object the junction of the Red and Mediterranean seas, by means of a canal through the isthmus of Suez: and in order to ascertain the practicability of such a plan, Buonaparte resolved to proceed thither himself, first sending a detachment of troops to take possession of the town and neighbourhood.

On the 2nd of November, General Bon set out on that expedition; and on the 8th the advanced division, under Eugene Beauharnois, entered the seaport of Suez, which is a small town situated at the northern extremity of the western arm of the Red Sea, distant about 30 leagues from Cairo, and nearly the same from the Mediterranean. Buonaparte was prevented following General Bon by the plague breaking out among his troops, and by the information he had just acquired of the hostile intentions of Turkey.

Buonaparte quitted Cairo on the 25th of December, and on the 27th arrived at Suez, attended by the members of the "Institute of Egypt." Immediately proceeding to reconnoitre the town, harbour, and the neighbouring coast, he afterwards crossed the Red Sea by means of a ford, only practicable at low water, in order to reach a spot which the Arabs still, (1845), call the "Fountain of Moses," and where, according to the traditions of the country, lie the rocks which, on being touched, produced water to the followers of the prophet. In their way back to Suez, the general and his escort nearly suffered the fate of Pharoah and his army: the ford, which had been crossed with such ease in the morning, being now covered by the rapid rise of the tide, the travellers were compelled to descend to the bottom of the gulph; and here, owing to some mistake about the depth of the water, Buonaparte was under the necessity of being carried on the shoulders of his guide, and it was not without difficulty that they succeeded in effecting their escape.

After various surveys of the locality of Suez, Buonaparte was unexpectedly called back to Cairo; for the officer, who a month previous to his departure for Suez had been sent to Achmet Djezzar, had returned without obtaining an audience. Indignant at this treatment, the general sent the following letter to Djezzar:—

I do not desire to make war if you are not my enemy, but you must explain yourself. Your continuing to afford refuge to Ibrahim Bey, and allowing him to remain on the frontiers of Egypt, will be considered by me as an act of hostility, and I shall in that case march to Acre. If you are disposed to live in peace with me, you will remove Ibrahim forty leagues from the frontiers of Egypt, and let there be a free commerce between Damietta and Syria. On those terms I shall respect your sovereignty, and allow a free commerce by land between Egypt and Syria.

This letter met with no better fate than the message sent by Colonel Beauvoisins; consequently Buonaparte determined on immediate preparations for fulfilling his promise to Djezzar; believing that by such proceeding he would gain favour with the *grand signior*, to whom the *pacha* of Acre had long been a rebellious subject. The arrival of a body of troops in the castle of El-Arish, situated just within the frontiers of Egypt, quickened the movements of Buonaparte, who marched from the neighbourhood of Cairo in the early part of January 1799, with an army of 13,000 men, accompanied by 37 field-pieces, and 11 howitzers, to effect the conquest of Syria; and Generals Regnier, Kléber, Bon, Lannes, and Murat had commands under Buonaparte in this expedition. The remainder of the army, about 17,000 men, was scattered over the different provinces of Lower Egypt; and by the 18th of February the whole of the army destined to invade Syria had assembled before El-Arish.

Commodore Sir Sidney Smith, who jointly with his brother, Mr. Spencer Smith, had been invested with the rank of minister-plenipotentiary to the Sublime Porte, and had recently been at Constantinople arranging a plan of active co-operation with the Turks in Egypt, arrived off Alexandria on the 3rd of March in the 74-gun ship *Tigre*, and superseded Captain Troubridge; who on the 7th sailed in the *Culloden*, leaving the *Theseus* 74, and *Alliance* frigate (*en flute*) on the station. On the same evening an express arrived from Djezzar with an account of the invasion of Syria by Buonaparte, and of his having that very day carried Jaffa by storm. In consequence of this intelligence, the commodore on the following day despatched the *Theseus* to Acre, with Colonel Phelipeaux, a French Royalist officer of engineers: the *Tigre* meanwhile remained off Alexandria, to observe the enemy's movements.

The removal of most of the vessels in the old port to the eastern or new harbour, gave intimation that some naval expedition was in preparation; and this supposition being confirmed by a neutral vessel which had sailed from Alexandria on the 9th, it determined the commodore to detach the *Marianne* gun-vessel on the following day to reconnoitre the coast to the eastward, and to join him in the road of Caïffa; a port about eight miles south-east of Acre, whither the *Tigre* immediately proceeded. Having been joined by the *Marianne* on the 15th off Caïffa, the *Tigre* anchored in the bay of Acre, where the *Theseus* had arrived two days before. On the 16th Sir Sidney landed, and commenced putting the town of Acre, with its rotten and ruined walls, in the best possible state to resist the attacks of an European army: and thus encouraged, the *pacha* and the garrison determined to make a vigorous defence.

The *Theseus* was detached on the 17th to reconnoitre the coast to the southward, while Sir Sydney proceeded with the boats of the *Tigre* to the anchorage of Caïffa, near the promontory of Mount Carmel, in order to intercept the maritime portion of the French expedition; but as the their advance-guard, mounted on asses and dromedaries, were discovered by the sea side, Sir Sydney returned to the *Tigre*, and sent the launch with a 32-pounder carronade, under Lieutenant John Bushby, to the mouth of the River Kerdanneh, to defend the fort.

On the 18th, at daybreak, the launch opened a fire on the French troops, which compelled them to retire precipitately to the skirts of Mount Carmel. The main body, finding the route near the sea thus exposed, approached by the Nazareth road, but not without being harassed by the Samaritan Arabs; and being driven by the fire from the British ships, directed at the trenches, from making an attack along the coast to the northward, the French invested the town of Acre to the north-east, where the defences were much stronger.

On the 18th a French flotilla, consisting of a corvette and nine sailing gun-vessels, were seen from the *Tigre*, who after a chase of three hours captured seven gun-vessels, mounting together 34 guns, laden with battering cannon and every kind of siege equipage, which they had brought from Damietta. The French guns intended for the attack of Acre were now landed for its defence, and the captured gunboats were manned and sent to co-operate in harassing the enemy and cutting off his supplies. For five successive days and nights the gun-vessels were occupied in annoying the French, and rendering assistance to the Turks. On the 21st an unsuccessful attempt was made to cut out of the port of Caïffa four *djerms*, or lighters, which had put in there on the 18th from Alexandria, having on board supplies for the French Army; and at 10 a.m. the boats of the two line of battle ships, covered by some of the gun-vessels, proceeded to the attack. In this gallant though unfortunate attempt, 4 midshipmen and 8 seamen were killed; 1 midshipman and 26 seamen wounded, 8 of whom, with twelve others, were taken prisoners. Among the officers who distinguished themselves on this occasion, we find the name of Lieutenant Charles Frederick Burton of the marines.

On the 20th of March, the French before Acre opened their trenches against the front or saliant angle, on the east side of the town, and a constant cannonade was kept upon that point until the 1st of April; when the breach which the enemy had made in the tower appearing to them practicable, and conceiving that the counterscarp had suffered from a mine they had sprung, the French troops resolutely advanced to the assault. On both these points they were deceived; whilst the Turks, stimulated by the heroic example of the British seamen and marines, continued to pour down a shower of stones and grenades upon the assailants, and drove them back with considerable loss.

The violence of the weather, and the unsheltered state of the anchorage, compelled the *Theseus* and *Tigre* to put to sea; and on their return, which was on the 6th of April, it was discovered that the French had pushed their approaches to the counterscarp, and even to the ditch of the north-east angle of the town, and were mining the tower, so as to increase the breach which they had made by the fire of their field-pieces.

Although the fire from the guns captured from the enemy, and which had been admirably mounted under the direction of Colonel Phelipeaux and Captain Wilmot of the *Alliance*, appeared to slacken the efforts of the enemy, yet much danger was apprehended from the mine. A sortie was therefore determined upon, and the seamen and marines of the squadron were to force their way into the mine, while the Turkish troops attacked the enemy's trenches on the right and left.

Just before daybreak on the 7th of April, the columns moved forward to the attack, but the impetuosity and noise of the Turks rendered abortive the attempt to surprise the besiegers; yet, in other respects, the Mahometans performed their part to admiration. Lieutenant J. W. Wright received two balls in his right arm, whilst leading the seamen pioneers; he nevertheless proceeded to the bottom of the mine, and pulling down the supporters, destroyed as much as could be effected in its present state. Major Douglas and the marines were highly distinguished in this enterprise; and they ably supported the seamen in the desperate service, bringing off the wounded under a tremendous fire from the enemy.

The loss sustained by the British was 1 major of marines, Thomas Oldfield, and 2 privates killed; Lieutenant John W. Wright of the navy, Lieutenant George Beatty of the marines, 2 midshipmen, 1 sergeant, 6 privates of marines, and 12 seamen wounded. The return of the detachment to the garrison was ably covered by the fire of the *Theseus*, in the excellent position she had taken for that purpose: the Turks, as proofs of their prowess, brought in 60 Frenchmen's heads, and a number of muskets and entrenching tools.

General Berthier, who commanded a division of the enemy, affords the best testimony of the merits of the marines upon this occasion; and we therefore, without comment, give an extract from a letter of that gallant officer, dated from the French camp:—

On the 18th *Germinal* (7th of April), the enemy at break of day attacked our left and centre; each column was headed by British marines belonging to the ships, and their colours were seen waving with those of the *Djezzar*, and the batteries were all manned by Englishmen. The enemy attempted to surprise our advanced posts, but their design was seen through: we received them with a brisk fire from our parallels, and all that appeared were either killed or wounded. The enemy ultimately retired without gaining an inch towards destroying our works. The central column acted with more obstinacy, and their object was to penetrate to the entrance of our mine; they were commanded by Major Thomas Oldfield, who advanced boldly towards the entrance of the mine at the head of some of his intrepid countrymen. They attacked like heroes, and were received by heroes,—death only checked their bold career: the remainder retreated, and took refuge in the fortress. The approaches of our parallels remained covered with the dead bodies of English and of Turks. The body of Major Oldfield was carried off by our grenadiers, who brought him to headquarters; but he had expired before their arrival. His sword, to which he had done so much honour, was also honoured after his fall: it remains in the hands of one of our grenadiers. He was buried amongst us, and has carried with him the esteem of the whole French Army.

This eulogium from an enemy, and a soldier whose proud renown is associated with that of Napoleon, is the noblest epitaph that the brave could aspire to.

Sir Sidney Smith, at a meeting of the anniversary of the Naval Asylum, held on the 2nd of June, 1802, offered a tribute to the memory of this gallant soldier. After speaking of the many virtues of Captain Miller, Sir Sidney thus enlarges upon the merits of his departed friend, Major Oldfield:—

The next is Major Oldfield of the marines. I will tell the company where the body of this brave man was contended for, and they will judge where, and how, he died. It was in a sortie of the garrison of St. Jean d'Acre, when attacked by General Buonaparte, that Major Oldfield, who commanded a column, was missing. On our troops advancing, he was found—his body was found at the mouth of one of the enemy's mines, and at the foot of their works: our brave men hooked him by the neck-cloth as he lay dead, to draw him off; the enemy at the same time pierced him with a halbert, and each party struggled for his body. The neck-cloth gave way, and the enemy succeeded in dragging to their works this brave man; and here I must do them the justice which such gallant foes are justly entitled to: they buried him with all the honours of war!

When Buonaparte commenced the siege of Acre, he had no other artillery than field-pieces; but the squadron of Admiral Perrée, which sailed from Alexandría, consisting of three frigates and two corvettes, having on board a quantity of battering cannon and other munitions of war, reached Jaffa in safety; and in addition to these, by Buonaparte's desire, he landed 4 eighteen-pounders from the *Junon.*

The garrison of Acre continued to make occasional sorties, under the protection of field-pieces in the ships' boats, until the evening of the 1st of May; when the French, after several hours' cannonade from 23 pieces of artillery, including 9 battering twenty-four and eighteen-pounders brought by Admiral Perrée's squadron, and which reached the besieging army on the 27th of April overland from Jaffa, made a fourth desperate attempt to mount the breach, which was now much extended. The *Tigre* and *Theseus* were stationed on either side of the town, so as to flank the walls; whilst the gunboats were moored in the best manner for opening on the enemy's trenches.

Opposed by this destructive fire, the French troops, notwithstanding their determined bravery, were repulsed with a heavy loss. On the part of the British, Captain David Wilmot of the *Alliance* was killed by a musket-shot, as he was mounting a howitzer on the breach; a midshipman and 4 seamen were also slain, and Lieutenant William Knight with 8 men wounded: in addition to this loss they had to regret the death of Colonel Phelipeaux, from excessive fatigue and anxiety. The French continued to batter in breach with progressive effect, although they had been repulsed with great slaughter in their several attempts to storm: nor were they more successful in their attacks on the two ravelins that had been erected by Sir Sidney to flank the nearest approaches of the besiegers, which were only a few yards distant. The frequent sorties from the garrison impeded the enemy in their covering works, and these were only suspended during the intervals which were caused by the excessive fatigue on both sides.

On the 7th of May, and the fifty-first day of the siege, the long-expected reinforcement from Rhodes made its appearance in the offing, consisting of some Turkish corvettes, and above twenty transports with troops on board. The approach of this reinforcement induced Buonaparte to order a vigorous attack, in the hope of getting possession of the town before the troops could disembark: the fire from the French batteries suddenly increased considerably, whilst the flanking fire from the British afloat was less effectual, owing to the *epaulments* and traverses of great thickness, which the enemy had thrown up to protect themselves. The attacking columns of the enemy suffered severely from the fire of a brass eighteen-pounder, under the direction of Mr. Schroder, master's mate, and a twenty-four pounder in the north ravelin under Mr. Jones, midshipman; these being within grape range, added to the Turkish musketry, did great execution.

Two *djerms* lying in the mole, mounting 2 sixty-eight pounders, worked under the able direction of Mr. James Bray, carpenter of the *Tigre*, threw shells into the centre of the attacking column with evident effect, and checked its advance; nevertheless, the besiegers gained ground, and effected a lodgement in the second story of the north-east tower, the upper part of which was entirely battered down, and its ruins formed the ascent from the ditch by which they mounted. As the day appeared on the 8th, the French standard was seen flying on the outer angle of the tower; and the enemy, having covered themselves by this lodgement, and the approach to it by traverses across the ditch, the fire from the besieged became of less effect, and even the flanking fire from the gunboats did but little execution. Those traverses were constructed by the French under the fire from the fortress during the preceding night, and were composed of sand-bags with the bodies of the dead built in with them, and were so high that their bayonets only were visible above them.

At this crisis the troops of Hassan Bey were in the boats, and half-way to the shore: an effort was therefore necessary, to preserve the place until this reinforcement could take their stations on the walls. Sir Sidney now landed with the ships' boats at the mole, and led the seamen, armed with pikes, to the breach, where they found a few Turks hurling stones on the heads of the assailants, who falling down the slope, impeded the progress of the rest. Fresh parties of the French ascended to the assault, the heap of ruins between the two contending forces serving as abreast-work for both; and here the muzzles of their muskets touched, and the spear-heads of the standards locked. Djezzar Pacha was sitting in his palace, rewarding those who brought him the heads of his enemies, and distributing musket cartridges with his own hands; but hearing that Sir Sidney and his brave companions were on the breach, the old man hastened thither and pulled them down with violence, saying, that if any harm happened to his English friends, all would be lost. This amicable contest occasioned a rush of Turks to the spot, which fortunate occurrence gained time for the arrival of the first division of Hassan Bey's troops.

Sir Sidney, having overcome the *pacha's* repugnance to the admission of any troops but his Albanians into the gardens of the seraglio, and as this spot was now an important post, as occupying the *terre-pleine* of the rampart, the commodore introduced 1000 men of the Chifflic regiment, armed with bayonets and disciplined after the European method. The garrison, animated by the appearance of such a reinforcement, were soon in sufficient numbers to defend the breach. Sir Sidney then proposed to the *pacha* to allow the Chifflic regiment to make a sally, and take the assailants in flank: the Turks rushed out with much bravery, but not being calculated for such a movement, they were driven back with great loss, whilst the town gate was efficaciously protected by the sixty-eight pounders of the *Tigre*.

The sortie had the effect of obliging the besiegers to show themselves above their parapets, and consequently exposed to the flanking fire of the British, which brought down numbers; while those remaining were killed, or dispersed by the grenades thrown among them.

After this repulse, the enemy commenced a new breach, by an incessant fire directed to the southward of the lodgement: every shot knocking down whole sheets of the wall, which was much less solid than that of the tower, and on which they had expended so much time and ammunition. At this moment, the group of French generals, which the shells from the sixty-eight pounders had frequently dispersed, was assembled on Richard Coeur-de-Lion's mount, and Buonaparte was distinguishable in the centre of them; his gesticulations indicated a renewal of the attack, and as an *aide-de-camp* was despatched to the camp, it showed he only waited a reinforcement. Sir Sidney immediately directed the ships of Hassan Bey to take their stations in the shoal water to the southward, and made the *Tigre* signal to get under weigh, and join the *Theseus* to the northward.

A little before sunset a dense column appeared advancing slowly to the breach, which they mounted unmolested, and then descended from the ramparts into the *pacha's* garden. Here, in a few minutes, the most advanced of the Frenchmen lay headless trunks,—the sabre, with the dagger in the other hand, proving more than a match for the bayonet. The rest of the assailants precipitately retreated, and their leader, General Lannes, who was seen daringly encouraging his men to mount the breach, was carried off wounded by a musket-ball, while General Rambeaud was among the killed.

In the dusk of the evening the British uniform was mistaken for the French by the newly arrived Turks, and in consequence of this confusion many a sabre blow was parried by the British officers; and Major Douglas, with Messrs. Ives and Jones, nearly lost their lives while forcing their way through a torrent of fugitives. At length the *pacha's* exertions restored confidence; and both parties being worn out with fatigue, an end was put to this contest, which had lasted twenty-five hours.

In this splendid defence the British had 1 seaman killed, 7 wounded, and Mr. Lamb, midshipman, with 3 seamen, drowned. Sir Sidney now addressed a circular to the princes and chiefs of the Christians of Mount Lebanon, and also to the *sheiks* of the Druses, exhorting them to cut off the supplies from the French camp. Two ambassadors were immediately sent by the Syrians, and active measures were taken to prevent any supplies arriving overland; while Buonaparte's career further northward was effectually stopped by a warlike people, inhabiting a country now become impenetrable by their determined resistance.

General Kléber's division, just arrived from the fords of the Jordan, was intended for the next attempt to mount the breach of Acre. To frustrate that movement, another sortie was resolved upon; and during the night of the 19th the Turkish Chifflic regiment, led by its Lieutenant-Colonel Soliman Aga, rushed out of the gates, and gained the third parallel of the besiegers; and their impetuosity carried them to the second trench, where, although they lost some of their standards, four of the enemy's cannon were spiked before they retreated. By this movement Kléber's division, instead of mounting the breach, had full occupation during three hours' conflict, nor did the French recover their works without sustaining a heavy loss.

Since their last failure, the French grenadiers refused to mount the breach over the dead bodies of their unburied countrymen; consequently a flag of truce was sent into the town by an Arab *dervise*, with a letter to the *pacha* proposing a cessation of arms for the purpose of burying the dead, the stench of which had become intolerable, and threatened the existence of every person on both sides. While the answer was under consideration, a discharge of shot and shells announced another assault; but, fortunately, the garrison was prepared to receive them, and the assailants only contributed to increase the number of the dead bodies under the walls. Sir Sidney rescued the Arab from the indignation of the Turks, by conveying him on board the *Tigre*, whence he was sent back to the French general with a message that must have made the army sensible of the well-merited reproof.

The French, having abandoned all hopes of success, raised the siege of Acre on the 20th; and on the 21st of May they made a precipitate retreat, leaving twenty-three pieces of cannon (after burning their carriages) in the hands of the besieged. The army reached Cantoura on the afternoon of the 21st, the ruins of Caesarea on the 22nd, and Jaffa on the 24th: here it rested three days, and reached Gaza on the 30th. On the 1st of June it entered the desert, and halted on the 2nd at El-Arish, where Buonaparte left a garrison: the main body then continued its march, arriving at Cairo on the 14th. Berthier states the loss of the French Army, during the last four months, at 700 men who died of disease, 500 killed in the different actions, and about 1800 wounded; it is probable, however, that it greatly exceeded this statement.

The British seamen and marines rejoined their ships, and Sir Sidney with his little squadron quitted the bay of Acre on the 12th of June.

Lord Nelson having urged the Sicilian Government to place the island in the best possible state of defence, a large body of troops assembled; and preparations were made under His Lordship's auspices to fit out the gunboats, and mount the batteries with 65 twenty-four pounders, which had been brought from Naples.

On the 18th of March, Captain Troubridge arriving at Palermo with four ships of the line, was immediately detached by Lord Nelson to blockade the port of Naples; and on the 2nd of April the squadron anchored off the island of Procida, of which they took possession, and hoisted the Sicilian colours: on the following day Ischia, Capraia, and all the other of the Ponza islands, followed the example of Procida. The squadron rejoined Lord Nelson on the 17th, and between that date and the 13th of June, his Lordship had collected a fleet of sixteen sail of the line under his immediate command. On the departure of Captain Troubridge, the blockade of the port of Naples devolved upon Captain James Foote, in the 38-gun frigate *Seahorse*, having under his orders the Perseus bomb, with two brigs. In the meantime, the immense Austro-Russian Army under General Suwarrow, which had entered Italy since the middle of April, was now bearing down all opposition in the Neapolitan territory. Cardinal Ruffo defeated the French near Naples on the 5th of June, and the fortified rock of Rivigliano capitulated to the *Seahorse* on the 14th. On the 15th the important fortress of Castel-a-Mare surrendered on the following terms:

> That the garrison should march out with the honours of war; and that such of them as chose, be allowed to avail themselves of the protection of the British flag.

The little squadron proceeded on the 17th to attack Castel del Uovo, which with Castel Nuovo constituted the principal sea defence of the capital. The latter is situated in the heart of the city, and has a communication with the palace; whilst the Castel del Uovo runs out into the bay, and is joined to the land by a narrow pass with a drawbridge: these two forts, and that of St. Elmo on the western side of the city, were the only strongholds possessed by the French in the immediate neighbourhood of Naples.

Captain Foote, after sending a summons to the commandant in Castel del Uovo, had commenced the attack of that fortress; when on the 19th he was requested by Cardinal Ruffo to cease hostilities while the flag of truce was flying, as negotiations had taken place on the part of the Russian minister, Count Micheroux. On the 20th the captain received from the cardinal a plan of the capitulation, already signed by him and the chief of the Russians, and required the signature of Captain Foote: that officer complied with the request, but at the same time expressed his opinion that the terms were too favourable to the republicans. On the 22nd the capitulation of the forts of Nuovo and Del Uovo was signed in form by the Cardinal Ruffo, by the Russian as well as Turkish commanders, and by Captain Foote as command- ing British officer in the bay of Naples; whilst Colonel Méjan, the French commandant at fort St. Elmo, had previously approved the terms, which stipulated that the two garrisons, consisting of about 1500 individuals, chiefly Neapolitans and revolutionists, should march out with the honours of war; that they should have the choice of embarking in *cartels* for Toulon, or of remaining at Naples; and that until such cartels were prepared, the garrisons should keep possession of their forts; whilst four hostages were to be detained at fort St. Elmo, until the arrival of the individuals at Toulon had been ascertained.

It necessarily required some days for assembling the transports to convey the garrisons to their destination,, and in the meantime the flags of truce remained hoisted as well at the two forts, as on board the British and Neapolitan ships of war in the bay. Whilst matters were in this state, on the 24th Lord Nelson, with sixteen sail of the line and a 64-gun ship, arrived in sight, and the *Foudroyant* made the signal to annul the flag of truce then flying on board the squadron of Captain Foote. On the same afternoon a conference was held on board the flag-ship, at which were present Sir William and Lady Hamilton, and Cardinal Ruffo: the latter insisted that the inviolability of the treaty ought to be held sacred; but Lord Nelson considered that as the treaty had been entered into with rebels, it ought not to be carried into execution without the approbation of His Sicilian Majesty. Upon this decision of the British admiral, the cardinal indignantly retired from the conference.

On the 26th the garrisons of the forts of Nuovo and del Uovo, in obedience to the ninth article of the treaty, set at liberty the state prisoners as well as the English prisoners of war; and then the garrison, as stipulated in the third article; marched out with the honours of war, and grounded their arms. The principal part embarked on board fourteen transports to be conveyed to Toulon, conformably with the fifth article; but in reality to be held as prisoners until the king of the two Sicilies, then at Palermo, determined how they should be disposed of. Thus the treaty was violated by the order of Lord Nelson; for had his fleet by any fortunate chance been prevented entering the bay until the 27th or 28th, those unhappy victims of violated faith would have been on their way to Toulon, and British honour preserved inviolate. On the 8th of July Ferdinand the Fourth and his queen arrived from Palermo, but the monarch was entirely under the influence of Lady Hamilton and his ministers, and through their perfidy the unhappy wretches on board the prison-ships (cartels that had been), underwent the greatest sufferings. A letter from one of these miserable victims of misguided policy says:

It is now twenty-four days that we are lying in this road, unprovided with everything necessary to existence: we have only bread to eat, and we drink nothing but putrid water, or wine mixed with sea-water, and have nothing but the bare planks to sleep upon. Our houses have been pillaged, and the greater part of our relations have been either imprisoned or massacred.

An apologist for Lord Nelson styles him "commander-in-chief," and considers that in such capacity, as representative of the King of

England, he might annul treaties. Lord Nelson was only third, or admitting that the Earl St. Vincent had resigned, second in command; but even the sovereign power did not extend to the enemies of his country, without whom as parties, a treaty could not exist. If Captain Foote, in signing the treaty, had exceeded his orders, he should have been tried and punished; but even then, the faith of the nation having been once solemnly pledged, it ought not to have been compromised.

Since the surrender of the castles of Nuovo and Del Uovo, the French troops had evacuated the city of Naples, but a detachment amounting to about 800 men, under Major-General Méjan, still remaining in the fort of St. Elmo, it was resolved to attack this fortress with the British and Portuguese marines, who had been landed from the squadron under the command of Captain Troubridge of the *Culloden.*

The battalion of marines amounted to about 800 men, comprising the following officers:—

Lieutenant-Colonel Strickland; Captain Creswell (temporary rank of major), Captains Weir, Dunsmuire, Minto, Knox, Wolfe, Torkington, and Williams; Lieutenants Noble, Hare, McCarthy, Pearce, Barford, Short, Witts, Harvey, Scobell, Adair, Bunce, Jones, Walker, Hart, Collins, Jewell, Toomer, Perrott, Miller, Bozon, Wright, Wheeler, Ross, and Wemyss and Tyldesley (adjutants), and Vyvion (quartermaster.) These, with the 400 Portuguese marines, 500 Swiss, 450 Russians, and 70 Greeks, formed a total of 2170 men, exclusive of officers.

The commandant of Fort St. Elmo having expressed his determination to defend the place entrusted to his charge to the last extremity, Captain Troubridge resolved to storm the fort as soon as two practicable breaches could be made. On the 3rd of July a battery, mounting 3 thirty-six pounders, and 4 mortars, was opened within 700 yards of the walls, and on the 5th another battery of 4 thirty-six pounders. On the same day the Russians opened a battery of 4 thirty-six pounders against the angle opposite to the point attacked by the British, to which 4 more mortars were subsequently added.

On the 11th, the three-gun battery being entirely destroyed, and the guns dismounted by the fire of the besieged, Captain Hallowell was directed to construct another battery of 6 thirty-pounders within 180 yards of the walls. Some trees intervened between the battery and the fort, which it was necessary to remove before the fire could be opened with effect; and although this was a service of great danger, it was gallantly performed under the cheering example of the British officers. A second battery of 1 eighteen-pounder and 2 howitzers, was getting ready, when an officer appeared on the walls with a flag of truce. A capitulation being agreed upon, the garrison marched out with the honours of war, and, in this instance, were honourably conveyed to Toulon. The loss sustained by the British, Russian, and Neapolitan forces, amounted to 5 officers and 32 rank and file killed; 5 officers and 79 rank and file wounded.

The fort of Capua, a small town on the River Volturno, and distant about fifteen miles from Naples, became the next object of attack. On the 20th Captain Troubridge, with the seamen and marines and Portuguese troops, marched from Naples, and encamped before Capua on the morning of the 22nd. On the same day a bridge of pontoons was thrown across the Volturno, to facilitate the communication between the different corps, and batteries of guns and mortars were constructed within 500 yards of the works. On the 25th a battery of 4 twenty-four pounders opened upon the fort, which was replied to by a fire from 11 guns. On the 26th fresh trenches were opened, and new batteries commenced within a few yards of the glacis, when the garrison proposed terms of capitulation, which were rejected; but others, sent back by Captain Troubridge, were acceded to by the French commandant. On the morning of the 29th, the French garrison, numbering 2800 officers and men, under Brigadier-General Girardon, marched out with the honours of war, and were conveyed to Toulon. The fort was mounted with 108 pieces of ordnance, exclusive of ten that were unserviceable.

The neighbouring fort of Gaeta surrendered on the 31st, and the French garrison, amounting to 1498 officers and men, were allowed to march out with their arms and personal effects, and they were to be sent to a French port. Here again the poor unhappy Neapolitan insurgents were handed over, without any effort to protect them, to those who would soon become their executioners. The fort of Gaeta mounted 72 pieces of cannon, including 58 brass twenty-four and eighteen-pounders, with 13 heavy mortars; and the magazines contained an immense quantity of powder and other garrison stores. On the 29th and 30th of September, 200 seamen and marines landed at Civita-Vecchia, and assisted by a detachment of Neapolitan troops, took possession of that town, as also of Corneto and Talfa. Since the 17th of July, Leghorn had been evacuated, and the persevering exertions of the British in a great degree assisted in freeing Naples, Rome, and Tuscany from the dominion of the French.

On the 29th of February, 1799, the 38-gun frigate *Sibylle*, Captain Edward Cooke, in the bay of Bengal, sustained a severe action with the French 40-gun frigate *Forte*. About 1 a.m. the *Sibylle* bore up and poured her broadside into the stern of her opponent, then luffed close alongside of her to leeward, and a furious night action was maintained within musket-shot for more than an hour. As the *Forte* endeavoured to make her escape at 2 h. 30 m., the action was renewed by the *Sibylle*, which brought down the three masts of the enemy's ship, and she then surrendered, with the loss of her captain and 65 killed, and 80 wounded. The *Sibylle* (who had only 9 private marines on board) had 5 killed and 17 wounded.

On the 30th of March the boats of the 36-gun frigate *Trent*, commanded by Lieutenant Nathaniel Belchier, with Lieutenant M'Gee of the marines, attacked a Spanish ship and three schooners, anchored under protection of a battery of 5 guns in a bay about seven leagues to the northward of Cape Roxo, in the island of Porto Rico. Lieutenant M'Gee, with the marines and some seamen under Lieutenant Belchier, landed and stormed the battery, which they carried in gallant style, after killing 5, and wounding several of the Spaniards who defended it. The ship and one of the schooners was brought out during the time occupied by the party on shore in spiking the guns. This exploit was effected with no greater loss than 3 men wounded.

On the 30th of May, while the 74-gun ship *Impetueux*, Captain Sir Edward Pellew, was lying in Bantry Bay in company with several sail of the line under Admiral Sir Alan Gardner, the seamen refused to assist in obeying the signal to unmoor, insisting upon having a boat to convey a letter to the admiral, complaining of tyranny and hard usage. Finding all endeavours to persuade the men to return to their duty of no avail, Sir Edward ordered Captain Wm. Henry Boys to get his detachment under arms, and the marines, who had previously withstood every attempt of the conspirators to seduce them from their duty, now displayed that unwavering loyalty and prompt obedience, for which in the most trying circumstances this valuable force has always been distinguished. The sailors finding themselves firmly opposed, ran below, exclaiming, "Put out the lights, and remove the ladders," but Sir Edward and the officers, following them closely, seized the ringleaders and dragged them aft to the quarter-deck. This decisive conduct had the desired effect, and the ship's company returned to their duty. Sir Edward Pellew, in his letter to Rear-Admiral Sir Charles Cotton, bart., applying for a court-martial on the mutineers, observes:

> I cannot in justice close my letter without informing you, sir, of the alert and manly conduct of the marines, in support of the king's service on this occasion.

On the 21st of October Captain Edward Hamilton, with the beats of the 32-gun frigate *Surprise*, containing 100 officers and men, put off from the ship at 8 p.m., to attempt the capture of the Spanish frigate *Hermione* (formerly British), mounting 44 guns, moored head and stern between two strong batteries situated at the entrance of the harbour of Puerto Cabello. Towards midnight the boats beat off the Spanish guard-boat when about three-quarters of a mile from the *Hermione*, who opened a fire from her bow guns, on hearing the alarm. The boats immediately dashed on; and about half-past midnight Captain Hamilton with eight or ten followers got on board the *Hermione*, and took possession of the forecastle without much resistance. Mr. McCullen in the gig boarded on the larboard bow, and joined the captain's party; but the two cutters, under the first-lieutenant and boatswain, were beaten back in their attempt at the gangways.

The second-lieutenant in the launch was directed to cut the bower, and the carpenter in the jolly-boat the stern-cable; and then both boats, after reinforcing the boarding-party with some men, were to go ahead and tow the ship. Captain Hamilton, after leaving the gunner with 12 men on the starboard gangway, proceeded with the surgeon's party to the quarter-deck, which was obstinately defended for a quarter of an hour with great loss on both sides; Captain Hamilton, the gunner, and several men being severely wounded. At this moment, the first-lieutenant with M. la Tour du Pin, acting lieutenant of marines, boarded with their respective divisions, and the boats under the second-lieutenant took the ship in tow, whilst the men ordered to go aloft, loosed the top-sails. The quarter-deck being in possession of the British, whose force was increased by the marines and others, no time was lost in attacking the main-deck.

Captain Hamilton and the gunner were so severely wounded, as to be incapable of further duty; but M. de la Tour du Pin and the surgeon leading the men down the after-ladder so quickly after the Spaniards, gave them no time to prepare for a regular defence; and after a severe struggle and dreadful slaughter on the part of the Spaniards, who were also fired at from the upper-deck, the survivors of the frigate's crew called for quarter. In passing the batteries the captured ship sustained a heavy fire, but fortunately without any loss; and at 2 a.m. she was out of gun-shot, and in entire possession of the British. In effecting this desperate service, not a man of the attacking party was killed, and only 12 wounded; whilst the Spaniards, out of a crew of 365, had 119 killed and 97 wounded.

A garrison of seamen and marines, amounting to 157 men, having been placed at Lemmertown, in West Friesland, under Captain Boorder of the *Espiègle* sloop of war, were attacked on the 11th of October at 5 a.m. by the advanced party of French and Batavians, consisting of an officer with 30 rank and file, who attempted to storm the north battery. The British soon got them between two fires, and so effectually surrounded them, that they laid down their arms with the loss of 2 killed. The prisoners had scarcely been secured, when the main body, amounting to 670 men, attacked the British, who after a contest of four hours and a-half, routed the enemy in every direction, with the loss of 5 killed and 9 wounded. The marines continuing the pursuit, killed and wounded more than 40; and if the allied forces had not broken down a bridge in their retreat, they would have lost their colours and two field-pieces. Captain Boorder, in his official letter, says:

> Lieutenants Wyburn, Howel, Higginson, and Gardner of the marines, behaved with honour to themselves and credit to their country; and their men distinguished themselves in the most gallant manner.

On the 24th of January, 1800, a convention was signed at the fort of El-Arish, by two commissioners from General Kléber and those sent by the *grand vizier*, for the evacuation of Egypt by the French Army. This treaty, consisting of twenty-two articles which was ratified by General Kléber on the 25th, stipulated that the French army should evacuate Egypt, embarking at Alexandria, Rosetta, and Aboukir; and that there should be an armistice of three months, or longer if necessary; that all subjects of the Sublime Porte prisoners among the French should be set at liberty; and that the vessels containing the French Army should have proper passports to go to France, and not be molested by any of the belligerents. Major Douglas, of the marines, was immediately sent to England by Sir Sidney Smith with a copy of the convention, and it was announced in the *London Gazette* on the 25th of March, 1800. This official notice of the treaty of El-Arish implied an approval of the measure; but long before its appearance in the *Gazette*, the convention had been disowned and denounced by a party, without whose entire concurrence it could not be carried into effect.

After making the necessary arrangements for the removal of the army according to the terms of the treaty, General Kléber learnt, to his surprise, that the captain of the *Theseus*, then cruising off Alexandria, by the express orders of Sir Sidney Smith would not allow any vessel to depart from the shores of Egypt; although, it should be observed, Generals Desaix, Davoust, and some other officers of distinction, had already sailed for France. Shortly afterwards, General Kléber received a letter from Sir Sidney, dated at the Isle of Cyprus on the 20th of February, informing that officer, that the commander-in-chief in the Mediterranean had received orders which opposed the immediate execution of the treaty of El-Arish. This was followed by a letter from Lord Keith, acquainting the general that he had received positive commands to consent to no capitulation with the French troops in Egypt and Syria, unless they laid down their arms and surrendered as prisoners of war, abandoning all their ships and stores in the port and citadel of Alexandria; that in case of such capitulation, the troops would not be allowed to return to France without exchange, and that all ships having troops on board, would be detained as prizes.

The instant General Kléber read this letter, he determined on giving battle to the *grand vizier;* he nevertheless calmly observed to Lieutenant Wright, the bearer of the letter, "You shall know my answer to your admiral tomorrow." That very night Kléber had the letter printed, and the next morning issued it to his army with the following postscript:

*Soldats! on ne repond à une telle insolence que par des victoires: préparez-vous à combattre!*

It is true that Sir Sidney Smith did not affix his signature to the formal convention concluded at El-Arish, but he signed, conjointly with General Desaix and M. Poussielgue, a preliminary document containing the basis of the treaty, of which the last article runs thus:

That the French Army evacuate Egypt with arms and baggage, whenever the necessary means for such evacuation shall have been procured, and to withdraw to the ports which shall be agreed upon.

This agreement bears date on board the *Tigre* "*8 Nivose,*" or 29th of December; and it was therefore very natural that Sir Sidney should feel indignant at the refusal of his superiors to ratify a treaty which

213

he had full power to sanction. This extraordinary proceeding, which had not the sanction of the British Government, evidently emanated from Lord Keith, and was contrary to the intention of the English cabinet; for in a letter from His Lordship addressed to M. Poussielgue, he states:

> I had received no orders on this head from the king's ministers, although I was of opinion that His Majesty should not take part in this convention; but since the treaty has been concluded, His Majesty, being desirous of showing his respect for his allies, I have received instructions to allow a free passage for the French troops.

The rupture of the treaty of El-Arish stimulated the injured party to wreak the most signal vengeance, upon the Turks, who were undeserving of such animosity, as they took no part in this breach of faith; but unluckily for them, they happened to be in immediate contact with the enraged French Army, for the *grand vizier* with his numerous force had taken possession of the different strong-holds the instant the French had quitted them on their way to the coast to embark, under the terms of the treaty.

On the 20th of March a battle was fought at the village of Matarieh (built upon the ruins of the ancient Heliopolis), between the French Army under General Kléber, stated at 10,000 men, and the Turkish Army under the Grand Vizier Jussuf, computed at 60,000, or some say 80,000 men. After five days' fighting, during which the Turks were driven from village to village, the French gained a complete victory; and the *grand vizier* fled with only 500 followers, leaving his camp, artillery, and baggage on the field of battle. The loss of the Turks is stated to have amounted to 50,000, whilst the French suffered comparatively but little.

After suppressing the revolt at Cairo, and the expulsion of a small British force under Lieutenant-Colonel Murray, which had disembarked from the 50-gun ship *Centurion*, and some smaller vessels at Suez, the French found themselves in possession of the posts they had formerly occupied in Egypt. In the month of June, General Kléber received an intimation of the desire of the British Government to renew the convention; but being now firmly established, and having no confidence in the promises of those who had once deceived him, the French general declined any negotiation, and instantly began to strengthen the principal defences along the coast, and to make preparations for repelling any attack which the British might probably undertake.

Unfortunately for the French-Egyptian Army, General Kléber was assassinated on the 14th of June: whilst walking on the terrace of his palace at Cairo, accompanied by the architect M. Protain, a stranger rushed out of an adjoining gallery, and stabbed the general with a poniard; and M. Protain, in endeavouring to hold the assassin, was wounded in six places, but not mortally. General Kléber was buried with military honours in a suburb of Cairo, and it will be only justice to the memory of this brave man to say, that among his enemies, no less than among his friends, he bore the character of a brave officer and an honourable man. The command of the army devolved on General Abdallah Jacques Menou, of whom we shall have occasion to speak in our account of the next year, in bringing to a close the French campaign in Egypt.

The garrison of Malta, under General Vaubois, consisting of 3000 sailors and seamen, had been shut up in the fortress of Valetta since the close of the year 1798, menaced on the land side by a powerful force of Maltese, Neapolitans, and British, and blockaded by a squadron of British and Portuguese ships. In the early part of 1799 the French garrison received some supplies by a frigate from Toulon, which had eluded the vigilance of the blockading squadron; but in the latter part of the year the troops began to experience the miseries of famine and disease. To alleviate the sufferings of the garrison, a portion of the inhabitants was from time to time ordered out of the city, and the original number of 45,000 was by this expedient reduced to barely 9000.

On the 1st of November, 1799, Lord Nelson, then with his flag on board the 80-gun ship *Vanguard*, sent in a summons of surrender; to which General Vaubois replied:

*Jaloux de mériter l'estime de votre nation, comme vous recherchez celle de la notre, nous sommes résolus de défendre cette forteresse jusqu'à l'extrémité.*

The blockade of the island was so rigidly maintained since the arrival of the frigate in the early part of the last year with the supplies, that the French were kept in ignorance of the revolution on the 9th of November, until the arrival of an *aviso* with despatches from the new government. The garrison of Valetta were so elated with the news of the advancement of Buonaparte to be chief consul, that they rashly swore never to deliver up the island to the enemies of France.

On the 15th of February Lord Keith, when cruising off Malta with the *Queen Charlotte* 100 guns, *Foudroyant* 80, *Audacious, Northumberland*, and *Alexander*, of 74 guns, and *Lion* 64, received intelligence from Captain Peard, of the 32-gun frigate *Success*, that a French squadron, consisting of the *Généreux* 74, bearing the flag of Admiral Perrée, with a frigate, two corvettes, and several transports having on board 3000 troops, had sailed from Toulon on the 7th, and would attempt throwing supplies into Valetta. In order to intercept this reinforcement the *Queen Charlotte* kept close to the entrance of the harbour, whilst the *Foudroyant, Audacious*, and *Northumberland* were stationed to windward in the south-east, the *Lion* off the passage between Goza and Malta, and the *Alexander* on the south-east side of the island.

On the 18th, at daylight, the *Alexander* chased the squadron of Admiral Perree, and captured a store-ship. The *Généreux*, to avoid the fire of the *Alexander*, bore up, and the *Success* being to leeward, raked her with several broadsides; but the frigate soon after became exposed to the fire of the *Généreux*, by which she had 1 man killed and 8 wounded. At 4 h. 30 m. p.m. the *Foudroyant*, bearing the flag of Rear-Admiral Nelson, followed closely by the *Northumberland*, having fired two shots at the *Généreux*, the latter discharged her broadside and struck her colours. The only loss she sustained was Rear-Admiral Perrée, who after being wounded by a splinter, lost his right leg, which occasioned the death of this gallant and upright man.

Some idea may be formed of the sufferings experienced by the French troops in Valetta, by the exorbitant prices of the following articles: a fowl sixteen *francs*, a rabbit twelve, an egg twenty *sous*, a rat forty *sous*, and fish six *francs* per pound: in addition to these privations the typhus fever was making destructive ravages among the troops, and the only *bouille* served to the sick in the hospitals was made of horseflesh. In this emergency, General Vaubois determined to despatch the *Guillaume Tell* to announce to the first consul that the place could not hold out another month.

Shortly after the capture of the *Généreux*, the *Queen Charlotte* proceeded to Leghorn, and we shall presently relate the distressing event which sealed her fate. In the early part of March, Lord Nelson returned to England, leaving the blockading squadron in charge of Captain Troubridge; and during that officer's temporary absence, the squadron cruising off Malta on the 30th of March consisted of the *Lion* 64, Captain Manley Dixon; *Foudroyant* 80, Captain Sir Edward Berry; *Alexander* 74, Lieutenant William Harrington (acting), and the

36-gun frigate *Penelope*, Captain Henry Blackwood.

On the 30th of March, at 11 p.m., the 80-gun ship *Guillaume Tell*, Captain Saulnier, bearing the flag of Rear-Admiral Denis Decrès, taking advantage of a strong southerly gale and the darkness that had succeeded the setting of the moon, sailed from the harbour of Valetta at 11 h. 55 m. p.m. The *Penelope*, then inshore of the *Lion* who lay at anchor, having discovered the French ship under a press of sail, Captain Blackwood sent a brig to apprise the commodore, and then stood after the stranger. At half-past midnight the *Penelope*, luffing up under the stern of the *Guillaume Tell*, gave her the larboard broadside. She then bore away under her larboard quarter, and discharged the starboard guns, receiving in return a fire from the 80-gun ship's stern chasers. The *Penelope* continued to harass her adversary by pouring in a raking fire with such effect, that before the dawn of day on the 31st the *Guillaume Tell's* main and mizen top-masts and main yard came down.

About 5 a.m. the *Lion*, steering between the *Penelope* and the enemy's ship, and within pistol-shot of the latter's larboard side, opened a destructive fire upon the crippled ship: then luffing up across the bows of the *Guillaume Tell*, the latter's jib-boom passed between the *Lion's* main and mizen shrouds; but as the jibboom was soon carried away, the 64 gained a position on the bow of her antagonist, where she continued until 5 h 30 m. a.m., by which time the *Lion* was so damaged by the heavy broadside of the French ship, that she dropped astern. At 6 a.m. the *Foudroyant* arrived up under a crowd of sail, and passing close to the starboard side of her antagonist, poured in her broadside, which the French ship immediately returned, and with such effect, as to cut away a great deal of the *Foudroyant's* rigging. The latter unavoidably shot ahead, but having regained her position, the firing recommenced.

The second broadside from the *Guillaume Tell* brought down the fore top-mast, main top-sail yard, jib-boom, and sprit-sail yard of the *Foudroyant*; and having her sails cut to pieces, the British 80 dropped astern, leaving the *Lion* upon the enemy's larboard side, whilst the *Penelope* upon the same quarter was occasionally firing at the enemy's ship. At 6 h. 30 m. a.m., just as the main and mizen-masts of the French ship came down, the *Foudroyant*, having partially refitted herself, again closed with her opponent. At 8 h. a.m. the *Guillaume Tell* lost her foremast, and at 8 h. 20 m. this nobly-defended ship, from her dismasted state rolled so heavily, that it became necessary to close the lower deck ports, and being incapable of further defence she struck her colours, having upwards of 200 men killed and wounded.

The *Foudroyant* had 8 killed and 64 wounded; the *Lion* 8 killed and 38 wounded; and the *Penelope* 1 killed and 3 wounded. The officers of marines belonging to these ships were as follows:—*Foudroyant*, Captain George Wolfe, Lieutenants Richard Bunce, Zaccheus Miller, and James Collins; *Lion*, Lieutenants Philip Patriarche and John C. Hoskins; and Lieutenant John Senhouse, *Penelope*; but as these officers composed part of the battalion landed at Malta, it is doubtful if they had returned to their ships previous to the action.

The brave garrison of Malta still holding out, a summons was again sent to General Vaubois by the officer commanding the blockading force, but the reply was in unison with that gallant veteran's former message:—

*Cette place est en trop bon état; et je suis moi-même trop jaloux de bien servir mon pays, et de conserver mon honneur, pour écouter vos propositions.*

By the beginning of August all the beasts of burden had been consumed, and dogs, cats, fowls, and rabbits, for want of nourishment, had disappeared. Firewood began likewise to fail, but this was remedied by breaking up the *Boudeuse* frigate. There was also a great want of water, and the troops were dying in numbers daily. The general being now convinced that he could not hold out much longer, wished to save two fine 40-gun frigates to the republic, and accordingly on the evening of the 24th the *Diane* and *Justice* put to sea; but they were soon discovered and chased by the British squadron, and after a short running fight with the *Success* frigate, the *Diane*, having only 114 men on board, struck her colours, but the *Justice* escaped and arrived at Toulon.

On the 3rd of September General Vaubois proposed terms for the surrender of the fortress, and on the 5th the articles of capitulation were agreed to by the respective chiefs. Of the two 64-gun ships in the port, the *Athenien*, the only one in a sea-worthy state, was brought away.

On the 16th of March the *Queen Charlotte* of 100 guns, Captain Todd, was ordered by Lord Keith to get under weigh from Leghorn roads, and proceed to reconnoitre the island of Capraia, then occupied by the French; and on the succeeding morning, when about three leagues from Leghorn, she was discovered to be on fire. Assistance was immediately forwarded from the shore, but many boats were deterred from approaching the ship, by the guns going off in all directions as they became heated by the flames. The fire is supposed to have originated in some hay on the booms, which had ignited by falling on the match-tub, usually kept there for firing signal-guns. The mainsail being set at the time was instantly in flames, even before the men could get at the clue garnets. Lieutenant Heneage Dundas went below from the forecastle, with as many hands as he could collect, to drown the lower deck; the ports of which were opened, the scuppers plugged, fore and main hatches secured, the cocks turned, water drawn in at the ports, and the pumps kept going, and by these exertions the lower deck was kept free from fire for a long time; nor did Lieutenant Dundas and Mr. John Baird, the carpenter, quit this station until the guns from the middle deck fell through.

About 9 o'clock, finding it impossible to remain below, these officers got out of the fore-mast lower deck port, and climbed over the bows to the forecastle, where there had assembled about 150 men, drawing water and throwing it as fast as possible upon the fire. Before 1 o'clock the heat was so insufferable that few remained in the head, and many, by jumping overboard, were saved by the boats from the shore. Captain Breedon and Lieutenant William Ferguson of the marines, jumped out of the stern-port, and swam towards one of the ship's boats, which the lieutenant reached in safety, but Captain Breedon sunk, and was seen no more. Lieutenant Thomas Peebles, of the marines, not being a swimmer, had no chance of reaching the boat, and therefore hastened forward, got up over the ship's bows to the head; and as the last extremity, when the flames had reached the forecastle and the heat became too intense to be borne, he dropped overboard, and was picked up after being some time in the water. There were saved from the wreck 3 lieutenants, 2 lieutenants of marines, 3 midshipmen, the clerk, and 146 seamen and marines. Those who perished were the captain, 3 lieutenants, 1 captain of marines, the master, purser, surgeon, boatswain, 4 master's mates, 18 midshipmen, 2 clerks, 3 surgeon's mates, and about 630 seamen and marines.

After the loss of the *Queen Charlotte*, Lord Keith hoisted his flag on board the *Audacious* 74, having under his orders the *Minotaur* 74, several frigates, sloops, and gunboats, which squadron on several occasions successfully co-operated with the Austrian Army in their attacks upon the outworks of Genoa; and within the first three weeks of May, the town had been thrice bombarded. The French, being much annoyed by those attacks, prepared a flotilla, consisting of a galley, rowing fifty-two oars and mounting 2 brass thirty-six pounders of extraordinary length, besides smaller pieces; an armed cutter, three armed settees, and several gunboats. On the 20th, in the afternoon, this flotilla, standing outside the mole-head, exchanged several shot with the British ships in passing, and the *Audacious* was twice hulled by the long guns of the galley. At sunset the flotilla took up a position under the guns of the two moles and the city bastions.

On the 21st, at 1 a.m., the English flotilla made another attack, when the batteries quickly returned the fire, particularly from the thirty-six pounders of the *Prima* galley, now lying chain-moored close to the inside of the old, or eastern molehead. Captain Beaver proposed carrying the galley by boarding, and after dark ten boats, containing about 100 officers and men, drew off from the flotilla, and proceeded to the immediate attack, in the hope of being able to reach the galley unperceived; but a boat stationed between the two mole-heads opened her fire upon them, and the British then dashed on towards the galley; the gun-whale of which projected upwards of three feet from the side of the hull, and was strengthened by a stout barricade, along the summit of which several wall-pieces and blunderbusses were mounted.

As an additional obstruction to the advance of boats, the oars were banked, or fixed in their places, with the handles secured to the benches or thwarts; and with a crew of 257 fighting men the *Prima* was thus lying prepared, under the protection of formidable batteries. She was first assaulted on the starboard-side a-midships by a boat of the *Haerlem*, commanded by midshipman John Caldwell, who was promptly supported by other boats; while the crew of the barge of the *Minotaur*, commanded by Captain Beaver, (who was accompanied by Lieutenant Thomas Peebles of the marines), and of the *Vestal's* launch, by Lieutenant William Gibson, got up over the quarter, and after a desperate struggle with the French soldiers on the poop, they drove the enemy at all points, the greater part jumping overboard; and in a few minutes the commodore's broad pendant was hauled down by Lieutenant Gibson, when all further resistance ceased.

The boats were then ordered ahead to take the captured vessel in tow, and the slaves in seeming cheerfulness manned the sweeps. After a little delay in clearing her from her chain moorings, the galley moved towards the entrance of the harbour under a tremendous fire of shot and shells, and from musketry on the mole-head, round which she passed within a dozen yards, with no greater loss than 5 men wounded.

Of the crew of the galley, 1 was killed and 15 wounded by the British when they boarded; some were drowned, and many others succeeded in reaching the shore. Before the galley was out of gun-shot, an alarm was raised of fire below; when a drunken French sailor was discovered attempting to break open the door of the magazine, for the purpose, as he unhesitatingly avowed, of blowing up the ship. Had the wretch succeeded, nearly 500 persons might have perished; for besides the British and the 70 French soldiers and seamen remaining on board, there were upwards of 300 miserable beings chained to the oars.

It is to be regretted that Lord Keith in his official letter should have been so regardless of the fair fame of his officers, as to have omitted the names of every individual engaged in this very gallant and well-conducted enterprise; but we have the gratification of recording the name of Lieutenant Thomas Peebles of the marines, who was one of the first on board the enemy.

On the 4th of June General Masséna consented to evacuate Genoa, and with his 8000 troops to retire to Nice; consequently, on the 5th the *Audacious, Minotaur,* and *Généreux* of 74 guns, and a small Neapolitan squadron entered the mole. On the very day on which the treaty was signed, Buonaparte after crossing the Alps with a powerful army, entered Milan, and proclaimed afresh the Cisalpine republic. On the 7th the first consul, still unacquainted with the surrender of Genoa, quitted Milan to attack the Austrians; and General d'Ott, who had quitted Genoa after three days' possession, was defeated by Buonaparte at Casteggio and Montebello.

On the 14th the famous Battle of Marengo was fought, where General Mélas was defeated with a loss of 4500 men left dead upon the field of battle, nearly 8000 wounded, above 6000 prisoners, 12 stands of colours, and 30 pieces of cannon; and on the part of the French, of 2000 killed, 3600 wounded, and 700 prisoners. A convention for a suspension of arms was signed on the 15th at Alexandria, by which France was put in possession of twelve important fortresses; Genoa was consequently re-occupied by the French, and General Masséna returned to that city on the 24th. The occupation was so sudden, that the *Minotaur* found some difficulty in warping out of the mole in time to make her escape.

Rear-Admiral Sir John Borlase Warren, cruising off the Penmarcks with the *Renown* and *Defence,* of 74 guns, *Fisgard* and *Unicorn* frigates, detached the boats of the squadron on the evening of the 10th of June, under command of Lieutenant Henry Burke, to cut out a convoy in the small harbour of St. Croix, known to be laden with provisions for the Brest fleet; and among the officers employed on this occasion, we find the name of Lieutenant Mark Anthony Gerrard of the marines, a volunteer on that service. The boats proceeded to the attack at 11 p.m., but owing to the freshness of the wind, they did not reach the enemy's anchorage until after daylight on the 11th; and notwithstanding they were opposed by a heavy battery, three armed vessels, and a constant fire of musketry from the shore, they captured a gunboat mounting 2 long twenty-four pounders, a *chasse marée* of 10, and another of 6 guns, and eight merchant vessels. The remainder of the convoy, amounting to twenty sail, escaped by running upon the rocks.

The boats of the same squadron, with the exception of the *Unicorn*, in which Lieutenant M. A. Gerrard of the marines was again a volunteer, attacked a corvette mounting 28 guns, a brig of 18, a lugger of 16, and a cutter of 10 guns, lying at anchor with several merchant vessels in Quimper River. At daylight on the 24th of June the boats arrived off the entrance of the river, and for their protection two divisions of marines were landed; that on the right commanded by Lieutenant Burke of the *Renown*, and that on the left by Lieutenant Gerrard. The boats in the meantime pulled with all expedition to the attack, but the enemy's vessels had retired far beyond their reach. After blowing up three batteries, the British returned to their ships without sustaining any loss.

Sir John B. Warren having received information that a large convoy from Sables-d'Olonne, bound to Brest, was lying within the island of Noirmontier, anchored the squadron in the bay of Bourgneuf on the 1st of July, with the intention of attacking the ship *Thérese* of 20 guns, a lugger of 12, a cutter, and two schooners of 6 guns each, moored within the sands of the bay, under the protection of six batteries on the south-east part of the island, besides flanking guns on several projecting points. The boats after assembling on board the *Fisgard*, proceeded in the evening in three divisions, amounting together to 192 officers and men under Lieutenant Burke, assisted by several officers, including Lieutenants of Marines John Thompson, Charles Henry Ballinghall, Mark Anthony Gerrard, and Hugh Hutton.

At midnight the British boarded, and after a spirited resistance, carried the ship and three other armed vessels, as well as fifteen sail of merchant-men,—the whole laden with provisions and ship-timber for the Brest fleet; but it being impossible to bring them off, Lieutenant Burke caused them to be effectually destroyed. Having performed this essential service without incurring any loss, the boats, in attempting to pass over the sand-banks, unfortunately grounded, and in less than ten minutes were left perfectly dry. In this helpless situation they were exposed to a continual fire from the forts on Noirmontier Island, and from the musketry of 400 French soldiers. But nothing daunted by this formidable opposition, the British attacked some vessels afloat near them, in the hope of securing one sufficiently large to carry them all off. Having accomplished this object, they by great exertion and intrepidity drew her upwards of two miles over the sands, until she floated, by which time the men were wading up to their middle in water. Notwithstanding this gallant perseverance, 92 officers and men were taken prisoners, including Lieutenants of Marines Thompson and Ballinghall, who were wounded; but the remainder, after compelling the enemy to retreat, got back to their ships.

On the 20th of August the 38-gun frigate *Seine*, Captain David Milne, when cruising in the Mona passage, at 8 h. 30 m. a.m. gave chase to the French 40-gun frigate *Vengéance*. At 4 p.m. the latter commenced firing her stern chasers, but it was not until 11 h. 30 m. p.m. that the *Seine* reached a position on the quarter of her opponent; and after exchanging some broadsides, the rigging of the British ship was so disabled as to cause her to drop astern. The remainder of the night was occupied in reeving fresh rigging, while the ship continued carrying all the sail she could in pursuit of the enemy. At 8 a.m. the *Seine* got close alongside her opponent, and the action continued with great spirit on both sides until 10 h. 30 m. a.m., when the *Vengéance*, having lost her fore-mast, mizen-mast, and main topmast, all of which had fallen in-board, with a loss of 35 killed and 70 wounded, out of a crew of 326, hailed the *Seine* from the bowsprit of the French ship that they had surrendered. The *Seine*, out of 281 men and boys, had one lieutenant, George Milne, and 12 killed; Lieutenant Archibald Macdonald of the marines, and 24 wounded. Captain Milne, in speaking of his officers, says,—

I am much indebted to the services of Lieutenant Archibald Macdonald of the marines, who was taken down wounded, and came up when dressed; but was obliged from a second wound to be taken below. Yet I am happy to state the life of this valuable officer will be saved, to render further services to His Majesty.

On the 29th of August, while the squadron under Sir John B. Warren, as already mentioned, with several transports in company, was proceeding along the coast of Spain, the French privateer *Guêpe*, mounting 18 long eight-pounders, and manned with 160 men, was seen to run into Vigo, and anchor near to some batteries in the narrows of Redondella. In the evening a division of twenty boats, under the orders of Lieutenant Burke of the *Renown*, proceeded to the attack of the privateer. About 40 minutes past midnight the enemy discovered the boats; and to show that they were prepared to receive them, the crew of the privateer cheered in defiance: the captain having laid over the hatches, to prevent his men from quitting their quarters. Notwithstanding these resolute preparations, the British gallantly boarded, and in 15 minutes carried the *Guêpe*, with the loss of 3 seamen and 1 marine killed; 3 lieutenants, Lieutenant John Wright of the marines, 12 seamen, and 5 marines wounded. The enemy's loss amounted to 25 killed and 40 wounded, including her brave commander, mortally wounded.

On the 3rd of September eight boats from the 74-gun ship *Minotaur* and 32-gun frigate *Niger* (*en flute*), under the command of Captain Hillyar of the latter, (in which Service Lieutenant John Jewell of the marines was a volunteer), proceeded at 8 p.m. to cut out two Spanish corvettes, the *Esmeralda* and *Paz*, each mounting 22 guns, anchored in Barcelona roads. At 9 p.m., after receiving the broadside of the *Esmeralda*, the boats dashed on, and were on board before the Spaniards had time to reload their guns, and after a short struggle carried the corvette. On hearing the cheers of the British, the *Paz* cut her cables to run under the battery at the mole-head; but the ship casting the wrong way, she was boarded and in possession before 10 p.m.; and in spite of a fire from ten gunboats, each armed with 2 thirty-six pounders, and a fort which threw shells from Montjouic, the prizes were brought off, with a loss of only 2 seamen and 1 marine killed, and 5 wounded. On board the *Paz*, 1 man was killed and 4 wounded; the *Esmeralda* had 2 killed and 17 wounded.

The *Phaeton* frigate of 38-guns, Captain J. N. Morris, cruising off Malaga, discovered the Spanish national *polacre*-ship *San Josef*, mounting 2 long twenty-four pounders in the bow, 2 brass long eighteen-pounders for stern chasers, with 4 twelve and 6 four-pounders on her sides, having on board 34 seamen and 24 soldiers, and moored under the protection of 5 guns mounted on the fort of Fuengirola. On the evening of the 27th of October, an attempt to cut out this formidable vessel being determined upon, the boats of the *Phaeton* were placed under the orders of Lieutenant Francis Beaufort, supported by Lieutenant George Huish and Lieutenant Duncan Campbell, of the marines. On the approach of the boats, they were fired upon by a French privateer-schooner that had entered during the night, and which lay in a position to flank the *polacre*; nevertheless, the British got alongside the latter at 5 a. m. on the 28th, and in spite of an obstinate resistance boarded and carried her. Lieutenant Beaufort was severely wounded in the head, and received several slugs through his left arm and body; and Lieutenant Campbell several slight sabre wounds. The total loss on the part of the British was 1 seaman killed, and 4 wounded. Of the crew of the *San Josef* 6 men were badly, and 13 slightly wounded.

On the 12th of October, Lieutenants of Marines Alexander, Montgomerie, Mitchell, and Jordan, assisted, in the boats of the *Montagu* and *Magnificent*, in capturing eleven vessels lying under the protection of a battery and two armed vessels in a harbour near l'Orient. Captain Knight, in reporting this exploit, concludes his letter by observing,—

This service, which was completely and expeditiously performed with the loss of only 1 killed and 3 wounded, has won my approbation, and will, I trust, merit Your Lordships'.

## CHAPTER 7

# From the Year 1801 to 1804

In this year, the naval strength was augmented to 135,000 men, including a considerable addition to the marines, which establishment was increased to 22,696, and subsequently to 30,000 men.

In consequence of an attack made by a small British squadron upon the Danish 40-gun frigate *Freija*, in September 1798, by enforcing a long recognised right of searching neutral ships for contraband of war, but more particularly for the passage of the Sound by a British squadron, the Emperor Paul of Russia issued an order for the sequestration of all British property in his dominions. This, however, was shortly afterwards rescinded; but on the 5th of November, the news of the capture of Malta by the British occasioned an embargo to be laid on all our shipping in the ports of Russia, amounting to more than 200 sail. A convention between Russia and Sweden soon followed, both parties agreeing to an armed neutrality; and Denmark, at the instigation of the former, was also induced to join the confederacy.

Whilst thus menaced by the threatening attitude of the three northern powers, their hostile preparations were met by a corresponding resistance on the part of Great Britain; and on the 12th of March Admiral Sir Hyde Parker was despatched from Yarmouth roads, with fifteen sail of the line, and as many frigates, sloops, and bombs as made the whole armament amount to fifty-three sail; and there were embarked on board a division of this fleet, under command of Colonel Stewart of the 49th regiment, two companies of rifles, and a detachment of artillery.

The nominal force of the three powers, against which the British fleet was destined to act, was as follows: Russia eighty-two, Denmark twenty-three, and Sweden eighteen sail of the line, having between them eighty frigates and corvettes; but Russia did not really possess more than sixty-one sail, thirty-one being in the Baltic, and the remainder in the Mediterranean and Black Seas. Of these thirty-one ships, which were divided between the different ports of Russia, not above twenty sail of the line could be brought to act as a fleet; and even these were badly equipped and wretchedly manned. The Swedes had eleven sail of the line at Carlscrona, and by all accounts tolerably manned; whilst the Danish force at Copenhagen consisted of ten sail of the line ready for sea, exclusive of about the same number in an unserviceable state. Thus, the reputed force, as stated by several writers, of eighty-eight sail, did not exceed forty-one of the line; and it must have been under fortunate circumstances that twenty-five of these forty-five sail, could be assembled on any particular time and place. Moreover, this reduced number made up of three different nations, and very little acquainted with naval tactics, were opposed to a fleet of fifteen sail of British, under Rear-Admiral Nelson.

In the hope that Denmark, in spite of her hostile demonstrations, would be inclined to negotiate, the Honourable Nicholas Vansittart took his departure for Copenhagen on the 12th. Owing to the blowing weather, the fleet did not reach the entrance of the Sound until the 21st, when the ships anchored off Knoll-point, on the Swedish shore. On the 23rd the *Blanche*, with Mr. Vansittart on board, returned to the fleet from Copenhagen, bringing also Mr. Drummond the British *chargé d'affaires* at that capital, who, instead of a reply of conciliation from the Danish Government, brought one of open defiance; and the Danes, taking advantage of the time which had been lost in negotiating, had considerably strengthened their means of defence.

At 6 a.m. on the 30th, with a fine breeze at north-north-west, the British fleet proceeded into the Sound, in line ahead. At 7 a.m. the batteries at Elsineur opened their fire upon the *Monarch* and the other ships in succession as they passed; but not a shot struck them, nor did any but the van ships fire in return. The seven bomb-vessels, however, threw shells, and about 200 are stated to have fallen in Cronenberg and Helsingen, where they did some damage. The British observing that there were only a few guns mounted on the Swedish shore, passed near the castle of Helsinburg, and thus avoided the fire from above 100 pieces of cannon on Cronenberg Castle.

At noon the fleet anchored, when about fifteen miles from the city of Copenhagen; and the commander-in-chief, accompanied by Vice-Admiral Lord Nelson and Rear-Admiral Graves, with the commanding-officer of the troops, proceeded in the *Lark* lugger to reconnoitre the enemy's defences. A council of war was held in the evening, at which it was proposed to delay the attack; but Lord Nelson, in urging immediate operations, offered to carry the business through in a proper manner with ten sail of the line, and a proportionate number of smaller vessels. This proposal met the approbation of Admiral Parker, who added two 50-gun ships to the number stipulated by his enterprising second in command.

The approach to Copenhagen was through an intricate channel, which the Danes had rendered more difficult by judiciously removing or misplacing the buoys on the shoals; but this was remedied by the anxious care of Lord Nelson, who proceeded on the same evening to re-buoy the outer channel,—a narrow passage lying between the island of Saltholm and the Middle Ground. It was at first intended to make the attack from the northward, but a second examination of the Danish position on the 31st, and a favourable change of wind, determined the vice-admiral to commence operations from the southward.

## The Battle of Copenhagen.

On the morning of the 1st of April the British fleet got under weigh, but shortly afterwards re-anchored off the western extremity of the Middle Ground,—a shoal extending along the whole sea-front of the city of Copenhagen, leaving an intervening channel of deep water, called the King's Channel, which is about three-quarters of a mile wide: in this channel, close to the town, the Danes had moored their line of defence, consisting of block-ships, *radeaus*, *prames*, and gun-vessels. Lord Nelson having embarked on board the *Amazon* during the forenoon, again reconnoitred the position he was about to attack; and soon after his return, at 1 p.m., the *Elephant* made the signal to weigh, which intimation was welcomed by a hearty cheer from the British fleet.

The vice-admiral's squadron, amounting in the whole to thirty-six square-rigged vessels, was soon under sail in two divisions, with a light but favourable wind, and, led by the *Amazon*, entered the upper channel, coasting along the edge of the Middle Ground until they had reached and partly rounded its southern extremity, where at about 8 p.m. they anchored: the north-westernmost ship was then about two miles distant from the southernmost of the Danish line.

British squadron under the command of Lord Nelson before Copenhagen, 2nd of April, 1801:

*Elephant*, 74 guns, Vice-Admiral Lord Nelson, Captain T. Foley, 10 killed, 13 wounded. Captain-Lieutenant Thomas Piers, First-Lieutenant John Claperton, Second-Lieut. W. B. Watts.

*Defiance*, 74 guns, Rear-Admiral T. Graves, Captain E. Retalick, 24 killed, 51 wounded. Captain Jos. Lambrecht, Second-Lieutenant James Duff, Second-Lieutenant William Furber.

*Edgar*, 74 guns, Captain G. Murray, 31 killed, 111 wounded. Captain Alexander Mackenzie, Second-Lieutenant Benjamin Spencer (killed), Second-Lieutenant James Campbell.

*Monarch*, 74 guns, Captain J. R. Mosse (killed), 56 killed, 164 wounded. Captain Anthony Stransham, First-Lieutenant James Marrie, Second-Lieutenant J. C. Urquhart.

*Bellona*, 74 guns, Captain Sir T. B. Thompson (wounded), 11 killed, 72 wounded. Captain Samuel Williams, First-Lieutenant Henry A. Durré, Second-Lieutenants Robert Hall and John George.

*Ganges*, 74 guns, Captain T. F. Freemantle, 7 killed, 1 wounded. Captain John B. Savage, First-Lieutenant Christopher Abbott, Second-Lieutenant Charles R. Miller.

*Russell*, 74 guns, Captain W. Cumming, 6 wounded. Captain-Lieutenant William Barry, Lieutenant George H. L. Crispin.

*Agamemnon*, 64 guns, Captain R. D. Fancourt.

*Ardent*, 64 guns, Captain T. Bertie, 30 killed, 64 wounded. Captain John Hopper, Second-Lieutenant Charles Symonds, Charles H. Ballinghall.

*Polyphemus*, 64 guns, Captain J. Lawford, 6 killed, 25 wounded. Captain George Edward Roby, Second-Lieutenant Joseph Langston.

*Glatton*, 50 guns, Captain W. Bligh, 18 killed, 37 wounded. First-Lieutenant Peter Lely, Second-Lieutenant. Richard Rouse.

*Isis*, 50 guns, Captain J. Walker, 33 killed, and 88 wounded. Lieutenant Henry Long (killed), Lieutenant Richard McCormick.

*Amazon*, 38 guns, Captain H. Riou (killed), 14 killed, 23 wounded. First-Lieutenant Demetrius Grevis James.

*Desirée*, 36 guns, Captain H. Inman, 4 wounded. Second-Lieutenant John Humphries.

*Blanche*, 36 guns, Captain G. E. Hammond, 7 killed, 9 wounded. Lieutenant Robert Clarke.

*Alcmene*, 32 guns, Captain S. Sutton, 5 killed, 19 wounded. First-Lieutenant Stephen M. Sandys (wounded).

*Jamaica*, 24 guns, Captain J. Rose.

*Arrow*, 28 guns, Captain W. Bolton.

*Dart*, 28 guns, Captain J. F. Devonshire, 3 killed, 1 wounded.

Total,— 255 killed, and 688 wounded.

Brigs: *Cruiser* and *Harpy*.

Bomb-vessels: *Discovery, Explosion, Hecla, Sulphur, Terror, Volcano*, and *Zebra*.

Fire-ships: *Otter* and *Zephyr*, and some gun brigs, &c.

Leaving at anchor, under Admiral Parker, the following: *London* 98, Admiral Sir Hyde Parker, *St. George* 98, *Warrior* 74, *Defence* 74, *Saturn* 74, *Ramillies, Raisonable*, and *Veteran*, of 64 guns.

Part of the night was passed in active preparations for the attack: Captain T. M. Hardy proceeded in a small boat to examine the channel, and approached so near the Danish line as to sound around the first ship, using a pole lest the heaving the lead should betray them.

The Danish force consisted of two-decked ships, chiefly old and in a dismantled state, frigates, *prames*, and *radeaus*, mounting altogether 628 guns; and these eighteen vessels were moored in a line extending more than a mile, flanked at the north end, or that nearest the town, by two artificial or pile-formed islands, called the Trekoner batteries; one of 30 twenty-four, the other of 38 thirty-six pounders, with furnaces for heating shot; and both these batteries were commanded by the two-decked block-ships *Mars* and *Elphanten*. Off the harbour and docks, which lie in the heart of the city, were moored two 74-gun ships, a 40-gun frigate, two large brigs, and several armed *xebecs*; and these vessels also had furnaces for heating shot. Along the shore of Amag Island, a little way to the southward of the floating line, were several gun and mortar batteries; and thus the extent of the line of defence in front of Copenhagen covered a space of between three and four miles.

On the 2nd of April a favourable breeze sprang up with the break of day, when all the captains were called on board the *Elephant* by signal, and the plan of attack determined upon; the ships being directed to anchor by the stern, abreast of their opponents in the Danish line. At 9 h. 30 m. a. m. Lord Nelson made the signal for the ships to weigh in succession. The *Edgar* was the leading ship, and the *Agamemnon* was to have followed, but having anchored outside the end of the great shoal, she was unable to weather it, and was consequently obliged again to anchor in six fathoms water. The *Polyphemus* now followed the *Edgar*, and the *Isis* was the third ship. The *Bellona*, in hugging too close to the Middle Ground, stuck fast when about 450 yards from the rear of the Danish line; and the *Bellona*, following close to the *Rus-*

*sell*, also grounded, with her jib-boom almost over her leader's taffrail. The *Elephant* was next to the *Russell*, and Lord Nelson, on perceiving the situation of that ship, ordered the helm to be put a-starboard, and passed to the westward, or along the *Russell's* larboard beam: all the successive ships followed the same course, and reached their stations in safety. Admiral Parker's squadron got under sail at the same time that Lord Nelson weighed, and took up a new position nearer to the mouth of the harbour, but still at too great a distance to do more than menace the north wing of defence.

At 10 a. m. the cannonade commenced, and for the first half hour the only ships engaged were *Polyphemus*, *Isis*, *Edgar*, *Ardent*, and *Monarch*. About 11 h. 30 m. a.m. the *Glatton*, *Elephant*, *Ganges*, and *Defiance* reached their stations, as did the several frigates, bombs, etc. The *Desirée*, by raking the *Provoosteen*, was of great service in drawing her attention from the *Polyphemus* and *Isis*; particularly from the latter, who bore the brunt of that ship's heavy fire, and suffered severely. Owing to the strength of the current, the *Jamaica*, with the gun-vessels and bombs, could not get near enough to do much execution.

The unfortunate circumstance of the *Bellona*, *Russell*, and *Agamemnon* remaining aground, occasioned several of the British ships to have a greater share of the enemy's fire than could have been anticipated, or that they were well able to bear: the *Amazon* was among the many sufferers on that account, as well as the four other smaller ships under the orders of Captain Riou, who consequently had to contend with the Trekoner batteries. The cannonade had continued three hours, when Sir Hyde Parker, considering that the *Defence*, *Ramillies*, and *Veteran* (which had been detached to reinforce Lord Nelson) were approaching but slowly, and that the three line of battle ships remained immoveable where they had grounded, while the *Agamemnon* continued in the same position with signal of inability flying, was induced to throw out the signal to discontinue the engagement.

It is related of Lord Nelson, that when the signal-lieutenant reported that No. 39, "leave off action," was flying on board the *London*, the vice-admiral continued to walk the deck and appeared not to notice it. The officer meeting him at the next turn, asked if he should repeat it: "No!" he sharply replied, "answer it."

Presently His Lordship called after him to know if the signal for close action was still hoisted; and on being answered in the affirmative, he quickly observed, "Mind you keep it so." Then reverting to the message of the commander-in-chief, he exclaimed, "Leave off action?

231

No, d—n me if I do! You know, Foley," turning to the captain, "I have only one eye: I have a right to be blind sometimes," and then putting the glass to the blind eye, in that mood of mind which sports with bitterness, he exclaimed, "I really do not see the signal." Presently he exclaimed, "D—n the signal! keep mine for closer action flying! That's the way I answer such signals;—nail mine to the mast!"

On board the *Elephant* the signal was never repeated; and although it did appear on board the *Defiance*, Rear-Admiral Graves would not suffer the flags to be hoisted anywhere but at the lee main top-sail yard-arm; whilst he kept "No. 16," the signal for close action, flying at the main top-gallant mast-head.

About this time the frigates and sloops had suffered so severely, as to be compelled to haul off from the Trekoner batteries; and while the *Amazon* was unavoidably exposed to their raking fire, Captain Riou and several men were killed. The fire of the Danes began to slacken at 1 h. 30 m., and by 2 p.m. it had nearly ceased along the whole line astern of the *Zealand*, the sixth ship from the rear. Some of the smaller craft had gone adrift, and but few of the vessels whose flags had been struck would allow themselves to be taken possession of; for reinforcements were constantly arriving from the shore, who did not inquire whether the flag had been struck or not; many of them had never been engaged in war before, knowing nothing of its laws, and thinking only of devoting themselves to the defence of their country.

Lord Nelson was so irritated by these proceedings, that he meditated sending in fire-ships to burn the surrendered vessels: as a preliminary measure, however, His Lordship wrote the celebrated letter to the Crown Prince of Denmark, wherein he says:

Vice-Admiral Lord Nelson has been commanded to spare Denmark when she no longer resists. The line of defence which covered her shores has struck to the British flag; but if the firing is continued on the part of Denmark, he must set on fire all the prizes he has taken, without having the power of saving the men who have so nobly defended them. The brave Danes are the brothers, and should never be the enemies of Englishmen.

A wafer was then brought, but Nelson ordered a candle, and sealing the letter with wax, His Lordship observed, "This is no time to appear hurried and informal." This letter was immediately despatched by Captain Sir Frederic Thesiger, acting as *aide-de-camp* to Lord Nelson, who found the crown prince at the sally-port. In the meantime, the destructive cannonade was still kept up by the *Defiance, Monarch,* and *Ganges,* who silenced the fire of several ships in the rear of the Danish line; but the great crown-battery, comparatively uninjured, still continued its fire, and as 1500 men had been thrown into it from the shore, it was considered too strong to be stormed. Preparations were making to withdraw the fleet from the intricate channel while the wind continued fair, when the Danish adjutant-general arrived with a flag of truce; upon sight of which the Trekoner ceased firing, and the cannonade, which had continued five hours, was brought to a close.

The message from the crown prince being to ascertain the precise object of Lord Nelson's note, the vice-admiral replied, in writing, that as humanity was his chief consideration, he consented to stay hostilities, and was desirous that the wounded Danes should be taken on shore. It was his intention to take his prisoners out of the captured vessels, and then burn or carry off the prizes as he might afterwards determine. In conclusion, his lordship expressed his hope, that the victory he had gained would lead to a conciliation between the two countries. Sir Frederic Thesiger returned with the adjutant-general, and the latter was referred to the British commander-in-chief for a final adjustment of the terms. The cessation of hostilities was a favourable moment, and readily taken advantage of by removing the leading British ships, all of whom were much crippled in their rigging and sails. The *Monarch* touched upon the shoal, but the *Ganges* taking her a-midships, pushed her over it.

The *Glatton,* drawing less water, passed clear, but the *Defiance* and *Elephant* grounded about a mile from the crown battery, and, notwithstanding the great exertion of their crews, remained immovable several hours; whilst the *Desirée,* who had gone to assist the *Bellona* at the opposite end of the line, became fixed on the same shoal. The *Bellona* was, however, soon afloat, having extricated herself by picking up the cable which the *Isis* had slipped, and by that means hove off the shoal. Soon after the *Elephant* grounded, Lord Nelson followed the Danish adjutant-general on board the *London* to attend the conference, which secured to England one of her brightest triumphs.

The Danish floating batteries were mostly knocked to pieces; and it is probable that they would have been reduced to that condition in far less time than four hours, had the pilots ventured to place the ships nearer than three and four hundred yards, in which case the heavy carronades of the *Ardent* and *Glatton* would have produced their full effect. It would be impossible to make an accurate return of the loss sustained by the Danes, as the ships were frequently re-peopled from the shore; but the aggregate of killed, wounded, and prisoners has been stated at 6000 men.

The night of the 2nd of April was employed by the British in bringing away the captured vessels, and in floating the grounded ships. The generality of the prizes were so defective and worthless, that the whole, with the exception of the *Holstein* of 60 guns, were, destroyed. On the 9th an armistice was agreed upon, which was to continue for fourteen weeks, and Denmark engaged to suspend all proceedings under the armed neutrality which she had entered into with Sweden and Russia.

The thanks of Parliament were voted to the officers, seamen, and marines in the fleet for the gallantry displayed before Copenhagen on the 2nd of April. Three commanders were promoted to post rank; the senior lieutenants of each ship engaged also gained a step, and the rank of brevet-major was conferred on Captain James Lambrecht, the senior Officer of Marines in the squadron.

On the 3rd of January 1801, at 9h. 30 m. p.m., five boats of the 38-gun frigate *Melpomene*, Captain Sir Charles Hamilton, manned with 55 volunteers from that ship, 5 from a transport in company, and Lieutenant Christie with 35 men from the African corps, under the orders of Lieutenant Thomas Dick, assisted by Lieutenant Wm. Palmer and Lieutenant Wm. Vyvian of the marines, proceeded to the attack of a French 18-gun brig-corvette and an armed schooner, at the entrance of the Senegal River. Having passed the heavy surf on the bar in safety, and without discovery by the battery on the point, the boats at 11 p.m. had arrived within a few yards of the brig; when by a single discharge of her 2 bow guns, two of them were sunk, and Lieutenant Palmer and 7 seamen were killed.

Notwithstanding this loss, the three remaining boats dashed alongside, boarded, and after a severe contest of twenty minutes carried the French brig *Sénegal*, of 18 long eight and twelve-pounder carronades and 60 men, whilst the schooner cut her cables and took shelter under the battery. The prize was immediately got under sail, but having unfortunately grounded on the bar, after several attempts to get her or! she was abandoned; and the three boats succeeded in reaching the ship across a heavy surf, and exposed to a severe fire of grape and musketry from the adjoining batteries. In this gallant affair Lieutenant Palmer, Lieutenant of Marines Wm. Vyvian, and 9 men were killed, and 18 wounded.

On the 19th of February, at 4 p. m., the 36-gun frigate *Phoebe*, Captain Robert Barlow, when about two leagues to the eastward of Gibraltar, discovered and chased a strange ship near Ceuta, steering up the Mediterranean under a press of sail. At 7 h. 30 m. p. m., the stranger finding an action unavoidable, shortened sail; and on the *Phoebe* firing a shot at her, a broadside was returned from the French 40-gun frigate *Africaine*, Commodore Le Saulnier, having 400 troops on board, bound to Egypt. The *Phoebe* steering a parallel course with the enemy, continued engaging within pistol-shot until 9 h. 30 m. p.m., when the *Africaine* being nearly unrigged, having five feet water in the hold, and having sustained a loss of 200 killed and 143 wounded, out of a crew of 715 men, struck her colours. Of the crew of 239 on board the *Phoebe*, only 1 man was killed; her First-Lieutenant J. W. Holland, her master Thomas Griffiths, and 10 men wounded. Lieutenant Thomas Weaver commanded the detachment of marines on board the *Phoebe*.

On the 3rd of April the 36-gun frigate *Trent*, Captain Sir Edward Hamilton, while lying at anchor off the Isle of Bréhat, at daylight discovered a ship with a cutter and lugger, steering towards Plampoul. The boats of the frigate were immediately despatched after the strangers, under the orders of Lieutenant George Chamberlayne, with the other officers of the frigate. Several boats from the shore took the ship in tow, but on the approach of the British they cast her off, and prepared to defend themselves. After a sharp conflict the French lugger and boats were driven on the rocks, and although protected by five batteries, the ship, which was a captured English vessel, was boarded and brought away. Lieutenant Taite of the marines unfortunately lost a leg upon this occasion; which accident, with 2 seamen killed, was the extent of the loss sustained by the British.

After Buonaparte had concluded the treaty of Luneville on the 9th of February with the emperor of Germany, the first consul seemed to entertain serious hopes of landing his victorious legions on the shores of Britain. The port of Boulogne was to be the central rendezvous of the grand flotilla; and in the month of July nine divisions of gun-vessels, with nine battalions of troops, besides artillery, were ordered to assemble. These preparations spread considerable alarm on the coast of England, and caused corresponding preparations for the defensive to be made by the British Government. Vice-Admiral Lord Nelson was appointed to the chief command from Orfordness to Beachy Head; and having his flag on board the 32-gun frigate *Medusa*, he sailed from the Downs with about thirty other vessels, and on the 4th of August bombarded the port of Boulogne.

On the night of the 15th the boats of the squadron, in four divisions, accompanied by several mortar-boats, made an attack on the French flotilla; but owing to the darkness of the night and the uncertainty of the tide, the attacking party separated. The first division, under Captain Somerville, was carried considerably to the eastward of Boulogne bay; and finding it impracticable to reach the flotilla in the order prescribed, the boats were ordered to cast each other off, and make the best of their way towards the enemy. A little before daybreak on the 16th, some of the leading boats attacked a brig lying close to the pier-head, and after a sharp conflict carried her; but owing to the vessel being secured with a chain, and the heavy fire of grape and musketry from the shore and four armed vessels within pistol-shot, they were compelled to abandon their prize. The boats now retreated with a loss of 18 killed and 55 wounded; among the latter was Captain George Young of the marines. The other three divisions attacked with equal determination, but were alike unsuccessful, and their combined loss amounted to 44 men killed and 71 wounded; making a total in this gallant enterprise of 62 men killed and 126 wounded.

On the 3rd of August the 38-gun frigate *Pomone*, Captain E. L. Gower, having outsailed the three other frigates with which she was cruising off Elba, at 8h. 10 m. p.m., after the interchange of a few shot from their chase guns, and a resistance of about ten minutes duration, captured the French 40-gun frigate *Carrère*. The *Pomone* had 2 men killed; Lieutenant Charles Douglas of the marines lost a leg, and 2 seamen were wounded.

On the 2nd of September the French frigates *Bravoure* and *Succès*, which had sailed from Leghorn on the 31st of August, were discovered by the British frigates *Minèrve*, *Pomone*, and *Phoenix*, then lying in the Piombino channel. After a pursuit of some hours, the *Succès* ran aground on the shore of Vada, and was taken possession of by the *Pomone*; whilst the *Bravoure* grounded under the battery of Antignano, and was totally wrecked.

Shortly after the disposal of these frigates, which had hitherto created great annoyance to the garrison of Porto-Ferrajo, Lieutenant-Colonel George Airey, commanding the British troops in that fortress, applied to Rear-Admiral Sir J. B. Warren for the assistance of the marines of the squadron under his command to attack some of the French batteries, and those especially which shut up the port. Immediate preparation was made for the active co-operation of the squadron, consisting of the *Renown, Gibraltar, Dragon, Alexander, Généreux,* and *Stately,* of the line, with *Pomone* and *Pearl* frigates, and *Vincejo* brig. On the 13th at daybreak the *Dragon* and *Généreux,* to create a diversion, opened a fire upon the round tower of Marciana; and on the 14th, a little before daylight, 449 marines, under the following officers, were landed:—

*Captains*: Robert Johnstone, John Richardson, and Francis Williams.

*Lieutenants*: James Fischatt, Joseph Coombs, John Clarke, Thomas M'Gill, Michael Burton, David Weir, William Ravenscroft, David Holt, W. D. Jervis, Beddingford Pagedon, Frederick William Mann, John Davidson, and George Peebles.

This battalion, in conjunction with 200 seamen and a party of Tuscans, amounting in the whole to about 1000 men, were formed into two divisions, under the direction of Captain J. C. White of the *Renown.* After a successful attack upon the batteries, which were destroyed, and taking 55 prisoners, including three captains and two subalterns, the allied force was opposed to very superior numbers, and compelled to retire with a loss of 32 men killed, 61 wounded, and 105 missing. Lieutenant Clarke of the marines was wounded and made prisoner. Captain James Weir commanded a Maltese corps, and distinguished himself on this occasion; and he again signalized himself in a subsequent sortie on the night of the 10th of October. The garrison continued to defend itself until the Treaty of Amiens produced a cessation of hostilities.

On the 25th of May, Lieutenant Wilson of the marines assisted in the boats of the 28-gun frigate *Mercury,* under the orders of Lieutenant William Mather, in attacking the late British bomb-vessel *Bull-dog,* lying moored off the mole of Ancona. She was boarded and the cables cut, when the alarm having spread, a heavy fire was opened upon the British of musketry and cannon. A favourable light breeze enabled the prize to gain sufficient offing as to be without the reach of the batteries, when it unfortunately fell calm; and the current carrying the captured vessel close to the shore, she was attacked by the gunboats, and Lieutenant Mather was reluctantly compelled to abandon his prize, with the loss of 2 killed, and 4 wounded.

Lieutenant Wilson was again employed in the boats in the attack of a pirate *tartan,* mounting 8 guns, and a crew of 60 men, lying among the rocks of the small islands of Tremiti, in the gulf of Venice. Notwithstanding the boats were exposed to a sharp fire of cannon and musketry, both from the vessel and from a four-pounder upon an eminence, they gallantly rowed in; and while Lieutenant Mather boarded the vessel, Lieutenant Wilson landed with the marines, and drove the enemy from the hill, taking several prisoners. The service being fully accomplished, the marines re-embarked, and the *tartan* was brought out without any loss on the part of the British.

In the month of July the *Beaulieu*, Doris, and *Uranie* frigates were lying at anchor about 3 miles to the south-south-east of St. Matthew's lighthouse, and in full view of the combined fleet of France and Spain, when the French 20-gun ship-corvette *Chevrette* was discovered also at anchor under some batteries in Camaret bay. It was resolved to make an attempt to cut her out from this position of apparent security; accordingly, on the night of the 20th the boats of the *Beaulieu* and *Doris*, manned entirely by volunteers, and placed under the orders of Lieutenant Woodley Losack of the *Ville de Paris*, proceeded on this enterprise. From the circumstance of the boats not pulling alike, the detachments separated, and some returned to their ships; whilst the remainder, having reached the entrance of the bay of Camaret, lay upon their oars until daylight on the 21st, and disappointed in not having been supported by their companions, they pulled back to the frigates.

As they had been discovered by the *Chevrette* as well as from the shore, so much of the plan as contemplated a surprise was defeated; consequently the corvette on the following morning got under weigh, and having run about a mile and a half further up the bay, she was moored close under some heavy batteries. The *Chevrette* then embarked a detachment of soldiers, sufficient to augment her number of men to 339, and made the most careful preparation to repel an attack; bringing the arms and ammunition upon deck, and loading the guns with grape and canister. Having thus profited by the discovery of the morning, the corvette, in defiance, displayed a large French ensign over the English colours. This insulting bravado, while it tended to inspire the British with increased ardour to renew the attack, made them more determined to reverse the position of the national flags.

At about 9 h. 30 m. p.m. the boats of the three frigates, joined by two from the *Robust*, numbering altogether fifteen boats, containing 280 officers and men, still under the command of Lieutenant Losack, proceeded again to the attack of the *Chevrette*. Shortly after their departure, the division of six boats under that officer went in chase of a boat supposed to be from the shore. The remainder lay on their oars, awaiting the return of the commanding officer; and after some time had elapsed, Lieutenant Keith Maxwell of the *Beaulieu*, the next officer in command, considering that they had at least six miles to pull, and that the night was far advanced, resolved, notwithstanding that his force was now reduced to 180 men, to proceed without further delay. He then gave orders, that whilst one party was engaged in disarming the enemy on deck, some of the smartest topmen of the *Beaulieu* should fight their way aloft and loose the sails; others to cut the cable, and a quartermaster was named, who was to take charge of the helm of the corvette.

It was about 1 p. m. on the 22nd when the boats arrived in sight of the *Chevrette*; who, after hailing, opened a heavy fire of musketry and grape, and presently there was a loud roll of musketry from the shore. In face of this determined preparation, the boats dashed nobly on towards the ship: those of the *Beaulieu*, under Lieutenants Maxwell and James Pasley, with Lieutenant James Sinclair of the marines, boarded on the starboard bow and quarter; those of the *Uranie* under Lieutenant Martin Neville, one of the *Robust's* under Midshipman Robert Warren, and one of the *Doris's* under Lieutenant Walter Burke, on the larboard bow. The French obstinately opposed the assailants, and in their turn boarded the boats; whilst in their efforts to overcome this formidable opposition, many of the British lost their fire-arms, and with their swords only succeeded in gaining a footing on the enemy's deck.

Those who had been selected for going aloft, fought their way to their respective stations, and although some were killed and wounded, the remainder gained the corvette's yards; and here, finding the foot ropes strapped up, the intrepid fellows had to scramble out upon their hands and knees: yet so quickly was this part of the service performed, that in less than three minutes after the boats got alongside, and in a conflict against numbers more than trebly superior, the three top-sails and courses were loosened, and the cable having been cut at the same time, the ship casted as a light breeze sprang up from off the land, and the *Chevrette* began drifting out of the bay. The Frenchmen perceiving their sails fall, and the ship under way, were seized with astonishment and consternation: some leaped overboard, whilst others threw away their arms, and ran down the hatchways.

The British had now possession of the upper deck, but those of the corvette's crew who had fled below, still maintained a smart fire of musketry; nevertheless, they were soon overpowered, and compelled to submit. The batteries continued to fire at the ship, and just as she cleared the point it fell calm, and she became exposed to a shower of shot and shell; but a light breeze from the north-east soon drove her out of their range. About this time some boats were seen approaching from the direction of Brest; and Lieutenant Maxwell, suspecting them to be enemies, was preparing for a new conflict, when the strangers were recognised as the division under Lieutenant Losack, to which officer Mr. Maxwell resigned the command.

This gallant and unequalled exploit was performed in the presence of the combined fleet of France and Spain, by an officer on his own judgment and responsibility; and whose intrepidity and presence of mind, seconded by the wonderful exertions of the officers and men under his command, succeeded in effecting an enterprise, which, by those who reflect .upon its peculiar circumstances, will ever be regarded with admiration and astonishment. Lieutenant of Marines James Sinclair, Mr. Robert Warren, midshipman, 7 seamen, and 2 marines were killed; Lieutenants Martin Neville and Walter Burke (the latter mortally), 3 Midshipmen, Edward Crofton, Edward Byrn, and Robert Finnis, 42 seamen, and 9 marines wounded; and 1 marine drowned in the *Beaulieu's* barge, which was sunk by the enemy's shot. Total,—11 killed, 57 wounded, and 1 drowned.

The *Chevrette* had her captain, 2 lieutenants, 3 midshipmen, 1 lieutenant of infantry, and 85 men killed; 1 lieutenant, 4 midshipmen, and 57 seamen and soldiers wounded. Total,—92 killed, and 62 wounded.

Lieutenants Rose and Sinclair of the marines were both volunteers in this enterprise, and the latter was killed in the act. of defending Mr. Crofton, midshipman of the *Doris*, who, in his efforts to get on board the corvette, was wounded in two places.

On the night of the 20th of August, the boats of the *Fisgard*, *Diamond*, and *Boadicea* frigates, under the orders of Lieutenant Philip Pipon, boarded and carried the Spanish ship *Neptune* of 20 guns, a gunboat mounting a long twenty-four pounder, and a merchant ship, all moored within the strong batteries of Corunna, and within pistol-shot of the shore. The three vessels were brought out without sustaining the slightest loss. Lieutenant Mark Anthony Gerrard of the marines was a volunteer in this gallant affair.

Lieutenant Gerrard was so much esteemed by his shipmates in the *Fisgard*, with whom he had so frequently acquitted himself with valour and honour, that a gratifying testimony was conferred upon him by his gallant companions. It consisted of a handsome sabre and belt, with the following inscription:—

This sabre and belt are presented to First-Lieutenant Gerrard of the marines, by those who served with him on board His Majesty's ship *Fisgard*, in memory of the action with *L'Immortalité*, on the 20th of October, 1798; the boarding expeditions at the Saintes, Penmarcks, Quimper, Noirmoutier, St. Matthew, St Andero, and Corunna, in which he served as a volunteer, and bore so distinguished a part.

This gallant officer was rewarded by the adjutancy at the Plymouth division, where he was highly respected and esteemed by his brother-officers.

On the 31st of January a squadron, consisting of the *Foudroyant* of 80 guns, *Kent, Ajax, Minotaur, Northumberland, Tigre,* and *Swiftsure,* with a fleet amounting to above sixty sail of vessels, conveying an army of 16,000 men under General Sir Ralph Abercromby, anchored in Marmorice Bay. On the 1st of February the expedition arrived in sight of Alexandria, and on the 2nd anchored in Aboukir Bay. A succession of strong northerly gales, attended by a heavy swell, set in, and lasted until the evening of the 7th; when the weather becoming moderate, preparations were made for landing the troops. At this time, according to the returns in the *Moniteur,* the French force in Egypt amounted to 21,000 fighting men; and there were also about 900 sick, 1000 sailors, 4 or 500 Greek auxiliaries, with perhaps 1200 persons in civil employments; and the whole was under the command of General Abdallah Jacques Menou.

At 2 a.m. on the 8th, the British troops began embarking, and at 9 a.m. the signal was made for the boats to advance towards the shore, which operation was promptly accomplished under the respective captains and agents of transports; while the launches, containing the field artillery, as well as the detachment of seamen to co-operate with the army, was under the immediate direction of Sir William Sidney Smith, assisted by several other officers.

The whole line moved forward under the direction of the Honourable Captain Cochrane, flanked by the smaller vessels; and the landing was covered by the *Tartarus* and *Fury* bombs, while the *Peterel, Minorca,* and *Cameleon* were moored as near as possible to the shore. The British force, amounting altogether to about 700 men, was opposed by the whole garrison of Alexandria, consisting of 1500 infantry and 180 cavalry, exclusive of several detachments from Rosetta and other places; forming a total of at least 2,500 men, under the command of General Friant, who had stationed a part of his men with 15 pieces of artillery upon an almost inaccessible hill, which commanded the whole space of debarkation; while others, with field pieces and mortars, were placed in such positions as the ground afforded. As the boats arrived near the shore, a heavy fire of grape and musketry was opened from behind the sand-hills, and the castle of Aboukir maintained a constant discharge of shot and shells on their right flank; but despite of all opposition the beach was attained, and the troops, having steadily formed, immediately advanced and compelled the enemy to relinquish all his advantageous positions. The boats returned without delay, and before the evening of the 9th the whole army, with a proportion of stores and provisions, was landed.

The brigade of seamen, amounting to about 1000 men, commanded by Sir William Sidney Smith, landed with the army; their duty was to drag the cannon up the heights,—a service they performed with their usual alacrity and determination, and in which they sustained a loss of 22 killed; 3 lieutenants, 4 midshipmen, and 63 wounded. The army on the same occasion had 4 officers, 4 sergeants, and 94 rank and file killed; 26 officers, 34 sergeants, 5 drummers, 450 rank and file wounded: making a total of 124 killed, 585 wounded, and 38 missing. On the 12th the army moved forward and came in sight of the French, whose force had been reinforced by 4000 men under General Lanusse, including upwards of 1000 cavalry; and now amounting to about 7000 men, formed upon an advantageous ridge, having their right on the canal of Alexandria, and their left towards the sea.

Several detachments of marines were landed from the squadron and formed into a battalion, consisting of 35 sergeants, 32 corporals, 22 drummers, and 500 privates, under the command of Lieutenant-Colonel Walter Smith, with the following officers:

*Major:* William Minto.

*Captains:* George Wolfe, Robert Torkington, and R. Roe.

*Lieutenants:* Paul Hussey, Thomas Mould, John Linzee Shea, Roger P. Symons, Walter Stubbe, James Short, Edward Bailie, Zaccheus Fayerman, Robert Stewart, Arthur Hall, Richard Hill, and John Witts.

*Second-Lieutenants:* John Jewell, Richard Parry, Charles F. Burton, George Peebles, James Jones, Alexander Murray, Zaccheus Miller, Richard Ekenhead, George A. Mayhew, Richard Turner, John Davenport, Thomas Hussey, Thomas Edensor, Thomas Appleton, Thomas A. Lascelles, M. L. Crofton, William Pridham, George Johns, Richard

Swale, and William Swyer.

*Adjutant*: Charles Tyldesley.

After the battalion had assisted in filling bags with sand for the batteries, they received orders to march at seven on that morning to join the army, then about 15 miles distant, which they effected, after much fatigue, at one on the morning of the 13th. At 5 the troops were under arms, and having made the necessary preparations for attacking the enemy, the army advanced in two lines, in order to turn their flank; but the French, anticipating this movement, descended from the heights they occupied, and at about 7 o'clock attacked the leading brigades of both lines. The engagement becoming general, the marines were somewhat crowded in their ranks by the regiments on their right and left, owing to the narrowing of the peninsula on which they acted; and it was at this moment, in their too great eagerness to cope with the enemy, they suffered a severe loss.

The brigade of seamen, under Sir Sidney Smith, emulated the brave troops with whom they were associated, and sustained a loss of 1 midshipman and 5 seamen killed, and 19 wounded. The battalion of marines had 2 lieutenants, Paul Hussey and John Linzee Shea, with 22 rank and file killed; 1 major, William Minto; 1 captain, Robert Torkington; 2 lieutenants, Richard Parry and George Peebles (both severely); 2 sergeants, 2 drummers, and 27 rank and file wounded. Total,—24 killed, and 35 wounded. On the part of the army, 6 officers and 150 killed; 66 officers, 61 sergeants, and 946 rank and file wounded.

The following appeared in public orders on the morning after the battle:—.

G. O. 14th of March, 1801.

The commander-in-chief has the greatest satisfaction in thanking the troops for their soldier-like and intrepid conduct in the action of yesterday. He feels it incumbent upon him particularly to express his most perfect satisfaction with the steady and gallant conduct of Major-General Craddock's brigade, and he desires that Major-General Craddock will assure the officers and men of the 90th regiment, that their meritorious conduct commands his admiration. To the 92nd and Dillon's regiment an equal share of praise is due: when it has been so well earned, the commander-in-chief has the greatest pleasure in bestowing it. Sir Ralph Abercromby desires that Lieutenant-Colonel Smith and the battalion of marines will accept his thanks, for their gallant conduct in the course of the service of yesterday.

At the request of Lord Keith, that corps will march this afternoon to Aboukir, and will place themselves under the command of colonel the Earl of Dalhousie.

Accordingly, in the afternoon the battalion marched to Aboukir, where it remained some time after the surrender of that fortress, which capitulated on the 18th, after a bombardment of two days. The castle mounted 10 guns and 2 heavy mortars, and was garrisoned with 300 men, under a *chef de bataillon.*

Although General Menou was officially apprized on the 4th of March of the arrival of the British expedition in Aboukir Bay, he did not quit his headquarters at Cairo until the 11th, nor did he arrive at the camp, under the eastern walls of Alexandria, before the evening of the 18th. The reinforcements he brought with him augmented the French force at Alexandria to 9730 men, including 1380 cavalry, with 46 pieces of cannon. The effective force of the British Army at Bedah did not exceed 10,000 men, including only 300 cavalry, with 12 pieces of moveable artillery, and 30 pieces in the different redoubts, thrown up to protect the encampment.

On the 21st, at about an hour before daylight, the French attacked the British with great impetuosity; but after an obstinate and sanguinary contest, were repulsed with a loss of 800 killed, 200 wounded, and 400 prisoners, according to their own account; but their loss has been estimated at 3000 in killed, wounded, and prisoners. Among the killed were Generals Lanusse, Roize, and Baudot; and among the wounded, General D'Estaing and several other distinguished officers.

The loss of the British was also very severe: it amounted to 10 officers and 233 killed; 60 officers and 1133 wounded, with 3 officers and 31 missing. The commander-in-chief was mortally wounded by a musket-ball in the upper part of the thigh; and Major-General Moore and Brigadier Hope were both wounded in the head, but not dangerously.

The marines were at Aboukir Castle at the period of the action, but the seamen under Sir Sidney Smith shared in the battle, and sustained a loss of 1 master's mate, Mr. Krebs, and 3 seamen killed; Sir Sidney himself, Lieutenant Davis, and 48 seamen wounded: making the grand total in the Battle of Canopus, so named by the French, amount to 247 killed, 1243 wounded, and 34 missing.

General Sir Ralph Abercromby, at his own request, was conveyed on board the *Foudroyant*, where he breathed his last on the 28th of March. Major-General J. H. Hutchinson, who succeeded to the command of the army, thus eloquently expresses himself on the death of the late commander-in-chief:—

> Were it permitted to a soldier to regret anyone who has fallen in the service of his country, I might be excused for lamenting him more than any other person; but it is some consolation to those who tenderly loved him, that as his life was honourable, so was his death glorious. His memory will be recorded in the annals of his country, will be sacred to every British soldier, and embalmed in the recollections of a grateful posterity.

On the 26th a second ottoman squadron arrived, having on board 5000 Turks and Albanians. This made the Turkish force in Aboukir Bay amount to six sail of the line, and eight frigates and corvettes. On the 3rd of April the Turkish troops were landed, and with a division of 800 British, and 8 pieces of cannon, under Colonel Spencer, after a fatiguing march across the desert, gained possession of the castle of Rosetta; which was a post of great importance, protecting an unmolested navigation of the Nile, and enabling the British, by a communication with the friendly inhabitants of the Delta, to obtain supplies and provisions. On the 16th the castle of Jullien, on the banks of the Nile, mounting 15 pieces of cannon, was attacked by a division of British and Turkish gunboats, and on the land side by the troops of Colonel Spencer's corps; but it was not until the 19th that the castle surrendered, after a brave resistance.

On the 15th of April the British cut the canal of Alexandria, and let the waters of Madieh into the basin of the ancient Lake Mareotis; which for ages past had been dry, except that a considerable portion of it, at certain seasons especially, was impassable, owing to the swampy nature of its bed. Although the first rush of water from its volume and impetuosity was awfully grand, some time elapsed before the whole area of the lake became covered. When this was accomplished, the troops under General Menou, amounting to about 6000 men, became shut up in Alexandria, and separated from the 4000 under General Lagrange, entrenched at El-Aft, and the 5000 under General Belliard in garrison at Cairo. Leaving Major-General Coote in command of the army before Alexandria, Major-General Hutchinson arrived at Rosetta on the 26th of April, to direct in person the operations against the French in the interior of the country; and on the 5th of May the major-general, with the combined British and Turks, in number about 8000, advanced towards the position of General Lagrange at El-Aft, accompanied by the gunboats on the river, under the command of Captain James Stevenson.

On the 7th the French general abandoned El-Aft and retreated towards Rahmineh, which place was attacked by the gunboats under Captain Curry on the 9th, in which affair the British sustained a loss of Lieutenant Hobbes and 3 seamen killed, and 7 wounded. During the night the enemy retreated towards Cairo, leaving in the fort 110 sick and wounded. The possession of this important post effectually cut off all communication between Alexandria and the interior of Egypt. Owing to various delays, the allied forces did not arrive at Embaeth, a village distant about a mile and half from the fortress of Giseh, until the 20th of June. On the 22nd, while preparations were making to besiege Cairo, General Belliard sent a flag of truce to Lieutenant-General Hutchinson, offering to capitulate upon honourable terms: these were signed by the respective parties on the 27th, stipulating that the French troops, amounting to 8000 effective, 1000 sick, and about 500 convalescent, should be conveyed to a port in France.

Whilst these operations were going forward, a force of 6000 men was approaching from Bombay, under the command of Major-General Baird, which landed in Kosseïr Bay on the 9th and 14th of May. Between the 10th and 15th of June, the two divisions of this army commenced their march across the desert by the valley of Kuittah, and on the 30th arrived at Kenneh, on the banks of the Nile; but owing to the difficulty in procuring boats to descend the river, the major-general did not effect a junction with the army under Lieutenant-General Hutchinson until several days after the surrender of Cairo. A detachment of 320 men, under Lieutenant-Colonel Lloyd of the 86th regiment, which marched across the desert, a distance of above eighty miles, reached Cairo on the 12th, after a painful and distressing journey, in which 3 officers and 20 men perished. The last division of the French troops, taken prisoners at Cairo and other places, amounting to nearly 13,500 men, having by the 10th of August sailed from the bay of Aboukir, immediate measures were adopted for the reduction of Alexandria, which was the last strong-hold of the French in Egypt.

On the night of the 16th, about 5000 troops, under Major-General Eyre Coote, embarked on Lake Mareotis, escorted by the flotilla of gunboats under Captain Stevenson; and having proceeded to a position westward of the town of Alexandria, disembarked early on the morning of the 17th without opposition; previous to which the French set fire to their flotilla of eighteen gunboats, stationed opposite to Pompey's Pillar, and protected by a battery of 3 long eighteen-pounders. After sustaining a combined naval and military attack, the island of Marabou capitulated on the 21st, and on the same evening a small squadron of the allies entered the harbour; soon after which the French sank several merchant vessels to impede the further progress of the British to the eastward, having previously moved their two 64-gun ships and corvettes close up to the town.

Four batteries on each side of the town opened upon the entrenched camp of the French on the morning of the 26th; and being pressed on all sides, General Menou, on the evening of the 27th, sent an *aide-de-camp* to Lieutenant-General Hutchinson requesting three days' armistice, in order to prepare a capitulation: this proposal was acceded to, and on the 2nd of September the city of Alexandria surrendered. The garrison, consisting of 8000 soldiers and 1300 sailors, were to be conveyed to France at British expense, as had already been the case with the garrison of Cairo. This concluding operation of the campaign was effected with a loss of 13 killed and 113 wounded; and to the British navy, in the attack on Marabou, of 2 killed and 2 wounded: making the total loss on the part of the British in the Egyptian campaign, of 330 killed, 1872 wounded, and 39 missing: that of the French, commencing at the disembarkation of the British troops in Aboukir Bay, between 3000 and 4000 men in killed alone.

The marines, as constituting a material proportion of the strength of Lord Keith's fleet, were continued on the coast, and their duties were confined to the blockade of Alexandria, where they might be ready to re-embark in case of emergency. They were withdrawn from the defence of Aboukir, and remained attached to the brigade of Major-General Coote until the 5th of August, when, at the desire of Lord Keith, they re-embarked on board their respective ships.

The following testimonials bespeak the exemplary conduct of the battalion in such flattering terms, that no comment, can enhance their merit, and we therefore subjoin the official report:—

*Foudroyant*, Bay of Aboukir, 5th July, 1801.

Sir,

I have had much satisfaction in receiving the commands of the Lords Commissioners of the Admiralty to make known to you Their Lordships' approbation of your conduct, and that of the officers, non-commissioned officers, and privates of the marine battalion, landed from the ships in the squadron to co-operate with the army on the coast of Egypt; and I have to request that you will, with the permission of Major-General Coote, communicate the approbation which Their Lordships have been pleased to express to the officers and men serving under your command.

I have the honour to be, sir,

Your very obedient humble servant,

(Signed)                                             Keith.

Lieut.-Col. Smith
&c. &c &c.

Previous to their embarkation, Major-General Coote issued the following:—

Camp, near Alexandria, 3rd August, 1801.
At the request of Admiral Lord Keith, it is Lieutenant-General Sir John Hely Hutchinson's directions that the battalion of marines, under your command, is to hold itself in readiness to return on board their respective ships. I cannot, however, suffer you to leave the division of the army, without assuring you how perfectly satisfied I am with the attention you have always paid to the marines. The good conduct of your corps whilst under my orders does them the greatest credit, and I beg you will be so obliging as to signify the same both to your officers and men.

I have the honour to be, &c.

Eyre Coote.

Lieut.-Col. Smith,
&c. &c &c.

The battalion having done duty during some time in the first brigade under Major-General Finch, that officer thus expressed his sentiments:—

Brigade Orders, August 5th, 1801.
Major-General Finch, in taking leave of Lieutenant-Colonel Smith and the marines under his command, requests him to accept his warmest thanks for the order, regularity, zeal, and attention that have uniformly marked their conduct during the period he had the honour of commanding the first brigade; and

he shall be happy, on all occasions, to bear testimony to their merit in the correct performance of their duty in every respect, which has come under his observation.

The following flattering communication from Lord Hutchinson, was sent to Lieutenant-Colonel Smith after his return to England:—

Jermyn-Street, 28th June, 1802.

Sir,

Your sudden departure from Egypt rendered it impossible for me to desire that you would communicate my thanks to the marines who served under your command during the campaign. May I now beg that you will assure the officers and men how highly sensible I am of their meritorious services, and of the zeal and exertion which ever marked their conduct. The order and discipline preserved by the battalion does great credit to your military character, and is equally honourable to the respectable corps which you had the good fortune to command.

I have the honour to be, &c.

Hutchinson,<br>Major-General.

Lieut.-Col. Smith,
Royal Marines.

The medals conferred by the *grand signior* upon every officer of the army, commemorative of their services during the Egyptian campaign, were, from some omission, withheld from the marines; but in consequence of a representation from Lord Keith to the Earl of Elgin, at that time the British ambassador at the Ottoman Porte, these honourable marks of distinction were conveyed to Sir Richard Bickerton, commanding the British naval forces at Malta, who transmitted them with the following letter:—

*Kent*, at Malta, March 18th, 1803.

Sir,

I have the honour of forwarding to you some Turkish medals, to be distributed among the officers of marines who served on shore, and in the squadron employed in the blockade of Alexandria, during the Egyptian campaign.

The accompanying letter and list will explain everything; it therefore only remains for me to add, that I feel a pleasure in having been made a medium in conveying what may be acceptable to a small part of your corps; and I should be much more gratified if it was in my power to congratulate you on the acquisition of more substantial advantages for the whole, being every day more fully convinced of its services and utility.

I have the honour to be, sir,

&c. &c. &c.

R. Bickerton.

Lieut.-Col. Smith,
Royal Marines.

On the 13th of June Rear-Admiral Linois, with the 80-gun ships *Formidable* and *Indomptable*, *Desaix* 74, and *Muiron* frigate, put to sea from Toulon, intending to proceed to Cadiz; but on learning that a superior force blockaded that port, the rear-admiral, at 5 p.m. on the 4th of July, anchored his squadron in front of the town of Algesiras. On the 5th Rear-Admiral Sir James Saumarez, commanding the British squadron before Cadiz, having been apprised of the appearance of the French ships off the rock of Gibraltar, immediately repaired in quest of them; and at 7 a.m. on the 6th, the *Venerable*, on opening Cabrita Point, discovered the French squadron, then warping further in shore to get under the protection of the batteries that defended the road, and moored in line ahead thus: the *Formidable*, nearly abreast of the San-Jago battery, mounting 5 long eighteen-pounders; the *Desaix* about 500 yards astern, and to the southward of the flag-ship; and the *Indomptable* about the same distance astern of the *Desaix*: the *Muiron* took her station a little within, and to the northward of the Isla-Verda, whilst fourteen heavy guns were placed in suitable situations to support the ships of the line.

At 8 a.m. the *Venerable* lay becalmed at a considerable distance on the starboard bow of the *Pompée*, and shortly afterwards the latter, followed by the *Audacious*, passed the *Venerable* to windward. At this time, the *Caesar* and the two remaining ships were upwards of three miles astern.

The following is a statement of the British squadron, with their loss of killed and wounded, showing the names of the officers of marines serving on board the respective ships.

*Caesar*, 80 guns, Rear-Admiral Sir James Saumarez, Captain Jahleel Brenton, 18 killed, 25 wounded. Captain James Maxwell, First-Lieutenant William Dymock, First-Lieutenant Philip Pipon, Second-Lieutenant Henry Grape.

*Pompée*, 74 guns, Captain Charles Stirling, 15 killed, 69 wounded. Captain Samuel Middleton, Lieutenant Alexander Anderson, Lieutenant George F. Skipp.

Spencer, 74 guns, Henry D'Esterre Darby, 6 killed, 27 wounded. Captain Thomas Abernethie, First-Lieutenant Robert Stevens, Second-Lieutenant Joseph Triscott.

*Venerable*, 74 guns, Captain Samuel Hood, 8 killed, 25 wounded. Captain John Wardlaw, Second-Lieutenant Walter S. Boyd, Second-Lieutenant John Cockell, Second-Lieutenant Alexander Smith.

*Superb*, 74 guns, Captain Richard G. Keats, Captain Benjamin Dickenson, First-Lieutenant Charles Rosville, Second-Lieutenant Joseph Britton, Second-Lieutenant W. Dorrington. *Hannibal*, 74 guns, Captain Solomon Ferris, 75 killed, 62 wounded. Captain John Victor, First-Lieutenant William Connolly, Lieutenant James D. Williams (killed), Second-Lieutenant George Dunford (wounded).

*Audacious*, 74 guns, Captain Shuldham Peard, 8 killed, 32 wounded. Captain Martin Horlock, Lieutenant Robert Hart, Second-Lieutenant Nathaniel Pitts, Second-Lieutenant Robert J. W. Day.

Total,—killed 130, wounded 240.

At 8 h. 30 m. a.m. the *Pompée*, hauling close up for the tower of Santa Garcia and the island battery, received the fire of the *Muiron*, and successively of the *Indomptable, Desaix*, and *Formidable*; and after firing a broadside at each of the two latter ships, dropped her anchor close to the *Formidable's* starboard bow, where she continued the action with great spirit. At 8 h. 50 m. the *Audacious*, and five minutes afterwards the *Venerable*, baffled by the want of wind, having dropped their anchors, the former abreast of the *Indomptable*, and the *Venerable* at a considerable distance from the quarter of the *Formidable*, a furious cannonade was maintained on both sides. At about 9 h. 15 m. the *Caesar* anchored ahead of the *Audacious*, and after sending a spring on board the *Venerable*, she opened her broadside upon the *Desaix*. A few minutes afterwards, the *Hannibal* also got into action, anchoring within hail, and on the starboard bow of the *Caesar*.

The *Spencer*, owing to the light winds, was far to leeward, and could not approach much nearer than was sufficient to expose her to the heavy fire of the Spanish batteries. At 10 a.m. the *Hannibal* was ordered by the rear-admiral to weigh, and take a position to rake the French admiral in order to support the *Pompée*, who was then in a very critical situation. The *Hannibal* immediately cut her cable, and casting herself by the spring, stood to the northward with the light air from the west-north-west, and then tacked for the *Formidable*; but at

11 a.m., just as she had arrived abreast of the tower of Almirante, and was in the act of hauling closer to the shore in order to cross the hawse of the French ship, the *Hannibal* took the ground. In this situation she opened a fire upon the *Formidable* with as many of her foremost guns as she could get to bear, and the remainder were directed with evident effect upon the tower of Almirante, the battery of San Jago, and the gunboats. An ineffectual effort was made to get the ship afloat, and a boat from the *Venerable* and *Caesar* had been sent to afford assistance; but finding every means unsuccessful, the boats returned to their respective ships, whilst the *Hannibal* continued to defend herself as she could bring her guns to bear upon the enemy.

Soon after the *Hannibal* grounded, a light breeze sprang up from the north-east, and Rear-Admiral Linois, to get further from the reach of his opponents, threw out the signal for his ships to cut, and run themselves on shore. This was immediately complied with; but the wind suddenly failing, the *Formidable* brought up again with her broadside towards the enemy: in the meanwhile the *Desaix* grounded upon a shoal in front of the town, and the *Indomptable* upon one to the north-east of Isla-Verda, with her larboard towards the sea.

The *Caesar* now made the signal for the British ships to cut, and then wearing round the *Audacious* and *Venerable*, she brought her broadside to bear upon the *Indomptable*, into whose bows the *Caesar* poured a destructive fire. At a little before noon the *Audacious* passed between the *Caesar* and *Indomptable*, and shortly afterwards the fore top-mast of the latter was shot away. The *Venerable* and *Spencer*, after cutting their cables, were incapable, on account of the calm that immediately ensued, of co-operating in the attack; and the *Venerable's* mizen top-mast was shot away just as she was in the act of casting. The *Pompée*, after remaining nearly an hour unable from her position to bring a gun to bear, had also cut, and was now towed out of action. The *Audacious* and *Caesar* were also prevented, by its falling calm, from taking their new position; and both these ships, exposed to a heavy fire from the guns of the island battery without the power of returning a shot, were drifting upon the reef that was near it.

Thus frustrated by the unfavourable state of the weather, and the serious opposition of the enemy's batteries and shipping, and being prevented, by the destruction of most of the boats and the absence of the remainder, which had gone to assist the *Pompée*, from an attempt to storm the island with the marines of the squadron, the *Caesar* and *Audacious* at 1 h. 30 m. p.m. cut their cables; and profiting by a light breeze from the shore, made sail on the starboard tack in company with the *Venerable* and *Spencer*, being reluctantly compelled to leave the dismasted and nobly-defended *Hannibal* as a trophy in the enemy's hands.

The loss and damage sustained by the British squadron was very considerable: the total killed amounted to 121, 240 wounded, and 14 missing. Lieutenant James D. Williams of the marines was killed on board the *Hannibal*, and Lieutenant George Dunford wounded.

As soon as Rear-Admiral Linois got his ships afloat, he sent an express to Admirals Massaredo and Dumanoir at Cadiz, requesting them to despatch a squadron to his assistance, before the British ships were sufficiently repaired to renew the attack. In compliance with this solicitation, Vice-Admiral Moreno with six sail of the line moved into the outer road of Cadiz on the 8th, ready to start with the land-wind on the next morning. This movement was observed by Captain Richard G. Keats, who with the *Superb* 74, *Thames* frigate, and *Pasley* brig, were watching the motions of the fleet in Cadiz. On the 9th, the enemy's squadron put to sea, consisting of five ships of the line and three frigates, steering towards the straits, and preceded by the British 74, frigate, and brig.

Early in the afternoon the *Pasley* came crowding into Gibraltar, with the signal flying for an enemy; and at 3 p.m., while the Spanish squadron was hauling round Cabrita Point, the *Superb* and *Thames* anchored by signal in the bay of Gibraltar. Shortly afterwards the Spanish squadron cast anchor in the road of Algesiras; and on the following morning the *St. Antoine* 74 joined them from Cadiz. As it was now evident that this reinforcement was to conduct the squadron of Admiral Linois to Cadiz, the utmost exertion was made by the men and officers of the British squadron to get their ships ready for sea. The *Pompée* was in too bad a state to admit of her being refitted in time, her men were therefore turned over to assist in the repairs of the other ships; and the *Caesar* was in so shattered a state, that the admiral shifted his flag to the *Audacious*; but when this circumstance was made known to the crew of the *Caesar*, and that unless she could be got ready in time they were to be distributed to the effective ships, the gallant fellows answered, with three cheers, "All hands to work, night and day, until she is ready."

By their extraordinary exertions, working all day, and watch and watch by night, the ship was warped into the mole and her masts shipped on the 8th; a new main-mast got in on the 9th; and on the

11th their energies were, if possible, increased by the enemy showing some symptoms of sailing. On Sunday the 12th, at dawn of day, the enemy loosed sails; whilst the *Caesar* was still refitting in the mole, receiving stores previous to hauling out. The wind was now fresh from the eastward, but it was not until noon that the combined squadron began to move: at 1 p.m. they were all under weigh, and the two Spanish first-rates off Cabrita point. At this moment the *Caesar* was warping out of the mole, and the line wall, mole-head, and batteries were crowded, from the dockyard to the ragged staff,—the *Caesar's* band playing, "Come cheer up, my lads, 'tis to glory we steer;" the military band of the garrison answering with "Britons, strike home!" It is impossible to describe the enthusiasm of this inspiring scene: all were eager to participate in the glorious struggle at hand, and even the wounded were desirous to be taken on board, to share in the honours of the approaching conflict.

The *Caesar*, as she passed under the stern of the *Audacious* in her way out of the mole, at 3 p.m. rehoisted the flag of Sir James Saumarez, and made the signal for the ships to weigh and prepare for battle. The squadron, consisting of the *Caesar, Venerable, Superb, Spencer,* and *Audacious* of the line, *Thames* 32, Captain A. P. Hollis, with 14-gun polacre *Calpe* and Portuguese frigate *Carlotta*, were soon under sail; and as they got from under the lee of the rock, they formed in line ahead. At 7 h. 45 m. p.m. they wore together, and stood on the starboard tack under easy sail. About 7 h. 50 m. the combined squadron cleared Cabrita point, with the exception of the *Hannibal*, who having top-masts for lower-masts, remained behind in tow of a frigate; and eventually, the two latter returned to Algesiras, leaving the following force:

### SPANISH.

*Real Carlos* 112, *Hermenegildo* 112, *San Fernando* 96, *Argonauta* 80, *San Augustin* 74, with the *Sabina* frigate; and on board of the latter were Vice-Admiral Moreno, and Rear-Admiral Linois.

### FRENCH.

*Formidable* 80, *Indomptable* 80, *St. Antoine* 74, *Desaix* 74, *Libre* and *Muiron*, frigates.

The British squadron bore away in chase soon after 8 p.m., and at 8h. 40 m. the *Superb*, having been directed to go ahead and attack the sternmost ships of the enemy, soon got sight of them; and at 11 p.m. she had so much increased her distance, that the *Caesar* was the only

British ship visible from her. At 11 h. 30 m. the *Superb* shortened sail, and when within 300 yards of the *Real Carlos*, opened her larboard broadside. In a short time the Spanish three-decker was observed to be on fire, just as her mizen top-mast had been shot away; soon afterwards she came suddenly to the wind, and dropped astern in great confusion. The *Superb* then made sail, and at 11 h. 50 m. p.m. brought to action the *St. Antoine*. After a close encounter of thirty minutes, the French 74 ceased firing, and hailed that she had surrendered; but from the circumstance of the broad pendant remaining flying on board of her, owing to the halliards having been shot away, she was fired into by *Caesar, Venerable, Spencer,* and *Thames,* as they successively arrived up.

At about fifteen minutes past midnight the *Real Carlos* blew up, but not until she had fallen foul of the *San Hermenegildo,* who, mistaking the *Real Carlos* for a British ship, had been engaging her; and in less than a quarter of an hour she also exploded. Only 300 were saved out of 2000 men composing the crews of these Spanish ships, but the *Superb* had no further loss than Lieutenant E. Waller and 14 men wounded.

During the latter part of the night it blew very hard, and on the 13th, at 4 a.m., the only ships in company with the *Caesar* were the *Venerable* and *Thames* ahead, in chase of the French 80-gun ship *Formidable* on their lee bow, standing towards the shoals of Conil, with a light air from off the land; at the same time the *Spencer* was in sight, far astern of the admiral's ship. As the *Formidable* had jury top-masts, the *Venerable* and *Thames* came up with her fast, and at 5 h. 15 m. the enemy's ship commenced firing; soon afterwards the *Thames* hauled up and raked her, but the *Venerable* did not open her fire until the lapse of five or six minutes, when the baffling airs threw the two ships broadside-to, within musket-shot of each other. At 5 h. 30 m. the *Venerable* lost her mizen top-mast; and at 6 h. 45. m. her main-mast having fallen by the board, she dropped from alongside her opponent, who stood on her course, keeping up a well-directed fire from her stern chasers.

At 7 h. 50 m. the *Venerable's* fore-mast fell over the side, just as the ship, driven by the strength of the current, struck upon the rocky shoals of San Pedro, about twelve miles to the southward of Cadiz; and at 8 a.m. her mizen-mast shared the fate of the other masts. At this time the *Caesar, Audacious,* and *Superb* making their appearance, the Spanish admiral was induced to haul up for Cadiz, whence the remaining ships of his squadron arrived in safety. By great exertion the *Venerable* was got afloat and towed into Gibraltar; having sustained a loss of her master and 17 killed, Lieutenant Thomas Church and 86 wounded.

For the service rendered to the country by the prompt and effective manner in which the combined squadron under Vice-Admiral Moreno was attacked by the British under Rear-Admiral Sir James Saumarez, the officers, seamen, and marines received the thanks of Parliament; the rear-admiral obtained the distinction of a knight of the bath, and several naval officers were promoted: yet no reward was extended to the marines.

On the 13th of December Captain Fanshawe, of the *Castor* frigate, having discovered some mutinous designs among the seamen, ordered the marines under arms. The command was instantly and cheerfully obeyed by Lieutenant J. S. Smith, who heading his party, drove the most determined of the disaffected to the larboard side of the lower deck, and then seized the ringleaders.

At the court-martial on these deluded men, Captain Western, the president, thus addressed Lieutenant Smith:

> I have it in command from this court, to express to you the high sense they entertain of your very officer-like conduct on the evening of the 13th December, and the good and steady conduct of the party of marines embarked under your orders. Your prompt and spirited execution of Captain Fanshawe's orders, appears to the court to have stopped a very dangerous mutiny; and this token of their approbation of your conduct will be transmitted to the commander-in-chief, and inserted in the minutes of the court-martial.

This flattering mark of approbation was much enhanced, by the following gratifying commendation of the commander-in-chief:

> Southampton, Fort Royal Bay, 26th December, 1801.
> Memorandum.—Whereas the members of the court-martial on the mutineers of His Majesty's ship *Castor* have felt called upon, in justice to the exemplary and meritorious conduct of Lieutenant J. S. Smith of the marines, and the party under his command, to express their high sense of such spirited behaviour;
> It is my directions that these sentiments of the court be read on board His Majesty's ship under my orders, to testify how fully I accord with the court in the commendation so deservedly bestowed.
> (Signed)                                    J. T. Duckworth.

A mutiny broke out on board the squadron in Bantry Bay on the 1st of December, 1801, which continued until the 11th. The marines remained firm to their allegiance, and it is probable that their zealous and loyal conduct deterred the seamen from further resistance of the commands of their officers. Six of the ringleaders were executed on the 5th of January, 1802, and five on the 19th of the same month.

The following letters are from the marines of two ships of the squadron:—

*Princess Royal*, Beerhaven, 12th December, 1801.

Sir,

We, the non-commissioned officers and privates serving as marines of a detachment under your command on board this ship, have heard with pleasure of the gallant conduct of our brother-soldiers on board His Majesty's ship *Téméraire*; and therefore beg leave to express, alike with them, our determination to oppose, with all our might and power, all unlawful combinations, and our readiness to obey our officers night or day.

(Signed by the whole party).

To Lieut.-Colonel Tench.

*Resolution*, Bantry Bay, 15th December, 1801.

Sir,

I hope you will pardon the liberty we take in addressing you, but as we understand that some ships' companies have disobeyed the just commands of their superior officers, and knowing as we do the dreadful consequences that formerly attended same practices, for our parts we abhor the idea; and we hope you will inform Captain Gardner, likewise the admiral, that it is our firm resolution to support and maintain our officers in every thing which they may think proper, and which is best calculated to promote the interests of our king and country.

I have the honour to subscribe myself, and in behalf of the detachment of marines, your most obedient servant,

William Heans,
Sergeant.

Captain Forshall, Marine forces.

GENERAL ORDERS.

The Lords of the Admiralty having expressed their high satisfaction of the good conduct of the marines of several of the ships under my command, with those at Beerhaven, in declaring their abhorrence of the mutinous proceedings which had lately taken place at that anchorage, and of their having come forward upon that occasion, so much to the honour of their corps and the interest of their country; I am to desire that you will be pleased to communicate the same to them, and assure them that I feel highly gratified on the present occasion.

   (Signed)       Wm. Cornwallis.

To Vice-Admiral Sir A. Mitchell,
   &c. &c. &c.

         Spithead, 29th December, 1801.

It is my directions to the captains of His Majesty's ships *Windsor Castle, Princess Royal, Malta, Glory, Resolution,* and *Vengéance,* under my orders, to communicate to the marines serving on board the respective ships under their command the above letter from the commander-in-chief: and I feel equally happy that their good conduct has merited such a mark of approbation from him, and the Lords Commissioners of the Admiralty

             A. Mitchell.

On the 1st of October preliminary articles of peace were signed in London by Lord Hawkesbury, the Secretary of State for Foreign Affairs, on the part of Great Britain, and by Citizen Louis Guillaume Otto, commissary for the exchange of prisoners in England, on the part of France. On the 10th the negotiations were duly exchanged, and on the 12th a proclamation was issued by His Britannic Majesty, ordering a cessation of arms. According to the preliminary articles, five months from the date of the exchange of ratifications was the longest period that hostilities could legally be continued in the most distant part of the globe.

On the 27th of March, 1802, the definitive treaty was signed at Amiens, which stipulated the restoration to France of all the colonies taken from her, except Trinidad and Ceylon. Egypt was restored to the Porte: the islands of Malta, Goza, and Comino were to be restored to the order of Jerusalem, as before the war; and the British troops were to quit those islands within three months after the exchange of the ratification. The French troops were to evacuate Naples and the roman territory; and the British, in like manner, to quit Ferrajo, as well as all the islands in the Mediterranean and Adriatic. The Cape of Good Hope and various other important colonies were restored to Holland;

and Denmark, as well as Sweden, regained their foreign possessions.

The distinguished services of the marines, and their unshaken loyalty, had frequently obtained for them the public expression of their country's gratitude; but no particular mark of the royal favour was extended to the corps, until the 29th of April, 1802, when the following gratifying communication was conveyed to their commandant by the Earl of St. Vincent:—

Admiralty Office, 29th April, 1802.

Sir,

The Earl of St. Vincent having signified to My Lords Commissioners of the Admiralty, that His Majesty, in order to mark his royal approbation of the very meritorious conduct of the corps of marines during the late war, has been graciously pleased to direct that in future the corps shall be styled the 'Royal Marines;' I have great satisfaction in obeying Their Lordships' commands to communicate this intelligence to you; and in offering Their Lordships' congratulations on this testimony of the opinion His Majesty entertains of the very distinguished services of that part of his forces to which you belong.

I am, sir, &c. &c.

(Signed)                    Evan Nepean.

Lieutenant-General Souter Johnstone,
Commandant of the Marines.

The unsettled state of affairs in Europe induced the British Government to keep up a large peace establishment, and consequently the marines retained 100 companies, making a total force of 12,119 men. Six field-officers, eight captains, one captain-lieutenant, three first-lieutenants, and three second-lieutenants, were allowed to retire; and the retired establishment was made an open list.

The detachment of marines under the command of Captain Johnstone, serving on board the 80-gun ship *Gibraltar* in the Mediterranean, was distinguished for its firmness in suppressing a mutiny. Two of the ringleaders were hung by sentence of a court-martial.

The following order was issued by the commander-in-chief:—

*Kent*, Oristagni Bay, 4th November, 1802.

Memorandum.—Whereas, it appears in the minutes of the late court-martial on the mutineers of the *Gibraltar*, that the detachment of marines serving on board that ship bore no part in the disgraceful proceedings of the 6th of October last; but, much to the credit of the officers and themselves, maintained the character of the loyal and respectable corps to which they belong, by a steady adherence to their duty; the rear-admiral takes this public method of expressing his approbation of their good and soldier-like conduct, and requests Captain Johnstone to accept his thanks.

(Signed)                                    Richard Bickerton.
To the respective Captains.

A similar instance of insubordination occurred on board the 74-gun ship *Excellent*, in the West Indies, which was subdued by the firmness and discipline of the marines, whose fidelity obtained the following commendation from Commodore Hood:

*Blenheim*, Carlisle Bay, Barbadoes, 30th Dec. 1802.
Memorandum.—The commander-in-chief had flattered himself in the hope, that all those ill-disposed acts of mutinous conduct were at an end in the Royal Navy, and that the seamen would endeavour to heighten their characters in the eyes of the rest of His Majesty's subjects; but he trusts the punishment he has been obliged to order to be carried into execution on those unfortunate men, may be sufficient example to deter a few evil-minded persons from disturbing the repose and good order amongst the seamen in future.

The commander-in-chief, (as well as the members of the court-martial), are highly sensible of the active exertions of the officers of His Majesty's ship *Excellent* in quelling the late mutiny on board her, and also the officers, non-commissioned officers, and private marines belonging to the said ship; who by their firmness in resisting the attempt to seduce them from their duty, and in opposing men in actual mutiny, have increased, if possible, the high character the corps has so justly acquired; and he begs to assure the whole of them, they have his best thanks, and he will not fail to represent their meritorious conduct to the Lords Commissioners of the Admiralty.

(Signed)                                    Samuel Hood.
To Captain Maxwell, *Blenheim*.

A detachment of 40 men, under Lieutenant O'Neal, from the 74-gun ship *Magnificent*, disembarked on the 10th of April on the island of Dominica, to assist in quelling an insurrection in the 8th West India regiment. This small party took post on a hill, and although opposed by a body of above 400 men, they maintained their position until reinforced by 25 men, under Lieutenants Lambert and Hawkins; and then, with the assistance of some colonial militia, they succeeded in rescuing several officers from the hands of the mutineers. On the following day the marines marched to Grand-Ance, and uniting with detachments of the Royal Scotch and 68th regiments, they entered the fort of Sirley on the 13th, and forming in front of the black corps, the latter, on being desired, grounded their arms; but when commanded to advance, they resumed their arms, which they instantly discharged. The detachment returned the fire, and then drove the mutineers with the bayonet, who, retreating up the Outer Cabaret, became exposed to a discharge of grape from the *Magnificent*. On the return of the detachment to Martinique, they received the thanks of General Johnstone, and of the presidency of Dominique.

In 1803 the peace of Amiens was so unpopular to both nations, that it was generally expected to be but of short duration: warlike preparations continued to increase with such activity, that it gave to the treaty the character of a truce or suspension of arms, in which both parties were striving to gain an advantageous position on a renewal of hostilities. Squadrons were preparing in the ports of France, Holland, and Spain; and a British fleet was in readiness to watch and follow their movements. France had long been desirous to gain possession of Malta, or to have that island placed under the protection of a power favourable to her interests; but England, in order to counteract that design, stipulated that this important island should be guaranteed by Great Britain, France, Austria, Russia, and Spain, and not under the protection of Russia alone. It was no longer concealed that Buonaparte's intentions were to occupy Egypt and the Ionian islands; and the augmentation of the French military establishments gave a clear indication of these warlike proceedings.

Negotiations were opened with a desire to remove the difficulties in the way of a continuance of peace; but the unfavourable aspect of affairs produced a message from His Majesty to Parliament, stating that the preparations in the ports of France rendered it necessary to increase our armaments by sea and land, although the French Government protested that it had no other view in these preparations, beyond subduing their own revolted colony of San Domingo.

In the ultimatum submitted by Great Britain, it was proposed to retain Malta for ten years, but France contended it should be ceded to Russia: Lord Whitworth consequently left Paris, and war was declared against France by His Britannic Majesty on the 18th of May, 1803;

On the night of the 27th of June, two boats from the 38-gun frigate *Loire*, Captain F. L. Maitland, under the orders of Lieutenant Francis Temple, attacked the French national brig *Venteux* of 10 guns, anchored close under the batteries of the Isle of Bas. Although fully prepared for the assault, she was gallantly boarded, and after a defence of ten minutes, carried and brought out, with the loss on the part of the British of 5 seamen and 1 marine wounded.

On the 2nd of July, in the evening, the 38-gun frigate *Minerve*, Captain Jahleel Brenton, being close in with the harbour of Cherbourg in a thick fog, grounded on the western conehead, and became exposed to the fire of two batteries, mounting together 170 guns and 40 mortars. After great exertion, the *Minerve* was got afloat at 4 a.m. on the 3rd, and would soon have been out of gunshot, when it unfortunately fell calm; and the last of the flood carrying the now helpless ship into the harbour, laid her upon a broken cone, where she remained until the top of high water, and then surrendered, having sustained a loss of 11 men killed and 16 wounded.

On the 4th of July, in the evening, Lieutenant Robert Irwin of the marines assisted in the boats of the *Naiad* frigate, under the orders of Lieutenant William Dean, in an attack and capture of the French national schooner *Providence*, mounting 2 guns, with a crew of 22 men, moored among the rocks and shoals of the Saintes.

The 36-gun frigate *Blanche*, Captain Z. Mudge, was lying anchored in Manunille bay, in St. Domingo, on the 3rd of November, when the French cutter *Albion*, having a crew of 43 men and officers, was discovered close to the battery of Monte Christe, mounting 4 long twenty-four pounders and 3 fieldpieces. During the day three boats, under the orders of Lieutenant Braithwaite, proceeded to attempt the capture of this vessel; but owing to the breeze blowing right on shore, the enterprise was abandoned. A night attack was then resolved upon, and Lieutenant Edward Nicolls of the marines volunteered to cut her out in a single boat. On the evening of the 4th that officer, accompanied by 12 men in the ship's cutter, pushed off from the frigate; but was shortly followed by the barge with 22 men, commanded by Lieutenant the Honourable Warwick Lake.

Lieutenant Nicolls soon afterwards pointed out the object of their pursuit to Lieutenant Lake; but the latter, considering that the French cutter lay on the opposite or north-east side of the bay, proceeded in that direction, leaving the other boat to watch the vessel that had been discovered. At about 2 h. 30 m. a. m. on the 5th, Lieutenant Nicolls pulled cautiously towards the cutter, whose crew expecting a second attack, had made preparations to meet it. On arriving within pistol-shot, and being hailed by the cutter, the British gave three hearty cheers and dashed at her, receiving in quick succession two volleys of musketry,—the second discharge wounding the coxswain severely, the man at the bow oar, and a marine; but before the enemy could fire a third time, Lieutenant Nicolls, at the head of his little party, sprang on board of her. The ball of the French captain's pistol entered the lieutenant's side, then passing under the skin, lodged in the fleshy part of his opposite arm; and almost at the same moment the captain was killed, either by the pistol of Lieutenant Nicolls, or by a marine standing near him. The crew were then driven below, after very little further resistance, with the loss, besides their captain killed, of 5 men wounded.

As yet the battery had not fired a shot, although only 100 yards distant from the cutter; for as the marines continued to fire their muskets while the seamen were getting the vessel under weigh, the enemy believed the *Albion* was still resisting. But Lieutenant Lake arriving at the moment the jib was hauled for casting, he ordered the musketry to be discontinued; whereupon the battery opened a fire of round and grape, which killed 2 of the *Blanche's* seamen. However, as there was a favourable breeze, the cutter, with the two boats towing her, soon ran out of gunshot, without incurring any further loss.

It can scarcely be credited that the captain of the *Blanche* should purposely detract from the merit of Lieutenant Nicolls, by not only omitting the name of that officer in the report of wounded, but even the credit of the gallant capture of the cutter is attributed to the joint attack under Lieutenant Lake, who certainly did not take part in the fight, nor did he arrive on board the prize until she was under way. Captain Mudge in his official letter, says:

At 2 this morning the enemy's cutter was masterly and gallantly attacked by Lieutenant Lake in the cutter, and Lieutenant Nicolls of the marines in the barge, who cut her out. She is 92 tons burthen, coppered close up and fastened; having 2 four-pounders, 6 swivels, and 20 muskets. The affair cost me 2 men killed, and 2 wounded.

From this report it would be impossible to infer that the "two men wounded," included a commissioned officer; but Lieutenant Nicolls, although omitted by his captain, was honoured by a sword of the value of £30 from the Patriotic Fund, for having commanded one of the boats; whilst Lieutenant Lake, *for his gallantry*, obtained one of £50! Another quarter, equally deceived, promoted Lieutenant Lake, but paid no attention to the claims of the officer who so nobly executed the service he had gallantly undertaken.

On the 16th of November a detachment from the *Blenheim* 74, consisting of 71 seamen, under Lieutenants Thomas Cole and Thomas Furber, with 60 marines under Lieutenants George Beatty and Walter S. Boyd, and the whole under the orders of Captain Ferris of the Drake sloop, proceeded at 11 p.m. to attempt the capture of the *Harmonie*, French privateer, mounting 8 carriage guns, with a crew of 66 men, in the harbour of Marin, island of Martinique. It was arranged, that while the seamen attacked the privateer, the marines were to surprise, or at all events to storm Fort Dunkirk, a battery of nine guns, situated on the starboard side of the harbour, and the possession of which was necessary, to prevent the island militia from collecting on Marin Point, whence they could have greatly annoyed the boats on their return. By judiciously timing their departure from the ship, both parties arrived at the same instant at their respective destinations. The marines surprised the fort, and took 15 prisoners, and having dismounted and spiked the guns, they destroyed the carriages and blew up the magazine. But Lieutenant Beatty humanely spared the barracks; for had they been set on fire, a large and ripe field of canes would have been destroyed. The seamen had 1 killed and 5 wounded.

On the 26th of November Captain Acheson Crozier and Lieutenant Walker, with the detachment of marines, were landed from the 74-gun ship *Centaur*, at the Petite Ance d'Arlette, Martinique, and carried a battery mounting 6 twenty-four pounders, which they destroyed, and threw the guns over the precipice. In exploding the magazine, one man was killed; Captain Crozier, Lieutenant Walker, and 6 men wounded.

Lieutenant McLauglan, of the marines of the *Centaur*, assisted at the destruction of a battery of 3 guns on the Pointe d'Arlette, between Grande and Petite Ance.

CHAPTER 8

# From January 1804, to October 1805

In the early part of the year 1804, a considerable military force assembled on the French coast, and the preparations for invading England were continued with the greatest activity, in the construction of 2000 *prames*, gun-vessels, and flat-bottomed boats, to convey the army across the Channel. Almost every department of the nation voted a ship of the line, each of the larger villages a frigate, and every commune gave its *prame*, gun-vessel, *peniche*, or flat-bottomed boat. Vessels for the flotilla were constructing, not only in all the naval ports and in the small harbours along the coast, but upon the banks of every river. Even Paris became for a time a maritime arsenal: two slips were erected there, and many vessels of the smaller kind were launched on that part of the Seine. At Antwerp, for the first time during a great many years, the keels of ships of the line were laid down; and at Brest, l'Orient, Rochefort, and Toulon, several ships of force and magnitude were ordered to be built.

The ports of reunion of the flotilla were seven: Ostend, Dunkerque, Calais, Ambleteuse, Vimereux, Boulogne, and Etaples; and Boulogne, being only twelve leagues from the low land between Dover and Hastings, was made the main depot. This port, until the projected invasion, possessed an insignificant harbour, formed by the estuary of a small river which was nearly dry at low water, having only one quay; but in a short time both banks of the river were lined with quays, moles were constructed, a capacious basin formed, and a bridge thrown across the river; and the water being confined by means of a dam, vessels were kept constantly afloat. Immense batteries were erected on all the commanding points, and a strong line of heavy gun-vessels moored across the road, which from the numerous shoals and sand-banks was difficult of approach: the tides, too, which cross each other in an extraordinary manner, were very serious obstacles in the way of a bombarding force.

Corresponding exertions were making on the British coast: a number of small vessels, each armed with one or two heavy long guns, were stationed at the Nore, and at all the most assailable parts of the shore; as were also several large ships, mounted with heavy carronades. Martello towers were erected along the coast, and a large army, composed of regulars, militia, and volunteers, was ready to meet the enemy, should he venture to place foot on English ground. In the Channel, and all along the French coast, our cruisers were constantly on the watch, ready to fall upon the divisions of the flotilla when they showed themselves outside the sands and batteries by which they were protected; and scarcely a day passed without some skirmish, either with the vessels under the protection of their numerous batteries, or by encounters with the flotilla.

On the 15th of January Captain John Bligh, of the 74-gun ship *Theseus*, was ordered by Sir John Duckworth to proceed from Port Royal, St. Domingo, and summons the garrison of Curaçoa, taking with him the 74 gun-ship *Hercule*, frigates *Blanche* and *Pique*, and *Gipsy* schooner. Owing to calms and variable winds, this squadron did not reach the island of Curaçoa until the 31st, when a summons was sent to the governor, who peremptorily refused the terms. The passage into the harbour is so narrow, that even with a fair wind, a line of battle ship can enter with difficulty; and the batteries, mounting nearly 100 pieces of cannon, entirely command the entrance.

Under these circumstances, no alternative remained but to try the effect of a landing. Captain Bligh therefore bore up with two seventy-fours for an eligible spot where the disembarkation might be effected, leaving the two frigates to cause a diversion of the enemy's force, and to blockade the harbour. According to a previous arrangement, the boats of the squadron, all the marines of the four ships, amounting to 199, including Lieutenants Edward Nicolls (senior-officer), William Henry Craig, Samuel Perrot, Earle Harwood, and Bertrand Cahuac, had assembled on board the *Hercule*, with a detachment of 406 seamen; numbering together 605 officers and men, under the order of Captain Richard D. Dunn.

Fort Amsterdam, situated on the south-east side of the entrance to St. Ann, fired at the ships as they passed, but the shot fell short. At 11h. 30 m. Fort Piscadero, mounting 10 twelve-pounders, and protecting the intended point of disembarkation, opened a fire, which was returned by the *Theseus* within half musket-shot; who, making short tacks, so effectually silenced the enemy, that at 1 p. m. the first division of seamen and marines landed, stormed the fort without sustaining any loss, and struck the Dutch colours. They then by a rapid movement gained the heights, and with the loss of only four or five killed drove the Dutch soldiers from the position: by this time, the remainder of the detachment had landed without opposition.

On the morning of the 13th of February, 2 eighteen-pounder carronades and a field-piece were landed from the *Theseus*, and with great difficulty and danger were dragged four miles to the advanced position on the height, situated about 800 yards to the westward of the town of St. Ann, which it in part overlooked; and this post was placed under the command of Lieutenant N. J. Willoughby, while the position between it and the place of disembarkation was under the orders of Lieutenant J. B. Hills. On the 2nd, 2 long eighteen-pounders and 1 twelve-pounder were placed in "Willoughby's battery;" but in effecting this, some loss was sustained from the heavy fire kept up by Fort République. Four eighteen-pounder carronades and another field-piece having been landed and mounted at the outposts, a constant interchange of firing was kept up between the British and Dutch batteries.

A smart skirmish took place between our advanced post and the enemy's sharp-shooters on the evening of the 4th, when the latter were repulsed; and on the morning of the 5th there was a serious affair between the marines under Lieutenant Nicolls, and a force of Dutch and French amounting to 500 men. Notwithstanding the inferiority of the British, Lieutenant Nicolls in the most gallant manner engaged the allied forces, and drove them under the guns of Fort République, from whose destructive fire, the marines sustained a loss of 20 in killed and wounded. On the 6th the cannonade was resumed on both sides, and the town partially set on fire. Many successive days were passed in this way, the British force decreasing, not only by the encounters with the enemy and the cannon of their heavy batteries, but from fatigue and sickness, 63 men had been embarked on account of dysentery. Thus circumstanced, and learning that the Dutch had already received a reinforcement, Captain Bligh determined on withdrawing the whole of his force; and at 11 p.m. on the 25th the detachment safely arrived on board the vessels appointed to receive them, having previously destroyed Fort Piscadero.

The loss of the British, in the different skirmishes with the enemy, amounted to 1 midshipman, 8 seamen, 2 sergeants, and 7 privates of marines killed; Lieutenants Harewood, Cahuac, and Perrot (the latter with the loss of an arm), 16 seamen, 2 sergeants, and 21 privates of marines, wounded. Total,—18 killed, and 42 wounded.

On the 11th of July, at 10 p.m., three boats of the 32-gun frigate *Narcissus*, three of the 38-gun frigate *Seahorse*, and four of the 32-gun frigate *Maidstone*, under the orders of Lieutenant Thompson, assisted by several officers, and among that number Lieutenant William Wiltshire of the marines, proceeded to the attack of twelve *settees* lying at La Vaudour, in the bay of Hyères, distant between four and five miles from the ships. The enemy's vessels were moored head and stern close to the beach, to which they were also completely secured, and covered by a battery of three guns. About midnight the *settees* were boarded under a tremendous fire of grape and musketry, as well from the vessels as from the batteries and the houses of the town: most of them were set fire to, and only one was brought off.

This gallant attack was unfortunately attended with severe loss: Lieutenant William Wiltshire of the marines, 1 midshipman, and 2 seamen, were killed; 1 lieutenant, 1 master's mate, 3 midshipmen, 15 seamen, and 3 marines wounded. We cannot refrain from an expression of astonishment, that in neither the letter of Lieutenant Thompson to Captain Donnelly, nor in the latter's official report, is there any mention of the officer of marines who gallantly fell in this enterprise; and but for the surgeon's return of the casualties, we should have been denied the opportunity of recording the name of Lieutenant Wiltshire.

In the latter part of September, the *Acasta* frigate, Captain Atholl Wood, was attached to the Channel fleet, and on regaining her station off the Black Rocks, after a heavy gale from the eastward, reconnoitred the French fleet lying in Brest harbour. Finding that five ships of the line had disappeared since the frigate's last visit, it became a matter of speculation to account for the departure of the French squadron; and as a means of ascertaining the cause of their absence, Lieutenant Thomas Peebles of the marines suggested the following scheme, which that officer carried into execution on the same evening. Soon after dark, the *Acasta* stood pretty close to the shore; and early on the following morning the lieutenant, with six marines in one of the cutters, and accompanied by Mr. Hemet, the master, put off from the frigate, directing their course for the point of Bertheaume, where it will be recollected there is a strong fort situated on a rock, and connected with the main land by a wooden bridge.

Under this bridge the fishing-boats from Brest were accustomed to assemble during the night, in readiness to pursue their occupation on the following morning. It was just daylight when the cutter arrived near the rock, and immediately gaining possession of a fishing-boat, and taking a man out of two others, she was brought off, unobserved by the sentries in the fort directly over their heads. On reaching the *Acasta*, the fishermen were separately examined, and as they concurred in their statement that the missing ships had moved into the inner harbour, the Frenchmen, after being well regaled, were allowed to proceed to Brest in their own boat.

On the 13th of August the 32-gun frigate *Galatea*, Captain Henry Heathcote, having discovered the late British sloop *Lily* (now the *Général Ernouf*), refitting as a French privateer near Anse à Mire in the Saintes' islands, and lying anchored near a French privateer-schooner; four boats, under the orders of Lieutenant Hayman, assisted by several officers, including Lieutenant Robert Hall of the marines, were sent to attempt her capture. At 10 p.m. the detachment left the *Galatea*, and pulled towards the harbour under cover of the night; but the enemy had placed a guard-boat in advance, which gave an intimation of their approach, and consequently they were fully prepared to receive the attack. About 1 a.m. on the 14th, Lieutenant Hayman in the barge, leading the party, was nearly alongside the *Lily*, when the firing commenced: heedless of this reception the boats dashed alongside, and in the dreadful conflict which ensued, Lieutenant Hayman fell mortally wounded; and only 3 out of the 26 men and officers in the barge were left free from dangerous wounds.

The three other boats tried in vain to overcome the numerous and still increasing force opposed to them; and after sustaining a fire for nearly an hour, they were compelled to abandon the enterprise, leaving the barge to her fate. On their return, they were exposed to a very destructive fire from the batteries, which continued until 3 h. 30 m. a.m.; and just as the day dawned the miserable remnant of the expedition reached the frigate. Out of the 90 officers and men who quitted the *Galatea*, not more than twenty returned unhurt: besides Lieutenant Hayman, Mr. Michael Birbeck, the master, and Mr. Wall, midshipman, were among the killed; and Lieutenant Robert Hall of the marines, who lost an arm, was made prisoner. The total loss on this occasion amounted to 65 in killed and wounded: it would be difficult to state the loss of the enemy, but they acknowledge having had four men killed.

On the 15th of September the 50-gun ship *Centurion*, when lying in Vizagapatam roads, at 10 a.m. was attacked by the French 74-gun ship *Marengo* and two 40-gun frigates, who, after an action of thirty minutes, hauled off to seaward; but at 11 h. 15 m. the *Marengo* and her consorts were again seen approaching, and the 74 having anchored about a mile from the *Centurion*, recommenced the cannonade, supported occasionally by the *Atalante*, under sail upon the quarter of the British ship. At 1 h. 15 m. a shot cut the cable of the *Centurion*, and about the same time the 74 made sail, accompanied by the frigates, and taking with them the *Princess Charlotte* Indiaman. The *Centurion* also got under weigh, and continued her fire until the enemy was out of gunshot, having 9 men wounded. Captain Lind, in his official letter, expresses himself much indebted to the zeal and energy of Lieutenant Waring of the marines.

Intelligence having reached the ministry that an armament was fitting out at Ferrol, and that French troops were on their way thither, the Admiralty despatched a squadron of four frigates, under Captain Graham Moore, to intercept four laden frigates, having treasure on board, from Monte Video, bound to Cadiz. On the 5th of October the squadrons met off Cape St. Mary's, and the Spanish rear-admiral refusing to be detained and conducted into an English port, an action ensued; during which one of their frigates exploded, and the other three surrendered, with a loss of 13 killed, and 80 wounded. The English squadron had 2 men killed, and 80 wounded.

That the British Government had any right to detain this squadron was more than doubtful, even to those who concurred in the expediency of the measure; but when the alternative was determined upon, it would have been only considerate to have sent a more formidable force to execute the service, in order to have justified the Spanish admiral in surrendering without an appeal to arms. This act of aggression produced an order from the court of Madrid on the 27th of November to make reprisals on English property; but it was not until the 12th of December that the King of Spain issued his formal declaration of war, nor until the 12th of January that Great Britain directed letters of marque to be granted against Spanish vessels and property.

Scarcely had the declaration of war been issued by the court of Madrid, than France began to put in requisition the fleets and armies of her new ally. On the 4th of January, 1805, three days actually before the Spanish declaration reached London, a secret treaty between the two courts was signed at Paris, by Vice-Admiral Decrès on behalf of

France, and by Vice-Admiral Gravina on the part of Spain. The first article contains a display of the force at the French emperor's disposal, describing the respective flotillas at Ostend, Dunkerque, Calais, Boulogne, and Havre as collectively capable of embarking 120,000 men, and 25,000 horses; whilst in the united ports of Brest, Rochefort, and Toulon, there were thirty-eight sail of the line affording a grand total of 188,000 men. On the part of Spain, she was to furnish twenty-nine ships of the line, and to have from 4000 to 5000 troops ready to embark at Cadiz, in conjunction with 20,000 French infantry.

The British Government took immediate measures for the increase of every branch of our force; and the number of seamen voted for this year, was 120,000, including 30,000 marines.

On the 13th of February the 36-gun frigate *San Fiorenzo*, Captain Henry Lambert, near Vizagapatam fell in with the French 32-gun frigate *Psyché*, having in her company two captured British vessels. After a long chase, the *San Fiorenzo* was enabled to bring the French frigate to action at 8 p.m. on the 14th, which continued with great fury on both sides until 9 p.m., when the *Psyché* fell on board her antagonist; but in about a quarter of an hour the ships got clear, and the cannonade recommenced. The French frigate's main-yard was shot away at 9 h. 40 m., but the firing continued with unabated fury until 11 h. 30 m. p.m., when the *San Fiorenzo* hauled off to reeve new braces, and repair her rigging. At midnight the latter bore up to renew the conflict, and just as she was about to open her broadside, a boat came on board from the *Psyché*, announcing her surrender.

The *San Fiorenzo*, out of a crew of 253 men and boys, had 12 killed and 36 wounded; among the latter, Lieutenant Samuel Ashmore of the marines. The *Psyché* had three lieutenants and 54 men killed, and 70 wounded, out of a crew of 240 men. The heroic defence of a ship of such inferior force during a close action of more than three hours, reflected the greatest credit on the gallant Captain Bergeret; and every Frenchman who is proud of his country's glory, should hold in honourable recollection the determined resistance of the *Psyché*. On the 16th of February, at daybreak, the 32-gun frigate *Cleopatra*, Captain Sir Robert Laurie, when in latitude 28° north, longitude 27° west, went in chase of the French 40-gun frigate *Ville de Milan*: both ships were under all sail, and the pursuit continued through the night.

At daybreak on the 17th they were only four miles apart, the *Cleopatra* still gaining on the enemy. At 10 h. 30 m. the *Ville de Milan* took in her studdingsails and hauled more up; and after some manoeuvre on the part of the French ship to get the weather-gage, a running fight was maintained until 2h. 30 m. p.m., when just as the *Cleopatra* had arrived within a hundred yards of her opponent, the latter luffed close to the wind and discharged her broadside, which was repeated before the British frigate returned the fire: a warm action then ensued, which continued with great spirit, both ships steering free. At 5 p.m. the main top-sail yard of the *Ville de Milan* was shot away, and the *Cleopatra*, being so much disabled as to be incapable of shortening sail, ranged ahead; Captain Laurie therefore prepared to cross the bows of his adversary, but just at that moment a shot struck the wheel of the *Cleopatra*, and rendered the rudder ungovernable.

Availing herself of the helpless condition of her opponent, the *Ville de Milan* bore up and gave her the stem, running her head and bowsprit over the latter's quarter-deck, just abaft the main rigging; and covered by a heavy fire of musketry the French crew attempted to board, but were repulsed. The *Cleopatra* was now incapable of further resistance, and in a second attempt the French boarded and took possession of their gallantly defended antagonist. Almost immediately afterwards, the *Cleopatra's* fore and main-masts went over the side, and her bowsprit soon followed. Out of a crew of 200 men and boys, she had 22 killed and 36 wounded, including among the latter Lieutenant Thomas Appleton of the marines. The *Ville de Milan*, out of a crew of 350, had 1 men killed and several severely wounded.

After refitting the captured ship, the *Ville de Milan* with her prize, continued her route towards a French port; and on the 23rd, at noon, they were discovered and chased by the 50-gun ship *Leander*, Captain John Talbot. About 3 p. m. the two frigates closed for mutual support, but on the arrival of the *Leander* within gun-shot, they separated,— the *Cleopatra* running before the wind, and the *Milan* with the wind on the starboard quarter. At 4h. 30 m. the *Cleopatra*, on receiving a shot from the *Leander*, hauled down her colours, and was immediately taken possession of by her original crew. Observing this, the *Leander* made sail after the *Ville de Milan*, and at 5h. 30 m. having arrived alongside, the French ship surrendered without firing a gun.

On the 6th of May, in the morning, the 32-gun frigate *Unicorn*, when about nine leagues to the northward of Cape Francois, St. Domingo, discovered the French cutter *Tape-à-bord*, of 4 long six-pounders, and 46 men. The prevailing calm rendering a chase by the ship impracticable, Captain Hardyman despatched four boats under the command of Lieutenant Henry Smith Wilson, assisted by several officers, and among that number Lieutenant Walter Powell of the marines. After a pull of several hours the boats reached the cutter, and, under a heavy fire of great guns and musketry, boarded and carried her without the slightest casualty.

On the 27th of May, Lieutenant Thomas Bland of the marines, in command of the barge of the 32-gun frigate *Seine*, Captain David Atkins, when off Aguadilla, island of Porto Rico, went in pursuit of the Spanish schooner *Concepcion*, mounting 2 long six-pounders, with a crew of 10 men besides several passengers, and captured her after some resistance. About three weeks afterwards the same enterprising officer, assisted by Midshipman Edward Cook, being on a cruise in the barge, destroyed a Spanish sloop; and after an action of three quarters of an hour captured a second *Concepcion*, a large *felucca*, bound from Porto Rico to Cadiz, and armed with 2 long four-pounders and 14 men, five of whom were severely wounded; but no loss was sustained by the British.

On the 1st of June the 38-gun frigate *Loire*, Captain F. L Maitland, being off the coast of Spain, chased a small privateer into the bay of Camarinas, near Cape Finisterre; and when it became dark, the launch and the two cutters, with 35 officers and men under Lieutenant James Lucas Yeo, assisted by Lieutenant Samuel Mallock of the marines, and three midshipmen, were sent to attempt her capture. Owing to the intricacy of the passage, the boats did not reach the point of attack until break of day on the 2nd, when they found two privateers moored under a battery of 10 guns. Lieutenant Yeo, with the two cutters, gallantly attacked and carried the Spanish *felucca Esperanza*, armed with long eighteen-pounders, 4 four-pounders, brass swivels, and 50 men; of these 19 were missing, including several that had been killed by the pike and sabre, the only weapon used by the British, to prevent discovery. The launch, commanded by Mr. Charles Clinch, master's-mate, had in the meantime attacked and captured a lugger of 2 six-pounders, and 32 men. No loss was sustained by the British in this affair.

Captain Maitland having received information that a French privateer of 26 guns was fitting out at Muros, and nearly ready for sea, he resolved to attempt the capture or destruction of that vessel. After arranging the plan of attack, the *Loire* at 9 a. m. on the 4th stood into the bay, having in tow the boats containing fifty officers and men, commanded by Lieutenant Yeo, assisted by Lieutenants of Marines Samuel Mallock and Joseph Douglas, and Master's Mate Charles Clinch.

As the *Loire* hauled round the point, a small battery of 2 long eighteen-pounders opened a fire upon her, and some shots were returned; but finding that the battery, from its commanding situation, would considerably annoy the ship, Lieutenant Yeo was directed to push for the shore and spike the guns.

As the *Loire* opened the bay, a corvette was discovered, pierced with 13 ports of a-side, apparently ready for sea, and a brig with 10, in a state of fitting; but neither had their guns mounted. These vessels were protected by a fort of 12 long eighteen-pounders, which now opened to view within less than a quarter of a mile, and which commenced a well-directed fire on the frigate. The *Loire* immediately anchored with a spring, and opened her broadside upon the fort; but with little effect, owing to its elevated situation, and from being protected by its embrasures. After a few minutes of this unequal warfare, during which the *Loire* had 9 men wounded, the fort ceased its annoyance; and just at that moment the British colours appeared above the walls.

As Lieutenant Yeo landed with his party to storm the battery on the point, the Spaniards, amounting to 18 men, abandoned their guns and fled; and scarcely had the seamen time to spike the 2 eighteen-pounders, when at the distance of a quarter of a mile, and close to the town of Muros, the fort, whose destructive fire upon the frigate we have just described, was observed to open upon the *Loire*. Notwithstanding the formidable appearance of the fort, Lieutenant Yeo determined to attempt its immediate reduction, and the detachment readily proceeded to the attack of this important post. Not suspecting an attack by land, and being wholly occupied in firing at the frigate, the garrison had left open the outer gate of the fort: the French sentinel, after discharging his musket, retreated through this gate, and was quickly followed by the advance of the storming party, led by Lieutenant Yeo, who attacked and killed the governor.

The contest then became severe, but the boldness and vigour of the assault was irresistible, and the remainder of the garrison, composed principally of the crew of the French corvette, and numbering above 90 men, fled to the further end of the fort; from the embrasures of which many of them leaped upon the rocks, a height of 25 feet. Shortly after this, the survivors in the fort having laid down their arms, the British colours were hoisted on the flagstaff, as we have described. Lieutenant Yeo, Mr. Clinch, 3 seamen, and 1 marine wounded, was the extent of the British loss in this daring enterprise. The loss on the part of the garrison was extremely severe: the governor and the second captain of the fort, with 10 others, were killed, and 30 wounded. The

12 eighteen-pounders being spiked and thrown over the parapet, and part of the fort blown up, the British re-embarked without sustaining any further loss; and the two privateers, together with a Spanish merchant brig, were brought away. Lieutenant Yeo was promoted to the rank of commander, and Lieutenant Mallock obtained the adjutancy of the Plymouth division.

On the 6th of July Lieutenant Pigot, of the *Cambrian* frigate, having proceeded twelve miles up the River St. Mary's, North America, in a small privateer which had been taken from the enemy, attacked and captured an armed ship and brig, protected by the militia from the shore. The British sustained a loss of 2 men killed, and 13 wounded.

Captain Beresford, in reporting this enterprise, observes:

Lieutenant Masterman of the marines, who most ably seconded all Mr. Pigot's views, escaped unhurt, to the wonder of all, for his clothes were shot through and through.

On the 19th of July the 36-gun frigate *Blanche*, Captain Z. Mudge, being in latitude 20° 20' north, and longitude 66° 44' west, at 8 a.m. discovered to windward the French 40-gun frigate *Topaze*, with a corvette of 22 guns, another of 18, and a 16-gun brig, who, under English colours, steered towards the *Blanche*; but the latter, on finding the private signal not answered, made sail from the strange ships. At 9 a.m. the *Topaze* had so far gained in the pursuit, as to discharge a broadside into the starboard quarter of the *Blanche*; who perceiving that she could not escape, shortened sail, and as soon as the *Topaze* had arrived within pistol-shot, the British frigate returned the fire.

The action continued with spirit, all the vessels being under easy sail, and never without hail of each other: the large corvette on the starboard-quarter, and two others close astern. At about 10 h. 15 m. a.m. the *Blanche* attempted to cross the bows of the *Topaze*; but the latter defeated the manoeuvre by putting her helm hard a-starboard, and passing under the stern of her opponent, raked her with effect. The engagement continued until 11 a.m., when having her sails and rigging cut to pieces, seven of her guns dismounted, and six feet of water in the hold, the *Blanche* struck her colours. At the commencement of the action she had only 215 men on board: of these 8 were killed; Lieutenant Thomas Peebles of the marines (his legs broken by a splinter), and 14 wounded. The captors finding their prize in a sinking state, set her on fire.

On the 26th of September the 50-gun ship *Calcutta*, Captain Daniel Woodriff, having under convoy the *Indus* Indiaman, with six other merchant vessels, when in the Bay of Biscay fell in with a French squadron of five sail of the line and three frigates, under Rear-Admiral Allemand. At 11 a.m. the *Calcutta* made the private signal, which not being answered, she directed the Indus to make all possible sail ahead with the convoy, and then stood for the 40-gun frigate *Armide*.

After having been distantly engaged with that ship for more than an hour, the *Calcutta* at 5 p.m. found a more powerful opponent in the 74-gun ship *Magnanime*, who began firing her chase guns at the British ship, as the latter was still running under all sail to the southward, with a light northerly breeze. Finding that the *Magnanime* was far ahead of her consorts, Captain Woodriff resolved to attack and endeavour to cripple her; and when within pistol-shot commenced an action, which was maintained for three-quarters of an hour without intermission. By this time being completely unrigged and unmanageable, the *Calcutta* hauled down her colours, having sustained a loss of 6 men killed and 6 wounded, out of a crew of 343 men and boys.

On the 10th of August the 36-gun frigate *Phoenix*, Captain Thomas Baker, cruising off Cape Ortegal, at 5 a. m. bore up in chase of the French 40-gun frigate *Didon*, who having shortened sail to await the approach of the *Phoenix*, at 8 h. 45 m. opened a smart fire, and then wore round and discharged her other broadside into the bows of the British frigate. This manoeuvre was thrice repeated, to the great annoyance of the *Phoenix*, who failing in her intention of passing astern of her opponent, and engaging her to leeward; and hopeless, from her inferior sailing, of being able to pass ahead of the *Didon*, ran right at her to windward. At 9 h. 15 m. the action was mutually maintained within pistol-shot, but owing to the press of sail under which the *Phoenix* had approached, she ranged considerably ahead. The *Didon* filled and stood on, and crossing the stern of the *Phoenix*, fired some distant shot; then profiting by the damaged state of her opponent's rigging, the French frigate bore up, passed under the stern of the *Phoenix*, and again raked her.

The *Didon* now hauled up on the larboard tack, intending to discharge her starboard broadside in a similar manner; but the *Phoenix* throwing all aback, defeated the attempt and brought her starboard quarter against the stern of the *Didon*, both ships lying nearly in a parallel direction. The instant they came in contact, each prepared to board; but the great superiority of numbers that advanced to the assault on board the *Didon*, made it necessary for the *Phoenix* to defend her own decks. Having repulsed the boarders, chiefly by the steady fire of the marines under First-Lieutenant Henry Steele, and Second-Lieutenant John Peter Pleydell, a main-deck gun was brought to bear upon her opponent out of the cabin window of the *Phoenix*, which at the first discharge swept the *Didon's* deck, and killed or wounded 24 men. Meanwhile the marines and small-arm men on the quarter-deck were exerting themselves in the most gallant manner; one party directing their attention to the troops on the enemy's gangway, while the other was fully occupied in preventing the men on the *Didon's* forecastle from discharging their thirty-six pounder carronade.

After the frigates had remained on board of each other for upwards of half an hour, and just as the *Didon* began to forereach, the fire of the second aftermost gun of the *Phoenix* knocked away the French ship's head-rails, and cut the gammoning of her bowsprit. As the *Didon* forged ahead, her guns were successively brought to bear, and a mutual cannonade recommenced, yard-arm and yard-arm, to the evident advantage of the British ship, until her opponent had passed out of range of her guns, with her main top-mast gone, and her fore-mast tottering. The rigging and sails of the *Phoenix* were so much cut up, as to render her almost unmanageable: her main-royal mast, main topsail yard and gaff, were shot away; but the English colours were still displayed, suspended from either cross jack yard-arm. Both ships were actively employed in repairing their damaged rigging; and about noon the *Phoenix*, having sufficiently refitted, closed with her opponent.

At about 15 minutes past noon, when about to renew the action, the *Didon*, from the fall of her foremast being incapable of offering further resistance, hauled down the French colours. Out of the 260 men and boys on board the *Phoenix*, her second-lieutenant, one master's mate, and 10 seamen were killed; Lieutenant Henry Steele of the marines (dangerously in the head), two midshipmen, 13 seamen, and 12 marines were wounded: total,—12 killed, and 28 wounded. The *Didon*, out of a crew of 330, had 27 killed and 44 badly wounded.

On the 29th of March a French squadron of eleven sail of the line and six frigates, under Vice-Admiral Villeneuve, having 3500 troops on board, sailed from Toulon; and on the 8th of April they stood into the bay of Cadiz, driving away Vice-Admiral Sir John Orde, with his five sail of the line.

Receiving a reinforcement of five Spanish and one French ship of the line, Vice-Admiral Villeneuve quitted Cadiz on the 9th; when this combined fleet, consisting of seventeen sail of the line, six frigates, and three brigs, steered a westerly course; but owing to contrary winds and calms, they did not reach Martinique until the 13th of May, and on the 16th they were joined by the Spanish 80-gun ship *San Rafael.* On the 3rd of April Vice-Admiral Lord Nelson was apprized by the *Phoebe* frigate of the French fleet being at sea: not gaining any intimation of their route, and surmising their course would be westward, His Lordship made sail in that direction; and on the 17th, information was obtained of the enemy having passed the straits. The prevalence of strong southerly and westerly winds made it the 30th ere Lord Nelson got sight of Gibraltar; and it was not until the 7th of May that the squadron passed through the straits. Having anchored in Lagos Bay, and obtained a supply of provisions from the British transports, the vice-admiral with the *Victory, Canopus, Superb, Spencer, Swiftsure, Belleisle, Conqueror, Tigre, Leviathan,* and three frigates, crowded sail to the westward on the 11th, in pursuit of the combined fleet.

After touching at Madeira on the 15th, the admiral gained intelligence on the 3rd of June, of the enemy being in the West Indies; and on the 4th, the British fleet anchored in Carlisle bay, where they were joined by the *Northumberland* and *Spartiate.* Here the squadron embarked 2000 troops, and then proceeded towards Tobago and Trinidad; but on the 7th the vice-admiral, finding that he had been misled, altered his course, and on the 9th arrived off Grenada, where Lord Nelson received accounts that the enemy had passed the island of Dominique on the 6th, steering to the northward, On the 13th the British fleet arrived at Antigua, where the troops were disembarked; and leaving the *Northumberland* as the flagship of Admiral Cochrane, Lord Nelson stood to the northward with his eleven ships of the line, in the hope of reaching the shores of Europe before the enemy could arrive there.

To return to Vice-Admiral Villeneuve: we find that two French line of battleships joined his fleet on the 5th of June, when at Martinique, and after embarking a portion of that garrison, he proceeded with an intention of reducing some of the windward islands; but learning that the British squadron was close upon his heels, the French admiral hastily got rid of his military force, and bent his course towards Ferrol. After capturing several English merchant-men, and having recaptured the Spanish galleon *Matilda,* the combined fleet of twenty sail of the line arrived off Cape Finisterre on the 9th of July. Lord Nelson also hastened towards Europe, and on the 18th fell in with three ships of the line under Vice-Admiral Collingwood. On the 19th the squadron arrived at Gibraltar, and having replenished the water and provisions, repassed the straits on the 28th, and reached England on the 16th of August.

Soon after the arrival of the combined fleet off Cape Finisterre on the 9th of July, a violent gale from the northeast sprang up, which slightly damaged some of the ships: the wind moderated, but continued to blow from the same adverse quarter until the 20th. On the 22nd, in the forenoon, the enemy's force of twenty sail of the line, consisting of seven ships of 80 guns, eleven of 74 guns, and two of 64 guns, seven frigates, two brigs, and the *galleon*, were steering in a thick fog towards Ferrol, in three divisions, with a light breeze from west-north-west; when on a sudden clearing up of the weather, ten sail of the line were signalled by their advanced ship, approaching on the starboard tack, and presently twenty-one were discovered. The strangers were fifteen British ships of the line, two frigates, a cutter, and a lugger, under Vice-Admiral sir Robert Calder, who after making the necessary preparatory signals, formed his fleet in line of battle as follows:—*Hero* 74, *Ajax* 74, *Triumph* 74, *Barfleur* 98, *Agamemnon* 64, *Windsor Castle* 98, *Defiance* 74, *Prince of Wales* 98 Vice-Admiral Sir Robert Calder, *Repulse* 74, *Raisonable* 64, *Dragon* 74, *Glory* 98 Rear-Admiral Stirling, *Warrior* 74, *Thunderer* 74, and *Malta* of 80 guns.

About the same time the combined fleet arranged themselves in line of battle, and under top-sails stood on upon the larboard tack, rather off the wind, in a close well-formed line; one frigate ahead, another astern with the galleon in tow, and the remaining five frigates to windward of the centre and rear. At this time the British were nearly a-beam, and about seven miles distant; but owing to the fog, neither fleet was more than partially in sight of each other.

At 3 h. 20 m. p.m. the signal was made to engage the enemy, and immediately afterwards for the fleet to tack together; but this was annulled, and the ships, having been ordered to make all possible sail and steer south-south-west, were at 4h. 21 m. directed to tack in succession. The signal to this effect was made by each commander-in-chief about the same time, but the weather being so foggy, neither fleet observed the commencement of the other's manoeuvre. The British tacked to prevent their opponents escaping them on the opposite tack, and the enemy, who had hauled close to the wind, on approaching within three miles of the British fleet wore round, in consequence of signal-guns in quick succession from the sternmost frigate, signifying that the rear was in danger.

This was occasioned by the bold approach of the *Sirius*, who had tacked with the intention of attempting to carry, by boarding, the galleon in tow of the frigate. At that moment the Spanish 80-gun ship *Argonauta* was discerned through the haze, approaching with the wind nearly a-beam: this compelled Captain Prowse to relinquish his design upon the *galleon*, and seek his own safety; and in effecting this, the *Sirius* had to pass to leeward of the enemy's line: fortunately, neither of the three Spanish line-of-battle ships considered her inferiority worthy of their notice. At about 5h. 15 m. the *Hero*, the British van-ship, hove in stays; and the Spanish ships, all of whom had royals and courses set, instantly hoisted their colours, and commenced the action, the *Argonauta* firing her larboard guns at the *Hero*, and the *España* hers at the *Sirius*, which killed two men, and wounded three on board the frigate. The *Ajax* tacked astern of the *Hero*, but instead of supporting Captain Gardner in his bold manoeuvre, Captain Brown bore away to acquaint the admiral with the change in the enemy's van, and the *Ajax* then fell into the line astern of the *Glory*; thus making herself the twelfth, instead of the second, ship from the van. The British ships successively tacked, and by 6 p.m., with the exception of the *Dragon*, who was still to leeward working up, the whole had got round on the starboard tack, and the greater part found opponents in the opposite line; but what with the fog and the smoke, no ship could see much beyond her own length.

Owing to the disorder arising from this circumstance, some ships in both fleets had several opponents at the same time. On the British side the *Windsor Castle* was the principal sufferer; and the *Ajax*, *Prince of Wales*, *Thunderer*, and *Malta*, the last especially, took part in this unequal contest. Of the combined fleet, the *San Rafael*, *Firme*, and *España*, having dropped to leeward, became generally exposed to the fire of the British. The *Firme's* critical situation called the attention of Captain Cosmao Kerjulien, of the French-74 *Pluton*, who gallantly bore up out of the line, and for awhile covered the Spanish ship from the destructive fire to which she was exposed; but the *Firme* was too powerfully opposed to profit by the aid of her ally, and the *Pluton* herself with difficulty regained her station. Shortly afterwards the French ship bore up a second time to interpose herself between the *España* and the powerful fire of the British line: and with the assistance of the *Mont Blanc* and *Atlas*, Captain Kerjulien succeeded in rescuing the *España*. The *Atlas* suffered most severely, and but for the support of the *Neptune* and some others, would certainly have been captured.

The *Firme*, having lost her mizen-masts, surrendered about 8 p.m., and shortly afterwards her fore-mast went over the side. The *San Rafael*, with loss of main top-mast, and subsequently of all her masts, also struck, and both ships were taken possession of. It was about 8 h. 30 m. when Sir Robert Calder made the night-signal to discontinue the action, at which time the British ships were much scattered, and the combined fleet barely within gunshot to windward; and as the signal of the British admiral was observed but by few ships of his fleet, the general firing did not cease until 9 h. 30 m. p.m. Shortly afterwards the fleet brought to on the starboard tack, and lay by repairing damages, in order to renew the contest on the morrow.

The total loss sustained by the British fleet amounted to 39 officers and men killed, and 159 wounded; while the gross amount of killed and wounded in the combined fleet is stated to have been 476.

At daybreak on the 23rd the two fleets were about seventeen miles apart; and owing to the hazy state of the morning they were but partially visible to each other: but the advanced squadrons of the respective fleets were within six miles. Far to leeward, and out of sight of the admiral, were the *Malta*, *Thunderer*, the two frigates and prizes; whilst between them and the main body lay the crippled *Windsor Castle*, in tow of the *Dragon*. Having concentrated his fleet, the British admiral, at 9 h. a.m., hauled up on the larboard tack, steering to the northeast, keeping between the enemy and his three disabled ships: the *Windsor Castle* being in tow of the *Dragon*, the *San Rafael* of the *Egyptienne*, and the *Firme* of the *Sirius*.

Towards noon the combined fleet, formed in order of battle, bore up towards the British, then about four leagues distant in the east-south-east; but owing to the lightness of the breeze, it was not until 3 h. 10 m. that their advance was noticed by their opponents, who immediately hoisted their colours, and by hauling closer to the wind, awaited the expected attack. At 4 p.m. the enemy, with colours also hoisted, and then distant about three leagues from the British, hauled to the wind on the same tack, thus declining a renewal of the engagement.

At 8 a.m. on the 24th the wind, having shifted to north-east, brought the combined fleet nearly astern of the British, now to windward, and might in all probability have recommenced the action; but Sir Robert continued with his prizes under easy sail, steering about south-east by east, working towards a British port, whilst the enemy edged away south-east by south; and by 6 p.m. the two fleets had wholly disappeared from each other. Admiral Villeneuve, with his eighteen sail of the line, reached the port of Vigo on the 26th, and having refitted his fleet, quitted that anchorage with thirteen French and two Spanish ships of the line on the 30th, and arrived at Corunna on the 1st of August. On the 11th the combined fleet, reinforced by a squadron from Ferrol, amounting to twenty-nine ships of the line, put to sea; and on the 20th this formidable armament anchored in Cadiz harbour, where they found six Spanish ships: thus forming a total of thirty-five sail of the line and several frigates.

The British squadron cruising off that port consisted of the *Dreadnought*, bearing the flag of Vice-Admiral Collingwood, and the two seventy-fours *Colossus* and *Achille*, who were reinforced by four sail of the line on the 22nd; and on the 30th Sir Robert Calder joined with eighteen line-of-battle ships. Lord Nelson, in the *Victory*, arrived from Portsmouth on the 28th of September, to take the chief command of the Mediterranean fleet, which now consisted of twenty-seven sail of the line; twenty-two of which cruised about fifteen miles off Cadiz, while the remaining five, under Rear-Admiral Louis, were stationed close to the harbour, to watch the motions of the enemy. Between the 1st and the 17th of October there had been several interchanges of ships: six were detached to Gibraltar for provisions and water, and Sir Robert Calder returned to England in the *Prince of Wales*; whilst on the other hand the *Royal Sovereign, Belleisle, Africa*, and *Agamemnon* had joined, so that the fleet still amounted to twenty-seven ships of the line, four frigates, a schooner, and a cutter.

It has been stated, that on the very day his Lordship arrived to take the command of the Mediterranean fleet, Vice-Admiral Villeneuve received the French emperor's commands to proceed to sea. These orders had been issued in the preceding month, requiring that the fleet should pass the straits; and having landed the troops on the coast of Italy, to sweep the Mediterranean of all British vessels, and then enter the port of Toulon to refit.

The French troops having embarked on the 10th of October, the combined fleet moved to the entrance of the harbour in readiness to start. From the 10th to the 17th it continued to blow hard from the westward, with but little intermission; but at midnight on the 17th the wind shifted to the eastward, and on the 18th Vice-Admiral Villeneuve determined on putting to sea. At 7 a.m. on the 19th, the combined fleet, by signal, got under way, with a light breeze at north by east; but owing to the lightness of the wind, only twelve ships succeeded in getting out, and these lay becalmed until early in the afternoon, when a breeze springing up from the west-north-west, they stood to the northward, accompanied by the British frigates, *Sirius* and *Euryalus*. At daylight on the morning of the 20th, the remainder of the combined fleet quitted the port with a light breeze at south-east, consisting, with the ships already outside, of thirty-three sail of the line, five frigates, and two brigs.

Every movement of the enemy was reported by the British frigates, and the communication conveyed to the commander-in-chief by intermediate ships, stationed at convenient distances from each other. It was on the 19th, at 9 h. 30m. a.m., while the British fleet was lying to, about sixteen leagues west-southwest from Cadiz, that the *Mars* came running down, with the signal flying that the enemy was coming out of port. All sail was immediately made in chase to the south-east, with a light breeze from the south-south-west; and some ships were ordered to lead the fleet, and to carry a light during the night.

At daylight on the 20th, the British found themselves at the entrance of the straits, but nothing of the enemy was to be seen: the fleet therefore wore, and made sail to the north-west, with a fresh breeze at south-south-west. At 7 the enemy was signalled north; and by noon the British fleet was about nine leagues south-west of Cadiz. At 2 p. m. they were taken aback by a breeze from west-north-west, and at 4 p.m. stood to the northward. At 8h. 40 m. a.m. the British fleet wore to the south-west; and at 4 a.m. on Monday the 21st they again wore, and steered under easy sail to the north by east.

At 6 a. m., Cape Trafalgar bearing east by south, distant about seven leagues, the combined fleet was seen from the *Victory*, and nearly at the same time by the whole British fleet, bearing about east and by south, and distant about ten miles. At 6h. 40m. a.m. the *Victory* made the signal to form the order of sailing in two columns, and to prepare for battle, and in another ten minutes to bear up. This prompt mode of attack had been previously directed by Lord Nelson, in order to avoid the inconvenience and delay of forming a line of battle in the usual manner.

The French admiral, considering the near approach of the British fleet rendered an action unavoidable, made the signal at 8 h. 30 m. for his ships to wear together, and form line in close order upon the larboard tack, thereby bringing the harbour of Cadiz on his lee-bow. Owing to the lightness of the wind, it was near 10 a.m. before the manoeuvre was completed; and even then the line was so very irregular, that it was more in the form of a crescent, particularly towards the rear. Some ships were to leeward, others to windward of their proper stations, and they were generally two, and in a few instances three deep; thus accidentally presenting a far more formidable opposition, than if each ship had been in the wake of her leader. They were mostly under top-sails and top-gallant sails, with the main-top sail shivering, steering a point or two off the wind. The British fleet made but slow progress, not going more than a knot and half an hour with all sail set: the *Victory* leading the weather, and the *Royal Sovereign* the lee column, in the following order of battle:—

### BATTLE OF TRAFALGAR.

### BRITISH FLEET.

*Victory*, 100 guns, Vice-Admiral Lord Nelson (killed), Captain T. M. Hardy, 57 killed, 102 wounded. Captain Charles Wm. Adair (killed), First-Lieutenant James G. Peake (wounded), Second-Lieutenant Lewis Buckle Reeves (wounded), Second-Lieutenant Lewis Rotely.

*Téméraire*, 98 guns, Captain E. Harvey, 47 killed, and 76 wounded. Captain Simon Busigny (mortally wounded), Second-Lieutenant William N. Roe, Second-Lieutenant Samuel J. Payne (wounded), Second-Lieutenant John Kingston (killed).

*Neptune*, 98 guns, Captain T. F. Freemantle, 10 killed, 34 wounded. First-Lieutenant George Kendall, Second-Lieutenant William Burton, second-Lieutenant Lewis Rooke.

*Leviathan*, 74 guns, Captain H. W. Bayntum, 4 killed, 22 wounded. Captain George P. Wingrove, First-Lieutenant Nathaniel Cole, First-Lieutenant Thomas J. W. Tane.

*Britannia*, 100 guns, Rear-Admiral Earl of Northesk, Captain C. Bullen, 10 killed, 42 wounded.. Captain Alexander Watson, First-Lieutenant William Jackson, Second-Lieutenant L. B. J. Halloran, Second-Lieutenant John Cooke.

*Conqueror*, 74 guns, Captain J. Pellew, 3 killed, 9 wounded. Captain James Atcherly, Second-Lieutenants Patrick Toole, and Thomas Wearing (wounded).

*Africa*, 64 guns, Captain Henry Digby, 18 killed, 44 wounded. Captain James Fynmore (wounded), First-Lieutenant Thomas Brattle.

*Agamemnon*, 64 guns, Captain Sir E. Berry, 2 killed, 7 wounded. Captain H. B. Downing, Second-Lieutenant Herbert Raban, Second-Lieutenant Donald Campbell.

*Ajax*, 74 guns, Lieutenant J. Pilfold, 2 killed, 9 wounded. Captain

David Boyd, Second-Lieutenant J. Cinnamond, Second-Lieutenant Samuel B. Ellis.

*Orion*, 74 guns, captain E. Codrington, 1 killed, 23 wounded. Captain Henry W. Creswell, Second-Lieutenant Stephen Bridgman.

*Minotaur*, 74 guns, Captain C. M. Mansfield, 3 killed, 22 wounded. Captain Paul Hunt, Second-Lieutenant Nathaniel B. Grigg, Second-Lieutenant Thomas Reeves.

*Spartiate*, 74 guns, Captain Sir F. Laforey, 3 killed, 20 wounded. First-Lieutenant Samuel Hawkins, First-Lieutenant John R. Coryton, Second-Lieutenant G. D. Hawkins.

## Lee Column.

*Royal Sovereign*, 100 guns, Vice-Admiral C. Collingwood, Captain E. Rotheram, 47 killed, 94 wounded. Captain Joseph Vallack, Second-Lieutenant Robert Green (killed), Second-Lieutenant Armiger Wm. Hubbard, Second-Lieutenant James Le Vescomte (wounded).

*Belleisle*, 74 guns, Captain W. Hargood (wounded), 34 killed, 96 wounded. First-Lieutenant John Owen (wounded), Second-Lieutenant John Weaver, Second-Lieutenant Paul Harris Nicolas.

*Mars*, 74 guns, Captain G. Duff (killed), 29 killed, 69 wounded. Captain Thos. Norman, Second-Lieutenant Charles Holmes, Second-Lieutenant Robert Guthrie.

*Tonnant*, 80 guns, Captain C. Tyler (wounded), 26 killed, 50 wounded. Captain Arthur Ball, Second-Lieutenant James Cottle, First-Lieutenant William Magin.

*Bellerophon*, 74 guns, Captain J. Cooke (killed), 27 killed, 123 wounded. Captain James Wemyss (wounded), Second-Lieutenants John Wilson (2nd), Peter Connolly, and Luke Higgins.

*Colossus*, 74 guns, Captain J. Morris (wounded), 40 killed, 160 wounded. Captain Elias Lawrence, Second-Lieutenant William Laurie, Second-Lieutenant John Benson (wounded).

*Achille*, 74 guns, Captain R. King, 13 killed, 59 wounded. Captain Palms Westropp (wounded), Second-Lieutenants William Liddon (wounded), and Francis Whalley.

*Dreadnought*, 98 guns, Captain J. Conn, 7 killed, 26 wounded. Captain Thomas Timmins, First-Lieutenants John M'Cullum and Thomas Lemon, Second-Lieutenant David Manley.

*Polyphemus*, 64 guns, Captain Robert Redmill, 2 killed, 4 wounded. Captain Michael Percival, First-Lieutenant John Mackintosh, Second-Lieutenant Charles Stewart.

*Revenge*, 74 guns, Captain R. Moorsom (wounded), 28 killed, 51 wounded. Captain Peter Lely (wounded), Second-Lieutenant Arthur Copperthwaite, Second-Lieutenant Henry Blackler Fairtlough.

*Swiftsure*, 74 guns, Captain H. G. Rutherford, 9 killed, 8 wounded. First-Lieutenant William Gibbins, First-Lieutenant Robert Gordon, Second-Lieutenant Henry Miller.

*Defiance*, 74 guns, Captain P. C. Durham (wounded), 17 killed, 53 wounded. Captain Basil Alves, Second-Lieutenant George Bristow.

*Thunderer*, 74 guns, Lieutenant J. Stockham, 4 killed, 12 wounded. Captain Gilbert Elliott, Second-Lieutenant William Hockley, Second-Lieutenant John Lister.

*Defence*, 74 guns, Captain G. Hope, 7 killed, 29 wounded. Captain Henry Cox, First-Lieutenant John Wilson (1st), Second-Lieutenant Alfred Burton.

*Prince*, 98 guns, Captain R. Grindall. Captain Francis Williams, Second-Lieutenant Edward Pengelley, Second-Lieutenant John Shillibeer.

Total,—450 killed, 1244 wounded.

### Officers of Marines on Board the Frigates.

*Phoebe*, First-Lieutenant Mortimer Timson; *Euryalus*, Lieutenant John Sandford; *Naiad*, Lieutenants Edward Jones and P. S. Perkins; *Sirius*, Lieutenants Thomas Moore and William Murray.

The direction in which the combined fleet now lay, with a home port scarcely seven leagues on their lee-bow, induced Lord Nelson to telegraph to his second in command:

> I intend to pass through the van of the enemy's line, to prevent him from getting into Cadiz.

And as the shoals of San Pedro and Trafalgar were under the lee of both fleets, his lordship, in order to guard against that danger, made the signal:

> Prepare to anchor after close of day.

Shortly afterwards that emphatic message of:

> England expects every man to do his duty.

. . . . was communicated to the fleet by telegraph. The inspiring sentiment excited the most lively enthusiasm, and was greeted by hearty cheers on board of every ship.

Having already described the formation of the combined line of battle, it is only necessary to observe, that the commander-in-chief in the *Bucentaure*, with the *Santissima Trinidada*, his second, ahead, were directly in front of the *Victory*; the *Santa Ana*, bearing the flag of Vice-Admiral D'Alava, was in the same direction from the *Royal Sovereign*; whilst the Spanish commander-in-chief, Admiral Gravina, in the Principe d'Asturias, was the rearmost ship of the combined fleet, which formed nearly as follows:—

### COMBINED FLEET.

*Neptuno* 80, *Scipion* 74, *Intrépide* 74, *Rayo* 100, *Formidable* 80, *Dugnay Trouin* 74, *Mont Blanc* 74, *San Francisco d'Asis* 74, *San Augustin* 74, *Heros* 74, *Santissima Trinidada* 130, *Bucentaure* 74, *Neptune* 80, *San Leandro* 64, *Redoutable* 74, *San Justo* 80, *Indomptable* 80, *Santa Aña* 112, *Fougueux* 74, *Monarca* 74, *Pluton* 74, *Algésiras* 74, *Bahama* 74, *Aigle* 74, *Swiftsure* 74, *Argonaute* 74, *Montanez* 74, *Argonauta* 80, *Berwick* 74, *San Juan Nepornuceno* 74, *San Ildefonso* 74, *Achille* 74, *Principe d'Asturias* 112.

It was just at noon, the wind very light, the sea smooth, with a heavy ground-swell setting from the westward, and the sun shining beautifully upon the fresh-painted sides of the long line of the French and Spanish ships, when the ship next to the *Santa Ana*, the *Fougueux*, opened her fire upon the *Royal Sovereign*. The British fleet immediately hoisted their colours, and the *Victory* made the signal for close action: about the same time the enemy also hoisted their ensigns, and the admirals, with the exception of Vice-Admiral Villeneuve, their flags.

At ten minutes past noon, the *Royal Sovereign* having reached a position close astern of the *Santa Ana*, discharged her guns double shotted into her, and with her starboard broadside distantly raked the *Fougueux*. It was just at this moment that Lord Nelson, observing the enviable position of his friend, exclaimed, "See, how nobly Collingwood carries his ship into action." The *Royal Sovereign* then ranged close alongside of the three-decker to leeward, and a tremendous cannonade ensued between these two powerful ships; but besides this equal contest the British ship had other opponents. About 400 yards ahead lay the *San Leandro*, who bearing away raked the *Sovereign*, while the *Fougueux* kept up a galling fire astern: she was also exposed to the occasional fire of the *San Justo* and *Indomptable*, within 300 yards, on her bow and quarter; but finding they were sustaining injury from their own cross fire, and the near approach of other British ships, the four two-deckers drew off from the *Royal Sovereign*, leaving her closely engaged with the *Santa Ana*.

For upwards of fifteen minutes the *Royal Sovereign* was the only British ship in close action, and she had taken a position upon the lee-bow of her opponent, when the *Belleisle* fired her broadside into the stern of the *Santa Ana*, and then bore away for the *Indomptable*. Just at this time the mizen topmast of the Spanish three-decker was shot away, and at the end of about an hour and a quarter from the commencement of the battle, her three masts had fallen over the side; and after a severe contest of a little more than two hours, the *Santa Ana* struck her colours. At this period the mizen-mast of the *Royal Sovereign* came down, and shortly afterwards her mainmast fell over the starboard side, tearing away two of her lower deck ports; whilst the tottering foremast was so disabled, that the British ship was almost in as unmanageable a state as the Spanish three-decker she had so gallantly captured. Lieutenant Robert Green and 13 marines were killed; Lieutenant James Le Vescomte and 16 marines wounded.

After sustaining the tremendous fire opened upon her from the centre and rear of the combined line for more than twenty minutes, and having, notwithstanding the precaution of the men lying down a-fore and aft, suffered a loss of above 50 in killed and wounded: her sails and rigging cut to pieces, and her mizen top-mast over the side, the *Belleisle*, at thirty minutes past noon discharged a treble-shotted broadside into the stern of the *Santa Ana*, and with her starboard guns exchanged some shot with the *Fougueux*; then bearing away a little, she passed under the stern of the *Indomptable*, who quickly wearing, exchanged a few broadsides with her, and bore away to the southeast. At about forty-five minutes past noon the *Belleisle's* main top-mast was shot away, and as the enemy's rear were now pressing forward to support the centre, the British ship's situation became extremely critical.

At 1 p.m. the *Fougueux* ranged up in the smoke on the *Belleisle's* starboard beam, and striking her at the gangway with her larboard bow, dropped alongside. After both ships had engaged for about a quarter of an hour, during which the mizen mast of the *Belleisle* fell over her larboard quarter, the *Fougueux* dropped astern, and hauling to the northward ran on board the *Téméraire*. At 1 h. 30 m. p.m. the French *Achille*, ranging past the stern of the *Belleisle*, stationed herself on the latter's larboard quarter, and kept up a steady fire with comparative impunity, while the *Aigle* engaged her, distantly, on the starboard side; and as the *Leandro* and *San Justo* passed ahead on their way to join Admiral Gravina in the rear, they opened a fire on the British ship.

Thus in a manner surrounded, the *Belleisle*, at 2 h. 10 m. p.m., had her main-mast shot away about four feet above the deck, which failing aft on the break of the poop, with the wreck already over her larboard side, disabled the guns, and prevented her from returning the *Achille's* destructive fire. At 2 h. 30 m. the French *Neptune*, driven from her station upon the bows of the *Victory* and *Téméraire* by the approach of the *Leviathan*, placed herself across the starboard bow of the *Belleisle*, who was still engaged by two other ships; and at 2 h. 45 m. the fore-mast and bowsprit of this almost helpless ship were shot away by the board.

At 3 h. 15 m. the *Polyphemus* having interposed herself between the *Belleisle* and the *Neptune*, the latter stood on towards the rear; and shortly afterwards the *Defiance* took off the fire of the *Aigle*. The British *Swiftsure* next approached, and passing close to the stern of the *Belleisle* as she lay covered in the wreck of her masts and sails, with the English colours fastened to the stump of her mizen-mast, manned her rigging, cheered the gallantly defended ship, and then opened her fire upon the *Achille*. Thus relieved by the timely arrival of her friends, from the overwhelm-ing force around her, the *Belleisle* ceased firing at about 3 h. 30 m. p.m.: Captain Hargood observing that a Spanish two-decker had already sur-rendered, sent the master and Lieutenant John Owen, the senior Officer of Marines (who volunteered, although wounded) to take possession of the 80 gun ship *Argonauta*. On board the *Belleisle* eight marines were killed; Lieutenant Owen, and 19 wounded.

The *Mars* following the *Belleisle*, suffered severely from the heavy raking fire to which she was exposed, particularly from the *San Juan, Monarca, Pluton,* and *Algesiras*; and directing her course to pass between the first two of these ships, the *Pluton* ranged ahead and became en-gaged with the *Mars*, who had also found opponents in the *Monarca* and *Algesiras*; but the *Tonnant* coming up, soon gave full employment for both those ships. The *Mars* then had her attention called to the *Fougueux*; and after receiving her broadside, as the latter hauled off from the *Belleisle*, she was severely raked astern by the *Pluton*, from which ship a cannon-shot killed Captain Duff, when standing on the break of the quarter-deck. By this time, on the approach of other British ships, the *Pluton* stood away to the south-east to join Admiral Gravina; whilst the *Fougueux* made off to the northward in the direc-tion of the *Téméraire*. The main top-mast and spanker-boom of the *Mars* were shot away, and her masts were so much injured that they all fell by the board during the gale on the following day. Eight marines were killed; Captain Thomas Norman and 16 wounded, on board the *Mars*.

The *Tonnant*, after firing at the ships which pressed upon the *Mars*, steered for the larboard bow of the *Algesiras*, then standing slowly onwards in the line, and very near to her leader, the *Monarca*; but the French ship backing her main and mizen top-sails as the *Tonnant* advanced, the latter was enabled to pass under the stern of the *Monarca*, and then range up alongside the Spanish ship, who soon dropped astern and struck her colours, although she afterwards rehoisted them. At this time the *Tonnant* had her fore top-mast and main-yard shot away, when the *Algesiras*, making sail, endeavoured to cross her stern; but the latter putting her helm a-port, defeated the manoeuvre, and ran the *Algesiras* on board. The bowsprit and anchors of the *Algesiras* getting entangled in her opponent's main rigging, the two ships remained fast together, greatly to the advantage of the *Tonnant*; who, while engaged with her principal antagonist, had to contend with the *San Juan* on her larboard bow, and the *Monarca*, who had rehoisted her colours, on her quarter. At about 1h. 10 m.

Captain Tyler received a severe wound, which compelled him to resign the command to Lieutenant John Bedford, and an animated fire was maintained by the two ships; during which the *Algesiras* lost her fore-mast, and the *Tonnant* her main and mizen top-masts. The French ship now made a serious attempt to board; but the marines of the *Tonnant* under Captain Arthur Ball, kept up so steady and well-directed a fire, that the assailants were repulsed. At about 2 h. 15 m. p.m., just as the main and mizen-masts of the *Algesiras* were about to share the fate of her fore-mast, the gallantly-defended ship struck her colours; and Lieutenant Bennett, with Captain Ball of the marines and 50 men, stepped on board and took possession of her. In another quarter of an hour the *San Juan* also surrendered. Nine marines were killed, and 16 wounded on board the *Tonnant*: the *Algésiras* had upwards of 200 men killed and wounded, including several officers; and among them, mortally wounded, the brave and respected Rear-Admiral Magon.

The *Bellerophon*, from being at some distance astern of the *Tonnant*, and owing to the lightness of the wind, did not cut through the enemy's line for more than a quarter of an hour after the latter; and passing under the stern of the *Monarca*, as the Spanish ship, with colours rehoisted, was dropping away from the *Tonnant*, the *Bellerophon*, at about 50 minutes past noon, ran foul of the *Aigle*, the latter's main-yard locking with her fore-yard; and whilst thus closely engaged with an opponent of equal force, the *Bellerophon* sustained the fire of the *Monarca* and *Montanez* to windward, and the *Bahama* and French *Swiftsure* on either quarter. In this unequal contest the *Bellerophon* suffered severely; and at 1 p.m. her main and mizen top-masts fell over the starboard side; shortly afterwards Captain Cooke was killed, and the command devolved on Lieutenant Pryce Camby. The *Swiftsure* and *Montanez* then became engaged with the *Colossus*; and at 1 h. 40 m. p.m. the *Aigle*, after several ineffectual attempts to board, having dropped astern, was exposed to a raking fire from her opponent, as well as from the *Revenge*. The *Bellerophon*, now in an unmanageable state, took possession of the *Monarca*, and subsequently of the *Bahama*, who had surrendered to the destructive fire of the *Colossus*. Four marines were killed, Captain Wemyss and 20 wounded, on board the *Bellerophon*.

At about 1 p.m. the *Colossus* ran past the starboard side of the French *Swiftsure*, as she edged away to bring her larboard guns to bear on the quarter of the *Bellerophon*, and owing to the density of the smoke, nothing was visible to leeward until the *Colossus* found herself close alongside the *Argonaute*, whose larboard yard-arms were locked in her starboard ones. After a smart cannonade, which lasted about a quarter of an hour, the *Argonaute's* fire slackened, and as she paid off, she received a heavy raking broadside from the *Colossus*. It was just as the French ship had receded, that Captain Morris received a severe wound a little above the knee; but the gallant officer, having applied a tourniquet, did not quit the deck. In the meanwhile the *Colossus* was warmly engaged with the *Swiftsure* on the larboard quarter, and with the *Bahama*, who kept up a galling fire across the *Swiftsure's* fore-foot; but on the latter dropping astern, the *Bahama* occupied the entire attention of the *Colossus*, whose well-directed fire soon brought down the main-mast of the Spanish ship, and compelled her to make signs of having; surrendered.

The French *Swiftsure* now endeavoured to bear up under the stern of the *Colossus*; but the latter wearing more quickly, poured in her starboard broadside, which brought down the *Swiftsure's* mizen-mast; and the *Bellerophon* in passing having knocked away her main-mast, the French ship surrendered to the *Colossus*, who, in hauling up to take possession of the two prizes, lost her wounded mizen-mast over the starboard side. Her other masts were much disabled, and the main-mast went during the ensuing night. Eight marines were killed on board the *Colossus*, and Lieutenant John Benson and 31 wounded.

The *Achille*, following closely after the *Colossus*, passed under the stern of the *Montanez*, and luffed up alongside of her to leeward; but in less than a quarter of an hour, the Spanish ship sheered off, and the *Achille* bore away to succour the *Belleisle*, then lying partly dismasted, with three enemy's ships upon her. On her way down, the *Achille* became engaged with the *Argonauta*, until the Spanish colours were hauled down. At that moment two French ships claimed the attention of the *Achille*, who had to contend with her French namesake to windward; whilst the *Berwick*, after being distantly engaged with the *Defence*, ranged up on the British ship's starboard side, between her and the *Argonauta*. The two ships continued in close action for upwards of an hour, when the *Berwick* hauled down her colours, and was taken possession of by the *Achille*.

In the meantime, the French *Achille* had passed on in the direction of the *Belleisle*, and the *Argonauta* dropped to leeward. Six marines were among the killed; Captain Palms Westropp lost an arm, Lieutenant William Liddon and 14 men wounded. The *Berwick* lost her captain, and above 200 men in killed and wounded. Continuing the proceedings of the lee division of the British fleet, the *Dreadnought* next claims our attention. It was about 2 p.m. when that ship got into action with the *San Juan*, who was then surrounded by the *Principe de Asturias*, *San Justo*, and the *Indomptable*. At about 2 h. 20 m. the *Dreadnought* ran on board of and captured the *San Juan,* who, having previously been engaged by the *Tonnant*, *Bellerophon*, and some other ships, was nearly in a defenceless state; the *Dreadnought*, therefore, without waiting to take possession of this severely-handled ship, stood on towards the *Principe de Asturias*; but after two or three broadsides the Spanish three-decker made sail, and with several other ships effected her escape. One marine was killed and 4 wounded on board the *Dreadnought*.

The *Polyphemus*, after hauling to starboard to allow the *Dreadnought* to close with the Spanish three-decker, was obliged to wait until the *Swiftsure* had passed ahead before she could resume her station. It was at about 3 h. 25 m. when the *Swiftsure*, after crossing the *Belleisle's* stern, opened her fire upon the French *Achille*, as the latter, passing along the larboard beam of the *Belleisle*, edged away to the south-east, followed and engaged by the *Swiftsure*, who presently succeeded in crossing her opponent's stern, and getting to leeward of her. The *Polyphemus* about this time, after receiving a heavy fire from the French *Neptune*, in passing between that ship and the *Belleisle*, had advanced on the *Achille's* weather-quarter. In about half an hour after the *Swiftsure* commenced firing on the *Achille*, the latter had her mizen-mast and fore-yard shot away, and having taken fire in the fore-top, she ceased to engage; but the *Prince* bore down in time to assist in silencing this nobly defended ship. The *Polyphemus* then stood away towards the *Defence*, who was engaged with the *San Ildefonso*; but the Spanish colours were hauled down before the *Polyphemus* could take part in the action. Two marines were killed on board the *Swiftsure*, and one marine wounded.

In attempting to pass through the enemy's line, the *Revenge* stood so close ahead of the *Aigle*, that the jib-boom of the French ship caught the mizen top-sail of her antagonist, and enabled her to pour two deliberate broadsides into her bows before the two ships got clear. The *Revenge* then stood on, and while hauling up on the larboard tack, received a destructive fire into her lee-quarter from the *Principe de Asturias*, who, in conjunction with three ships around her, continued to cannonade the *Revenge*, until the *Dreadnought* and *Thunderer* took off the fire of the Spanish three-decker. From the exposed situation of the *Revenge*, her loss was very severe, and her masts and rigging were much disabled. Eight of her marines were killed; Captain Lely and nine marines wounded.

The *Defence* commenced engaging the *Berwick* at 2 h. 30 m. p.m., but in less than half an hour the French ship hauled off, and sustained a sharp contest with the *Achille*, as we have already related. The *San Ildefonso* was the next opponent of the *Defence*, and after engaging for upwards of an hour, the Spanish ship struck her colours. Three marines were killed on board the *Defence*, and six wounded. The *San Ildefonso* had been engaged by several ships before the *Defence* came up; and consequently her loss was very great, having nearly a third of her crew killed or wounded.

About 3 p. m. the *Thunderer* stood athwart the hawse of the *Principe de Asturias*, and having raked her distantly, brought to on the starboard tack. The *Dreadnought* had also opened her fire on the three-decker, when the French *Neptune* came to her assistance, and after engaging the *Thunderer* a short time, the two ships, with others near them, bore away towards Cadiz. Two marines were killed and one wounded on board the *Thunderer*. The *Principe de Asturias* having contended with several opponents, her damages and loss were comparatively severe: she had suffered so considerably, that her main and mizen-masts went in the gale that ensued, and she had 40 men killed, and 107 badly wounded.

The *Defiance*, after engaging the Spanish admiral and the *San Juan*, stood towards the *Aigle*, whose crippled state, from her encounter with the *Bellerophon*, and then with the *Revenge* and others, had prevented her from making sail; and at 3 h. p. m. she ran alongside, boarded with little resistance, and got possession of the *Aigle's* poop and quarter-deck. The French colours were hauled down, and when in the act of hoisting the English in their stead, so destructive a fire of musketry was opened upon the boarders from the forecastle, waist, and tops of the *Aigle*, that the British were glad to escape back to their ship. The *Defiance* having sheered off to the distance of pistolshot, a sharp action between the two ships continued for about twenty minutes, when the *Aigle* being very much shattered, and having sustained a loss of 270 in killed and wounded, called for quarter. On board the *Defiance* six marines were killed, and nine wounded.

Having detailed the proceedings of the ships composing the larboard division of the fleet, the operations of the column led by the commander-in-chief will commence in the next volume.

# Appendix

## No. 1.

*To the Right-Honourable the Lords Commissioners of the Admiralty.*

The memorial of the lieutenant-colonels, majors, captains, and subalterns of His Majesty's marine forces:

Humbly sheweth,—That in establishment, rank, promotion, and every other circumstance, honorary as well as beneficial, the officers of the marines employed in the former war were exactly on the same footing with the officers of other corps; and had equal intercourse, by removals, exchanges, and sales with and into the army, as any other part thereof. After their reduction in 1748, the half-pay marine officers were equally considered, in point of right and favour, with other reduced officers of the army, in consequence of which, many Of them have since risen to the highest military ranks and honours; and at the first formation of the present body of marines, they had the most solemn assurances given them by the then board of Admiralty, that they should be put on as advantageous a footing as any other corps in His Majesty's service.

That, on the faith of these assurances, the officers with spirit and alacrity proceeded for years to do their duty every where, and upon all occasions with general satisfaction, with honour to themselves and credit to their country; in the meantime the intercourse between the army and themselves remained open, whereby several captains from the marines have arrived at the rank of colonels, lieutenant-colonels, and majors in the army; the several ranks of colonel downwards, in their own corps, were given amongst themselves, and therefore they went on without repining in firm and daily expectation, that as respectable an establishment as had been promised would be settled for them.

That, in the year 1760, on a representation from Your Lordships to the king in council that more colonels were wanted for the better discipline of the marines, a colonel, with the appointment of forty-shillings a-day, was put upon the establishment of each of the three divisions; but to the unspeakable mortification of your memorialists, their own only marine colonel was removed, and the commissions were given to three gentlemen of the nary, who though very respectable in their own profession, yet, their starting for the first time with a land command, were certainly not so fit for conducting the discipline and detail of troops on shore as old, experienced military officers then in the marines, who from their services and seniority were entitled to this rank: this step at once destroyed that laudable spirit of emulation which is the soul and life of a soldier, and without which he becomes languid and uninterested: by it all hopes of future higher preferment than that of lieutenant-colonel are cut off from your memorialists, whilst every officer in His Majesty's other corps can look forward to the command of an army, and support himself with these flattering hopes under the greatest distresses of service.

Your memorialists can with the strictest truth affirm, that Europe does not afford an instance of a corps on so discouraging an establishment as theirs; and therefore they humbly hope your lordships will take their unhappy situation into consideration, and procure them such an establishment as will put them on a more eligible footing, by making a provision for superannuated and worn-out officers in the service, and appointing a proportionate number of colonels and field-officers with the rest of the army, which they flatter themselves may be done with a very little more expense to government, will make nearly 300 officers happy, and will greatly contribute to the better order and discipline of so large a body of men without injury to anyone.

## No. 2.

*By the Commissioners for executing the office of Lord High Admiral of Great Britain, Ireland, &c.*

Whereas His Majesty by his order in council dated the 21st of January last, was pleased to direct a new establishment of his marine forces to be formed, (a copy of which we send you enclosed,) consisting of seventy companies, with sixteen field and staff officers, instead of the establishment now in force, and that the same be forthwith carried into execution: And we having in consequence thereof given directions that the recruiting parties should be called in, and that all the detachments of marines serving on board ships under orders to be paid off should be disembarked to quarters, in order to their being assembled, and reduced agreeable to His Majesty's pleasure: We do therefore hereby require and direct you immediately to repair to Chatham, where you are to cause all the officers and men of the marine forces stationed at that port to be drawn out under arms before you; after which you are to proceed in reviewing the whole, and discharging such of the non-commission officers and private marines as hereafter directed, observing the following rules therein:

1. You are carefully to review the officers present, and to transmit an exact return of them to us; you are likewise to cause a return of the absent officers to be laid before you, specifying how long they have been absent, whether by leave or otherwise, and to report the same, together with your observations thereupon. And we rely on your care and punctuality, as well as upon your regard for the honour of the service, that you will not omit to acquaint us with the merit of any officer in your division who shall at any time have eminently distinguished himself, that we may be enabled to express our just approbation thereof, and to reward the same upon any occasion that shall offer; on the other hand, we must recommend it to you to be equally punctual in informing us of the misbehaviour of any officer, whose bad example may reflect disgrace upon the whole.

2. Having reviewed the non-commission officers and private men, and taken an account of their condition and numbers, to be laid before us, you are to proceed in discharging all such of them as shall appear to you unfit to serve through infirmities or otherwise; and also all above forty years of age.

3. You are to take care that the quarters of each company be duly satisfied, and also that all accounts between the non-commission officers and private men hereby to be discharged and their officers be made up to the day of their discharge; and that the said non-commission officers and private men be fully satisfied, and paid their sea-pay, arrears, and other just pretensions; whereof to the commissioner of His Majesty's yard the said officers and deputy paymasters are to produce acquittances and discharges from them respectively.

4. You are to take care that the arms of such marines as shall be discharged, which were delivered out of His Majesty's stores of ordnance, be returned into the charge of the store-keeper of the ordnance at Chatham, taking his acquittances for the same.

5. Each non-commission officer and private marine discharged, is

to be permitted to carry away with him the clothes, belt, and knapsack he now wears. They are likewise to be allowed twenty-one days' pay each, from the date of their discharge, to carry them home, for which their receipts are to be taken; and you are also to cause passes to be delivered to them, in case they shall desire the same, to the places of their former residence, allowing them a convenient time to repair thither, and giving them a strict charge that they do not presume to travel with any arms, nor more than three in a company, upon pain of the severest punishment.

And to the end that the said non-commission officers and private men may be sensible of the care taken of them on this occasion, you are to cause these our directions to be read at the head of the said corps.

At the same time you will please to acquaint all the officers and men, that we desire to return our thanks to them and the marine corps in general, for the signal good conduct and bravery shown by them on all occasions during the course of the war; and for the share they have had in the many eminent and meritorious services performed by the fleet and army for their king and country, which has always been highly satisfactory to us.

Given under our hands the 12th of March, 1763.

> George Grenville,
> G. Hay,
> James Harris.

To the Right-Hon. Lord Howe, &c.
Colonel of Marines.

## No. 3.

Admiralty Office, April 26th, 1763.

Sir,

The king having done me the honour to appoint me one of the commissioners for executing the office of His Lord High Admiral, and my attendance at the marine headquarters of the division being therefore dispensed with, I send you enclosed, for your better information, the orders issued under the late commission of the admiralty that yet remain unexecuted in part; and to the contents of which you may be referred occasionally, in my absence from quarters in future.

I am at the same time authorised to declare, for the information of the officers of the division, that by the resolution respecting the time of absence proposed to be allowed them upon their application occasionally, the lords do not mean to restrain themselves from granting such further extension of that indulgence, as from the nature of the case in any particular instance they may see fitting; wherein the officers wall perceive their ground of apprehension on that head will be, in all reasonable degree, removed.

I have it moreover in charge to signify to you, that you are to direct the several officers now at the headquarters at Chatham to repair to the different divisions, according as they are respectively classed in the enclosed lists, where their commissions will be sent to them, and to which they are in future to belong.

You will also please to make known to the officers appointed to your division as they arrive, that their applications to the board of Admiralty occasionally, are in future to be made through the commanding officer for the time being, as the person best able to judge of, and state to the board, the merit of their claims.

I am, &c.

Howe

To Col. Bendyshe, or the Commanding.
Officer of Marines at Chatham.

## No. 4.

*To the Right-Honourable the Earl Sandwich, &c. &c*

The memorial of the field-officers, captains, and subalterns of His Majesty's marine forces:

Most humbly sheweth,—That we are impressed with sentiments of the greatest respect and gratitude for the many marks of your lordship's patronage and support; and relying on the assurances of your great condescension and kindness, though we are restrained by gratitude, we cannot in justice to ourselves as military men, omit the present occasion of most humbly laying our case before your lordship. The recent and second promotion of rank which our most gracious sovereign has so generously bestowed upon his land officers, and his marine corps not enjoying his royal favour in the same manner, are events which deeply affect us as military men, and fill our breasts with the most anxious concern and mortification; and though, from the establishment of our service, the promotion is slow, yet we humbly hope our length of faithful services, and our rank, will be considered an equal plea to partake of the preferment with His Majesty's land forces, artillery, and engineers.

We cannot but hope that the services of the marine corps on all occasions, and in the present unnatural rebellion in America, has met with the approbation of His Majesty, so as to entitle them to every mark of his distinguishing favour with his other officers, with whom he has been graciously pleased to enrol us. The officers of the marine corps are the oldest of their rank now serving in America, or elsewhere; and while they are risking their lives and fortunes in the service of their country, they will have the great mortification to find they are precluded from His Majesty's royal favour, while officers on the same service, of not half their standing in the army, arrive at the rank of field-officer.

These afflicting truths your memorialists most humbly hope will incite Your Lordship's kind representation and interposition in their favour, entreating Your Lordship to lay their case at His Majesty's feet, craving they may be partakers of his royal bounty with his other officers of equal rank, which only can enable them to perform their duty with that spirit, courage, order, and good discipline that ever characterized marine officers.

The following letter from Colonel Mackenzie accompanied the memorial:—

Chatham, September 4th, 1777.

My Lord,

The memorial I have the honour of enclosing you with this, contains no other than candid truths, joined to the most just and reasonable requests; as such, I am to beseech Your Lordship's earliest and most friendly attention to its prayer, as what will for ever hereafter render the marine service either acceptable or desirable for any officer of worth or spirit.

Your Lordship's benevolent compliance will, if possible, still further endear your former goodness to them and me, who am, with the most sincere respect,

Your Lordship's obedient humble servant,

John Mackenzie.

To the Right Hon. the Earl of Sandwich.

## No. 5.

*To the Right-Honourable the Lords Commissioners of the Admiralty.*

The memorial unanimously agreed to by the officers of His Majesty's marine forces:

Most humbly sheweth,—That your memorialists trust their services to their king and country have been as zealous and as faithful as any other of His Majesty's forces.

That your memorialists have it singularly and grievously to feel, that the service of the marines labours under a great many disadvantages not felt by any other corps in His Majesty's service. That they alone, of all His Majesty's forces, are without that establishment necessary to give animation to their service. That they are without an adequate proportion of field-officers, and an invalid provision for their worn-out officers.

That they have not had, in common with the army, any of their death vacancies filled up by the serving corps, all casualties having been supplied from the half-pay.

Your Lordships' wisdom must easily discern between the services of a corps animated by prospects of rank and honour, and the services of a corps acting solely on the principles of duty.

Your memorialists consider themselves as much entitled to Your Lordships' protection as His Majesty's Royal Navy, as the line to that of the commander-in-chief, or as the royal engineers to that of their present master-general.

Your memorialists trust their most gracious sovereign need but know their grievances to redress them; they are alike confident of his royal favour, and the gratitude of their country; and finally, your memorialists are persuaded, that Your Lordships' favourable attention only is wanting to give effect to their prayer; and in the humble hope that they shall obtain Your Lordships' good offices, your memorialists place their confidence of support and relief."

A copy of this letter was sent to Lord Chatham, with the following letter:

My Lord,

The memorial we have the honour to transmit to your lordship, it has been judged most proper to render as concise as possible in its appearance before the board at which Your Lordship presides; but as it involves in its detail much important matter, we solicit Your Lordship's attention whilst we explain more at large the grounds on which we prefer our prayer: indeed we feel it a duty, at the time we look to Your Lordship as our rightful patron, to make you more fully acquainted with those grievances of which we hope a redress.

In former wars the officers of marines were established on an equality with those of the line; they had an equal intercourse with them by sale and exchange of commissions. At the reduction in 1748 the half-pay officers of marines were considered as reduced officers of the army, and in consequence many of them have since attained the highest rank and command.

The first fifty companies of marines, raised in 1733, consisted mostly of experienced officers of the line and former marines, and received assurances from the then board of Admiralty, that they should be placed on as advantageous a footing as the marching regiments; however, at the end of the war they found that these assurances were unfulfilled, and from the circumscribed establishment on the peace of 1763, the service was rendered so far from respectable, that great discontent ensued; many officers solicited half-pay; memorial followed memorial to the board, without effect; all emulation was destroyed, the spirit of discipline was at an end, a heavy languor continued in every rank of the corps, till the Earl of Sandwich came to the head of the board in 1770.

His Lordship received their memorial with favour, and accounting their complaints just, very soon began to relieve them: the spirit of the corps, relying on their patron, revived in proportion, and their discipline soon became an object of admiration.

His Lordship, pleased with a corps that had improved under his protection, sent two battalions to the American war. Their behaviour during the course of the late war, serving in their double capacity on board and on shore, and their adherence to their duty at the conclusion of it, need not be particularly pointed out to your lordship: you in part witnessed it, the records of the Admiralty can fully attest it. At the close of the late war, the corps began to feel themselves neglected: a claim was more than once preferred by some officers, who in a former brevet-promotion had been omitted, but ineffectually; the vacancies of the corps, (even of those slain in battle,) when peace was determined on, were not filled up, notwithstanding all vacancies in the army (even in the youngest corps) were filled up, and very considerable promotion in the navy took place.

But Lord Keppel could not have adverted to that hardship, for he soon after, in an instance glorious to his memory, showed a mind superior to oppression; and judging the army an example for his conduct towards the marines, *seconded* an officer upon them, not more respectable for his high rank than his character: His Lordship's reduction was to the same establishment as had been fixed for the corps in

1771 by the Earl of Sandwich; from that, and the instance alluded to, the marines believed that, under His Lordship's auspices, they should one day obtain what remained to be done for them.

The corps continued to be trained with assiduity and spirit, till the reduction caused by Viscount Howe in March 1786 took place. It was bitter, My Lord, to part with officers who had commanded us in detachment and in battalion, with credit and honour, whom we loved as men and admired as officers; but it was more severe to have so unjust a proportion lopped off from the corps, by which it was so considerably animated.

This reduction was attended with a circumstance still more cruel: His Lordship, in a personal address to them, saw it in such a point of view as to delay his intentions nearly twelve months; then (first promising a compensation) carried them into execution. That compensation has never since been heard of; but the establishment of the marines being afterwards considered by his lordship unequal to the services required of them, a sergeant to each company, and four new companies were added, so that the field-officers' companies *alone* remained reduced, a circumstance felt by every rank of officers as an unparalleled oppression.

The corps is dispirited; even the private men, from the smallness of the establishment, are harassed beyond example in time of peace, having seldom two nights. Further, My Lord, the corps feel themselves neglected in not having shared His Majesty's royal favour, with all other corps, at the appearance of hostilities, and during the commotions in Holland, when every service under His Majesty received some promotion, some augmentation, themselves excepted; even the indulgence of leave of absence, which they heretofore enjoyed equally with other corps, His Lordship restricted to six months (field-officers excepted), under pain of being put on half-pay on not returning to quarters at the expiration of that period, making no allowance for accident or want of health.

My Lord, you are a soldier, and acquainted with the feelings that actuate them. What can be expected from troops sensible of such impressions? They feel themselves contemptible, because they know they are rendered less respectable in every point of view.

The services, My Lord, of the marines are constant, peace or war; their quick transition from clime to clime naturally soon enfeebles them: no corps can then more require an asylum for the disabled and worn out. The Royal Navy have sinecure places, civil appointments, military governments, invalid retreats, &c.; the line have sinecure places, civil appointments, military governments, invalid retreats, &c; the royal artillery their invalid battalion, and royal engineers as ample an invalid provision; but what has the marine veteran, when worn out in defence of his king and country? "The miserable pittance of half-pay!"

Your Lordship will undoubtedly hear it with surprise, that not one commission has been signed for the marine service (except from the half-pay) since the peace, notwithstanding the promotions in the army, navy, artillery, and engineers.

What the memorial before Your Lordship prays is, that the grievances, thus more fully stated, may by Your Lordship's wisdom and favour be so represented to our most gracious sovereign, as to obtain a due measure of redress; that in proportion to the strength of the corps it may be completed with field-officers, whom we humbly conceive may be as usefully employed in this corps as in any other, from the necessity of their attending the constant discipline at each of the head-quarters, by distributing them to regulate in the several recruiting districts, and by embarking them according to the strength of detachments serving on board each fleet, which would certainly be of the greatest benefit to the service, and give the corps due respectability when occasionally landed to co-operate with the line.

That the corps may obtain rank in the line, whenever their services require it, from the first establishment in 1755.

The memorial further prays an invalid establishment, formed in Your Lordship's wisdom, and proportioned to the contingencies the corps is subject to.

That the serving officers may be partakers in promotion.

It prays that all ranks of marine officers may enjoy leave of absence under the same liberal indulgence as other corps.

And, My Lord, permit us to hope, that the magnanimity of His Majesty will not suffer his marine forces to be *alone* aggrieved, *alone* oppressed.

Will not, my lord, our country equally bear the expense of those troops who equally fought her battles?

My Lord, believe it, that the marine service is in general reduced to a service of mere necessity; the present officers have only served too long to seek with advantage other professions: their case is hard,— it wants but representation; they trust it to Your Lordship's wisdom and Your Lordship's feelings.

We are, with the highest respect, in name of the whole corps,

Your lordship's most obedient servants,

Commandants   Henry Smith,

A. T. Collins,

W. Carruthers.

The Right Hon. the Earl of Chatham.

## No. 6.

To the Right-Honourable the Earl of Chatham, First Lord of the Admiralty.

The memorial of the officers of His Majesty's marine forces:

Humbly sheweth,—That many of your memorialists, from *age, long services*, and *infirmities* acquired in foreign climates, are rendered incapable of doing their duty agreeable to their wishes; and to add to their mortification, the present establishment affords not one comfortable retreat for the most deserving.

The memorialists have likewise the additional mortification of finding themselves excluded from the advantages all former marine officers enjoyed; your memorialists do not even benefit from the stoppages they have continued to pay from the first establishment of the present corps in 1755, under the denominations of Chelsea Hospital. Your memorialists beg leave to observe, that every military branch has now an established retreat for the worn-out officers.

The present Master-General of the Ordnance, His Grace the Duke of Richmond, found the corps of engineers in a similar situation to that your memorialists are now in. Humanity, and the rectitude of the measure, induced his grace to make a proper establishment, by selecting the young and healthy to do the executive part of the duty.

Relying on the justness of our application, we, whose names are hereunto subscribed, in behalf of the officers of the corps, most humbly entreat Your Lordship's protection; and we flatter ourselves Your Lordship will think our services merit an establishment for our worn-out officers, equally with every other part of His Majesty's forces by sea and land.

## No. 7.

*To the Earl of Chatham, First Lord of the Admiralty.*

The memorial of His Majesty's marine corps on full pay:

Humbly sheweth,—That your memorialists are impressed with

305

the deepest sense of gratitude for the many liberal proofs they have experienced of Your Lordship's generous patronage and protection.

The objects for promotion extended by the establishment of the field-officers; the prospects for the young and active advanced; those worn out by length of service rewarded by the comfortable provision made for the aged and infirm; the determination that every officer shall take rank and promotion in the corps from the date of his last commission, as in the case of Colonel Spry; the promotion that has taken place under Your Lordship's auspices, have all tended to excite a spirit of exertion throughout every rank, and must naturally be productive of advantage to His Majesty's service.

These objects, so flattering to the serving corps, have attracted the notice and attention of those officers on the half-pay list, who threw themselves into that situation, or were compelled for particular reasons to embrace it, prior or subsequent to the reduction in 1783, and many have avowed an intention of soliciting full-pay again, with a view of sharing those advantages, which the serving corps has been considered by Your Lordship so justly to merit. Your memorialists, with great submission, beg leave to observe, that should these solicitations have effect, the captains, lieutenants, and subalterns who have been constantly serving without promotion in any instance since the peace, will have to look forward to a period still more dreary and uncertain than ever: a circumstance aggravated by the sanguine hopes they entertained, that when the officers reduced at the peace in 1783 were provided for, they would certainly succeed to all vacancies in the serving corps.

Your memorialists presume to observe to your lordship, that the practice of bringing such officers from the half-pay list, at the same time that it is discouraging and injurious to the serving corps, has never been found of any advantage to the service; they will not, however, attempt to point out the trouble that such applications, when countenanced, must occasion Your Lordship, or any future board of Admiralty, and the constant alarm that must agitate the corps by the return of officers to the service so circumstanced; but they beg leave to submit to Your Lordship, that should purchase and sale of commissions be allowed in the marine service, the officers on half-pay might be admitted, by paying to the officers they exchanged with the difference between full and half-pay, and be placed last for promotion in their respective ranks, which your memorialists conceive would be a fair compensation, considering the short period they have *actually* served.

And your memorialists further presume to hope, that your lordship will see the propriety of placing all officers upon the marine list according to the dates of their last commissions, which will give universal satisfaction to the corps and demonstrate that the rule of promotion which Your Lordship has so justly established, is carried into complete effect.

Relying on that liberality with which your lordship has treated their just requests, and your perfect knowledge of military rules, your memorialists are happy in submitting their situation to your favourable attention; resting on the hope, that Your Lordship will not admit those officers into the service again who solicited or chose to remain on half-pay for various reasons, or who were indulged with that alternative for causes of too serious a nature to be inserted in this memorial; and that Your Lordship will be pleased to direct officers to be placed on the marine list agreeable to the date of their last commissions.

## No. 8.

### To the Right-Honourable Earl Spencer.

The memorial of His Majesty's marine forces:

Humbly sheweth,—That your memorialists trust their services to their king and country have been as zealous and faithful as any other of His Majesty's forces. They have it singularly and grievously to feel, that the service of the marines labours under a great many disadvantages not felt by other corps in His Majesty's service. They consider themselves as much entitled to your lordship's protection as His Majesty's Royal Navy, as the line to that of the commander-in-chief, or as the Royal Artillery and engineers to that of the master-general of the ordnance. Your memorialists have the mortification to find, that when equally engaged in fighting the battles of their country with His Majesty's other officers, *they alone* are precluded from a share of the royal favour.

Your Lordship's wisdom will easily discern between the services of a corps animated by prospects of rank and honour, and the services of a corps acting solely on the principles of duty. Your memorialists cannot but trust, that their country is disposed to be equally liberal in its provision for their service as for that of any other corps, and therefore hope that their long and faithful services may entitle them to partake of preferment equally with His Majesty's Royal Navy, army, and Royal Artillery. They conceive that an extension of the invalid establishment, an augmentation of field-officers, and promotion of the subalterns who served during the last war, would materially tend to remove their present grievances, and enable them to perform their duty with that spirit, order, and good discipline which have ever characterized His Majesty's marine forces.

The subalterns of from fifteen to seventeen years' standing submit their present hopeless case to Your Lordship's feelings.

Your memorialists submit to your lordship's consideration the propriety of holding out to marines a bounty equal to that of other corps, by which they may be able to complete, with dispatch, any augmentation His Majesty may be pleased to grant. That, finally, your memorialists are persuaded that Your Lordship's favourable attention only is wanting to give effect to their prayer. And in humble hope that they will obtain Your Lordship's good offices, your memorialists place their confidence of support and relief.

## No. 9.

### To the Right-Honourable the Earl Spencer, First Lord-Commissioner of the Admiralty.

The memorial of the officers of His Majesty's marine forces:

Humbly sheweth,—That your memorialists, conscious that zeal and loyalty have ever actuated their service, presume to entreat Your Lordship's attention to the senior officers of the corps.

That your memorialists, viewing the vote of Parliament for the service of the present year, are led to hope there is an ample provision to fulfil their utmost expectations, and confide in Your Lordship's justice, acknowledged zeal, and liberality, that those captains whose commissions are dated in 1778, and subalterns of 1779, who are grown old in expectation of that promotion which is the object of our present solicitation, may not be left a prey to disappointment, after steady and faithful services of thirty-five and seventeen years. Your memorialists experience a most singular mortification at being deprived of that rank in the line, which they trust their faithful and steady services would well justify.

That your memorialists therefore humbly hope, through your lordship's favourable representation and influence with their royal master, that their services may be animated with some portion of His Majesty's most gracious favour.

That, finally, your memorialists are persuaded Your Lordship's good offices *only* are wanting to give effect to their prayer, and in the hope they shall obtain Your Lordship's countenance they place their confidence of support.

No. 10.

Horse Guards, 25th May, 1797

Sir,

I have Field-Marshal the Duke of York's commands to acknowledge the receipt of your letter of the 23rd instant, with its enclosures, for which communication His Royal Highness desires that you will be pleased to accept his best thanks. His Royal Highness has felt great satisfaction at the highly praiseworthy conduct of the division of marines under your command, in having in such proper terms evinced their detestation and abhorrence of the vile acts that are now practising by wicked incendiaries with a view to shake the allegiance of the soldiery. But His Royal Highness trusts that the honourable example set by the Chatham division of marines will be followed by every individual of their brother-soldiers, and that the British Army will, to the latest period, preserve its love and attachment to their king and country, and that they will be as desirous to distinguish themselves for their loyalty, as they have ever been emulous to excel all other nations in courage when opposed to the enemy.

I have the honour to be, &c.

Robert Brownrigg.

Major-General Innes, Commanding
Chatham Division of Marines.

Admiralty Office, 23rd May, 1797

Sir,

I have received and communicated to My Lords Commissioners of the Admiralty your letter to me of yesterday's date, enclosing a printed hand-bill which appears to have been distributed amongst the marines at Chatham under your command, and an answer thereto, which had been transmitted to you signed by the non-commissioned officers of the division now in barracks at that place; and I have it in command from their lordships to acquaint you, that they view with great satisfaction the spirit, and loyalty and zeal so strongly manifested by the non-commissioned officers and privates of that division, and which it is their direction you should communicate to them in a proper manner.

I have at the same time the pleasure to add, that their lordships fully approve of all your proceedings on the occasion,

And have the honour to be, sir, &c,

Evan Nepean.

Major-General Innes, Chatham.

## No. 11

*To the Right-Honourable the Lords Commissioners of the Admiralty.*

The memorial of the senior captains of His Majesty's Royal Marine forces: Most humbly sheweth,—That your memorialists, members of a corps which forms a considerable portion of the national force at the present crisis of extended hostility, presume to obtrude their feelings and hopes on the notice of your right-honourable board, for to your lordships your memorialists must ever look up as to their constitutional guardians and protectors, and in whose justice they repose the fullest confidence.

Under these impressions, your memorialists beg to state to Your Lordships that the forty-nine senior captains of marines, who entered the service during the American war, many of them as early as 1778 and 1779, have served seventeen and eighteen years as subalterns, in addition to twelve and thirteen as captains. Thus circumstanced, your memorialists trust it will not excite surprise that they should express the severe mortification they feel in contrasting their situation with that of officers of other corps, who, with fewer years standing in the service, have attained and continue to attain considerable rank, with its attendant advantages.

Your memorialists have earnestly to entreat that Your Lordships will not ascribe to any improper motive their adducing the corps of Royal Artillery and Royal Engineers in proof of their assertion: in those corps (whose constitution with regard to promotion is exactly similar with that of the marines,) officers who have entered the service long after the first twenty-four captains on the marine list, have some time since been field-officers, and many of them lieutenant-colonels.

But besides this protraction of promotion, which your memorialists have grievously to lament, they feel a redoubled severity when they reflect they are almost without a hope of ever attaining any higher rank in the corps, while they daily witness the promotion of their juniors in every other branch of His Majesty's service.

The hardships of your memorialists' case will appear with still greater force, when it is considered that from the lapse of so many of their best years in the service of their country, they are necessarily deprived of that consolatory hope which time and some future changes in the corps may afford to their juniors. Such is the situation of Your Lordships' memorialists, while every subaltern officer and soldier throughout His Majesty's forces derive advantage from length of service.

Stimulated by the severe pressure of the circumstances which mark their case, and while it is with reluctance they intrude at the present moment, your memorialists, confiding in the candour and liberality of Your Lordships, indulge a hope that you will take their case into serious consideration, and grant them such relief as Your Lordships shall deem it to deserve.

In the name and behalf of the old captains,

(Signed)                William Henry Boys,
                                    Senior Captain.

18th March, 1808.

## No. 12.

*To the Right-Honourable the Lords Commissioners of the Admiralty.*

The memorial of the second-commandants, field-officers, and senior captains of royal marines: Humbly showeth,—That they have grievously to lament that the length of their services has been entirely overlooked in the late augmentation of the corps. The field-officers had been induced to hope, that the late memorial of the senior captains would have drawn the attention of the board to the forlorn situation of the superior ranks in the corps, when they had every reason to expect, for all the vigour and prime of their lives so exhausted in the service of their country, that some ample reward in the line of promotion would have been granted them, especially at a time when every other part of His Majesty's forces has been properly attended to and rewarded.

Your memorialists feel the proud distinction of forming an essential branch of the Royal Navy, and can never consider their services of inferior value to the state to those of any other corps in His Majesty's service; and they looked forward with confidence that the late promotion in the Royal Navy was the prelude to one in the higher classes in the royal marines. The only corps that your memorialists can assimilate themselves to are the Royal Artillery and Royal Engineers, to both of which they have, during the late and present war, become much inferior, as well in rank and appointment as in everything that can stimulate the pride and attention of a soldier.

Your memorialists will never regret that deserving officers of the royal navy are rewarded by nominal appointments on their establishment; yet they cannot but feel they have a claim to participate in such honourable remuneration for distinguished services.

Your memorialists therefore trust that Their Lordships will humbly represent to His Majesty the extreme mortification that the senior part of the faithful and loyal marine officers experienced on the late augmentation of the corps, when their services were unfortunately overlooked, and entreat His Majesty to grant such appointments as may reward lives spent in his service. They are properly sensible of and grateful to His Majesty for the honour he condescended to bestow on them in making them a Royal Corps; and they are so fully confident of His Majesty's gracious and good intentions at all times to reward the services of the Royal Marines, that their grievances need only to be properly brought before His Majesty by your lordships to obtain every redress they merit.

And as there are appointments of general, lieutenant-general, and major-general of marines to reward the services of distinguished naval officers; they trust that, as next in consequence, they may have a lieutenant-general and two major-generals appointed from the corps, and the same allowances with those of that rank in the Royal Navy; and that the commandants of divisions (to meet the expense of the present times) may be put upon the same footing with those of the royal artillery; that the field-officers and staff of the Royal Marines may have the same allowances as are granted to every other field and staff officer in His Majesty's service; and that the pay-captains of Royal Marines may have the same allowances for the payment of the grand divisions as are granted to the captains of the Royal Artillery.

(Signed by)

| A. Burn, | T. Davey, | R. Lee, |
| W. H. Boys, | R. H. Foley, | T. Guildford, |
| D. Ballinghall, | R. Smith, | F. Williams. |

## No. 13.

Admiralty Office, July 5th, 1814.

Sir,

My Lords Commissioners of the Admiralty observing that many marines who have been discharged from His Majesty's service, from time to time attend at this office as candidates for the out-pension of Greenwich Hospital who, not being worn out and become decrepit in the service of their country," are not entitled thereto, and that their proper age and cause of their discharge are frequently very inaccurately stated, I have Their Lordships' command, with a view to prevent the said men being put to unnecessary trouble and expense, to signify their directions to you, to acquaint such marines as may from time to time be discharged from your division, that they cannot be allowed pensions unless they come within the description above mentioned; and you are to cause the proper age and real cause of discharge of the said men to be stated; forbearing in future to insert therein any recommendation to the benefits of the said hospital, to prevent the possibility of disappointment, their lordships being disposed at all times to give due consideration to their respective cases.

I am, Sir, &c.

## No. 14.

*To the Right-Honourable the Lords Commissioners of the Admiralty.*

The memorial of the field-officers and senior captains of His Majesty's Royal Marine forces: Most humbly showeth,—That your memorialists have served longer to obtain the rank they at present hold in the corps than any officer in His Majesty's service; many of the senior captains having served thirty-one years and upwards during the course of those wars, and who are still without a prospect of promotion. Yet, as your memorialists presume to look forward to a reward for their services upon an increase of the establishment of the corps, they trust that when Your Lordships may recommend it to His Majesty in council to form the large body of supernumeraries (now attached to the corps) into companies, that you will at the same time be pleased to bring the length of service of that class of officers under His Majesty's gracious consideration, and recommend the establishment of two field-officers to every three thousand men in the corps, that not being half the proportion of field-officers in the army or artillery.

The senior field-officers are fully sensible of and grateful for the promotion conferred on them, and the increase of pay to the commandants; but should Your Lordships consider the services of the present senior field-officers deserving any further reward, they trust that Your Lordships will recommend the appointment of one second commandant to every two thousand men; which would either give promotion, or place as resident captains of divisions all those captains who have served during those wars, and who now continue to serve as such in every part of the world.

Your memorialists are aware it may be urged, that there is not any mode of employing any more commandants and field-officers; but the services of all are at the disposal of the board of Admiralty, and they are all anxious to be actively employed, and to have their services adequately rewarded; whereas a colonel in the line with the rank of general, colonels and colonels-commandant of the Royal Artillery (unless upon the staff), are not required to do any duty.

In the navy, in the army, in the Royal Artillery, and Royal Engineers, your memorialists could enumerate various appointments unconnected with the officers of those corps, by which the services of old and meritorious officers are rewarded. The Royal Marines alone are without any such appointments, or any superior staff; and as they are persuaded that their services are as useful to the state as any other body of men, they trust that they will not longer remain unrewarded.

Your memorialists appeal to your lordships with peculiar confidence as perfect judges of what meritorious officers may deserve after such a series of constant service, by which the health and constitution of all have in some degree been impaired.

Your memorialists rely upon Your Lordships' liberality, and trust that when their services are compared with those of other corps, or with those of the civil branch of the department over which your lordships preside, they will be considered deserving of an equal reward.

In a full persuasion that the humble petition of your memorialists will meet with Your Lordships' favourable consideration, and the approbation of their sovereign, &c. &c.

## No. 15.

*To the Right-Honourable the Lords Commissioners of the Admiralty.*

The memorial of the field-officers and senior captains of His Majesty's Royal Marine forces:

Humbly sheweth,—That the corps to which they belong, an integral part of the Royal Navy, is now and ever has been conspicuous for its eminent services to the state, which the marked approbation of the various superior officers whom it has since its institution served under, if such reference were required to establish a well-known fact, would amply testify; that notwithstanding this, and the honourable distinction of "Royal" lately conferred on it by His Majesty, in reward of its zealous and very meritorious services, it is still unquestionably held in a state of unexampled depression, reducing it far beneath the level of any other regular military establishment; and in proof of this assertion your memorialists, with all due deference to Your Lordships, beg leave to submit, that the causes productive of this depreciated effect are as follows, and until they cease to operate, their condition cannot possibly, in any shape, be materially ameliorated.

The causes of the corps' depression are, that although consisting of upwards of 30,000 men, it alone of all His Majesty's forces is destitute of a superior staff, and consequently both of that respectability it confers, and those remunerations which are bestowed upon the line, the Royal Artillery, and the Royal Engineers. That it is the only one whose post, when acting with the line, is equivocal and undefined, and wherein officers, by imposed restraints, are restricted to the exercise of mere regimental rank, notwithstanding their commissions, signed by the king and entered at the War Office for the purpose of giving them rank with the line, authorise their asserting their claims to command in any garrison, or elsewhere, when such command should by seniority devolve upon them; and what renders this recently-introduced exclusion of their corps from the most material and valuable privilege of the profession peculiarly grating to their feelings is, that prior to the distinguished notice of His Majesty it was in the full and unquestionable possession of a right common to every military body, without even excepting the militia or honourable East India Company's service.

Whereas, the now Royal Marine Corps, deprived of that for which in the estimation of professional men there can be no equivalent, and subjected in consequence thereof to repeated galling humiliations, has the mortification of beholding its laurels shaded, and its sovereign's gracious approbation overcast by a most extraordinary and unaccountable exclusion from that chain of command in which it was recently comprehended, and this its insulated condition rendered doubly painful by frequently viewing, not only junior officers of regular corps, but even of the militia, assuming those temporary commands at its respective headquarters in the absence of the generals or the staff, which its veteran officers have an indisputable right, by their superior rank, to exercise. That it is the only corps in the king's service where officers are eligible to nothing but regimental staff appointments, and there is none beside it so limited in its number of field-officers as to

315

almost bar the door of promotion against its junior captains, who, grown grey in the service, have served their country three wars, and in every climate.

Under such peculiar degrading mortifications, disadvantages, and disabilities, which exclusively operate on a corps whose distinguished services have attracted the notice of its sovereign, your memorialists must ever feel depressed; and they cannot refrain from expressing their firm belief, that the aggregate of their situation imposed upon a military body deserving of censure instead of commendation, would be deemed a most exemplary punishment. And here they pause to lament and deplore; glorying however in their attachment to a corps constituting an important branch of England's best defence, that its very annexation to the Royal Navy should seem, as it were, to plunge it into obscurity, rather than, as it ought, to raise it into consequence.

Your memorialists having now submitted to your right-honourable board the most prominent features of their grievances which bear exclusively upon them alone, together with their corps' depression, the causes of which are but too glaring, most earnestly entreat Your Lordships to lay them before His Majesty, who, when their unparalleled situation is known, will, they confidently trust, be graciously pleased to direct that *his faithful, zealous, and loyal corps of marines* shall be placed on a footing and raised to a level with the rest of the forces of this realm.

And towards the attainment of this but just and equitable end, your memorialists express a hope that Your Lordships, as their patrons, may be pleased to advise, that the senior commandant, resident in London, may be placed on the staff with such suitable establishment as his rank entitles him to; that the commandants of divisions, having the rank of general officers, who are of sixty and fifty years standing in the service, may be allowed to retire on the same pay as is enjoyed by the naval marine-generals; that the next in seniority may succeed to their vacancies; and that such a number of additional field-officers be added to the corps as to promote their senior captains, whose services, had chance thrown them into the Royal Artillery instead of the marines, would long since have been remunerated with lieutenant-colonelcies.

## No. 16.

*Minutes of the Board of Admiralty relative to the Royal Marine Artillery.*
Clause 5.

We now beg leave to call the attention of your Royal Highness to the companies of Royal Marine Artillery.

These companies were formed, one at each division, in 1804, for the purpose, in the first instance, of supplying the service of His Majesty's bomb-vessels, before that time performed by the Royal Artillery; but it was also intended that these companies should, particularly in time of peace, be employed at the respective divisions in drilling the whole of the marines in gunnery. We are so well satisfied of the great utility of having a considerable body of marines trained to gunnery, that we are inclined to recommend that the Royal Marine Artillery be increased to eight companies, as well for the purpose of encouraging and training the other marines, as to enable us to embark a certain number of well-trained artillery-men in others of His Majesty's ships as well as in the bombs, experience having proved the great advantage to be derived to the service from this practice, which has been tried of late to a small extent.

We therefore humbly propose to Your Royal Highness to be pleased to sanction the establishment of eight companies of Royal Marine Artillery; but in order that the whole establishment may not exceed what Your Royal Highness was pleased to declare to be a fit peace establishment of marines, we humbly propose to transfer a certain number of officers and men from the ordinary marines to the artillery respectively, which we think proper for the present period; by which the corps will consist of eighty companies, of which eight will be artillery. This measure, which will give great efficiency to the corps of marines, and to use the expression of the original promoters of the marine artillery, double its utility both ashore and afloat, will be very inconsiderable, if any expense to the public; because we have proposed to reduce an equivalent number of marines, and shall submit some further reductions in the number of officers attached to the artillery companies; and in time of war a further diminution of expense from what it would be under the present system will, if Your Royal Highness shall be pleased to adopt our suggestions, arise from the following circumstances:

The Royal Artillery, when embarked in bombs, had certain advantages granted them in consideration, we presume, of being taken out of their natural course of shore service; these advantages the Royal Marine Artillery have claimed and hitherto enjoyed, under, we think, an erroneous construction of His Majesty's order in council, establishing the pay and allowances of these companies.

It is evident, that however just it was to grant these allowances to the Royal Artillery when removed from their ordinary duties, it was certainly unnecessary to give them to the marine artillery, whose natural course of service it was to embark, and which, in fact, was formed for this special purpose. We trust, therefore, that Your Royal Highness will see the expediency of correcting this error at this favourable opportunity, when it can be done without any immediate injury to individuals, because at present none of the marine artillery are embarked, nor according to the original regulation would they have been embarked in time of peace. While we therefore propose to continue the increased shore pay, and to encourage the artillery, and the corps in general, by doubling the number who will receive this increased pay, we think we may fairly propose to abolish the distant and contingent advantages of the extra sea pay, to which in fact we doubt that any other right has hitherto existed than an erroneous construction of His Majesty's order in council. We therefore propose, that when the Royal Marine Artillery shall embark, the sea pay of all ranks shall bear to their pay on shore the same proportion that the sea pay of the marines in general bears to their shore pay.

## No. 17.

*Copy of a letter from Colonels Desborough and Tench to the Right Honourable Charles Yorke, First Lord of the Admiralty:—*

13th March, 1811.

Sir

We respectfully beg leave to introduce ourselves again to your notice, and to solicit your further attention to the subject on which you honoured us with a conference last September. Six months have since elapsed, during which period we have anxiously expected that some testimony of that approbation you were then pleased to express to us of the services and general good conduct of the Royal Marines, would have been conferred on the corps. This cheering anticipation has not been confined within our own breasts; as the advocate of our corps, at whose request we made ourselves then prominent, we held it incumbent upon us to communicate, through their commandants, to the officers of the several divisions, not only a detail of the subject we had submitted to your consideration, with your observations upon them, but likewise the more valuable and important account of those spontaneous views you were pleased to take of the deficiencies of the marine services, when you graciously suggested the practicability, and held out the prospect, of placing our chief commandant and general officers commanding divisions on the staff, and stated the public advantages which would arise from assigning to that part of the corps stationed on shore, at the great naval depots, a share of the garrison duties of those places.

Such intimations naturally awakened in the bosom of every marine officer the most sanguine and grateful emotion, and when they called to mind in conjunction with them your former favourable sentiments of their corps, and your flattering marks of attention to its interests when not a minister, it will not create surprise that such impressions should cause them to reason with that ardour, which promises itself the accomplishment of its object on finding a patron. And yet it was not altogether from your most candid and obliging reception of us and our representation that we presumed to deduce those favourable conclusions, and to impart encouragement to our brother-officers, but also, in a high degree, from the answer which the board of Admiralty condescended to return to the memorial of the corps, which we forwarded to them on taking our leave of you, after having previously had the honour of presenting to you the copy of its contents.

In that reply Their Lordships were pleased to acquaint us that our application should be taken into consideration. To the language of official communication we are not strangers, nor unaware of official circumspection; we know that refusal is sometimes conveyed by silence, and disapprobation sometimes accompanied with rebuke; but in this instance the style of Their Lordships' letter, and the assurance it contains, justifies us in believing that our appeal was regarded by them as neither frivolous nor intrusive. We, who know from authority that this case is under consideration, naturally look for a decision upon it. For half a year we have waited, and continue to wait for this mark of favour, not less with painful anxiety than respectful submission. And here, sir, permit us to remark to you, that during so long a period of expectancy the Royal Marine Corps, both collectively and individually, have endeavoured to evince the highest possible sense of deference for the public feeling and situation of yourself and that great board under whom they serve, by observing the most profound silence and exemplary forbearance on the merit of their cause and probable attainment of their hopes, out of their own immediate circle.

Excepting amongst themselves, they have been scrupulously solicitous not to agitate this subject, and by their prudent conduct have wholly prevented its discussion in pamphlets and newspapers. Sensible of the difficulties and embarrassments under which the executive government has been placed from the lamented malady of their sovereign, they have forborne not only from complaint, but enquiry. Nevertheless, it were to relinquish the best energies of our nature, and to stifle every military feeling and recollection, if we did not distinctly but respectfully mark to you, that the marines were more than disappointed when they found the fifth anniversary (21st October, 1810,) of the glorious victory of Trafalgar commemorated by a naval promotion only.

But we should neither convey the sentiments of our corps, nor execute our own intentions, if we presumed to make this letter the vehicle of accusation: we aim but to impress upon your mind the reasonableness and moderation of our pretensions, and to entreat you, in pity to the limits of human patience, to decide upon them. We humbly presume to hope that no obstacles which may not be surmounted oppose the placing of our chief commandant, and the commandants of divisions who are general officers, on the staff. All these veterans have been in the service of their country more than fifty years; and yet their appointments are so scanty as to degrade their high rank, by precluding them from the exercise of common hospitality in the expensive quarters where they are stationed.

If we turn our eyes to the other departments of service, we behold five ordnance generals on the staff at Portsmouth, Plymouth, and Chatham only; on the other hand, we recall military governments and lucrative appointments, partly civil, partly military, bestowed on officers of the army. Towards our brethren of the navy, what sentiments have we ever cherished but respect and good will? and yet, without a wish to infringe on what they enjoy, can it be justly affirmed that the marines are selfish or unreasonable, when they request that those officers who perform all the real duties of marine service should be placed on an equal footing of emolument with those who are but nominal members of their establishment? We shall advance yet a step further, sir, and presume to ask whether a colonel of militia, commanding a battalion of 1000 men, does not hold a more profitable appointment than the commandant of a marine division? In recording the reflection arising from the prospect of our performing garrison duty, if we should be found rather prolix, we trust to your indulgence on a subject so near our hearts, and inwoven with a review of our past lives and feelings.

When the inferior public consideration which as a body we receive on all occasions is recollected, what but that ardent, innate bravery, which you did us the honour to point out and commend,—that *esprit du corps*, which strings every nerve and beats in every artery of a marine, could enable us to sustain that reputation which is coeval with the establishment of our service. We would have an academy similar to those at Marlowe, Woolwich, and Portsmouth for the candidates of the navy, army, and artillery, where the intellect may be cultivated, the sciences taught, and the principles fixed, of the young persons who are introduced into our corps. They join headquarters without any previous examination of their mental acquirements or progress in education, where they are put through the ordinary drill of a parade, on which perhaps not a hundred men are daily assembled, and generally embark on naval duty in a few weeks after.

Of the field evolutions and regimental internal economy, they go away of course almost entirely uninformed. In two or three years, or after a longer period, they commonly rejoin their divisions, obtain leave to pay a short visit to their friends, and are then ordered to repair to a recruiting quarter, where they remain until their turn for sea duty again approaches. During this interim they have no duties to perform, but the occasional mounting a barrack guard, attendance at morning and evening roll calls, and a nominal superintendence of their companies, whose real management is vested (and wisely) with stationary officers,—the pay captains; who have an arduous task to fulfil, accompanied with a heavy pecuniary responsibility, for the executing of which, they are worse paid than a captain of militia.

Within this humble and circumscribed path are almost entirely restricted the duties of a marine officer on shore. Under circumstances of such peculiar depression, suffer us to intrude upon you a description of our private feelings and situation. A field-officer of marines, with rank, certainly with as much zeal and ardour, and possibly with an equal share of talent if not of practical acquirement with his brethren of the line or artillery, is seen wandering round the fortifications of Portsmouth, Plymouth, and Chatham, without object, interest, or employment; if a foreigner or a stranger of his own country, struck by a dress that is supposed to denote a share of command and consequence, inquires of this *nondescript character* the charge he sustains or the post he fills in the general scale of military arrangement, he blushes, in acknowledging he has none, to expose the state of insufficiency to which the injudicious regulations of service have condemned him.

Does a prince of the blood review the troops, and inspect the works of the garrison? He is not only an idle spectator of a scene in which he ought to act, but is left almost without an avenue by which he can approach royalty. At the levee of the governor he is never seen, and, from not being under his command, has no right to feel offended that he seldom partakes of his hospitality or, unless from personal considerations, is never found at the tables of the general officers,— privations of too small importance to cause one uneasy emotion if abstractedly regarded only, but not devoid of consequence when viewed by a reference to those principles by which, in some degree, the scale of rank and estimation in society is measured; besides that it narrows the acknowledged privilege attached to long and honourable military servitude of mingling with high rank, and associating with distinguished character.

Amidst these mortifying humiliations, it has occasionally happened that our strength of officers and men at headquarters has nearly equalled that of all the other troops within the lines of the place in which instance we form a most curious and preposterous spectacle for military consideration,—a corps in the heart of his garrison, almost as numerous as that appointed for its defence, not subject to the orders and control of the governor. Well might a former governor of Portsmouth demonstrate this anomalous body an "*imperium in imperio.*"

We draw, sir, towards an end, not without hoping that the fidelity of the description will apologise for the familiarity of the detail we have furnished. In conclusion, it becomes us to state, that although the tenor of our letter is almost exclusively confined to the description of the two important positions laid down by yourself, and the reflections which unavoidably accompanied them, yet we entreat, with equal earnestness and respect, your attention to many other points set forth in the memorial of the corps and our former letter to you. Our small artillery establishment wants but a continuance of that regard it has hitherto experienced, and an extension of its numbers, to become one of the most valuable appendages of the Royal Navy. But the claims of the senior captains are paramount with us

All these gallant, neglected officers commenced their career of service during the American war; and those at the head of the list have served their country between thirty and forty years,—a case which we can confidently affirm is without precedent in the military history of Britain, and we believe we should not risk contradiction if we marked it as unexampled in the military history of Europe. An appeal in behalf of our sergeants admitted into Greenwich Hospital being placed on a footing with the sergeants of the line at Chelsea, we conceive to be an obligation due from us to those brave and useful men; and the opulent state of the funds of Greenwich Hospital justify us in asking for this extension of liberality towards our non-commission officers.

It is a fact as curious as unparalleled, that the commissioned officers of marines furnish a day's pay towards the support of Chelsea Hospital, and a proportion of their prize-money to that of Greenwich, without receiving any advantage or emolument whatever from these great national institutions. One more repetition were yet necessary, if in appealing to the magnanimity and disinterested government of Mr. Yorke all repetition were not superfluous: should the plea of increased public expenditure be advanced against the prayer of our petition, we have already pointed out the means by which the argument can be obviated. If the marine establishment consisted of one hundred second-lieutenants less than are found upon it, the public service would not suffer by its diminution.

******

Mr. Yorke acknowledged the receipt of this letter to Colonel Desborough, acquainting him that the subject thereof was still under the consideration of the Board of Admiralty, and there it still remains.

## No. 18.

### Singular Illegal Sentence of a Naval Court-Martial.

Lieutenant Frye of the marines, when serving on board a frigate in the West Indies in 1743, was charged with contempt of orders, for having refused, when ordered by his captain, to assist another lieutenant in taking an officer prisoner on board the ship; the two lieutenants requesting to have the order given in writing. For this, Lieutenant Frye was tried at Jamaica by a court-martial, and sentenced to fifteen years imprisonment, besides being declared incapable of serving the king. He was brought home, and his case (after being laid before the privy-council) appearing in a justifiable light, he was released. Sometime after, he brought an action against Sir Chaloner Ogle, who had been president of the above court-martial, and had a verdict in his favour for one thousand pounds damages, as it was also proved that he had been kept fourteen months in the most severe confinement before he was brought to his trial. The judge, moreover, informed him that he was at liberty to bring his action against any of the members of the said court-martial he could meet with. The following part of the affair is still more remarkable.

Upon application made by Lieutenant Frye, Sir John Willes, Lord

Chief Justice of the common pleas, issued his writ against Admiral Mayne and Captain Rentone, two of the persons who had composed the above court-martial, who happened to be in England, and members of a court-martial then sitting at Deptford, and they were arrested on the breaking up of the court. The other members resented highly what they thought an insult; they met twice on the subject, and came to certain *resolutions*, which the judge-advocate was directed to deliver to the board of Admiralty, in order to their being laid before the king. In these resolutions they demanded "satisfaction for the high insult on their president from all persons, how high soever in office, who have set on foot this arrest, or in any degree advised or promoted it;" moreover complaining, that by the said arrest "the order, discipline, and government of His Majesty's armies by sea were dissolved, and the statute 13. Car. II. made null and void."

The altercations on that account lasted some months. At length the court-martial thought it necessary to submit; and they sent to Lord Chief Justice Willes a letter, signed by the seventeen officers (admirals and commanders) who composed it, in which they acknowledged that "the resolutions of the 16th and 21st May, were *unjust and unreasonable,* and to ask pardon of His Lordship and the whole court of common pleas, for the indignity offered to him and the court." This letter Judge Willes read in the open court, and directed the same to be registered in the remembrance office, "as a memorial to the present and future ages, that whoever set themselves above the law, will in the end find themselves mistaken." The letter from the court-martial, and Judge Willes's acceptation, were inserted in the next *Gazette,* 15th November, 1746.

## No 19.

### Garrisons held by Marine Officers.

The foreign, commands entrusted to the officers of the Royal Marines have been few, and but of doubtful advantage to the individuals who were selected to hold them, more than it has afforded them opportunities of displaying much zeal, courage, and fidelity, under very trying circumstances.

### EXPEDITION TO BOTANY BAY.

In 1787 a detachment under the command of Major W. W. Tench, consisting of 4 captains, 12 subalterns, 24 sergeants and corporals, 8 drummers, and 160 privates, making the whole of the military force, including the major-commandant and staff, 212 persons, sailed from Portsmouth on the 13th of May, on board the *Sirius*, *Hyaena*, and *Supply*, conveying 565 male and 192 female convicts, and 18 children. The expedition was under the direction of Captain Phillip of the Royal Navy, who was appointed governor of the colony.

On the 21st of January, 1788, the fleet anchored in Botany Bay, and on the 23rd moved to Port Jackson, where the convicts and the guard were landed and established. The governor read his commission on the 7th of February, in presence of the marines and convicts; and expressed his thanks to the battalion in public orders for their exemplary conduct from the time of embarkation. As winter was approaching, the marines hastened the building of a temporary barrack, and the plan of a town was laid out by the governor.

### ISLAND OF ASCENSION.

When St. Helena became the prison of Napoleon, the occupation of Ascension necessarily followed; and Sir George Cockburn, the commander-in-chief on the station, immediately sent an officer with a number of men under his command to hold the island. But the Lords Commissioners of the Admiralty were not long in forwarding a different establishment, and a detachment of marines was sent from England, under Major Campbell, to form the garrison. It was in October 1823 that Major Nicolls succeeded to the command of the Island of Ascension, which was then a mere rock overrun by immense rats, and incapable of producing any vegetation; having scarcely sufficient water for its small garrison, and the road from the barracks to the spring which furnished the supply almost impassable for the water-cart.

But by the unremitted exertions of the marines on the island, convenient roads were made, and water-tanks built, affording not only an ample supply for the garrison, but for the ships of the African squadron, and numerous merchant vessels that came to the island in distress. Vegetables were cultivated with so much success, that a plentiful supply was obtained by our cruisers; and previous to the recall of Major Nicolls from his command in 1828, (on his promotion to the rank of major in the corps,) he had so improved the cultivation of the island, that there were 800 head of cattle of his own rearing, consisting of cows, oxen, sheep, goats, and swine, besides about 500 that had been slaughtered.

The ingenuity and perseverance of the marines who served on

the Island of Ascension, and particularly those who were its earliest inhabitants, convey to the admiring and astonished visitor of the colony a flattering impression of the discipline and internal economy of the corps.

Captain William Bate succeeded Major Nicolls, and this officer, after years of exertion, vexation, and difficulty, died on the island. Captain Tinklar was the next commandant; and this zealous officer soon became a victim to his anxious desire to promote the welfare of the service. Captain Bennett was the next appointed; but the period of that officer's command was even more brief than his predecessor, and he died in a still more sudden manner.

The death of three commandants within so short a period leads us to infer, that their removal was not entirely attributable to the malignity of the climate,, for we do not find its fatal influence extending to the subordinate ranks; but we believe that the duties of the commanding officers were of a most tantalizing character, involving contradictions, vexations, and anomalies that but few constitutions could long resist in such a climate as that of Ascension.

The last officer of marines in command at this seemingly fatal colony was Captain R. P. Dwyer, and he all but shared the fate of his predecessors; for in little more than two years from his appointment, he was, through the excitement and vexations inseparable from his duties, seized with such severe illness, that, as the only chance of saving his life, he was sent to England by the first ship that touched at the island. But some time previous to his illness Captain Dwyer had solicited permission to resign his command, under the persuasion that no exertions, no line of conduct however upright and honourable, could guarantee him from annoyances which could not be overcome.

Thus ended the command which had been so long held by officers of the Royal Marines on the Island of Ascension,—that gloomy cinder in the distant ocean, which has been forced into its actual state of usefulness and importance by the perseverance, the skill, and the zeal of the marines. This fact so forcibly struck the Prince de Joinville when he visited the island in the early part of 1843, that His Royal Highness observed to Captain Dwyer:

The marines deserve great credit. They have performed wonders here; for out of nothing, less than nothing, you have created a great deal,—a very useful little colony.